Realism and Antirealism

:

Realism
&
Antirealism

Edited by
WILLIAM P. ALSTON

⋮

Cornell University Press
Ithaca and London

First published 2002 by Cornell University Press
First printing, Cornell Paperbacks, 2002

Printed in the United States of America

Library of Congress Cataloging-in-Publication Data

Realism and antirealism / edited by William P. Alston.
     p. cm.
Includes bibliographical references and index.
    ISBN 0-8014-4028-9 (alk. paper) — ISBN 0-8014-8790-0 (pbk. : alk. paper)
    1. Realism. I. Alston, William P.
    B835 .R315 2002
    149' .2—dc21

                                                      2002009210

Cornell University Press strives to use environmentally responsible suppliers and materials to the fullest extent possible in the publishing of its books. Such materials include vegetable-based, low-VOC inks, and acid-free papers that are recycled, totally chlorine-free, or partly composed of nonwood fibers. For further information, visit our website at www.cornellpress.cornell.edu.

Cloth printing   10 9 8 7 6 5 4 3 2 1
Paperback printing   10 9 8 7 6 5 4 3 2 1

Contents

IV. DEPARTMENTAL REALISMS AND ANTIREALISMS

A. Religion

B. Science and Religion

C. Literature and Morality

Preface

The original impetus for this volume was a summer seminar for college and university faculty on realism and antirealism that I directed in 1999 at Calvin College, Grand Rapids, Michigan. This seminar was one in a series of Calvin College Seminars in Christian Scholarship, funded by the Pew Charitable Trusts. For each of these seminars there is a conference the following spring at which participants in the seminar present papers they have written in connection with their work for the seminar. The conferences also feature addresses by invited speakers, in this case Ernest Sosa of Brown University and Nicholas Wolterstorff of Yale University. The bulk of the chapters in this book grew out of papers by the seminar participants presented at that conference. The only exceptions are chapters by David Anderson, Michael Lynch, and myself. Anderson and Lynch had been invited to the conference as, so to say, "designated commentators", and they greatly enriched the discussions, as did Sosa and Wolterstorff.

Hearty thanks are due to many people for directly or indirectly contributing to this volume. The success of the seminar itself was attributable, in no small part, to the wonderful support given by the staff of the Calvin Faculty Summer Seminars—the director, Professor Susan Felch of the Calvin English Department; Anna Mae Bush, coordinator of the seminars; and Anna Mae's hardworking and unfailingly cheerful student assistants. All these people together created an ideal environment for the seminar, not only in terms of facilities and accommodations and other nuts-and-bolts matters but also in terms of interpersonal atmosphere, helpfulness, and hospitality. As someone who has been visiting innumerable campuses in innumerable capacities for more than fifty years, I can say without any qualification that I have never experienced such a cordial and affectionate welcome as we received at Calvin in the summer of 1999. And I believe I speak for everyone in the seminar in saying this.

Appreciation is due to all the conference participants for their comments on the papers that were presented and also to two anonymous referees for Cornell University Press for useful suggestions to the editor. And speaking of the Press, we are all grateful to John G. Ackerman, director of Cornell University Press, who took personal charge of this project and displayed exemplary patience during what were sometimes trying times. And last but the reverse of least, I would like to express great appreciation to the participants in the seminar for making it a memorable and rewarding intellectual experience. I have no hesitation is saying that I learned *at least* as much from them about our topic as they learned from me. And they not only contributed to the intellectual value of the seminar; they made it a remarkably congenial and enjoyable group experience. (One of the participants in another summer seminar, who often walked by the room where we were meeting, said to me, "You people seem to be having a lot more fun than we are".) It was a privilege working with this group of philosophers.

WILLIAM P. ALSTON

Syracuse University

Realism and Antirealism

:

Introduction

WILLIAM P. ALSTON

I

Issues concerning realism figure prominently in recent philosophical literature, both in English-speaking countries and elsewhere. And not just in writings that bear a philosophical label: these are hot topics in literary theory, the social sciences, history, and religious studies. This book is designed as a contribution to that discussion. But since 'realism' is a term used variously even within philosophy, I will need to make a number of distinctions before being more specific as to what is to be found here.

Let's begin with the intuitive idea that a realist is one who takes us to be confronted with "hard facts" that are what they are, whatever we think, believe, feel about them, however we conceptualize them or talk about them. This is often put by saying that the things we encounter are "mind-independent". (Of course, we have to except minds and their contents, states, powers, etc. They could hardly be "mind-independent"!) But since there are different ways of being mind-independent, we have to distinguish different varieties of realism.

Realism has often been contrasted with *idealism*, the view that nothing exists except minds and their states and contents. The most prominent idealist in English speaking philosophy was the eighteenth-century thinker Bishop Berkeley, who held that the only things that exist independently of human (and other creaturely) minds are God's mind and its contents. But an opposition to realism that is much more prominent in contemporary thought is one that stems from the later-eighteenth-century philosopher Immanuel Kant. Kant held that anything of which we can have knowledge owes at least its basic structure to the categories in terms of which we think it—substance, causality, and the like—rather than to the way it is in itself. This kind of antirealism picks up on another part of my initial characterization of realism, namely, things being what they are however we think of them or conceptualize them. Kant's denial of realism in this sense was not global, for he recognized that there is an "an sich" (in itself) reality (noumena), though he denied that we can have any knowledge of it. What we can know are things as they appear to us (phenomena), which are

what they are, at least in good part, because of the way the human mind is pro-
grammed to conceptually structure them.

The contemporary heirs of Kant's antirealism, particularly Hilary Putnam
and Richard Rorty, want nothing to do with unknowable noumena. They unrestrictedly globalize Kant's treatment of phenomena, holding that nothing exists
or is what it is independently of the ways in which we conceptualize it, think of
it, talk about it. Moreover, whereas Kant thought that there is one unique way
in which the human mind imposes structure on its objects, the contemporary
post-Kantians think in terms of a plurality of "conceptual schemes" that are
available to and used by humans for structuring the objects of their thought.

It is the post-Kantian kind of antirealism, not the Berkeleyan idealist kind,
that is the focus of discussion in much of this book. For concision of reference I
use Putnam's term "conceptual relativity" for this kind of antirealism. But before looking at how this plays out in the essays collected here, I wish to make
some further points about the realist-antirealist territory.

First, there is the often overlooked point that the two kinds of realism-antirealism contrasts I have identified are independent of each other. On the antirealism side it is fairly obvious that one can be a conceptual relativist without
embracing idealism. At least Putnam, Rorty, and numerous other philosophers
claim this. One can hold that everything that exists does so and is what it is only
relative to one or another of a plurality of equally acceptable conceptual
schemes, without also holding that all those things are mental in character.
What is less often noticed is that one can embrace Berkeleyan idealism without
being a conceptual relativist and without even taking the less global position of
Kant. Though Berkeley thinks that only minds and what is ontologically mind-
dependent exist, he does not think that what exists is dependent on our way(s)
of conceptualizing it. The "tree in the quad" doesn't exist independently of
God's ideas, but it is in no way dependent for existing and being what it is on
our thinking of it as we do.

Second, there is the distinction between global and departmental versions of
realism. So far we have been dealing with the former. Both Berkeley and Putnam have unrestrictedly general views as to what it takes for something to exist
and be what it is. But there are also views of a realist or nonrealist sort about
particular stretches of reality: perceivable physical objects, abstract objects, universals, propositions, the objects of pure mathematics, moral obligation, meanings, God, and so on. We can have realist-antirealist oppositions of both post-
Kantian and Berkeleyan kinds on particular topics such as these. Berkeley is an
idealist about physical objects whereas Locke is a realist. Kant is antirealist in
his way about the physical world, again in opposition to Locke, Descartes, and
many others.

Third, there are still other sorts of opposed views on particular domains that
go under the 'realist-antirealist' label. Note that the realism-antirealism controversies we have been considering so far are not over whether something exists at
all but rather over what kind of status it has. Putnam no more doubts that trees

and rocks exist than does a staunch realist like John Searle; it is just a question as to what kind of existence and nature they enjoy. And so it is with Berkeley vs. Locke over perceivable physical objects. But theists and (straightforward) atheists do not differ on what sort of status God has. They disagree as to whether there is any such thing at all. Strangely enough, questions as to whether something(s) of a given kind exists at all are subsumed under the realist-antirealist rubric for some subject matters but not others. Atheists are not generally termed 'antirealists' about God any more than disbelievers in alien spacecrafts are termed 'antirealists' about such things. But one who denies that there are (really) any such things as universals or propositions, or theoretical scientific entities like electrons or negative matter, is commonly called an 'antirealist' about such matters. This kind of opposition appears in this book, to an extent, only in Chapters 13, 14, and 15.

Fourth, there is another kind of departmental opposition over what there is. This involves not a flat-out disagreement as to whether X's exist but rather an attempt to "reduce" X's to something that, on the face of it, seems to be completely different. Thus phenomenalists seek to reduce physical objects to actual and hypothetical patterns of sense experience. (To say that there is a table there is to say that under certain conditions one would have such-and-such kinds of sensory experience.) Nominalists seek to reduce propositions to sets of sentences, and properties to classes of particulars. Extreme physicalists would like to be able to reduce mental states to neurophysiological states. And so on. Some of these reductionist claims, for example the phenomenalist ones, are semantic claims, claims as to what it *means* to say so-and-so. We have something like this in Chapter 8, in Anderson's "semantic antirealism". But others are more ontological in character. The physicalist's physiological reduction of mental states is couched not in terms of what someone means in saying 'I feel sleepy' but rather in terms of what feeling sleepy really is.

Fifth, though it is obvious on the face of it, it is worth mentioning that the existence of departmental realisms and antirealisms gives rise to the possibility of global views of a mixed sort: for example, being realist for physical objects and antirealist for propositions.

Though the reader's head may already be swimming from a plethora of distinctions, there is one more complication that requires mention. Thus far, with the possible exception of semantic reductionist views, I have been dealing with what is properly called metaphysical realism and antirealism. But another opposition that goes under the realism-antirealism label is one concerning *truth*. Nor is this simply another departmental controversy, for it has implications all over the map. Let me explain.

A natural commonsense view of (propositional) truth is the following. What it is for a statement to be true is for what the statement is about to be as it is stated to be. The statement that *salt is sodium chloride* is true if and only if salt *is* sodium chloride. I have termed this a "realist" conception of truth, though some have quibbled at the designation. I call it 'realist' because it makes the truth value of a statement depend on how it is with something the statement is about, something that is *objective* in that way. The most prominent antirealist construals of truth are *epistemic*, making the truth value of the statement depend on how well it fits into a coherent overall system, is adequately supported by evidence or reasons, or has some other positive epistemic status. Whether or not we use the terms 'realist' and 'antirealist' for this opposition, it is an important one. And as I suggested above, the position one takes on the nature of truth has global implications for all domains of thought; for the truth conditions of a statement, any statement about anything, are intimately connected with the content of the statement, what it is that it states.

But although one's view of the nature of truth has extensive ramifications, I cannot agree with Putnam and others that an epistemic conception of truth logically implies and is implied by an antirealist metaphysics. Nor is my "realist" conception of truth related in this tight fashion to a realist metaphysics. Both these claims can be refuted by showing that conceptual relativity is compatible with a realist conception of truth. That can be shown as follows. On that conception of truth whether it is true that *water is wet* is wholly determined by whether water *is* wet. But that doesn't tell us *what it is* for water to be wet. In particular, it doesn't tell us what metaphysical status is enjoyed by the fact that water is wet. Still more specifically, it doesn't tell us whether or not water's being wet is constituted, at least in part, by how we conceptualize it. That is, it doesn't tell us whether or not a conceptual relativity or an opposed metaphysical realism applies to the truth maker in question. Hence the issue over the nature of truth is logically independent of the metaphysics of facts, of truth makers. No doubt, a realist metaphysics of facts is more congenial to a realist conception of truth than conceptual relativism. But there is no logical implication involved.

II

I will use the framework just sketched to organize and interrelate the diverse treatments of realism and antirealism in this book. In the course of doing so I will give a preliminary idea of the contents of the various chapters. But before turning to each particular chapter I will make a few points about the book as a whole.

First, in terms of the distinctions just laid out, the main focus of the book is on the Putnam sort of antirealism, *conceptual relativity*, and its realist opposition. Indeed, Putnam himself figures prominently in several of the chapters (3, 4, 5, 6, 7, 11). But even where he is not present in person, it is often his version of antirealism, and its opposite number, that is posing the issues. The main exceptions to this are Chapters 9, 10, 13, 14, and 15.

Second, here is a bird's-eye view of the organization of the book as a whole. Part I is concerned with basic issues concerning the opposition between metaphysical realism and antirealism. Part II explores the relation of issues concerning truth to the metaphysical realism-antirealism opposition. Part III deals with relations between epistemology and the realism problem. Part IV is made up of discussions of issues concerning realism in particular domains—religion, science, literature, and morality.

Finally, a point about the dominant orientation of the book. An overwhelming majority of the authors are realists of one sort or another, though this comes out more explicitly in some cases than in others. More or less sympathetic treatments of one or another sort of antirealism are to be found in Chapters 2, 4, 5, 8, and 13, though none of these amounts to an unqualified endorsement of a strong antirealism. So far as this polling sample goes, realism wins the argument!

Now let's look in more detail at what we have in Part I. Altering the order in which the chapters appear, we find a natural starting point in Chapter 6, my own chapter. I am concerned there to distinguish what does and does not belong to metaphysical realism. I identify a number of gratuitous accretions with which one or another author saddles metaphysical realism. These include, among others, the thesis that reality is inaccessible to us, the claim that there is a unique true description of the world, the causal theory of reference, and physicalism. It is important to realize that these views are not required by a robust metaphysical realism, because the latter is often criticized by way of an attack on the alleged components just listed. If metaphysical realism is not committed to them, refuting any (or all) of them fails to touch that position.

We find another "how to understand it" contribution in Chapter 3. Andrew Cortens, after despairing of other attempts to make sense of talk about different ways of "dividing" or "slicing" reality into distinct objects, turns to a linguistic interpretation, which he terms "Ontological Pluralism". This is the view that there is a plurality of languages equal in expressive power that differ in their devices for expressing quantification and identity. As a result, what can be truly said to exist in one of the languages can be truly said not to exist in another. And there is, in principle, no way of adjudicating the (apparent) dispute. Cortens does not endorse this position, but he considers it to make more sense of the idea of equally acceptable ways of dividing reality into objects than any alternatives.

Chapter 1 stands alone in seeking to give a straightforward argument for metaphysical realism. Caleb Miller does not exactly argue that the position is true. He contents himself with showing it to be supported by common sense. This being the case, he claims, it is more rational than antirealism, since any argument against realism has much less plausibility for most people than the deliverances of common sense.

In Chapter 4 Michael Lynch argues against Michael Devitt, Hilary Putnam, and others that many of the main intuitions behind metaphysical realism are compatible with a radical form of conceptual relativity, or what he calls "metaphysical pluralism". Along the way, he distinguishes several different forms of both metaphysical realism and metaphysical pluralism and discusses the nature of mind-independence. He also defends his claim that a relativism about content entails a relativism about fact against a recent critique by Ernest Sosa.

Chapters 2 and 5 both seek to support positions intermediate between realism and antirealism. In Chapter 2, which is in the form of a dialogue, Mark McLeod presents a series of arguments for what he calls 'irrealism'. The dialogue does not lend itself to brief summary, but I take the main argument to be that where our epistemic situation is such that two contradictory views are equally well supported, we have to recognize both as true. (This position bears an obvious family resemblance to Cortens's "ontological pluralism" in Chapter 3 and Lynch's "horizontal pluralism" in Chapter 4.) But since they can't both be true in the same world, we have to recognize a distinction of worlds, in one of which one view is true and in the other of which the other is. This argument clearly sides with those who take truth to be equivalent to a sufficiently positive epistemic status of a proposition. One interesting feature of McLeod's dialogue is the way in which it engages Miller's commonsense argument for realism in Chapter 1.

Michael Murray's version of an intermediate position in Chapter 5 is inspired by Leibniz. This is a "moderate theistic realism" in which natural kinds and individual substances exist independently, as realism maintains. But other things we recognize, such as artifacts like footballs and social entities like money, exist and are what they are because our conceptual thought is what it is. This is an example of what I called in Section I a "mixed" view; realism holds for a basic stratum of reality, but our cognitive activity is partly determinative of higher strata.

III

Part II contains two chapters, each of which in one way or another deals with the relation of truth to metaphysical realism. In Chapter 7 René van Woudenberg challenges my view that an acceptance of a realist conception of truth ("alethic realism") is neutral between metaphysical realism and antirealism. He argues that alethic realism is incompatible with Putnam's conceptual relativity. For example, he points out that whereas Putnam holds, on one interpretation, that all properties are mind-dependent, alethic realism is committed to denying this. Again, assuming that Putnam holds that a given property exists relative to some conceptual schemes and not others, it would follow that there are schemes relative to which the property of truth does not exist. But alethic realism is committed to an absolute status for the property of truth.

In Chapter 8 David Anderson is concerned with the kinds of truth *conditions* statements about perceptible middle-sized objects have rather than with the *nature* of truth. He distinguishes between *realistic* truth conditions, or how things are in themselves independently of our cognition of them, and *antirealist* truth conditions, or how things stand with respect to our "epistemic perspective". Although he holds that all sentences about perceptible objects *can* be used to make statements with realist truth conditions, he also thinks that statements about perceptible objects, as people normally make them, are subject to antirealist truth conditions. He calls the latter view "semantic antirealism". The point of the title is that Anderson holds that God, as the author of our epistemic situation, has deliberately and with set purpose arranged things so that we normally make such statements with antirealist truth conditions. Thus God has ordained that we live in a (partially) antirealist world.

IV

Part III comprises two chapters that explore epistemology from a realist perspective. In Chapter 9 Christopher Tollefsen deploys several concepts from moral discourse—*coercion, coordination,* and *cooperation*—in order to articulate different ways of conceptualizing cognitive relations between persons and the world. The first two of these concepts do not, he holds, give us enough of, or the right kind of, relation between persons and the world. But, he suggests, the notion of cooperation, if it is viable for the understanding of the relations in question, might allow us to see through to a broadly realist position of our cognitive relations to the objects of our thought.

Chapter 10 differs from the rest of the book in focusing on the epistemology of a major medieval philosopher-theologian, Saint Bonaventure, a position Laura Smit presents as a pervasively Christocentric form of realism. The person of Christ is the key both to knowing ourselves and to knowing the external, sensible world. All human knowers participate in Christ in the act of knowing. Christ is the source of all knowledge because all essences are contained in him. In the incarnation this immutable truth enters time and becomes accessible. The true nature of all created things is available for knowledge through this communication.

There are three particular mental operations that require divine illumination: memory, understanding, and an intrinsic love of goodness. Bonaventure establishes a typology by which the knower is connected to each person of the Godhead. The innate memory of Being per se accounts for the existence of a priori knowledge and connects the soul to the Father. The innate understanding of Truth by which we come to know objects in terms of their essences is a direct perception of the mind of Christ, in whom all forms are hid. The innate love for goodness is expressed in every soul as a desire to be happy, a desire animated by the Holy Spirit, who—as love—is the bond uniting us to God.

V

Part IV is devoted to applications of the realism-antirealism opposition to particular domains. Section A deals with religion. Chapter 11 is Gavin Colvert's response to Putnam's invitation to Thomists to discuss with him the status of religious discourse. Putnam's view is that it is meaningful but "incommensurable" with scientific and other empirical discourse. The meaningfulness of religious language stems from religious forms of life, and hence religious language cannot be translated into a neutral descriptive language. But despite the incommensurability, the different languages are not committed to incompatible claims.

Colvert points out that these views are remarkably congenial to the Thomist metaphysical realism that Putnam rejects. Aquinas can accommodate a modest form of the nonreducibility of religious language and its dependence on a religious form of life. For Aquinas the development of moral and intellectual virtues is required for grasping certain kinds of theoretical and practical truths. But, contrary to Putnam, once those virtues have been acquired, the unity of reality and truth required by Aquinas's metaphysical realism will ensure that reflection in one domain can and will influence reflection in other domains.

Aquinas also figures in Chapter 12. Philip Rolnick notes that since the Middle Ages the main understandings of how words we originally learn with respect to creatures refer to God have been univocity (same meaning in both applications) and analogy. In this chapter he argues that analogy offers the best case for realistic reference to God. He goes on to point out that the analogical account shows how God and creatures can share certain transcendental predicates, such as *being*, *good*, and *true*. He explores Aquinas's reasons for denying the possibility of univocity by engaging my critique of Aquinas. He then shows problems in my proposal of a functionalist account of a univocal application of psychological terms to God and creatures. Finally, he explores the commonality between the two approaches.

In Section B, dealing with science, there is a single chapter (13). There Anne Hiskes points out that using science as a model, Van Fraassen has proposed a new form of empiricism called "constructive empiricism", which corrects what are now acknowledged as defects of previous empiricist views of knowledge and science while preserving their spirit. She critically discusses four distinctive features of this new version of empiricism and their application to the domain of religious epistemology: (1) its representation of empiricism as a cluster of values and attitudes rather than a set of beliefs, (2) its acceptance of the theory-ladenness of observation reports, (3) the importance of the epistemic community in fixing the limits of observability, and (4) an emphasis on a distinction between criteria for acceptance versus criteria for belief. Hiskes argues that the application of a constructive empiricist framework to science and religion provides an illuminating picture of the interactions between experience and theory, and between belief and values, in both domains, as well as a strategy for the peaceful coexistence of science and religion.

Section C deals with literature and, in Chapter 15, its connections with morality. In Chapter 14 Frances Howard-Snyder discusses "fictional realism". She considers questions like "Does Macbeth meet three witches?". Fictional realism says that there are objective and determinate answers to such questions. They have answers that aren't simply a matter of whatever the viewer or reader happens to think about the matter. But if so, what is it that makes one rather than another answer correct? Howard-Snyder argues against several proposals for answering that question and then defends (in a somewhat modified version she develops) a view she takes from David Lewis, namely, the Reality Principle, which in its original form is formulated as: "In fiction F, phi is true if and only if were the story told as known fact phi would be true".

In Chapter 15 Kelly James Clark defends the importance of narrative for moral philosophy, in particular for moral realism, the position that there are moral truths independent of human beliefs. He contends that narrative is often necessary for change of belief and that through such change one can attain moral truth. Thus narrative is important for both individual moral improvement and societal moral progress. Clark opposes his account to that of fellow narrativalist Richard Rorty, who denies moral realism and its concomitants. Since Clark believes that the clash between realists and antirealists in morals is essentially a clash of intuitions, he does not attempt to give a conclusive argument in favor of realism. Instead, like Rorty, he draws a word-picture, one that stands in stark contrast to the word-picture Rorty draws for stories. Finally, he gives some reasons for preferring his picture to Rorty's.

PART I

Basic Issues for Realism and Antirealism

Realism, Antirealism, and Common Sense

CALEB MILLER

DEFINITIONS

In this chapter I will argue that common sense makes it more rational for most of us to accept realism than to accept antirealism. Although there is a considerable philosophical literature about realism and antirealism, there is no consensus about the meanings of the central terms or criteria for identifying views as versions of realism or antirealism. In view of this situation, I shall resort to stipulation. By "realism" I shall mean the view that reality, and the truth about it, are what they are, independently of our cognition of them. I would be happy in some contexts to defend a universal or nearly universal version of such realism. But common sense seems to me germane only to a version of realism with a more limited scope. For purposes of this chapter I shall, then, use the term "realism" to denote the view that the reality of the external world of concrete objects, and the truth about such reality, are what they are independently of our cognition of them. They are what they are independently of human beliefs, conceptualizations, descriptions, sentences, perceptions, conventions, languages, and so on. Thus, for example, realism entails the view that the tree on the green is what it is independently of our human conceptualizations, thoughts, beliefs, and so on about it. Furthermore, it's being *true* that the tree is the particular height that it is, is independent of our belief that it is that height, our conceptualizing or perceiving that it is, and so on. By "antirealism" I shall mean the denial of realism. On this understanding there are quite a number of different ways to be an antirealist, including the views of some philosophers who have explicitly renounced the label. But in the idiom of this chapter, for better or worse, they will be antirealists, whether they like it or not.

So, for example, C. S. Peirce endorsed an antirealist view of reality and truth when he said, "The opinion which is fated to be ultimately agreed to by all who investigate is what we mean by truth, and the object represented in this opinion is the real."[1] Richard Rorty endorsed an antirealist conception of truth when he

---

[1] Charles S. Peirce, "How to Make Our Ideas Clear," in Charles S. Peirce, *Selected Writings: Values in a Universe of Chance*, ed. Philip Wiener (New York: Dover, 1966), 133.

said that it is no more than "what our peers will, ceteris paribus, let us get away with saying."[2] The Christian theologian Phillip Kenneson, in an article titled "There's No Such Thing as Objective Truth, and It's a Good Thing, Too," said, "It simply does not make sense to think of reality as it is in itself, apart from human judgment."[3] Hilary Putnam endorses a similar view when he says, "Objects do not exist independently of conceptual schemes."[4] Nelson Goodman endorsed an antirealist view of truth when he espoused the views that truth is relative to worlds and that worlds are made by cognizers.[5] Jacques Derrida, the enormously influential father of deconstruction, appeared to endorse a linguistic form of antirealism when he said, "There is nothing outside of texts." But after a vigorous critique by John Searle, Derrida appeared to take it all back, saying that he really meant only that there is nothing outside of *con*texts.[6] In the ordinary sense of the term, it is obvious that everything is in some context or other; that banality has no antirealist implications at all. Although it is unwise to stake much on any particular interpretation of Derrida, I suspect that what he meant was less trivial than that. I suspect that he meant something like the claim that everything is what it is *in virtue of* its context or its *relation to texts*, where the term "texts" is understood as including the whole gamut of our cognitive life and its extensions, such as language, concepts, beliefs, conventions, speech, literal texts, and so on. In that case, Derrida would be endorsing a form of antirealism about reality. In any case, I think it safe to say that many of his *followers* are antirealists and take their antirealism to be an appropriation of his views.

The rough idea of what I shall mean by "common sense" is that body of beliefs that are generally shared because they generally seem to be obvious. Thus, for example, the beliefs that plants grow in soil, that newborn infants are incapable of providing for their own needs, that most dogs can see, that most birds can fly, and that sunlight is brighter than moonlight are among the beliefs of common sense. But the beliefs that Jesus Christ is God incarnate, that Jupiter is larger than the moon, and that viruses and bacteria cause diseases are *not* among the commonsense beliefs of North American culture. Although they are widely held in this culture, their being held so widely is due not to their seeming obvious or overwhelmingly plausible but rather to their being widely taught in the culture. It is also not a matter of common sense that Jean is a better philosophy student than Tom, even if it is utterly obvious to me that she is. That be-

---

[2] Richard Rorty, *Philosophy and the Mirror of Nature* (Princeton: Princeton University Press, 1979), 176.

[3] Phillip Kenneson, "There's No Such Thing as Objective Truth, and It's a Good Thing, Too," in *Christian Apologetics in the Postmodern World*, ed. Timothy R. Phillips and Dennis L. Olkholm (Downers Grove, Ill.: InterVarsity Press, 1995), 164.

[4] Hilary Putnam, *Reason, Truth, and History* (Cambridge: Cambridge University Press, 1981), 52.

[5] These are central themes in his *Ways of Worldmaking* (Indianapolis: Hackett, 1978).

[6] Jacques Derrida, *Limited, Inc.* (Evanston: Northwestern University Press, 1988), 136.

lief fails to be an item of common sense because it is not widely shared, in part because the grounds of making that judgment obvious to me are not widely available. I also intend my use of the term "common sense" to include what *would* seem obvious to most of us upon minimal reflection. Thus, it is a matter of common sense that no human being is more than 465 feet, 7 5/23 inches tall and that the number '37' is not a reptile, despite the fact that neither belief is likely to be held by anyone who has not read this sentence.

I will also use the term "common sense" to refer to the shared grounds that lead most of us to regard the beliefs of common sense as obvious. It is this sense of the term that is used when we say such things as "He was a man of common sense" or "Common sense tells you that she would not eat something she believed to be poisonous." Common sense, as I intend it, varies from culture to culture. It is an item of common sense in twenty-first-century North American culture that light bulbs typically require electricity to be illuminated but was not in seventeenth-century North America or in various isolated tribal cultures of the twenty-first century.

I intend the terms "seem" and "appear" and their cognates and synonyms in the foregoing and in the rest of the chapter to be understood as phenomenological terms, not as normative epistemological terms. Thus, when a claim seems obvious to us, our consideration of it has the sort of phenomenal quality that typically leads us to believe it with a high degree of confidence. Its seeming obvious doesn't itself constitute our believing it or being justified, warranted, or rational in believing it.

RATIONALITY

I do not intend to offer a "proof of the external world" or even to argue for the truth of realism. I shall rather argue that realism is a more rational belief than antirealism. The sort of rationality I have in mind is epistemic rationality, or rationality from the epistemic perspective. The epistemic perspective on a particular belief is that of one who seeks to hold that belief if and only if it is true. Unfortunately, this way of characterizing the perspective begs the question against versions of antirealism which deny that there is such a property as truth. To mollify such antirealists, I am willing to accept a paraphrase according to which the epistemic perspective on a given declarative sentence, p, is that of a person who seeks to believe that p iff p. Although I shall continue to describe rationality and the epistemic perspective in terms of truth, nothing will be lost to the argument if the reader substitutes the foregoing paraphrase, or any grammatically appropriate transformation of it, wherever I employ the concept of truth in those discussions.

For a belief to be *rational*, from the epistemic perspective, is for it to be a fitting means to the fulfillment of one's epistemic goal regarding that belief. For example, the belief that there is a tree on the green is rational for a person from the epistemic perspective iff believing that there is a tree on the green is well suited to achieving her goal of holding that belief if and only if it is true. There remains an ambiguity between subjective and objective ways of understanding what it is for a belief to be well suited to accomplishing one's epistemic goal. In the objective sense, a belief is well suited to accomplishing that goal, iff it is true, or alternatively, iff it is formed by an objectively reliable means of seeking the truth while avoiding falsehood, or perhaps iff it is formed by properly functioning cognitive faculties. In the subjective sense, a belief is rational iff it seems to the agent, by her own best lights, to be well suited to accomplishing her epistemic goal of holding that belief iff it is true. I intend my use of the term "rational" and its cognates to reflect this subjective sense of epistemic rationality. It is this subjective epistemic rationality that is most pertinent to the project of honest truth-seeking. To be rational in this sense is to do the best we can to have an accurate view of the world. To seek rationality in this sense is to answer for oneself the question, What should I believe about this, if I want as much as possible to hold true beliefs and avoid false ones? Epistemologists will recognize my debt to Richard Foley, who developed an impressive account of this sort of rationality in his book *The Theory of Epistemic Rationality*.[7]

THE ARGUMENT

What I will argue is that realism is more rational for most of us, in this subjective epistemic sense, than is antirealism. That is, insofar as we are motivated to seek the truth and to avoid error on the question of realism, we would do better, by our own best lights, to accept realism than to accept antirealism. The first point I want to establish is that common sense makes it prima facie more rational to accept realism than to accept its denial, antirealism. From the commonsense view of the world, there is no question that there is reality external to and independent of our minds. According to common sense, the tree on the green is not a feature of our cognitive life even if it is cognized by us. It is not within our cognitive control. Its existence does not depend on our cognitions, descriptions, possible perceptions, or any such thing. Common sense tells us that when we come to know something, it doesn't thereby become true. If we came to know, say, that the tree on the green is more than ten feet tall, it is patently obvious, on the *commonsense* picture of the world, the tree did not then, or thereby, *become* more than ten feet tall. Neither did it become *true* then that it is more than ten feet tall. If the tree was more than ten feet tall before anyone became aware of it, then it was true before then that it was more than ten feet tall: we have only discovered the truth of what was already true. I hope that it is not controversial that common sense makes realism prima facie rational. Even Rorty concedes something of this sort when he says: "What really needs debate between the pragmatist and the intuitive realist is *not* whether we have intuitions to the effect that 'truth is more than assertability'. . . . Of course we have such intuitions. How could we escape having them? We have been edu-

    [7] Richard Foley, *The Theory of Epistemic Rationality* (Cambridge: Harvard University Press, 1987).

cated within an intellectual tradition built around such claims. . . . The pragmatist is urging that we do our best to stop having such intuitions, that we develop a new intellectual tradition."[8]

Let's review where the argument stands. I have argued for the prima facie rationality of accepting realism over antirealism. That means that, given only the considerations of common sense, realism is more plausible to those of us for whom common sense is intuitively compelling than is antirealism. I will argue eventually that common sense makes realism more rational than antirealism, all things considered, for those of us who share the initial commonsense intuitions about realism. What stands in the way is the possibility of defeaters. Defeaters of a belief are other beliefs such that its being rational to hold them undermines the rationality of the defeated belief. There are two different kinds of defeaters that I shall, following John Pollock, call "rebutting defeaters" and "undercutting defeaters." An undercutting defeater undermines the rationality of holding a belief not by entailing or supporting its denial but rather by calling into question the soundness of its grounds. Rebutting defeaters override the rationality of holding a belief by way of grounds directly relevant to the truth of the belief. Such a defeater paradigmatically takes the form of a premise of an implicit or explicit argument for the denial of the belief.

Is there a rebutting defeater of the rationality of realism? Are there grounds for antirealism as strong or nearly as strong as the commonsense grounds for realism? Are there grounds, in other words, for the denial of realism which honestly seem to us as strong as the ground for thinking, say, that the reality of the tree on the green is independent of our cognition? That is a tall order. To be an item of common sense constitutes an enormous rational presumption in its favor. It must seem utterly obvious to most of us. It is not that the rational presumption in favor of common sense is indefeasible. The beliefs that the earth is flat, that the sun revolves around the earth, and that "solid" objects contain no empty space were all once commonsense beliefs. Yet the scientific grounds for denying them are, for most of us, clearly stronger than the grounds in their favor. Still, such a defeater will be very hard to come by. In the case of realism, it is not clear what a good candidate for such grounds would be. If the defeater is the premise of an argument for antirealism, it is easy enough to establish an *incompatibility* between a premise or conjunction of premises and our commonsense realist intuitions. But we must then face the question, Which of the incompatible claims honestly seems to us more likely to be true, our realist commonsense intuitions on the one hand or the premise or conjunction of premises for the antirealist argument on the other hand? Unlike the foregoing examples of defeated commonsense beliefs, realism is a metaphysical view. If we grant the logical coherence of realism, it is fairly uncontroversially compatible with any possible empirical observations. The same goes for any scientific theory. The

[8] Richard Rorty, *Consequences of Pragmatism* (Minneapolis: University of Minnesota Press, 1982), xxix–xxx.

only candidates for claims incompatible with realism are metaphysical claims. Yet metaphysical theories are, as a rule, notoriously lacking in compelling plausibility. I doubt that there are any interesting metaphysical views, not themselves derived from common sense, which have the intuitive pull on us that common sense has. Let's consider some possibilities. "All reality is socially constructed." "To be is to be perceived."[9] "There is nothing outside of texts." "There is no such thing as reality as it is in itself." When those of us for whom the realist intuitions of common sense are initially compelling ask ourselves whether it seems to us more likely that "all reality is socially constructed" or that the tree on the green is what it is, independently of any cognition of it, we will surely have trouble taking the former possibility seriously.

The most likely exceptions are reductio ad absurdum arguments and other arguments according to which realism has internal problems that render it implausible. That is, realism itself has consequences that are so implausible as to render the view unacceptable. But upon closer inspection, such arguments are not really internal arguments. They require assumptions not entailed by realism which, like the assumptions listed above, fall considerably short of the plausibility required to defeat realism, given its grounding in common sense.

Let's consider an argument of that sort. Nelson Goodman argues that if realism were true, then there would be true contradictions, a conclusion that any realist would regard as a refutation. He offers the following pair of statements as an example:

(1) The sun always moves.
(2) The sun never moves.

But the incompatibility and truth of these claims does not follow from realism itself. Those are additional assumptions. To do the work to which Goodman puts this example, the following must be true:

(a) (1) and (2) are both true.
(b) The conjunction of (1) and (2) is inconsistent.

But neither (a), (b), nor their conjunction is entailed by realism. It is quite consistent with realism to deny (a), (b), or their conjunction. The alleged defeater of realism is then the conjunction of (a) and (b). Does it defeat the rationality of realism? Not at all. We can, for example, help ourselves to the idea that motion is relative to frames of reference and deny (b). The concept of relative motion is well established in physics and is well known to many speakers of English. Given that, it is quite plausible to think that anyone uttering both (1) and (2) would be making compatible claims. The truth asserted in (1) is likely that

---

[9] I do not mean to imply that the theistic idealism of Berkeley, from whom this quotation was taken, is itself antirealist in my sense of the term. It is not.

the sun always moves relative to one frame of reference whereas the one as-serted in (2) is that the sun never moves relative to another frame of reference. If, however, the context of utterance makes it clear that both claims involve the concept of absolute motion, then clearly (a) is false, since obviously it is either false that the sun always moves absolutely or false that it never moves ab-solutely. We might want to leave it to the physicists to sort out which of (1) or (2), so understood, is false, but a bit of logic makes it obvious that their con-junction is false. So either (1) and (2) make claims involving relative motion, in which case they are obviously compatible, or they make claims involving ab-solute motion, in which case their conjunction is obviously false. Either way, the conjunction of (a) and (b)—the alleged defeater of realism is—false. Even if the realist has no good reason to believe of either (a) or (b) that *it* is false, she need not fear that their conjunction defeats the rationality of realism. After all, realism has common sense going for it whereas the conjunction of (a) and (b) is logically impossible. It doesn't really seem like a close call to me. The same strategy can be employed to rebut the alleged truth and incompatibility of any of the other pairs of claims that Goodman offers. It can also be used to defuse Putnam's claim of incompatibility and truth for the Carnapian claim that there are only three objects in a room and the Polish logician's claim that there are seven objects, namely, the original three plus the mereological sums of those ob-jects. Without delving deeper into the question, we can see the possible rebut-tals. Either the Polish logician's claim is compatible with the Carnapian claim, as I am inclined to think, or at least one of them is false, as realists such as Peter van Inwagen and David Lewis think. But we realists should not even be tempted by the suggestion that the claims are both true and incompatible with each other. That suggestion certainly has less intuitive appeal than does common sense.

Although I obviously cannot do a complete inventory of arguments against the truth of realism, they seem to come in two categories. Those of the first cat-egory are explicitly based on metaphysical premises inconsistent with realism but much less intuitively plausible than are the realist deliverances of common sense. Arguments in the second category purport to show that realism itself has implausible consequences. But these arguments turn out to have implicit prem-ises that are both independent of realism and not at all plausible to the realist who finds common sense intuitively compelling. So grim do the prospects ap-pear to me that I think it reasonable not to treat most arguments for antirealism most basically as offering purported rebutting defeaters of realism. Such argu-ments typically seem to me much more naturally understood as purporting to undermine the soundness of the commonsense basis of realism or, at any rate, most basically motivated by the conviction that it has been undermined. In other words, antirealist arguments are typically best understood to be, or to be motivated by, purported undercutting defeaters of realism. Goodman suggests something of the sort when he says, " 'The world' supposedly being that which all right versions describe, all we learn about the world is contained in right versions of it; and while the underlying world, bereft of these, need not be denied to those who love it, it is perhaps on the whole a world well lost."[10] In other words, he seems to acknowledge that the realist can easily stick to her guns in the face of his argument, but doing so is somehow misplaced. The reason seems to be that since all we can ever know is contained in versions of the world, we have no good reason for thinking that there is anything else.

Indeed, most antirealist arguments are most basically, explicitly or implicitly, motivated by considerations of this sort. They are epistemic arguments according to which the epistemic basis of realism is challenged. The rough idea of such arguments is something like this. Even if realism were true, we could have no way of knowing that it is. And this is not just because we can never be justifiably sure enough of realism to count as knowledge. It is rather that we can have no cognitive access to anything that is even relevant to the question. The realist convictions of common sense are, then, simply not indicative of the truth. But if we cannot have any reason for believing that realism is true, we should just stick to that to which we *do* have cognitive access. That to which we do have access are such things as our own cognitive life and concepts, our own conceptual schemes, language, reality as known by us or conceptualized by us, and the like. Sometimes it is further argued that our epistemic situation with respect to realism is so bad that any attempt to make a realist claim is incoherent. I take Putnam to be making such a claim when he writes that "the notion of a 'thing in itself' makes no sense; and not because 'we cannot know the things in themselves'." It is rather that "we don't know what we are talking about" when we talk about the thing in itself.[11] The point here is, I think, that we can make no sense of how things are in themselves or of what is true of the world in itself because we make sense of things and of the world only by means of our conceptualizations of it. To claim to make sense of the truth in itself or of things in themselves is tantamount to the incoherent claim that we can conceptualize without concepts, or something like that. There is, then, according to Putnam as I understand him, an incoherence of some sort in the kind of realism that claims that things in themselves have the properties they do apart from any conceptualization, or as he would prefer to put it, apart from any conceptual scheme. Other antirealists say or imply similarly that realist claims are tantamount to claims to know the unknown, to perceive something other than perception, and so forth.

The epistemic argument against realism, as I have presented it, really offers two potential defeaters of realism. The first is the claim that we cannot have cognitive access to anything that could justify the claim that realism is true. The second, which is taken to follow from the first, is the claim that realism is committed to an incoherence. If the cognitive access claim is rational, it is an undercutting defeater. The incoherence claim, if rational, is a rebutting defeater.

---

[10] Goodman, *Ways of Worldmaking*, 4.

[11] Hilary Putnam, *The Many Faces of Realism* (La Salle, Ill.: Open Court, 1987), 36.

Let's consider the incoherence claim first. This claim makes an important difference to the significance of the argument. Absent that claim, the epistemic argument gives us no reason to deny realism or to accept its denial, antirealism. If the problem with realism is just that we have no way of knowing that it is true, that, in itself, is not a reason for believing that it is not true. The epistemologically better response would be to say that we really have nothing to guide us with respect to whether realism is true or not. For example, if the problem is only that we have no reason to think that there is a way that things are in themselves, we should be agnostic about whether there is, not deny that there is. But if realism doesn't even manage to be coherent, then it is of course not true.

But is it incoherent? Not at all. There is nothing incoherent in saying the following: The tree on the green is 47 feet tall. Its being 47 feet tall is a property that the tree has, in itself. Furthermore, it is true of the world, as it is in itself, that the tree is 47 feet tall. It is, of course, not a property of the tree, in itself, that its height is expressed in feet. The world as it is in itself, apart from our conceptualizations, is not such that the truth about the tree's height is expressed in the English sentence "The tree on the green is 47 feet tall." It is, of course, also true of the world as we know it, or as we conceptualize it, and the like, that the tree is 47 feet tall. But nothing prevents us from coherently adding that it is part of the way the world is in itself. The world itself, apart from our characterizations of it, is such that what we have expressed in the sentence "The tree on the green is 47 feet tall" is true. It is, of course, also true that the tree has a height of 47 feet as we measure height. But nothing prevents us from coherently adding that the property we attribute to the tree by saying that it is 47 feet tall is a property that it has quite apart from our attribution, and even apart from our having the conceptual ability to make it. We are still left, of course, with the question whether this realist view of things is correct. But having disposed of this incoherence objection, we have one less potential defeater of realism to worry about. The example just given also refutes the weaker claim, typically based on epistemic grounds, that realism is unintelligible. Surely, the description just made of the tree on the green is intelligible as well as coherent.

But what of the problem of cognitive access? The allegations of access problems take many different forms. The basic idea is that the human mind has access only to what is already cognitively shaped or constituted. Given that we are the ones who conceptualize, know, believe, perceive, and so on, we can have access only to things as we conceptualize them, know them, describe them, perceive them, and so on. We cannot have any access to things as they are in themselves, apart from our cognitions.

There are, I think, two confusions that give arguments like this their apparent cogency. The first is a confusion between cognitive states or processes and cognitive content. Let me illustrate by considering perception. What sorts of things do human beings perceive? One answer is to say that whatever they are, they must be some form of perception. After all, what could we possibly perceive other than perceptions? But that doesn't follow. We might say, for example, that we perceive objects, such as trees and tables. Although we cannot perceive without perception, it doesn't follow we can perceive only perceptions. Similarly, although we can speak, and perhaps think, only in language, it does not follow that we can speak or think only *about* language. Although beliefs and knowledge are cognitive states, it does not follow that we can have beliefs only about, or knowledge only of, cognitive states. But of course, antirealists need not make those mistakes, and many of them do not. Many of them agree that we perceive objects, that we have knowledge of the truth, and so forth. What they deny is that we can perceive objects in themselves or have knowledge of the truth as it is in itself. After all, how can we possibly perceive objects other than as we perceive them, have knowledge of the truth other than as we know it, and so forth? That brings us to the second confusion. Of course, we can't perceive anything except as we perceive it. But it does not follow that we cannot perceive anything as it is in itself. That inference requires the assumption that the way we perceive it can't be the way it is in itself. But that assumption simply begs the question against the realist who takes herself to have cognitive access to reality and truth in themselves. And that includes most of us. Whether we have this sort of access is itself part of what is usually at issue between realists and antirealists. Shorn of these confusions, this argument against cognitive access seems to have very little to recommend it, although I have not yet given any grounds for doubting its conclusion.

As I indicated, realists typically take us to have the relevant sort of cognitive access to reality that would enable us to have knowledge of things in themselves. Consider perception, for example. Realists have at least two standard ways of understanding perception, according to which we have access to reality beyond our perception: representationalism and direct realism. According to representationalism, we have indirect access to objects by means of direct access to mental items, such as ideas and perceptions. The access to the objects is by means of some appropriate relation, such as representation or similarity, between the mental item and the object. Now I think representationalism has problems of its own with common sense, so I will not linger longer over this view of perception.

The other major view of perception according to which we have cognitive access to objects beyond perception is direct realism. This seems to me much more promising. According to direct realism, the objects of our awareness in perception are the objects themselves, and not by means of any awareness of a mental item. Although there might be an associated idea of which we could be aware, upon introspection, what we are directly aware of in perception are external objects. And that sort of access is quite compatible with the rationality of realism.

Where does that leave us with respect to cognitive access? I have offered reasons to doubt the cogency of a standard sort of argument against the existence of such access and the brief description of an alternative view, direct realism, according to which we do. I have not said anything yet about what it is rational to *believe* about such access. How does it, or should it, seem to us from the epistemic perspective? Well, it so happens that common sense has a clear answer to this question. That is why direct realism is often called commonsense realism. According to common sense, we do have the kind of cognitive access to reality that supports realism. It is patently obvious that we can see a tree and that we can see that it has certain properties, for example, that it is leafy, wooden, and so forth. On the commonsense view, it is obvious that the tree exists and has those properties quite apart from our cognition of its existence with those properties. So, just as in the case of realism itself, it is prima facie rational, or rational, absent a defeater, to believe that we do have the requisite cognitive access. But we have already had a look at the argument against cognitive access and found it wanting. So, I conclude, it is not only prima facie rational but also rational, all things considered, to believe that we have cognitive access to reality in itself. But if it is rational to believe that we have cognitive access, we have also completed our larger task of establishing the rationality, all things considered, of realism itself, since we have now disposed of the best hope of an undercutting defeater of realism.

SUMMARY OF THE ARGUMENT
I have argued that common sense makes it prima facie much more rational for most of us (i.e., those of us who find common sense intuitively compelling) to accept realism than to accept antirealism. I have argued that rebutting defeaters are either obviously false or much less plausible for such people than is realism, given its basis in common sense. I have further argued that the best candidate for an undercutting defeater, the claim that we lack cognitive access to any truth maker of realism, is implausible for those of us who find common sense intuitively compelling. Therefore, the prima facie rational preference for realism over antirealism stands undefeated. In short, common sense makes it more rational, all things considered, to believe that realism is true than to believe its denial, antirealism.

AN OBJECTION
It might be objected that my argument leaves me open to an obvious sort of rejoinder. The antirealist can simply dig in her heels and insist that she doesn't find the counsel of common sense intuitively compelling. The quick answer, of course, is to point out that my argument is not meant to convince such a person. But that response is appropriate only to those who do not find the realist implications of common sense initially compelling. If I am right, those people are quite rare. The more troublesome, and more common, objector is the person who finds that realism is, given common sense, initially intuitively compelling but who professes not to find it compelling upon careful consideration of its purported defeaters. We may, in the end, need to decide that the most basic intuitions upon which we must rely are just different. But I think that often the better explanation is that philosophy tends to be somewhat misleading in ques-

tions like this. Philosophers, especially contemporary analytic philosophers, are in thrall to arguments. Arguing is our specialty. Most of us are pretty good at offering and evaluating arguments. Experience has taught us to be impressed by the power of arguments to change minds, to clarify, illuminate, and debunk. Much of this appreciation is justified. But philosophers, like other specialists, are prone also to exaggerate the importance of their own enterprise. Specifically, I think philosophers tend to exaggerate the epistemic significance of arguments. In a dispute between opposing views on a major philosophic question, we tend to look almost exclusively at arguments on both sides of the question. But of course, philosophers not only are adept at the making of arguments; they also tend to be pretty good at formulating and revising their views in such a way as to avoid refutation by arguments. As a result, it typically becomes clear to all the parties to a major philosophical dispute that neither a theory nor its denial follows by valid deductive inference from the stock of beliefs common to the disputants. The dispute between realism and antirealism is no exception. Both realists and antirealists typically recognize that no argument for either view delivers a knockout punch. Realists typically think that realism has the better of the argument, and antirealists typically give the advantage to antirealism. Some philosophers seem to think that their judgments about realism and antirealism are epistemically unencumbered because none of the arguments on either side is much good. But in any case, philosophers tend to treat the question as though the epistemic status of their beliefs depended entirely on the arguments.

To take such an approach is to spurn the richness of our epistemic resources. Arguments are only part of what is relevant to an honest assessment of this question. This point is perhaps more obvious with respect to nonphilosophic beliefs. My belief that I am sitting in a chair is, I think, eminently rational. But it is not grounded in any argument. It is rather, quite properly, grounded in my perceptual experience. If I were called upon to convince someone who doubted my claim, I could, of course, produce an argument. I could say, for example, that it felt and looked to me as if I was sitting in a chair, that most likely if it feels to me and looks to me as if I am sitting in a chair, then I am sitting in a chair, and so on. Were I confronted by a genuine skeptic about my claim, such an argument might represent my best effort to convince *her*. But it would be a serious epistemological mistake to think that such an argument could be *my* only ground for thinking that I am sitting in a chair. That would be to confuse rational belief with rational persuasion. The epistemic force of such an argument would be minuscule compared with the epistemic force of my experience itself. My experience properly makes it seem much more obvious to me that I am sitting in a chair than any such argument could.

Arguments properly play an important role in our common consideration of whether or not realism is true. Given that we disagree about this, we need to be concerned with what might help us resolve our disagreement. Arguments typically are our best epistemic resources for the resolution of controversies. Furthermore, in our own case, arguments play an important clarifying role. They help us understand realism and antirealism in light of their logical relations to other beliefs or claims. It is helpful to learn what other claims might entail realism or antirealism and what claims might follow from realism or antirealism. Arguments can also disabuse us of false assumptions about such implications. The awareness of these logical relations is potentially quite helpful to an honest consideration of realism and antirealism. It helps us evaluate realism and antirealism in light of our honest consideration of the claims to which they are logically related. For example, if one has been laboring under the impression that realism *necessarily* follows from the phenomena of perceptual experience, it is helpful to learn that it does not. It is helpful to learn, if it is a revelation, that an object's having a property, *as we know it*, is not incompatible with its having that property *in itself*. The problem is that we tend to get lost in the arguments. We get stuck on the question, "How, in light of the arguments on both sides of the question, does it honestly seem to me?" Too often, we never get around to asking the question, "How, *all things considered*, does it honestly seem to me?" One important epistemic resource the former question ignores is the epistemic weight of perceptual experiences themselves. Arguments may avail themselves of *descriptions* of experiences. But as we have seen, the difference between the epistemic weight of experiences and that of their descriptions is often great. Although I am aware that I can't prove realism is true and that there are antirealist explanations of the phenomena of my experience, my everyday perceptual experience nevertheless makes it seem obvious to me that realism is true. When I consider the question, it seems utterly obvious to me that the existence of the tree and its having the properties that it does is quite independent of our cognition of it. I suspect that more philosophers would agree, were we not habituated by our preoccupation with arguments to disregard the intuitive pull of other considerations such as the phenomena of perceptual experience.

Realism and Irrealism: A Dialogue

MARK S. MCLEOD

IRREALIST: Why do you realists think there is a singular, real world?

REALIST: By "real" we mean that there exists a world and that it is what it is completely independent of how I (or we) think about it, cognize about it, believe about it, know about it, and so forth. The relationship between the world and our cognitive dealings with it, although not worked out in some final sense, is basically one of the world's existing in some mind-independent manner and its causing or influencing our thinking, believing, cognizing, and so forth about it.

IRREALIST: You've told me what you believe, but not why. The assumptions you make in what you just said are typically taken to be common sense, but what argument is there for them?

REALIST: I don't need an argument to defend common sense since the other position, antirealism, is so counterintuitive and itself without any decent argument.

IRREALIST: Counterintuitive it is. I agree. But it's not without argument. Consider this one, for example. Take any two apparently contradictory metaphysical claims. Suppose, for the moment, each claim is equally well epistemically justified (warranted, known, etc.). Add to those claims the additional premise that contradictions are impossible. What metaphysical conclusion should one reach? The most straightforward result is that there is more than one world and that truth is world-relative.

> For example:
> (1) Contradictions are impossible.
> (2) Metaphysical freedom exists.
> (3) Metaphysical freedom does not exist.
> (4) Therefore, there are at least two worlds, one in which metaphysical freedom exists, one in which it does not.
> (5) Therefore, truth is world-relative.

REALIST: Before I give you what I take to be the obvious solution to the problem, let me ask what you mean by "world." How can there be two or more worlds? For example, is the action I'm now performing both free and not free?

Well, I guess you'd say not. But then how are there two worlds? Do they over-lap in space and time? Do they somehow mysteriously coalesce? The notion of two or more worlds that are somehow coextensive seems to be just crazy.

IRREALIST: The term "worlds" is Nelson Goodman's, and I must admit that he isn't very clear about what it comes to. And I don't want to get bogged down on this issue. Perhaps we can work on it some other day. But I will say that if you don't prefer the multiple world talk, we could restate the argument in terms of Michael Lynch's account of a singular world presenting itself to various "conceptualizers" in radically distinct and incompatible ways. He cashes out his view by giving an account of "world," "object," and "existence" as fluid. He says that just as we can apply terms such as "object" and "existence" in a fluid manner, so we can apply terms such as "world" fluidly. We haven't switched concepts. We've just extended, implicitly, our shared notion of reality.[1] For sim-plicity's sake, however, we can keep talking about worlds. The force of the ar-gument can still be seen.

REALIST: Well, I'm not sure that Lynch's position works either, but let's pass over the issue of worlds. Your argument still fails because we all know that (2) and (3) cannot both be true. You ask us to suppose that (2) and (3) are equally epistemically justified. Why should we accept that, if it gives us an absurd con-clusion? And even if we do accept it, it doesn't follow that both are true. That our epistemic or cognitive abilities can't help us decide between two claims doesn't ever entail that both are true. Epistemology isn't metaphysics. Indeed, the common error of a good many antirealists is to confuse our epistemic limits with the way the world really is.

IRREALIST: First of all, let me say that I'm neither fish nor foul. I think the best position might lie not in antirealism nor in realism but in irrealism, somewhere between antirealism and realism. I take antirealists to have taken things into their own hands, or minds, so to speak. I'm not willing to follow them there, for it leads one to a kind of radical relativism I can't bring myself to hold. I'm not willing for just anything that a person happens to believe to be true. Neverthe-less, I can't see that the world is only "one way" without any kind of contribu-tion from our epistemic activity. Somehow our rational activity influences the way the world is (or the ways they are).

In particular, the argument indicates that our epistemic activity, our "epis-temizing," if you will, contributes to the world—or worlds. Here I must say that I'm not prepared to say exactly *how* our epistemizing contributes to the world(s), simply that it does. But I will have to be cautious here and note that the argument is about epistemizing and not cognizing. I want to set aside the "mere cognizing" of the world for our discussion and talk just about how our evaluating claims vis-à-vis truth might "make worlds." I set aside "mere cogniz-ing" not because I think it doesn't play a role but because the argument I've pre-

---

[1] Michael Lynch, *Truth in Context: An Essay on Pluralism and Objectivity* (Cambridge: MIT Press, 1998), 95.

sented doesn't apply to mere cognizing in the neat way it applies to epistemiz-ing. It may be helpful just to start with the neater argument before moving to the messier one.

So, as I've said, I'm not happy with the crazy position that simply believing *p* makes *p* true. But neither am I happy with the so-called commonsense position that the world is merely "lying around out there" for us to form beliefs about it, with us humans then hoping that there is some sort of accurate connection be-tween the "way the world is" and our "justified" beliefs about it. So my posi-tion isn't as clearly developed as I'd like it to be. I will suggest, without spelling out in detail, the notion that truth is (in part, at least) an epistemic notion so that somehow the world's being the way it is (or the worlds' being the ways they are) is due to our epistemic contributions. I'm not willing to say with Rorty that truth is what our peers will let us get away with, nor would I finally want to say that some individual human's epistemizing is enough to "make a world," but neither am I willing to say that truth is completely independent of our epistemic activity, where by "epistemic" I mean the rational activity of forming and justi-fying (or warranting, etc.) beliefs. So I think the argument is instructive to help us get onto the right track about some of these matters.

For clarity's sake, what do I want to argue and how do I want to approach it? First, the approach. I want us to take your typical realist claim that episte-mology and metaphysics are two different things seriously and not slip and slide between the two. At first blush, it certainly seems as if our epistemizing activi-ties are distinct from the metaphysics of the world. So, prima facie, to say that *p* is *true*—a term most straightforwardly understood as metaphysical and not epistemic—is not the same as saying that *p* is believed, justified, known, taken to be true, thought to be true, accepted, and so forth. These latter terms are best understood as epistemic. We can say these terms are epistemizing terms, terms of epistemic evaluations or weightings. I take it that the realist wants to keep a stark line drawn between metaphysics (truth) and epistemology. The issue whether the epistemizing of humans influences the truth of a statement simply doesn't arise for the realist. So let's keep the issues separate. My question is, then, what happens when we strip (1), (2), and (3) of epistemic evaluations and weightings? The argument concludes that what follows logically, given the truth of (1), (2), and (3), is (4) and (5). I want to argue, then, that a strict keeping of the dichotomy between our epistemizing and reality puts pressure on the notion that truth is purely a metaphysical concept.

REALIST: My reply is easy to see. We should simply take some one of (1), (2), and (3) to be false.

IRREALIST: Why?

REALIST: Because the laws of logic demand it. If (2) and (3) really do contra-dict each other, one must be false. That's the law of noncontradiction. I heard Peter van Inwagen give a simple argument against this position once. It goes like this. First, if W_1 is actual, then freewill exists. Second, if W_2 is actual, then freewill does not exist. Third, it is not both the case that freewill exists and that freewill does not exist. Therefore, it's either not the case that freewill exists or it's not the case that freewill does not exist.

IRREALIST: So van Inwagen is a realist, and he says that my (1), (2), and (3) cannot all be true. Since contradictions are impossible, either (2) or (3) must be false. It makes more sense to reject as false one of (2) or (3) than to reach the absurd conclusion that there is more than one world. But that argument surely misses my point. First, van Inwagen's third premise rests on an interpretation of the law of noncontradiction, namely, a realist interpretation. Without that realist interpretation, his third premise doesn't go together with his first and second to give his conclusion. Furthermore, van Inwagen's argument is legitimate if we epistemically value the negation of (4) or (5) more highly than (1), (2), or (3). But then he slips in some epistemic rankings again, precisely what we agreed to keep out of our discussion.

REALIST: I admit that we cannot access the world without epistemizing. That is implied by the realist position. The world is "out there" independent of our epistemizing it, but if one is to know about it, one must engage in some epistemological enterprise or other. Neither irrealism nor antirealism follows from that fact. Furthermore, that neither irrealism nor antirealism follows from the necessity of epistemizing to access the world doesn't show that we can talk about metaphysical matters stripped of all epistemizing. *Of course* we know that (1) is true and that therefore either (2) or (3) is false. So we don't have to buy (4) or (5). In fact, there is no pair of contradictory statements both of which we *must* admit is true. We can always take one of them to be false. So this kind of argument will never force us to the conclusion that there is more than one world.

IRREALIST: Your reply begs the question against irrealism. You say the world is the way it is and that our epistemizing has nothing to do with it, thus setting aside any role for epistemic weighting or ranking. But when I want to agree with you and actually set aside epistemic rankings, you reject my suggestion. You cannot say that epistemizing must be set aside when doing so favors realism and yet appeal to it when the argument runs against realism. Either we can use epistemizing to decide metaphysical issues or not. If we can epistemically rank-order the premises and thereby decide metaphysical issues, then our epistemizing contributes to the way the world is and irrealism wins. If we cannot, then my foregoing irrealist argument goes through, pure logic wins, and there is more than one world. Either way, irrealism wins.

REALIST: Aren't you trading on an ambiguity among two distinct meanings of "decision"? One is an epistemic sense of decision, as in "I decide which statement is true," that is, I decide which way to *believe*. The other is a metaphysical sense, as in "I decide which way the world is going to be," that is, the world is caused to be the way it is by my believing it to be so. On the one hand, if you take the latter meaning, then your argument might find success, but I see no reason to take the latter, as it is surely an absurd notion. On the other hand, the former allows that the world is what it is, all the while keeping our discovery of the world a completely independent enterprise. We can take our best epistemic shot at the world, but our believing one way rather than another has no causal link (from belief to world) at all.

IRREALIST: Perhaps. But if that is the case, then at best you realists are left with being able to discuss only worlds as you epistemize them and not the world itself. Your realism precludes ever getting at the world, and we are left with a very radical form of skepticism. The world known (reasoned about, argued over, etc.) is the world epistemized and not the world as it is in itself. Realism can never claim to know or, for that matter, rationally to surmise that the world itself is a realist world. What grounds could you produce except grounds filtered through your epistemic weightings and rankings? You can never talk about the world itself. You can only talk about the world as you rank-order it. And isn't that what so many antirealists are saying these days? There is no difference between the world we talk about and the world as it is. To suggest that the world is a singular, fixed way is to assume something we cannot show without epistemizing. Either there is no functional difference between "the world" and "the world epistemized by me (or us)" or "the world" is simply beyond our means and we cannot talk about it.

But perhaps I should have been more circumspect earlier. Let's get rid of the "decision" talk and consider this way of putting the irrealist argument.

(1) Contradictions are impossible.
(2') P
(3') -P
(4') Therefore, there is more than one world, one in which P is true, another in which -P is true.
(5) Therefore, truth is world-relative.

Consider also this supporting argument.

(A) Either our epistemizing (1–3') contributes (somehow) to the truth of (1–3') or it does not.
(B) If our epistemizing (1–3') contributes (somehow) to the truth of (1–3'), then irrealism obtains.
(C) If our epistemizing (1–3') does not contribute (somehow) to the truth of (1–3'), then the irrealist argument is successful, and irrealism obtains.
(D) Therefore, irrealism obtains.

REALIST: I don't see how (B) or (C) are to go.

IRREALIST: Taken straightforwardly, premise (B) simply gives us irrealism. Suppose we epistemize (1–3'). The antecedent of (B) then is either true or false. If it is true, then the truth of (1–3') depends somehow on our epistemizing them, in which case there is surely more than one way the world is, for there is more than one way to epistemize (1–3'). Truth thus is world-relative. Irrealism obtains. But if the antecedent of (B) is false, then the truth of (1–3') has nothing to do with epistemizing and thus epistemizing is irrelevant to the irrealist argument just presented. This irrelevance drives a large wedge between epistemology and metaphysics, precisely what the realist typically claims. Thus (C) comes into play.

REALIST: I can grant that, but (C) appears to be the truly controversial move.

IRREALIST: The antecedent of (C) says that the truth of (1–3') is in no way shaped by our epistemic stance toward (1–3'). So if we do not in any way epistemize the premises in the irrealist argument, then we cannot appeal to reasons to reject any of the premises. That leaves three possibilities with regard to the truth or falsity of (1–3'). Before we explore those possibilities, however, it is important to note that the discussion is focused not on defending the truth of (1–3') (that would be to rank them epistemically) but rather on understanding what true epistemic neutrality looks like in regard to this argument.

REALIST: I see. So the issue isn't whether we actually have evidence for or against the truth of any of the premises. Rather, the question is, since we aren't allowed to appeal to such evidence, how are we to treat (1–3')?

IRREALIST: That's it. And as it turns out, it looks as if the position that claims all the premises are true is at least as viable as any other position—in fact superior to some—and therefore the argument goes through.

REALIST: I don't see why I should buy that conclusion.

IRREALIST: Here's why. Let's consider the possible combinations of truth values for the premises. First, let's suppose all the premises are false. There is no solace for realism here. Because all three are false, (1) is false. But then contradictions would be possible and that is a fate worse than irrealism, for then anything goes. We are left with a true and complete antirealism that is no better than a radical relativism. So if we get irrealism if (1–3') are true, we get a kind of antirealism if (1) is false. Taking this route won't help you.

REALIST: I'll surely admit that.

IRREALIST: The second possibility is that some of (1–3') are true and others false. But which ones? We can tell right away that it won't be (1) that is false, without rendering the worlds not only multiple but completely relative. That leaves us with (2') and (3'). Although it is possible that one is true and the other not, without introducing some reason to pick one over another (which, by assumption, we cannot do, for that is to epistemize them), we look to be on shaky ground. Why should we take the situation one way rather than another? According to the realist dichotomy between epistemizing and reality, believing, knowing, taking, accepting, and so forth have nothing to do with the way reality is, as you've been wont to point out. We must remain epistemically neutral. We cannot, by supposition, epistemically rank-order the premises one way or another.

REALIST: I guess that's all right.

IRREALIST: That leaves the third possibility, that (1–3') are all true. But then (4') and (5) follow, and irrealism obtains! One could suggest that evidence can be marshaled against (1), (2'), or (3'). But to marshal such evidence is to epistemize the premises. Again, we can't do that, by supposition. Hence if we are consistent in not introducing epistemic rank-ordering, then the irrealist argument is successful, and irrealism obtains.

REALIST: I still say that the world is the way it is completely independent of the way we relate to it epistemically. I see how the first and third possibilities go. But I'm not really convinced by the second. Why can't we just retreat to the position that we don't know which of (2') and (3') is false, but that one must be true while the other is false? We don't have to introduce epistemic rankings here. We just have to admit that one isn't true.

IRREALIST: So you would be willing to admit that realism is stuck between the rock of admitting that epistemizing contributes to the metaphysical nature of the world and the hard place of skepticism.

REALIST: Yes, I think that's fine. My realism may leave the world a little mysterious, but that isn't anything new.

IRREALIST: Yes. But I believe you are actually worse off than that. As it turns out, there is no noncircular way of being a realist, once you retreat to the position of admitting that you could be wrong about the way the world is.

REALIST: Now you accuse us realists not only of skepticism but of circularity?

IRREALIST: Yes. My premise (1) is actually metaphysically neutral between there being a singular world and multiple worlds. That is, although (1) is taken to be true, there is no built-in commitment to a realist interpretation of the law of noncontradiction over against an irrealist interpretation. We irrealists can, and desire to, hold onto (1). One difference between you realists and we irrealists on this score is that we, following the strict distinction between epistemological projects and the metaphysics of the situation, want to remain epistemically neutral about (1) through (5). By remaining neutral in this way, we get the conclusions (4') and (5). About this, we irrealists are quite sanguine. How can you realists avoid these irrealist conclusions? What reason can you proffer to defend the single-world interpretation of (1)? None. Except, perhaps, to assert that there is only one world, and along with it the realist interpretation of the law of noncontradiction. But that is the realist thesis itself. And surely that begs the question against us irrealists. Realism is not the default position on these matters. Irrealism is on ground just as solid. Unless, of course, you introduce some epistemic ranking among the premises. But that puts us back to the earlier challenge.

REALIST: Well, can't I offer some set of reasons for realism?

IRREALIST: What would those be, except more already epistemized reasons? And therein lies the rub. Any reasons you realists offer will in fact count toward irrealism's truth, for they will all be epistemized reasons. When they are stripped of epistemic rankings, there simply is no reason to opt for realism over irrealism, without circularity.

REALIST: Well, on the grounds you've appealed to, circular reasoning is acceptable, for we know that any proposition follows from that proposition if we stick to logic. "p therefore p" is perfectly valid, deductively.

IRREALIST: Yes, but that proves my point and doesn't help yours at all. There are all kinds of odd things about deductive logic, stripped of all epistemic concerns. One of them is that logic alone cannot tell us anything about the world . . . or the worlds. Logic is at best neutral vis-à-vis these matters.

REALIST: But aren't you irrealists in the same skeptical boat? Why should we realists accept your conclusion? What evidence have you provided?

IRREALIST: We've provided (1), (2') and (3'). And you can substitute whatever you wish for P and-P. Perhaps that there is a God and that there isn't a God will do. Or maybe that humans have rights based in our natures and that humans do not have rights based in our natures. And so on. Pick your favorite metaphysical issue and draw from it two contradictory claims. All we need is some argument with contradictory statements substituted for P and-P. We do not offer those as epistemically ranked propositions. We offer the bare logic of the situation. We need no other reason. The strict separation of epistemic concerns from metaphysical ones opens the door to irrealism, just the opposite result from what realists often claim.

REALIST: But aren't you, too, slipping in some epistemology here? You, after all, *take* (1), (2'), and (3') to be true. Why should we realists accept this presupposition?

IRREALIST: We've already gone over that ground. What alternative have you got? You are down to (2') and (3'). If you rank-order them, then you, too, are *taking* one to be true over the other and then irrealism's won. If you simply say that one must be false, although you have no way to determine which one, you've slipped in a realist interpretation of (1). Our taking (1), (2'), and (3') to be true is simply admitting that irrealism is correct, that truth is world-relative, and that our epistemizing the world is world-shaping.

REALIST: Still, the world is the way it is independent of my epistemizing it.

IRREALIST: Do I detect a little metaphysical foot stomping here? Why should I accept that?

REALIST: Why should I accept your absurd position, with more than one world?

IRREALIST: Because I was just following your rules and trying to describe the world without epistemically weighting the description. The onus is on you to show the superiority of your position. I've given my argument. What's yours?

REALIST: Well, I know the law of noncontradiction is true.

IRREALIST: I agree, but it's metaphysically neutral vis-à-vis realism and irrealism, so that's not going to help you much.

REALIST: Sure. But the law of noncontradiction applies in all worlds, right?

IRREALIST: That depends on what you mean. It applies in all the worlds there are, I suppose. I'm not talking about merely possible worlds. I mean the actual worlds.

REALIST: Precisely. There is no world such that the law of noncontradiction doesn't apply. What about the world of worlds, or if you like, the superworld? Does the law of noncontradiction apply there? Your argument seems to operate that way. (1) seems to be true universally, and therefore you can allow for the contradiction between (2') and (3') and yet also for both to be true. You can do this because there is a kind of superworld of worlds for it to range over.

IRREALIST: Let's grant that for the moment.

REALIST: But then how about this argument?

(1) Contradictions are impossible.
(2") There is only one world.
(3") There is more than one world.
(4") Therefore, there are at least two superworlds, one in which there is only one world, one in which there is more than one.
(5') Therefore, truth is superworld-relative.

You can see where this is going. First superworlds, then supersuperworlds, then supersupersuperworlds, and so on. Pretty soon, we are in infinitely bad shape, with more worlds than we can shake a metaphysical stick at. There is a reason to reject your initial argument. It shows far too much.

IRREALIST: I don't think so.

REALIST: Don't tell me you're willing to buy an infinite regress too.

IRREALIST: I'm not sure. I've always wondered exactly what is wrong with them. As a realist, I suppose I would be worried. But as an irrealist, it's a whole lot less clear. Does it matter whether there are just two worlds or an infinite number of worlds? Once we've planted the garden, let a thousand flowers bloom—or maybe even an infinite number of flowers! There is no logical inconsistency in superworlds or supersuperworlds. It's a little uncomfortable and certainly more than I can imagine. But philosophers ought to be used to that.

But then again, I'm not sure that superworlds are the same as worlds. Perhaps we should put a stop to your argument before it gets off the ground. Perhaps we should just say that superworlds don't function like worlds at all, for then we'd have problems with the law of noncontradiction.

REALIST: How so?

IRREALIST: What I am concerned with is that by holding so fast to the law of noncontradiction I've admitted too much. Perhaps there is some single facet of all worlds that is common among them. And isn't that a sort of singular, realist superworld?

REALIST: Precisely. I was coming back to that. Not only does your argument seem to allow for an infinite regress of worlds; it also seems to admit that there is at least one singular facet of the worlds that is fixed, namely, the law of noncontradiction. Maybe that is all the world *really is* independent of us, and the rest we add. But then we realists have gotten our lever, and although perhaps we won't move the world, we can at least show that there is some aspect of the world that doesn't depend upon our epistemizing.

IRREALIST: Maybe you are right. But have you gotten a piece of the world without epistemizing? Don't you, as well as I, just hold the law of noncontradiction to be true? Haven't we "made the world" by believing that that is the only way we can make sense of the world? Perhaps that was inchoately behind your earlier point that we irrealists too beg the question, simply in the opposite direction from you. We assume the law of noncontradiction, as do you. We take it one way, with lots of worlds. You take it the other way, with only one world. Who is "right," and how do we decide? I've been thinking that taking things to be true by assumption, as we do in working logic proofs, is not an epistemic issue. But by assuming that, wasn't I giving away my store? Wasn't I leaving the world simply beyond my reach, which is what I've been accusing you of all along? So maybe the world really is mysterious, even on my irrealist view.

REALIST: Precisely.

IRREALIST: But we shouldn't move too quickly here. There may be a good response. Haven't we just admitted that we have to epistemize the law of noncontradiction in order to solve anything here? We have to *take* it to be true?

REALIST: Well, you have, at any rate.

IRREALIST: But what is the force of that "have to"? I said, "We have to, in order to solve anything here." That is, we have to in order to describe the world. But isn't the law of noncontradiction itself then nothing more than an epistemic principle, a way of constructing the world? Why take it to be a metaphysical statement? Or if it is, its metaphysical status is identical to its epistemological status. What I mean is that the law of noncontradiction has the ontological status it has because it has the epistemic status it has. That is, it is true because it coheres with the rest of our epistemic web of belief, warrant, rationality, knowledge, or what have you. It is true *because* we take it as fundamental to getting around in the world, that is, for describing the world. Its not being true would be too weird epistemically and metaphysically. Now of course you realists will want to introduce your "but we could be wrong" strategy here. However, it isn't clear how to do that. What we all need is for the law of noncontradiction simply to be (part of) the way the world is. It looks, however, as if it can't have that status, even on the grounds of logic alone, without our epistemizing. In some sense, it is true because it is the "way things are," and yet it is true because that is the way we take it. It is hard to tell the difference. In fact, I see no difference in this case. But then that falls right into our irrealist hands and we win. The world is the way we take it to be. Or the world makes us take it this way. There is one thing we can't be mistaken about, and that is the law of noncontradiction. But that isn't because that is the way the world is and therefore our minds are caused to think that way. Instead, as Kant saw long ago, the world is the way it is with regard to the law of noncontradiction because our minds "make it" so. We epistemize the world. Indeed, there is no distinction between the way the world is and the way we epistemize it, at least on the most fundamental of levels. No, irrealism still comes through in the end. I take back my earlier hesitation. The world is not beyond our ken, not because it's "out there" and we have minds that can conform to it. Rather, because we are here, and the world or worlds conform to us.

REALIST: Two comments. First, Kant at least believed in some sort of universality for the rational mind's operations. Your position seems no better off, in the final analysis, than the kind of radical relativism you rejected earlier. Surely something isn't true simply because I believe it is. Second, and this I want to explore a bit, don't we still have to account for the infinite regress problem? It's one thing to say that there are many worlds and truth is relative to them. It is another to say that there are many, perhaps infinitely many, superworlds and that truth is relative to them. Aren't we just forced into the kind of radical relativism you earlier wanted to avoid by affirming the law of noncontradiction? Isn't the notion of truth here just getting a little too thin? It seems more like make-believe—I believe it and therefore I make it so.

IRREALIST: Well, all right. I wasn't really happy with my earlier response to this issue either. Perhaps I have gotten us into an *unhappy* infinite regress. Is there some way to avoid this unhappiness?

REALIST: Let me suggest something, in the unlikely hope that you'll agree.

IRREALIST: I'm not opposed to taking help from my metaphysical enemies. Go ahead!

REALIST: What if you stop the regress with God?

IRREALIST: Surely you jest. Irrealists are trying to get away from a "God's eye" point of view.

REALIST: Hear me out. Following your arguments, there are many worlds because there are conflicting true statements about the world taken as a singular world. Similarly, just as there are apparent conflicts that generate the various worlds with their various contents, so are there apparent conflicts among world-descriptions that generate various superworlds. This is the source of the infinite regress.

IRREALIST: Yes.

REALIST: On your grounds, we can't stop the infinite regress by reducing all the worlds to one, as the materialist might be accused of. Instead, let's look for some unifying (as opposed to reducing) feature.

IRREALIST: What do you mean?

REALIST: Goodman says that we build worlds out of other worlds.[2] One might thus suppose that there is a first world. Whence this first world? Goodman suggests that the search for a universal or necessary beginning world is best left to theology. Taking our cue from Goodman, but applying the suggestion to the "superworld problem," let's turn to theology to help us avoid the infinite regress of worlds.

IRREALIST: Go ahead.

REALIST: In short, God is going to help you. God, too, is a world maker, although he has a different sort of ontological status than we do. And he provides the unification of all the worlds created by us.

IRREALIST: But how can God help? Isn't God just one more person making up

---

[2] See Nelson Goodman, *Ways of Worldmaking* (Indianapolis: Hackett, 1978).

worlds? How can God be a unifying factor without himself getting caught up in the beliefs and attitudes and other world-making activities?

REALIST: We have to go back to something earlier in our conversation first. At one point you suggested that any two contradictory pairs of statements would get your argument off the ground. One of your examples was "God exists" and "God doesn't exist." Obviously, if we are to use God as the ground of unity, God can't be "in" one world and not in another.

IRREALIST: True enough. But I don't see how you can treat God differently from any other controversial piece of metaphysical furniture.

REALIST: Well, I can because God isn't a piece of metaphysical furniture. He is beyond our world or worlds and yet in the worlds. Just as for a while we thought the law of noncontradiction might resolve our debate on the side of realism, so now God might.

IRREALIST: Well, I said that the law of noncontradiction was an epistemic principle and therefore counted on the irrealist side. How are you to keep God from falling into the same problem? Why isn't God just an epistemic posit, just as the law of noncontradiction is?

REALIST: One of the things that bothers realists about irrealism is its tendency toward relativism. Even if your position avoids the radical relativism created when one denies the law of noncontradiction, your final conclusion, (5), has truth relative to worlds.

IRREALIST: True enough. But I think I can avoid relativism of a radical sort at least, noting that we all, realist and irrealist alike, appeal to the law of noncontradiction, thus making the world or worlds one way rather than another.

REALIST: But that doesn't seem to be enough. For if the law of noncontradiction is epistemic, then what is to stop someone, or all of us, from simply denying it?

IRREALIST: Yes, I have to worry about that.

REALIST: And doesn't your position simply give us humans far too much ability to shape the world?

IRREALIST: Yes, I worry about that too.

REALIST: Perhaps these two worries are connected.

IRREALIST: Yes, I suspect so. But on my irrealism, not just anything will go. There are limits to what will count as true in any given singular world, even if statements ruled as false in one world are true in some other world.

REALIST: I understand that. But that is grounded in your acceptance of the law of noncontradiction.

IRREALIST: Yes, I suppose it is.

REALIST: So we face a dilemma. Either realism obtains and there are objective limits to the way a world can be but we are stuck with (potential) skepticism about the world, or irrealism obtains and we avoid skepticism, but only at the cost of (potential) radical relativism.

IRREALIST: I think that is the best we can do.

REALIST: That is where God enters the picture.

IRREALIST: How so?

REALIST: God is not part of the world, or any world, in the sense that God is just another thing in the world. God, put in Platonic terms, is like the Good—beyond simple being. God is the underlying ground of contingent being, but he isn't a being as we are.

IRREALIST: So is God real or not? That is to say, is God something that is what God is, independent of our thinking about him, conceptualizing him, believing things about him, and so forth?

REALIST: Yes, God is real, but he is not just another thing. God is the ultimate Reality. God is the objectivity in an otherwise nonobjective world.

IRREALIST: Surely God is just another epistemic posit, though.

REALIST: No. God is needed not just epistemically but metaphysically. Here's why. If irrealism obtains, then the world is as it is, or worlds are as they are, because of our epistemic contributions.

IRREALIST: Yes.

REALIST: And if irrealism obtains, it's possible for us to deny the law of non-contradiction and so remove the so-called objective limits on what can be in a world.

IRREALIST: Yes.

REALIST: I have questions, then. If I (or we) make the world, then how do I (or we) get here? What is my source?

IRREALIST: So irrealism is a sort of underground argument for God's existence?

REALIST: Yes, but we have to careful about the notion of existence. I think one of the oddities of irrealism, at least atheistic irrealism, is that it leaves unexplained, and perhaps unexplainable, the age-old question of why there is anything at all. It may be right that I contribute something to the world's being the way it is. But if that's all there is to the story, I am the creator of the world, and even the creator of myself. Yet we are deeply suspicious that the world doesn't depend in this way upon me. I am simply part of the world, and I can't make myself up. I am contingent. There must be something outside the world, so to speak, to account for it. And the existence of that outside "something" can't just be contingent. And yet that something must be able to bring things about in the world.

IRREALIST: I see. And there is the place for God, the Being beyond simple being.

REALIST: Yes. Now if God made the world and then made us, we don't have to bear the burden of causing the world. But we can't take God's involvement in our world to follow the rules we are used to. But if your argument about our epistemic contribution to world-making is correct, we have to allow that God would make us as creative beings who can influence the way the world is as well. But we all recognize that there are limits to what we can do. Those limits, I suggest, derive from God, the Being beyond simple being.

IRREALIST: What becomes of the dilemma you stated earlier? Is it true that either realism obtains and there are objective limits to the way a world can be but we are stuck with skepticism about the world, or irrealism obtains and we avoid skepticism, but only at the cost of radical relativism?

REALIST: We go between the horns. There is a middle position between realism and irrealism. It is something like irrealism but it is theistic. Not only does God provide the first world(s) into which we then enter and build and change and make, but God also is the unifier of the worlds. He controls how things finally are. For one thing, he epistemizes the law of noncontradiction, so it isn't just left up to us. But then neither is God's existence left up to us. God is a metaphysical requirement to avoid radical relativism, but he is also a requirement to avoid skepticism about the world(s).

IRREALIST: How do you remove skepticism?

REALIST: That is not so obvious, is it? There are a couple of things worth pointing out. First, now that we have God, we have some reason to think that God would make our epistemic abilities conducive, generally, to getting truth about the world. Second, the worlds are, to some extent, the way they are by our epistemizing them. So there isn't such an extreme gap, so to say, between the way the world is, or at least certain aspects of the world, and one's epistemizing it.

IRREALIST: Would we need to worry about the first point if the second is true? Indeed, isn't the first true trivially because of the second?

REALIST: Perhaps that is right. But none of this will work without God, and one might say that because God made our epistemic abilities conducive to knowledge, he made us as irrealist contributors to the world(s). But on this kind of theistic irrealism, there are some things, or aspects of things, that are beyond our contributions—the law of noncontradiction being contributed by God to the worlds, for example. And if you want to get beyond the worlds, God himself is not made up by us.

IRREALIST: How do we know God, then?

REALIST: God, as outside the world, can reveal himself to us through some means other than our typical epistemic abilities. I think, for example, this is what happens in Christian, and perhaps all theistic, mystical experience. There is often no skepticism left in the recipient of God's showing himself this way. A common report among recipients of mystical experiences is that they know God more assuredly than they know anything else. One reason for that might just be that instead of simply knowing about God, the mystic knows God as God knows himself, at least in part. That explains all the mystic's talk of union with God. But the mystic also has a heightened sense of being known by God. But God's knowing is a making of the world, and when God makes a world, he makes it well. Perhaps in the mystical revelation, God simply lets the mystic experience, even if not understand, how God's knowing the world(s) is also the making of the world(s). This extends to the mystic as well. So God's revelation of his knowing the mystic, changes the mystic. The mystic, in some way beyond our usual ken, knows the way God knows, for the mystic is known by God, and in God's knowing, the mystic knows himself and God as well. All other knowledge of worldly things ceases to be of import, except as filtered through the primary knowing granted in the mystical experience.

IRREALIST: So what we have suggested, according to my contribution, is that human epistemizing does to some extent influence the world(s). But then that comes at the price of infinite regress and potential radical relativism. Your realist contribution is the objectivity that God supplies, and that objectivity both stops the regress and the radical relativism while admitting that there is an irrealist aspect of the world(s).

REALIST: Yes, that seems a fair summary.[3]

---

[3] The irrealist argument presented here was uncovered when I was considering what is wrong with Goodman's argument for irrealism. In a way, this argument is what I think Goodman *should* have said. I have him to thank, posthumously, for his inspiration. I also owe a debt of gratitude to Nicholas Wolterstorff for his criticism of Goodman. It was his way of putting Goodman off that indicated the direction to go. I want to thank William P. Alston, René van Woudenberg, Caleb Miller, and Laura Smit for pushing me to state what the real issue is. I might add that not one of Bill, René, Caleb, or Laura is an irrealist. I'm not even sure I am. Neither am I sure, nevertheless, how to respond to the argument presented by the irrealist here, without begging the question against irrealism.

·3·

Dividing the World into Objects

ANDREW CORTENS

I. THE DIVISION METAPHOR

In several places Michael Dummett expresses sympathy with the idea that "the world does not come to us already dissected into discrete objects." Rather, he suggests, "it is we who, by adopting particular criteria for what is to count as being presented with the same object as before, slice it up into objects in one manner or another."[1] In a similar vein, Hilary Putnam claimed in *Reason, Truth, and History* that objects "do not exist independently of conceptual schemes. We cut up the world into objects when we introduce one scheme or another."[2] Even in later years, after Putnam had toned down his antirealist rhetoric somewhat, we still find him insisting that "it makes no sense to think of the world as dividing itself into 'objects' (or 'entities') independently of our use of language. It is *we* who divide up the world—that is, the events, states of affairs, and physical, social, etc. systems that we talk about—into 'objects', 'properties' and 'relations', and we do this in a variety of ways."[3]

Clearly, all this talk of "dividing", "cutting", and "slicing" reality is metaphorical in character. We do not literally slice up reality with language as we slice bread with a knife or dough with a cookie cutter. The philosopher who embraces such talk therefore owes us a nonmetaphorical statement of his position. The main aim of this chapter is to do just that, to articulate in nonmetaphorical terms a philosophical position of which the division metaphor is the natural expression. I call the view 'ontological pluralism', or 'OP' for short. Unlike other positions in the same ballpark, OP does *not* imply that

I am indebted to the following people for their many helpful criticisms and comments on earlier versions of this chapter: William P. Alston, George Knight, Kris McDaniel, and Michael C. Rea.

[1] Michael Dummett, "Wittgenstein on Necessity: Some Reflections", in *The Seas of Language* (Oxford: Oxford University Press, 1993), 458. Reprinted as Essay 3 in *Reading Putnam*, ed. Peter Clark and Bob Hales (Oxford: Blackwell, 1994).

[2] Hilary Putnam, *Reason, Truth, and History* (Cambridge: Cambridge University Press, 1981), 52.

[3] *Reading Putnam*, ed. Clark and Hales, 243.

everything literally depends for its existence on our linguistic or conceptual activity, that existence and truth are always "relative to a conceptual scheme", or that truth is an epistemic notion. The fact that OP has none of these implications, I suggest, makes it far more worthy of serious consideration than standard ways of cashing out the division metaphor. Yet this same fact about OP suggests that it may be far too *tame* a view to justify all this talk of dividing reality, talk that seems, on the face of it, to have a distinctively antirealist flavor. If I am correct in saying that OP is *compatible* with affirming the mind-independent character of much of what exists, the absoluteness of existence, and a nonepistemic conception of truth, then to many it will seem to be wholly *devoid* of antirealist implications. I will address this concern in the final section of the chapter.

Before proceeding, a disclaimer: I myself am constitutionally unable to accept OP. What bothers me most about it, I think, is its consequences for metaphysics. OP strongly suggests (by design) that a great deal of metaphysical debate is *merely verbal*. And personally, I regard this as a rather depressing result, if true. But however much I might hope and believe in my heart that OP is false, here I am mainly concerned to ensure that it gets a fair shake.

II. ILLUSTRATING THE METAPHOR

Let's begin our inquiry by looking at some cases that might tempt people to embrace the division metaphor in the first place. Each case involves apparently incompatible ways of describing a certain situation. It is helpful to divide these cases into three categories. First, there are those in which we feel rather reluctant to prefer one description to an alternative description; neither of the options before us seems obviously wrong or out of sync with our usual ways of thinking and speaking. Second, there are those cases in which one description does seem preferable but in which the alternative description doesn't strike us as being particularly weird or crazy. And finally, there are those cases in which the alternative mode of description *does* strike us as downright weird and crazy. Let's refer to these as 'Type 1', 'Type 2', and 'Type 3' cases, respectively.

Here is a Type 1 case. At noon an ice cube measuring 2 cm × 2 cm × 2 cm is placed on a table. Slowly it melts, so that after an hour has passed, all that remains on the table is a small puddle of water. One person—call him 'A'—describes the situation in the following words: "At noon a single thing measuring 2 cm × 2 cm × 2 cm was placed on the table—namely, an ice cube. Shortly afterward it began to shrink and eventually—sometime between noon and 1 p.m.—it ceased to exist altogether. Just as the ice cube began getting smaller, a new thing came into existence: a puddle of water. Although it began as a very tiny puddle of water, its volume is now roughly equal to that of the ice cube at its largest." Another person, B, provides a strikingly different account of the facts. "The one and only 2 cm × 2 cm × 2 cm object that was placed on the table at noon still exists," says B. "It has merely ceased to be an ice cube. Now it is merely a puddle of water." Doubtless we can think up still other descriptions of the situation that might be offered. One can imagine, for example, someone insisting that *two* cubical objects of the same size were placed on the table at noon, one of them an ice cube that went out of existence shortly thereafter, the other a quantity of water that went right on existing but in a different state. But I trust I have said enough to give you a feel for the various "versions" of the facts that might be offered in this situation. And I suspect that many will agree that none of these versions is obviously incorrect.

Now consider a Type 2 case. A man buys an orange at the grocery store. He peels it and drops the peel in the garbage disposal, which promptly chews it up. One person—again, I'll call him 'A'—describes what has happened as follows:

> A: Initially, the peel was a part of the orange. It ceased to be a part of the orange when it was peeled off and destroyed. Thus, the orange is smaller than it used to be.

In contrast, B describes the situation as follows:

> B: The orange purchased by the man was once covered by a peel but now is not. But the peel was never a part of the orange; it was just a covering. Nor were the orange and the peel ever parts of a single material object, any more than a child with a towel wrapped tightly around her together compose an object. So even after the peel was removed, the orange remained pretty much the same size as when it was bought.

I think most of us would find A's description of the situation to be the most natural one. Yet B's version, though perhaps incorrect, doesn't seem crazy. Indeed, one suspects that had our own training been just slightly different, we might well have regarded A's reaction as the less natural of the two.[4]

---

[4] We can also imagine a third party, C, who agrees with A in saying that the largest piece of citrus fruit now in the man's possession weighs less the largest piece of fruit the man was holding in his hand as he left the store. But unlike A, C claims that the piece of fruit the man was holding earlier ceased to exist upon the removal and destruction of the peel. What remains before us now, says C, is something that used to be a rather large and tasty part of that now defunct piece of fruit. We might suppose that C holds, quite generally, that *nothing* can survive the removal and destruction of even its seemingly most insignificant parts. But I think that perhaps C's views are beginning to look more like an illustration of a Type 3 case than a Type 2 case. Incidentally, although A's description seems like the most natural one, it might turn out to be somewhat trickier to defend, owing to some familiar—but deeply perplexing—philosophical puzzles. Suppose, for the sake of argument, that the orange once had a peel as a part. Surely, we must admit that at that time it also had another part—"all of it but the peel", the pulpy part, as it were. Call that part 'Orange Minus'. What was the fate of Orange Minus? It lost no part as a result of the peeling. Apparently, it survived the peeling more or less intact. But if Orange Minus is still with us, and if, as A supposes, the orange itself is also still on the scene, then it appears to follow that the region of space currently occupied by a once-unpeeled-but-now-peeled orange is simultaneously occupied by *another* material object, Orange Minus. But how is it possible that two material objects should exactly occupy the same place at the

Eli Hirsch's writings are a rich source of Type 3 cases.[5] One of my favorites is his fanciful example of the "incar/outcar" speakers. Consider the following sequence of events. At t1 a car is situated in a garage. It begins to back out gradually so that at t2 it is half in the garage and half out. At t3 the car is completely out of the garage. The incar/outcar speakers describe this situation as follows: "At t1 an incar was situated in a garage. Shortly thereafter, it began to shrink, and at the same moment an outcar came into existence. The outcar proceeded to grow. By t2, the incar had shrunk, and the outcar had grown, to the point that they were the same in length—exactly half as long as the incar had originally been, in fact. But the respective shrinking and growing continued, until at t3, the incar had disappeared completely and the outcar was just as long as the incar had been at t1."

The description just given of the mundane event of a car moving out of a garage strikes most of us as pretty weird. Matters become weirder still if we suppose that the members of this community are quite unwilling to affirm the following sentence: "There is something that was in the garage at t1 and out of it at t3." In other words, their way of speaking suggests that they do not reckon ordinary cars as objects at all. To make things still weirder, we may suppose that these peculiar folk would describe the events of a dog emerging from a doghouse, a person emerging from a house, and so on in analogous ways. Clearly, we have a Type 3 case on our hands.[6]

One prima facie coherent response to these cases is this: metaphysical questions are difficult and often deeply puzzling. If you want to know which of the alternative descriptions is correct, or simply *why* a particular description is the correct one to give, roll up your sleeves and start working out a theory of identity over time, a theory of parts and wholes, and so forth. But of course, the proponent of the division metaphor wants to draw a very different lesson from

---

same time? I shall simply assume for now that A has a principled and consistent set of answers to such queries. A helpful collection of essays devoted to these issues is *Material Constitution*, ed. Michael C. Rea (Lanham, Md.: Rowman and Littlefield, 1997), especially Rea's introduction.

[5] See especially Hirsch's *The Concept of Identity* (Oxford: Oxford University Press, 1982) as well as his *Dividing Reality* (Oxford: Oxford University Press, 1993).

[6] Here is one more case to bear in mind, although I'm not sure where it fits in terms of my threefold classification. This well-known example is taken from Putnam's *The Many Faces of Realism* (La Salle, Ill.: Open Court, 1987), 18–20. (I have slightly altered Putnam's formulation to avoid needless distractions.) Consider a world containing three "mereological simples": individual things having no parts. Call them 'x', 'y', and 'z'. These simples bear no particularly interesting causal relations to one another, and no other concrete things exist at this world except such things as might be composed of some or all of the simples that exist there. According to what Putnam calls the "Carnapian" version of the situation, this world contains just three things, x, y, and z (ignoring such abstract items as sets and properties). But according to what Putnam calls the "Polish logician's version", the world contains, in addition to the three simples x, y, and z, four more things: one that has x, y, and z as parts, a thing having just x and y as parts, and so on. I'm inclined to regard this example as a Type 2 case, but you can decide the matter for yourself.

such cases. As he sees it, there is no substantive issue between the adherents of these rival descriptions. One person describes the situation in accordance with one way of dividing up the world into objects; another person describes it in accordance with another way of dividing up the world into objects. Although we may not be able to avoid dividing up the world one way or another, there is no uniquely right way to do it. In cases of Type 2 and 3, we are shown ways of dividing the world that are at variance with our own—*wildly* at variance with our own in Type 3 cases. But the fact that those ways of dividing the world seem wrong or even crazy to us merely reflects the fact that they are not *our* ways. And Type 1 cases illustrate that we ourselves haven't settled definitively on a single way of dividing the world into objects.

III. CASHING OUT THE METAPHOR: POTENTIAL PITFALLS

Before I turn to the task of trying to figure out how best to construe this talk of dividing the world, let me point out several pitfalls we should try very hard to avoid.

First, we should try to formulate a position that doesn't conflict with any well-established empirical facts. We have all heard people suggest that everything depends for its existence on human cognition. It is sometimes said, for example, that were it not for the fact that we associate the word 'star' with certain criteria of identity, there would be no stars. It seems to me that people who say such things are guilty of taking a running jump into the first pitfall. Are we to swallow the claim that there were no stars around before humans arrived on the scene? Even the dimmest student of astronomy will tell you that this is nonsense. Are we to believe, then, that the effects of human conceptual activity extend back to times before there were any humans? Well, *I* certainly don't want to be the one to inform the physicists that backward causation is not only physically possible but actual![7]

Another familiar way of explaining the metaphor is by appealing to the idea that nothing can be said to exist or to be true absolutely, but only relative to this or that conceptual scheme. Again, I suspect that one is going to have trouble taking this view without running into direct conflict with some well-established empirical facts. For suppose that in uttering the sentence "There are

---

[7] In an earlier version of this chapter I asserted that such mind-dependency views *imply* that either there were no stars before there were humans or humans can causally affect the past. Michael Rea convinced me that this stronger claim is unwarranted by raising the following point. Suppose the mind-dependency theorist takes the following view: the fact that a certain parcel of matter composed a star a billion years ago is result of the fact that the matter in question "timelessly" stands in a certain relation to human mental activity occurring at a much later time. Clearly, this carries with it no commitment to the claim that *the relation in question is causal*. Although Rea is clearly correct on this point, I am inclined to think that the counterfactual ("There would have been no stars had there been no humans") itself contradicts well-established empirical facts. If you accept it, you've already landed in the first pitfall even if you don't hold that there were no stars before there were humans or that humans possess the power to causally affect the past. But I shall not attempt to establish this here.

stars", I am really reporting a *relative* fact: the fact that stars exist relative to a certain conceptual scheme, C. It is difficult to see how the fact in question could have obtained if there had been no minds and hence no conceptual schemes.[8]

The second pitfall to avoid is *unintelligibility*. Thus, if we plan to make use of such ill-defined technical terms as 'conceptual scheme', 'ontological framework', and the like, we had better be prepared to give a clear account of such notions. Many relativists run into serious trouble on this score; rarely do they provide a satisfactory explanation of just what sort of thing a conceptual scheme is.[9] I have argued elsewhere that even if the notion of a conceptual scheme is taken for granted, the view that existence is always relative to a conceptual scheme has the absurd consequence that we can never explicitly state the content of a sentence that has existential implications.[10] Whether or not my argument was successful, many will agree that there are legitimate worries about the intelligibility of relativism about truth or existence.

The third potential pitfall is somewhat more difficult to state precisely. But the basic thought is one to which I alluded in the introduction: we shouldn't count an attempt to articulate the division metaphor as a success unless the position that emerges has a sufficiently "antirealist" or "antimetaphysical" feel to it. A corollary of this is that we won't be satisfied by any mere truism like "You can't describe the world without describing it."[11] The division metaphor, on its face, seems to be the expression of a substantive claim, one whose falsity is tacitly presupposed by all those old-fashioned metaphysicians who aim to "limn the structure of the world", in Quine's memorable phrase. It would be a big disappointment if the only remotely plausible claim behind the metaphor turned out to be an utterly "toothless" claim that no one would think of denying.

It is sometimes suggested that if the proponent of the division metaphor is to avoid the charge of triviality, he had better have in mind something more exciting than mere *linguistic relativism*, that is, the relativity of what a sentence means to a language.[12] For example, suppose that the proponent of the metaphor suggests

---

[8] But for an interesting attempt to disassociate relativism about existence from objectionable forms of mind-dependency, see Ernest Sosa, "Addendum to 'Nonabsolute Existence and Conceptual Relativity': Objections and Replies," in *Metaphysics: The Big Questions*, ed. Peter van Inwagen and Dean Zimmerman (Melden: Blackwell, 1998), 407–10. Another interesting attempt occurs in the first of Nicholas Wolterstorff's 1995 Gifford Lectures (unpublished).

[9] For a noble attempt to explicate this notion, however, see Michael Lynch, *Truth in Context* (Cambridge: MIT Press, 1998), particularly chap. 2.

[10] *Global Anti-Realism: A Metaphilosophical Inquiry* (Boulder, Colo.: Westview Press, 2000), 34 and 70 n. 5.

[11] This particular truism is due to Putnam. Surprisingly enough, he seems to think that it reveals the essence of what he calls "the phenomena of conceptual relativity". See Putnam, *Renewing Philosophy* (Cambridge: Harvard University Press), 123.

[12] Anthony Brueckner is one writer who insists on this point. See his "Conceptual Relativism," *Pacific Philosophical Quarterly* 79 (1998): 295–301. Another is Susan Haack; see her "Reflections on Relativism: From Momentous Tautology to Seductive Contradiction," *Philosophical Perspectives 10: Metaphysics* (1996): 297–315.

that the apparent disagreement between A and B in the orange case is a result of the fact that A and B are *speaking different languages*. In A's language 'The orange got smaller' expresses a proposition that is true; in B's it expresses a different proposition, one that is false. "Big deal!" the critic will retort. "This is relativity of the most trivial sort; it hardly justifies extravagant talk of dividing reality."

On closer inspection, however, the critic's reaction is rather shallow. Admittedly, *some* kinds of linguistic relativity are wholly uncontroversial and unexciting. Suppose the apparent dispute between A and B could be explained merely by supposing that by 'orange', B means what you and I mean by 'pulpy part of an orange'; so when B says, "The orange remains the same size after it was peeled", he speaks truly, since the pulpy part of the orange *did* remain the same size. Then we would have a pretty boring case of linguistic relativity on our hands. But in fact, this does not even begin to explain the dispute between A and B as characterized earlier. Recall that we had B insisting that the peel and (what he called) the orange never succeeded in composing a material object. Thus, A will accept whereas B will reject the following sentence:

S1: Something the man purchased at the store is smaller now than it was at the time of purchase.

Likewise, B will accept whereas A will reject this sentence:

S2: Nothing the man purchased at the store is smaller now than it was at the time of its purchase.

The word 'orange' nowhere appears in either S1 or S2. Obviously, then, mere differences in how A and B employ the term 'orange' cannot explain how both A and B could be correct when it comes to these sentences. It seems plausible to suppose that the same holds for any nonlogical predicate we might care to select: we will always be able to point to a pair of general (i.e., "quantified") sentences about which the parties disagree and which do *not* employ the predicate in question.[13] This suggests that if linguistic relativity is to do any work here, it must run deeper than differences over how the parties use certain nonlogical predicates. It seems like it will have to involve differences in how the parties employ *quantifiers* and also—perhaps—differences in how they employ expressions of the form 'a is identical with b' (given the intimate connection between quantification and identity).

As we'll see in the next section, OP posits a form of linguistic relativity that is deeper in just this way. But before I get to OP, its worth pausing to note a

---

[13] By a "nonlogical predicate" I mean, roughly, any predicate that is neither (a) the identity predicate nor (b) definable in terms of purely logical vocabulary (the identity predicate, quantifiers, and connectives).

very different type of appeal to linguistic relativity.[14] The basic idea is fairly simple: apparent disagreements like the ones just encountered can be explained by supposing that one party customarily restricts his quantifiers in a way the other doesn't. Thus, in the orange case, the suggestion is that B's quantifiers are customarily restricted in such a way that unpeeled oranges are effectively excluded from the domain of discourse. Given such a restriction, S2 will indeed express a truth in B's mouth. Since A's quantifiers are not so restricted, S1 expresses a truth when he utters it.

It is important to realize, however, that this strategy will be available to us only if we are willing to come down firmly in favor of a particular ontology— one that is (roughly speaking) *maximally permissive* when it comes to questions about what there is. Take the ice cube case, for example. To get all the parties "coming out right" in this case, one will have to suppose that *two* objects were placed on the table initially, one that survived the melting and one that did not. Then we will say that A's quantifiers are restricted in way that excludes things that can survive melting whereas B's are restricted in a way that excludes things that cannot survive melting, or some such thing. Or take the case of the incar/outcar people. On the present view, we will have to admit that there *really are* incars and outcars, *in addition to* cars. A typical car exactly shares its location with an incar at some times, with an outcar at others. But although there really are incars and outcars, they don't fall within the domains over which we usually quantify in the ordinary business of life. (And likewise, ordinary cars do not fall within the domains over which the incar/outcar people normally quantify.)

In sum, this way of handling cases of Types 1, 2, and 3 requires us to countenance a distinct individual for every distinct filled region of space-time. No wonder Ernest Sosa dubs this type of view "the explosion of reality" approach! Indeed, if pushed to its logical limit, a view of this kind will end up countenancing indefinitely many distinct individuals *for each region of spacetime*. In a variant of the ice cube case, the relevant quantity of water remains in a frozen state throughout its existence. Here A and B will give different verdicts, not over when the ice cube ceases to exist but over such *modal* questions as whether the ice cube *could* have existed if the relevant quantity of water had been in an unfrozen state at a certain time. The natural extension of the present view would have us recognize two things that exactly share their spatial *and temporal* boundaries but that differ only in their *modal* properties. Talk about the explosion of reality![15]

---

[14] What follows is a somewhat simplified version of what Ernest Sosa refers to as "the explosion of reality" view. See Sosa, "Putnam's Pragmatic Realism," *Journal of Philosophy* 90 (1990): 605–26, and "Existential Relativity," *Midwest Studies in Philosophy* 23 (1999): 132–43.

[15] Of course, there is a well-known way to avoid this extreme: we may adopt a counterpart-theoretic analysis of *de re* modality. On this view, talk of what a given thing would have been like in alternative circumstances should be understood as talk about how it is with that thing's "counterpart" in those circumstances. Thus, instead of supposing that A and B are referring to

Now I have nothing to say against such a view here. It is not part of my purpose to suggest that the "explosion of reality" approach is unworkable. I raise it only to draw attention to two important points. (1) Clearly, to adopt a "linguistic relativity" approach to these disputes is not necessarily to advocate a position that boils down to an uninteresting truism. The explosion of reality approach requires an elaborate and highly controversial ontology. (2) The explosion of reality approach—whatever its merits or defects—will not do as an attempt to explicate the division metaphor. The division metaphor is meant to suggest that a certain range of metaphysical disagreements are "empty", without substantive content. But to embrace the explosion of reality is not to dissolve metaphysical debate; it is to take sides. Though the advocate of the division metaphor will probably be happy to concede that a maximally permissive ontology is a feasible option, he will firmly resist any attempt to dignify it as the ultimate truth about matters metaphysical. Instead, he will see it as simply one more respectable way to divide reality, neither better nor worse than others. In short, the explosion of reality approach, although certainly not trivial, lacks the antirealist, antimetaphysical flavor we associate with the division metaphor.[16]

Having said this, however, I don't think we should expect to be able to derive *too much* antirealism from the metaphor. In the quotation with which this chapter began, Dummett is giving his interpretation of the views of his favorite arch-*realist*: Gottlob Frege. As Dummett sees matters, Frege's insistence on the need for "criteria of identity" betrays a deep sympathy with the division metaphor, a sympathy that functions as a moderating influence on the predominantly realist tendencies in Frege's thought. As a further caution against reading too much antirealism into the metaphor, note that defenders of an objective, mind-independent external reality as ardent as John Searle are often quite happy to embrace the metaphor.[17]

My hope, of course, is that OP will turn out to avoid all the pitfalls discussed in this section. So let's get down to the business of characterizing OP.

---

different things in the modified ice cube case, we need only suppose that they are in the habit of invoking different "counterpart relations". I suspect that counterpart theory will be hard to resist, from the present point of view anyway. For consider: (1) The explosion of reality solution requires us to recognize indefinitely many things that exactly share a certain location at a certain time. (2) Rampant multiple occupancy of this sort is much easier to swallow if one "tames it" by embracing four-dimensionalism and treating it as the sharing of temporal parts. (3) As Peter van Inwagen persuasively argues, four-dimensionalists are under considerable pressure to adopt counterpart theory ("Four-Dimensional Objects," *Noûs* 24 [1990]: 245–55). My guess, then, is that the most viable version of the explosion of reality solution will presume four-dimensionalism in conjunction with counterpart theory. This, however, doesn't seem to be the way Sosa was thinking of the explosion of reality; he seemed to be thinking of it as committed to the existence of distinct and constantly co-located objects that differ only in their modal properties.

[16] Sosa is not under any illusions on this point; when he first introduced the explosion of reality approach in "Putnam's Pragmatic Realism", it was explicitly intended as a *realist alternative* to Putnam's conceptual relativism.

[17] See Searle, *The Construction of Social Reality* (New York: Free Press, 1995), 160–67.

IV. FORMULATING ONTOLOGICAL PLURALISM

According to the explosion of reality approach, the parties to these apparent disputes are really talking about distinct (though in some cases overlapping) things. The cost of embracing this solution (at least, to some of us it seems a cost) is a highly permissive ontology, one that countenances all sorts of criss-crossing, overlapping things. Note that according to this approach, *at least one of the parties will be incapable of conveying certain truths that the other can convey—or at least he will be incapable of doing so as long as he persists in tacitly restricting his quantifiers (or his domain of quantification) in the manner to which he is accustomed.* The ontological pluralist, in contrast, will locate the linguistic differences between the parties in a more fundamental place: in the very meaning of the idioms of quantification and identity employed by each party. As we shall see, this will put the OP-ist in a position to say that *neither* one needs to change his way of talking in order to convey all the truths the other is capable of conveying.

To a first approximation, OP is comprised of three theses, the first of which is presupposed by the second and third. I call the first of them the "Multiplicity Thesis" (MT):

> MT: Where $L1$ is any possible language containing words that function syntactically like quantifier and identity symbols, there is a syntactically similar language $L2$ that is (a) equal in expressive power to $L1$ but (b) whose idioms of quantification and identity differ systematically in meaning from those of $L1$. (Note: the same goes for lexical items that function syntactically like names and predicates. The only subsentential units whose meaning is the same in both languages are sentential operators.) Furthermore, as a consequence of these differences, there are sentences of the form 'There are Fs' that express a truth in one of the languages while expressing a falsehood in the other, and likewise for some sentences of the form 'x is identical with y.'

Here I am thinking of a language as an abstract entity, a function that assigns propositions to strings of marks or noises, let's say. When I say that two languages are "expressively equivalent", I mean roughly that any proposition that is assigned to a particular string by either one of these languages will also be assigned to some particular string by the other—but of course, it will often be a different string in each case. Thus, to say that two languages are expressively equivalent amounts to saying that any proposition that can be expressed in one of them can also be expressed in the other and vice versa. When I say that a language contains terms that "function syntactically like quantifiers and the identity sign", I mean that the inferential behavior of these signs perfectly mimics the inferential behavior of our own idioms of quantification and identity. (I am assuming, of course, that formally valid principles of inference involving a certain word or phrase are identifiable on the basis of purely syntactic criteria, without a semantics for the language having to be specified first.) The fact that such a language contains signs that function in this way is no guarantee that those signs mean just what they do in our language. MT in effect tells us that you can have a pair of expressively equivalent languages that are "uncalibratable"—not in the sense that sentence-by-sentence translation between them is impossible but only in the sense that translation at the level of *individual words* is bound to fail (with the exception of words that function as sentential connectives).

Let's return to S1 and S2, the two sentences that were assigned different truth values by A and B in the example of the orange that was peeled. MT requires us to acknowledge the possibility that whereas A speaks a language in which the idioms of quantification and identity function in such a way that S1 expresses a truth while S2 expresses a falsehood, B speaks a language in which the idioms of quantification and identity have precisely the opposite result.[18]

How might this work? How, for example, would B express the truth that A expresses by uttering S1 ('Something the man purchased at the store is smaller now than it was at the time of purchase.')? To know the answer to this question, we would need to know a lot more about how both A and B answer a whole host of questions concerning composition and identity over time. But here is at least one possibility: perhaps B uses the following sentence to express what A expresses by means of S1:

- Something the man purchased either (a) is smaller now than it was when it was purchased or (b) was firmly attached to something else when it was purchased but is no longer so attached.

Admittedly, this suggestion is more likely to be right if the following sentences both happen to express truths in A's language:

- Whenever two things are firmly attached, they compose a third thing.
- Whenever two things that were firmly attached become detached, something gets smaller.

The present suggestion also assumes that whenever A and B agree that 'x exists' and 'y exists' both express true propositions, and whenever they are provided with all the same information about the relevant physical circumstances, they

---

[18] MT does *not* imply that this possibility *must* be realized whenever A and B offer such seemingly incompatible descriptions. There may be a possible world in which A and B say the things I have attributed to them yet speak the same language. In such a world one party would simply be wrong. But I take it that the OP-ist will want to insist that in such a world the party in error is in some sense guilty of nothing more than a "verbal mistake"; his error stems not from any misapprehension about the character of nonlinguistic reality but rather from the fact that he has false beliefs about what the words of his own language mean. In any case, all MT requires is that it is at least possible that A and B are speaking languages that are expressively equivalent but uncalibratable.

can be expected to agree about whether 'x and y are firmly attached' expresses a truth, too.

Similar remarks apply to the question of how A will express the truth B expresses by means of S2—'Nothing the man purchased at the store is smaller now than it was at the time of its purchase.' Here too, in order to hazard a decent guess, we'd have to know much more about how the parties would answer a whole host of questions. We should need to know, for example, under what circumstances B is prepared to admit that some things compose a further thing. So the whole matter is rather complicated. But to the extent that a set of principled answers to questions about composition and identity over time could be elicited from A and B, it seems plausible to think that one could in principle devise a "translation" scheme for moving back and forth between the two languages posited by MT.

Let us turn now to the second thesis comprising OP:

> ET: The Egalitarian Thesis: For any pair of languages that are related in the manner described by MT, neither is an objectively better tool for describing reality than the other.

We have seen that given MT, it may be that the different descriptions of the ice cube offered by A and B are couched in different languages—languages that are expressively equivalent but uncalibratable with each other. If this is indeed the case, then according to ET there is no respect in which A's is an objectively better description than B's or vice versa. We will return to the question of just what sorts of "good-making" features are at issue here in the final section. Let's look now at the third and last component of OP.

> SI: The Semantic Indeterminacy Thesis: For some pairs of languages related in the manner just described, our linguistic conventions leave it indeterminate which of them is the language of *our* community. Consequently, for some sentences of the form 'There are Fs' and some sentences of the form 'x is identical with y', it is indeterminate whether those sentences express a truth or a falsehood in our mouths.

SI is designed to explain Type 1 cases. In such cases, our hesitancy to prefer one description over a seemingly incompatible alternative is explained by the fact that our linguistic conventions fail to settle which of two uncalibratable languages counts as the language of our community. This move is exactly parallel to one popular account of vagueness: the reason "Mel Tormé is bald" fails to be definitely true or false is that the conventions governing the use of the word 'bald' leave it indeterminate which of a certain range of properties are expressed by that term (properties like *having fewer than 10,000 hairs on one's head, having fewer than 9,999 hairs on one's head*, and so on). Some of those properties are possessed by Tormé, but others are not. The SI thesis makes a similar claim about our use of quantifiers and identity expressions. But here, of course, we cannot think in terms of distinct sets of objects, each of which is an equally good candidate for being the extension of a certain predicate. Rather, we must think in terms of distinct propositions, all of which are equally good candidates for the office of *the proposition expressed by 'Something that was placed on the table at noon had ceased by 1 P.M.'* Some of the candidate propositions are true, their truth being guaranteed by the fact that an ice cube that was placed on the table at noon had completely melted by 1 P.M. But others are false, requiring for their truth more drastic changes in the arrangement of material particles that composed the ice cube at noon.[19]

V. ONTOLOGICAL PLURALISM AND ANTIREALISM

OP is compatible with the claim that there would have been stars even if language users had not existed. True enough, the OP-ist is likely to believe that the

---

[19] Having reached the end of the section intended to explain OP, I am painfully aware of the need for further clarifications on a number of points. To mention just two: (1) How is the OP-ist thinking of word meaning? (2) How is he thinking of propositions and their individuation? These two questions are connected. The OP-ist insists that two sentences drawn from different languages may express the same proposition in spite of the fact that none of the individual words in one language (sentential connectives aside) can be translated into the other language. How can translation at the level of whole sentences be so much as possible when translation at the level of individual words fails so drastically? I cannot hope to adequately address such worries here, but let me briefly indicate the broad outlines of a response. The OP-ist is thinking of the meaning of a word as something that supervenes on the facts about what propositions are expressed by all the sentences in which the word occurs (in a given language). Word meaning is, in this sense, less basic than and derivative from sentence meaning. The OP-ist is thinking of propositions, meanwhile, as (a) unstructured and (b) "coarse-grained". (How coarse-grained? I think it would suffice to hold that propositions are identical when and only when they are a priori necessarily equivalent.) This combination of views, I believe, makes it plausible to suppose that two sentences composed of words that (taken individually) mean radically different things may express the same proposition. (It is somewhat analogous to the fact that two identical pictures might be formed from two different puzzle sets with differently shaped pieces.) Furthermore, the "unstructured" line seems to me to be demanded by the Egalitarian Thesis. For if propositions possessed intrinsic structure, then a language whose sentences better mirrored that structure would be objectively better than one whose sentences did not. Having said that, the OP-ist must tread very carefully here. On the one hand, he seems to require a coarse-grained conception of propositional content; on the other, he probably won't want to be firmly committed to any particular theory of what propositions are and how they are individuated. For if OP is on the right track, these are just the sort of abstract metaphysical questions to which alternative and equally acceptable answers should be possible—the sort that can be answered only by choosing one manner of speaking over another. His best course of action, I suspect, is to first articulate OP against the background of a particular theory of propositions (a coarse-grained theory) and then to indicate how his whole theory may be reformulated in terms of a rival ontological framework for discussing questions of meaning and content—for example, a framework that dispensed with propositions entirely and made do with a coarse-grained "sameness of content" relation that can hold between pairs of sentences or belief-states. I hope to address these and other pressing issues concerning how OP should be formulated at a later time.

proposition that we express by saying 'There are stars' is one that we might well have expressed in alternative language by saying (for example) 'There are some material objects arranged starwise'.[20] In *that* language the sentence 'There are stars' might well express a falsehood (for it may be that in the alternative language, things arranged starwise are not—so to speak—"counted" as composing a larger whole). But however expressed, the proposition we express by saying 'There are stars' presumably would have been true regardless of which language we speak—indeed, regardless of whether we exist at all. So OP in no way threatens the idea of a common world describable by various alternative languages, a world whose character is largely independent of our linguistic and conceptual activity.

In light of this, I suspect that many contemporary antirealists will view OP as a rather stodgy and old-fashioned view. The OP-ist who retains the notion of a mind-independent world will be accused of buying into a mysterious realm of "things in themselves" whose intrinsic character must remain forever beyond our grasp—a "world well lost" if ever there was one. From the point of view of these antirealists, OP will seem like a last-ditch but ultimately futile effort to save realism. They will insist that the real lesson of the phenomena OP hopes to explain is that there is only a multiplicity of "world-versions" and no common underlying world at all. Or if one insists on continuing to distinguish versions from what those versions describe, we may just as well say that there is a *multiplicity* of worlds *à la* Nelson Goodman, each of which is an artifact of a particular mode of description.

You can probably guess what *I* think of the idea that "all there is are texts", or that we literally *make* the world(s!) we inhabit by adopting this or that mode of description. I take such views to be simply crazy, not serious options at all, in the light of certain obvious empirical facts. If I thought I had to choose between this sort of linguistic idealism and accepting a mysterious ding an sich, I know what *I'd* do: I'd pick the latter, without hesitation. But is the OP-ist faced with this choice? Is there any justice to the antirealist's charge that if one accepts OP while affirming the existence of a mind-independent world, one will be forced to say that it is impossible for us to describe the world "as it is in itself"?

Well, if by "describing the world as it is in itself" one simply means making claims the truth of which in no way depends upon the fact that we cognize or describe the world in certain ways, then, as we have already seen, the OP-ist is under no pressure to deny our ability to describe things as they are in themselves. But I think there is perhaps another sense that is commonly attached to this phrase, a sense that may better serve the antirealist's purposes. In this second sense, to say that a language is suitable for describing the world as it is in itself is not a way of commenting on the mind-independence of what the lan-

---

[20] Compare with van Inwagen's proposal for paraphrasing ordinary talk of chairs into sentences that refer only to simples "arranged chairwise". See his *Material Beings* (Ithaca: Cornell University Press, 1990), sections 10 and 11.

guage describes. Rather, it is to make a claim about how the language *relates* to what it describes—whether the latter be mind-dependent or not. In this sense, a language can be said to describe the world as it is in itself only if there is an appropriate structural isomorphism between it and the world. The requisite isomorphism, moreover, needs to be displayed at the level of the individual sentence; each must be structured in such a way that if it is true, it serves as a kind of "mirror" of the things, events, or conditions that make it true.

Laugh all you like at such talk of "mirroring". But notice how easily philosophers lapse into something very much like this way of thinking, as when they distinguish between "perspicuous" and "unperspicuous" ways of saying something, or when they contrast a sentence's "surface grammar" with its "deep logical form". Consider, for example, the sorts of things a nominalist might be expected to say about a sentence like 'Wisdom is rare.' The nominalist holds, of course, that there is nothing designated by the term 'Wisdom'. Yet he is not likely to deny that a typical utterance of this sentence expresses a truth. Instead, he will probably contend that the truth expressed by such an utterance would be more perspicuously conveyed by means of the sentence 'Few people are wise.' If we regard the latter as a more perspicuous way of expressing what the original sentence is ordinarily used to express, we will realize that there doesn't need to be anything designated by the term 'wisdom' in order for an utterance of 'Wisdom is rare' to express a truth.

It seems to me that the contrast invoked here between perspicuous and unperspicuous ways of putting things is very close indeed to the contrast between sentences that "mirror" the structure of what they are about and those that do not. I see the contemporary philosopher who continually seeks to paraphrase certain sentences in more perspicuous terms as someone who is deeply committed to what is perhaps one of the central aims of traditional metaphysics: the aim of describing things as they are in themselves—not just in the sense of describing the cognition-independent aspects of the world but in the sense of providing us with a description that accurately mirrors the structure of that world.

Now recall the accusation that if one combines OP with a belief in a common world that may be described equally well by various uncalibratable languages, one is committed to the view that we can't describe reality as it is in itself. We are now in a position to see that there is some justice in this charge. For suppose that we have a pair of expressively equivalent yet uncalibratable languages. On the one hand, we can hardly say that *both* languages faithfully mirror the true structure of reality, on pain of attributing incompatible structures to reality itself. On the other hand, the OP-ist is also barred from saying that one of the two languages serves as an effective mirror whereas the other does not. For that would contradict ET, which says that of any two expressively equivalent yet uncalibratable languages, neither is objectively better than the other. (Whatever exactly might be involved in "mirroring the structure of reality", it surely constitutes a good-making feature of a language.) Thus (unsurprisingly, perhaps) the OP-ist seems forced to say that no language can rightly be regarded as mirroring the structure of reality. And since his central claims range over all possible languages, he appears to be committed to the view that it is impossible for there to be a language that would allow us to describe the world as it is in itself in the sense that concerns us here. This encourages the thought that for the OP-ist, the structure of reality is ineffable or, perhaps worse still, that it is entirely devoid of structure, forming a sort "amorphous lump". No wonder some complain that this is a world well lost!

Having said all that, however, I don't think there is any need for the OP-ist to panic. He can put a halt to this line of thought by making a very simple move. Instead of acknowledging our second sense of 'describing the world as it is in itself' and withholding this compliment from all languages, he can simply dismiss the whole notion of a language that mirrors the structure of reality as *utterly senseless*. It doesn't seem unreasonable to suggest, moreover, that the onus is on the *opponent* of OP to make this notion intelligible. (And note that the linguistic idealist who lodged the original complaint against OP is hardly in a position to offer any clarification of this notion. *He* probably regards it as ultimately senseless, too!)

I have been at pains to distinguish OP from all forms of linguistic idealism, but the question arises whether OP is nevertheless opposed to realism in some way. And this, as I remarked at the outset, is relevant to the question whether OP is a sufficiently bold doctrine to justify metaphorical talk of dividing the world into objects. Well, suppose for a moment that we concede that talk of mirroring makes sense. Suppose further that you think that sentences containing predicates like 'x is a table' and 'x is a chair' mirror the structure of reality just as they stand. I, however, maintain that although such sentences are normally used to convey truths, they do so in an *unperspicuous* fashion. According to me, the relevant truths would all be more perspicuously conveyed by means of sentences that spoke only of "simples arranged tablewise" (or "chairwise", as the case may be). Under these circumstances, would it not be natural for you regard me as something less than a full-fledged realist about tables and chairs— *even though I am prepared to agree that sentences containing the words 'table' and 'chair' are often used to depict cognition-independent facts about the world*? Now the OP-ist is unwilling to regard *any* sentence as "mirroring the structure of reality". Thus, *relative to a perspective from which it makes sense to talk of such mirroring*, at least, the OP-ist is naturally regarded as something less than a full-fledged realist about objects of *any* kind. There is, then, an identifiable philosophical standpoint relative to which OP represents at least a modest form of antirealism. This, I think, is sufficient to rebut the charge that OP is too tame a doctrine to serve as the underpinning for the division metaphor. But having said that, we must remember that the OP-ist has the option of dismissing all talk of language mirroring reality as senseless. If he takes this line, he will probably have difficulty appreciating that there is *any* intelligible sort of realism to which his position stands opposed. But I don't see why that should prevent him from employing the division metaphor.

Pluralism, Metaphysical Realism, and Ultimate Reality

MICHAEL P. LYNCH

> How exquisitely the individual Mind
> (And the progressive powers perhaps no less
> Of the whole species) to the external World
> Is fitted:—and how exquisitely too—
> Theme this but little heard among men—
> The external World is fitted to the Mind

—WILLIAM WORDSWORTH

I. PLURALISM AND REALISM

1. Pluralism is a familiar idea running through contemporary culture. Its root is the intuition that there can be more than one true story of the world. Many philosophers, even those who consider themselves metaphysical realists, acknowledge the force of this intuition. Some even leave room for it in their metaphysical theories or, failing that, try to explain it away or otherwise mollify its force. Simply ignoring it, however, is rare.

Discussions of these matters often confuse two ways of understanding the pluralist's intuition. There are two dimensions—we might label them "horizontal" and "vertical"—along which it can be addressed.[1] The vertical pluralist believes there is more than one true story of the world in that there are different

Portions of this chapter were presented at the December 2000 Meeting of the American Philosophical Association during an "author meets critics" session on my book *Truth in Context* (MIT Press, 1998) sponsored by the Society for Realist and Antirealist Discussion. I thank my critics at that session, Michael Devitt, Henry Jackman, and Ernest Sosa, as well as the Chair, Terence Horgan, and members of the audience for helpful comments. I benefited from further conversations with Steven Hales, William Lawhead, Paul Bloomfield, Andrew Cortens, David Anderson, and William Alston.

[1] The vertical and horizontal dimensions of pluralism were distinguished by H. Price, "Metaphysical Pluralism," *Journal of Philosophy* 89, 8 (1992): 387–409.

sorts of truths about that world that cannot be reduced to one another. Thus a vertical pluralist may believe that moral truths or religious truths are irreducible to truths about the physical world, or that economic or legal truths constitute their own domain distinct from either physical or moral discourse. Considered along the vertical axis, the question of pluralism concerns the relationship between propositions about different subjects.[2]

Considered horizontally, the issue of pluralism is whether there can be more than one true account of a single subject. Pluralism along this dimension is the idea that incompatible propositions from the same domain can both be true. With regard to morality, a horizontal pluralist might hold that could be more than one true answer to the question of what one should do in a particular situation. On a broader, metaphysical level, horizontal pluralism is the idea that there can be more than one true account of the ultimate nature of reality. Since contradictions can't be true, positions like this are committed to conceptual or content relativism—that is, that claims about what exists are relative to differing conceptual schemes or worldviews. Call this position metaphysical pluralism, and its opposite, that there can be only one true story of ultimate reality, metaphysical absolutism.

2. Metaphysical pluralism holds a distinctive and somewhat curious place in current debates in metaphysics. On the one hand, it is frequently endorsed—or at least paid lip service to—by many nonphilosophers, including distinguished intellectuals in other fields. Indeed, it often appears to be the standard position in the humanities, and people who maintain that there may be only one true story of the world can find themselves being referred to as "metaphysical fascists" (as I once heard someone called). Yet even while it is praised in disciplines such as literature and cultural anthropology, metaphysical pluralism is almost universally reviled among analytic metaphysicians. It is frequently referred to as "absurd", "crazy", or as one prominent nonpluralist put it recently, simply "very bad news".[3]

The fact that an otherwise abstract metaphysical debate can give rise to such strong emotional reactions should give us pause. These matters are more complicated than they first appear. Both sides are on to something, yet each misses

---

[2] I discuss and defend a form of vertical pluralism—involving a pluralism about the nature of truth—in my "Alethic Pluralism and the Functionalist Theory of Truth," *Acta Analytica* 24 (2000): 195–214, and "The Functionalist Theory of Truth," in *The Nature of Truth: Classic and Contemporary Perspectives*, ed. Michael P. Lynch (Cambridge: MIT Press, 2001), 723–51. An influential version of vertical pluralism is defended by Crispin Wright in his *Truth and Objectivity* (Cambridge: Harvard University Press, 1992) and in "Minimalism, Deflationism, Pluralism, Pragmatism," in *Nature of Truth*, ed. Lynch, 751–58.

[3] Michael Devitt, during our spirited—but constructive—debate at the December 2000 Meeting of the American Philosophical Association. See also Devitt, forthcoming, "An Unmade World."

that fact owing to certain confusions inherent in the way the debate is often framed.[4]

In my view a chief source of confusion is the assumption that metaphysical pluralism implies a denial of realism. We can distinguish two main forms of realism: *alethic realism* and *metaphysical realism*. Alethic realism is realism about truth and related notions like reference. According to alethic realism, truth is a robust, nonepistemic, objective property of propositions. A proposition is true on this view just when the world is as that proposition "says" that it is; the truth (of most propositions, anyway) does not depend on what anyone believes or knows.[5] Contemporary pluralists have often claimed that pluralism implies a denial of realism in this sense. Hilary Putnam, for example, once argued that giving up on the absolutist idea that there is only one possible true description of the world entailed that "truth comes to no more than idealized rational acceptability".[6] The idea is that if there can be equally true but incompatible descriptions of the world, then truth cannot consist in correspondence with reality.

I have argued at length elsewhere that this is not the case.[7] Metaphysical pluralism is in fact compatible with alethic realism. This makes pluralism a more attractive view. In this essay, however, I intend to concentrate on whether metaphysical pluralism is consistent with the other sort of realism: ontological or metaphysical realism.

To anticipate, I shall argue three main points. First, pluralism's compatibility with metaphysical realism is not a trivial question. Against several philosophers, most prominently Ernest Sosa, I argue that the conceptual half of pluralism—what I call content relativism—entails a radical form of fact relativism. Yet second, I claim that even the most thoroughgoing pluralist can, at least by the lights of her own position, endorse a form of metaphysical realism. Third, this endorsement makes pluralism more Kantian in nature.

3. Metaphysical realism is difficult to state without begging one question or another. Nonetheless, the core of the position is clear enough. It is the idea that the measure of ultimate reality is mind-independence. One expression of this thought is this:

Basic Metaphysical Realism (BMR): There is a world that exists independently of the mental.

---

[4] Another reason these debates are so heated, I think, is that politics, and not just metaphysics, is often on the mind of participants on both sides.

[5] The best recent defense of this position is William P. Alston, *A Realist Conception of Truth* (Ithaca: Cornell University Press, 1996).

[6] Hilary Putnam, *Realism with a Human Face* (Cambridge: Harvard University Press, 1990), 41.

[7] Michael Lynch, *Truth in Context* (Cambridge: MIT Press, 1998); see also Alston, *Realist Conception of Truth*.

Though simple, this formulation will be too bland for most tastes. For BMR says nothing about the specific nature of this mind-independent world, nothing about the number of objects, the status of properties or kinds of objects, or even the extent to which they have the properties they do independently of the mental. Further, BMR is consistent with the broadly Kantian view that the kinds and individual objects of our everyday life are phenomenal and mind-dependent even while noumenal, mind-independent reality remains beyond cognitive reach.

Therefore, most metaphysical realists, following Michael Devitt, make the doctrine more specific:

Commonsense Metaphysical Realism (CMR): Tokens of most commonsense and scientific physical types objectively exist independently of the mental.[8]

Both BMR and CMR rely on the concept "mind-independence". For now, I'll leave that notion undefined and hope that it has some intuitive content. We'll confront this issue directly in Section V.

Many philosophers write as if either BMR or CMR is obviously incompatible with pluralism. Putnam, who originated the term "metaphysical realism", *defines* it as follows:

The world consists of some fixed totality of mind-independent objects. There is exactly one and only one true description of "the way the world is". Truth involves some sort of correspondence relation between words and thought-signs and external things and sets of things.[9]

According to Putnam, then, metaphysical realism is the conjunction of three views. BMR (the first claim) is part of a theoretical package that includes absolutism (the second claim) and even the correspondence theory of truth (the third claim). As such, pluralism and metaphysical realism are incompatible by definition. Similarly, Devitt, from the realist end of things, explicitly argues that CMR is incompatible with pluralism and other "constructivist" views.[10] In short, it is orthodoxy on both sides that pluralism is inconsistent not only with alethic realism but with metaphysical realism.

II. PLURALISM AND CONTENT RELATIVITY

1. Whether Putnam and Devitt are right depends on the details of both metaphysical pluralism and metaphysical realism. So far we've defined pluralism in only vague terms. We need to get a bit more specific, and a good first step is to

---

[8] Michael Devitt, *Realism and Truth*, 2d ed. (Princeton: Princeton University Press, 1997), 24.

[9] Hilary Putnam, *Reason, Truth, and History* (Cambridge: Cambridge University Press, 1981), 49.

[10] Devitt, *Realism and Truth*, chap. 13.

examine why someone would believe pluralism. I will present two arguments for the position that have been raised in the literature. Since the focus of the present chapter is the compatibility of pluralism with metaphysical realism, and not the truth of metaphysical pluralism itself, my discussion of these arguments will be somewhat brief. The point of this section is to give an overview of the pluralist's position.

2. *Putnam's argument from conceptual relativity.* Imagine that two philosophers, Smith and Johnson, are asked to look in a bag containing some marbles and count how many objects there are in the bag. Johnson looks inside and announces,

Johnson: There are exactly three objects in the bag: X, Y, and Z.

Suppose that Smith is a "mereologist", that is, a logician who believes that every part of an object is an object and that the sum of any two objects is an object. When Smith looks in the bag, she says,

Smith: There are *really* exactly seven objects in the bag: X, Y, and Z, X + Y, X + Z, Y + Z, and X + Y + Z.

If they are contemporary metaphysicians, Smith and Johnson will not be equivocating over "object"—at least not in the ordinary sense of "equivocation". For they will each employ the same "logical" concept of an object, according to which anything we can quantify over is an object. Yet if we suppose that Smith and Johnson's answers are equally coherent, it is difficult to see what objective fact about the world is going to decide this matter. Neither view is ruled out by empirical evidence. Neither need deny that the ordinary statement 'this is a chair' is true. Each can claim to be giving a more perspicuous paraphrase of that sentence.

Putnam has used similar examples to point out what he calls the phenomenon of conceptual relativity.[11] Consider the historically important debate over substance. Roughly speaking, a substance is basic or fundamental in that it *has* properties but is itself not a property of something else. According to a philosopher like Aristotle, many substances and types of substances exist, all of which endure through time, have identity conditions, possess properties both accidentally and essentially, and so on. A particular person, on the Aristotelian view, is just one of these substances. But to a monist like Spinoza, persons are not basic enough to be substances. According to Spinoza, there is ultimately only *one* substance: the universe as a whole. He calls this one substance both "God" and

---

[11] Hilary Putnam, *Representation and Reality* (Cambridge: MIT Press, 1989), 112–14, and *Realism with a Human Face*, x–xi.

"Nature". Of course, it may *appear* to us that trees and humans are different substances, but ultimately, trees, persons, and mountains are just different modes or properties of the one *underlying* substance. Individual persons exist, of course, but they are "substances" only loosely speaking; strictly speaking, there is only the one substance, and a person such as yourself is simply a mode of that substance—a way it is at a particular time.

Or consider numbers. Are they to be identified with the scratches we make on a blackboard, or the ideas we have when making those marks, or something altogether different, as Plato thought, existing outside space and time? Or take points on a Euclidean plane. Points can be taken to be (a) basic abstract particulars, (b) sets of convergent spheres, (c) composed of intersecting lines, or (d) logical constructions out of volumes.[12] Every one of these answers would seem to be in conflict with the others; to say that points are particulars, for instance, is meant to rule out that they are "really" intersecting lines. Similar debates can take place over the ontological status of sets, functions, propositions, possible worlds, and properties.

Putnam argues that such examples should encourage us to see metaphysical concepts like object as fluid in a certain sense.

> "Identical", "individual", and "abstract" are notions with a variety of different uses. The difference between, say, describing space-time in a language that takes points as individuals and describing space-time in a language that takes points as mere limits is a difference in the choice of a language, and neither language is the "one true description".[13]

The absolutist idea is that there is only one right answer to Smith and Johnson's debate. Putnam's point is that this position assumes that there is only one correct way to apply the concept of an object or similar metaphysical concepts like "individual". It assumes our metaphysical concepts are made of Fregean crystal, that they are areas with precise boundaries, whose application conditions are determinate in all present and future cases of use. But why should we make these assumptions? For if we do so, we face the embarrassing fact that there seems to be no way to resolve these debates. Here, as in ethics, the alternative idea—that the concepts in question are fluid or open to divergent application—seems more faithful to our practice.

3. *Sosa's explosion of reality argument.*[14] Consider a common snowball B, constituted by some piece of snow P. This same piece of snow also constitutes a

---

[12] See Nelson Goodman, *The Ways of Worldmaking* (Indianapolis: Hackett, 1978), 113–15; and Hilary Putnam, *Renewing Philosophy* (Cambridge: Harvard University Press, 1992), 118–19, and *Meaning and the Moral Sciences* (New York: Routledge, 1978), 130–33.

[13] Putnam, *Representation and Reality*, 114–15.

[14] Sosa's original presentation of the argument can be found in his "Putnam's Pragmatic Realism," *Journal of Philosophy* 90 (1993): 605–26. He replies to some objections in "Addendum to Nonabsolute Existence and Conceptual Relativity," in *Metaphysics: The Big Ques-*

snowdiscball, D, where a snowdiscball is any piece of snow whose shape is somewhere between round and disc-shaped. Now P is clearly distinct from B since B would not survive squashing but P would. Similarly, B is also not D, since B again would not survive a partial flattening but D would. Yet there are infinitely many shapes between being round and being flat that our piece of snow can take on. And just as our snowdiscball is a distinct object from our snowball, so each of these entities will be distinct from our snowball, our snowdiscball, and one another. It follows, Sosa argues, that if P constitutes a snowball, it also constitutes infinitely many entities, all located in the same space, and any change in the snowball will have the effect of destroying as many entities as it creates. We seem to be left with what Sosa calls the "explosion of reality."[15]

Our natural temptation, of course, is to respond that not just any shape constitutes a real object. Our snowball is real, we want to say, but snowdisc-balls are not. But what objective fact about the world makes us prejudice snowballs over the infinitely many other types of objects a particular piece of snow can compose? There seems to be no such fact. Rather, Sosa argues, our conceptual scheme implicitly recognizes some matter/form combinations and does not recognize others. If our interests or needs were other than what they were (if we wished to play snow Frisbee, for instance), we might recognize snowdiscballs. But there is nothing in the world itself that demands that we privilege one way of carving up the world over another. Obviously, the argument isn't meant to apply only to snow. Sosa argues that it can be applied to matter/form combinations generally. For any hunk of matter M that composes some object O, Sosa claims, one can always recognize another object O1 that is also composed of M such that O1 and O are distinct from both M and each other.

If, as Sosa suggests, it is arbitrary to take one matter/form pair (or composed object O) as more fundamentally real than any other, we are left with three choices. We can remain absolutists and accept the explosion of reality. There is only one absolute way reality is, but there is much more to reality that we previously imagined. Yet if we go this route, we must accept that any attempt to state which objects exist is bound to capture only part of the truth. Second, we can remain absolutists but adopt a form of eliminativism. Here we say again that there is only one absolute way the world is but deny that there are any composed or derived objects. All that exists are the basic, simple components of the universe, or if there are no such things, nothing at all.

Neither of these options seems particularly attractive. Thus Sosa suggests we adopt a form of relativism and hold that our claims about what exist are relative to a particular context of speech or thought. On this view the claim that P

---

tions, ed. P. van Inwagen and D. Zimmerman (Oxford: Blackwell, 1998), 407–11, and in his forthcoming "Ontological and Conceptual Relativity, and the Self," in *Oxford Handbook of Metaphysics*, ed. M. Loux and D. Zimmerman (Oxford: Oxford University Press).

[15] Sosa, "Putnam's Pragmatic Realism."

composes a snowball and the claim that P composes a snowdiscball are both true relative to different conceptual schemes.

4. Sosa and Putnam suggest that conceptual relativity is a reasonable way of responding to certain metaphysical puzzles. Our brief discussion of their arguments indicates that a certain view of metaphysical concepts is at the heart of metaphysical pluralism.

The following analogy may help illuminate the pluralist's account of metaphysical concepts. Suppose we ask several different artists to fill in a very minimal sketch of a landscape—to turn it from a sketch into a complete painting. Very possibly, many of the finished paintings will look quite different, since each artist may take the lines of the sketch to suggest very different formations in the landscape. Perhaps some will not be a filling-in of the sketch at all (e.g., one that painted over the lines of the sketch with a single color). But there may be some that, although different paintings, are equally good enrichments of our sketch.

According to the metaphysical pluralist, we are in an analogous situation with regard to our most basic metaphysical concepts—concepts like *object*, *substance*, and *identity*. Our metaphysical concepts are sketches that can be filled in or extended in distinct but equally correct ways. As a result, propositions composed of those concepts are indeterminate unless indexed or relativized to a particular way of enriching their conceptual content. These ways of enriching our minimal metaphysical concepts can be called conceptual schemes.

Clearly, the fluidity of our metaphysical concepts—the fact that we can enrich them in different but equally acceptable ways—has global implications. If the logical concept of an object is fluid, for example, then "the very meaning of existential quantification is left indeterminate" unless indexed to a particular way of enriching that concept.[16] This implies that our existential assertions themselves will be relative. According to the pluralist, my claim that *there is an x that is F* actually expresses a proposition of the form *There is an x that is F relative to C*, where "C" denotes my conceptual scheme. And if existential propositions are relative to a conceptual scheme, so, it seems, must every proposition. Thus a relativism of metaphysical concepts globally expands. I can express determinate propositions only relative to conceptual schemes.

This isn't quite as mysterious as it sounds. As Sosa notes, content relativism "can be viewed as a doctrine rather like the relativity involved in the evaluation of the truth of indexical sentences or thoughts".[17] Just as the proposition that Chicago is more than one hundred miles away must be evaluated relative to my present position, so thoughts about whether something exists will be evaluated "relative to the position of the speaker or thinker in 'ontological space'". In both cases, the propositional content of my thought is indeterminate unless rel-

[16] Putnam, *Representation and Reality*, 112.
[17] Sosa, "Addendum," 409.

ativized—in the one case to my position in space, in the metaphysical case to my network of robust concepts and associated standards for identity, persistence, and objecthood. Nonetheless, *given* my "ontological position", it is objectively true or false that X's exist relative to that position. It is not, in most cases, up to me. Internal to a scheme, it is a completely objective matter whether a particular proposition is true or false. Such schemes are therefore not simply lists of beliefs, or the set of declarative sentences I accept, but structured networks of interrelated concepts. These concepts implicitly define criteria for object individuation and persistence. I may or may not be aware of these criteria; I may be confused about what they are. But given that they are in place, what I say about the world—the propositions I express—are true or false relative to them. In short, it is the proposition that is relativized, not its truth or falsity. As a result, this position is perhaps best labeled *content relativism.*

5. So far, we've discussed only the conceptual face of metaphysical pluralism—content relativism. Arguably, however, pluralism also has an explicitly ontological face: *fact relativism.* This is the view that states of affairs, obtaining or not, are relative or indexed to a conceptual scheme. By a "state of affairs" I mean a way the world is or could be. Thus snow's being white is an actual state of affairs or a fact.

According to fact relativism, there is no state of affairs of snow's being white simpliciter; there is only the fact that snow is white relative to some conceptual scheme. Just as propositional content is implicitly indexed to a scheme or schemes, so states of affairs are internally related to a network of concepts. The point can be put in a more material mode as well. The world is a certain way just when some object has some property. If so, then fact relativism implies that there are objects and sorts of objects with the properties they have only relative to conceptual schemes. As Putnam remarks, "It is characteristic of [my] view to hold that *what objects does the world consist of?* is a question which only makes sense to ask within a theory or description".[18]

Fact relativism is naturally opposed by fact absolutism, or the idea that the world is absolutely the way it is. In the absolutist view, all facts, except facts about minds or concepts, are as they are independently of any relation to any mind or conceptual scheme. Since fact relativism holds that the world is the way it is only relative to conceptual schemes, fact relativism is prima facie inconsistent with metaphysical realism. Thus it may seem that if metaphysical pluralism entails a relativity of both content and fact, metaphysical pluralism is inconsistent with metaphysical realism.

III. DOES CONTENT RELATIVITY ENTAIL FACT RELATIVITY?

1. Some philosophers believe that one can grant content relativism and deny fact relativism. That is, one can grant that propositional content is deeply per-

---

[18] Putnam, *Reason, Truth, and History*, 49.

spectival but deny that the facts that make our thoughts true are perspectival. Thus, Mark Heller says:

> Even if we have no nonrelative way to refer to the world, there is still a non-relative fact about what the world is like. It is our descriptions of the world that are relative to our conceptual schemes, not the world itself.[19]

And Sosa:

> From the fundamentally and ineliminably perspectival character of our thought it does not follow that reality itself is fundamentally perspectival.[20]

And Paul Moser:

> Saying and asking are, naturally enough, "relative to some background language" but it does not follow that the objects about which one says or asks something are similarly relative.[21]

The point of all of these passages is that one can grant the relativist's point about representation—at the level of concept and content—but reject it at the metaphysical level.

What I call the T-argument shows that this 'having one's cake and eating it too' is impossible.[22] If one wishes to admit that propositional content is relative or contextual, then the facts must be relative as well. The core of the argument can be summarized as follows. Assume, for the sake of argument, that some claim of the form x *is* F is true. According to the content relativist, the proposition expressed by that claim is that x *is* F *relative to* C. It is an a priori platitude that the content of a statement determines the necessary and sufficient conditions for that statement's truth. This is the lesson of the T-schema, or the principle

TS: it is true that p IFF p.

Now if the content of a statement (the proposition it expresses) is relative, it follows from our platitude that the conditions under which that content is true

---

[19] Mark Heller, "Putnam, Reference, and Realism," in *Midwest Studies in Philosophy XII*, ed. P. French, T. Uehling, and H. Wettstein (Minneapolis: University of Minnesota Press, 1988), 118.

[20] Sosa, "Putnam's Pragmatic Realism," 608. For similar remarks, see Hartry Field, "Realism and Relativism," in *Journal of Philosophy* 79 (1982): 553–67, and Terence Horgan, "Metaphysical Realism and Psychologistic Semantics," *Erkenntnis* 34 (1991): 297–322.

[21] Paul Moser, *Philosophy after Objectivity: Making Sense in Perspective* (Oxford: Oxford University Press, 1997), 37.

[22] A detailed presentation of the argument, along with responses to several objections, can be found in Lynch, "Relativity of Fact and Content," *Southern Journal of Philosophy* 38 (1999): 579–94.

must also be relative. That is, substituting for "p" gets us (together with our assumption):

(1) it is true that x is F relative to C IFF x is F relative to C.

Yet it also clearly a priori that

(2) x is F relative to C IFF it is a fact that x is F relative to C.

By transitivity of the biconditional, we obtain from (1) and (2) that

(3) it is true that x is F relative to C IFF it is a fact that x is F relative to C.

From which it follows, together with our assumption that our proposition is true, that there is a relative fact. Content relativism entails fact relativism.

2. We need to be clear about what this argument shows and what it does not. The T-argument shows that

For every relative true proposition, there is a relative fact.

This by itself does not entail that there are no absolute facts or that:

If every true proposition is relative, then every fact is a relative fact.

Sosa has recently objected on this basis to the T-argument.[23] Sosa has considerable sympathy with metaphysical pluralism; indeed, as noted above, he takes the content of existential claims to be relative to conceptual schemes. Sosa agrees that there must be relative facts, yet he argues that this is consistent with holding that there are absolute or scheme-independent facts as well. Further, he argues that we can even state such facts, in a certain sense:

> Even if I have no way to state [a fact] except perspectivally; so that the truth of the thought or proposition that I thereby state is not objective or mind-independent, it simply does not follow that the fact itself must therefore be mind-dependent. . . . Statements and thoughts are of course mind-dependent, at least in the sense that they are truth-evaluable only relative to their users. However, this does not entail that no mind-independent fact is thereby stated, even if our access to that fact must be perspectivally mind-dependent.[24]

---

[23] Sosa responded to the argument in his paper at the APA session on Lynch 1998 in December 2000; his response appears in "Ontological and Conceptual Relativity."

[24] Sosa, "Ontological and Conceptual Relativity," 10–11.

Therefore, content relativism does not entail that "the things around us and their states of being and interrelations are somehow, in some sense, also relative to context."[25]

How can we refer to an absolute fact about the world when every true proposition we utter is itself relative to a scheme? Sosa argues that scheme-relative facts and states of affairs are dependent on the existence of nonrelative facts and states of affairs. Thus we may be able to indirectly state or refer to absolute facts via stating the relative facts that depend upon them. In particular, he argues that even if it is a fact relative to our conceptual scheme that some snowball is white, it is possible also that

> (E) Relative to our conceptual scheme, A is white IFF there is an existing entity consisting of that snowball A and the property whiteness, where A exemplifies whiteness independently of anyone's thought or speech or conceptual scheme.[26]

Now suppose that we grant that the interdependency between a relative state of affairs and an absolute state of affairs imagined in (E) is possible. The question is where this gets the defender of absolute facts. If (E) is to have any bite, it must itself be an absolute fact. But if all content is relative, then it apparently follows that we cannot express *this* fact except via a proposition relative to a scheme. How can we avoid saying that (E) is simply a fact relative to some conceptual scheme or schemes?

Sosa is well aware of this problem. He responds by distinguishing between "everyday" contexts and "philosophical" contexts. In Sosa's view our everyday thought about what exists is indexed to a conceptual scheme with certain implicit persistence and identity conditions for objects. But in a philosophical context "we can abstract away from the object-delimitations normally presupposed in our ordinary speech and thought."[27] Within this special philosophical context we hold to a "latitudinarian", absolutist metaphysics according to which "ontologically anything goes". On this view the absolute truth about the world is that there are plenty of things beyond the delimitations presupposed in ordinary contexts. What's more, we can say, relative to this philosophical context, that the great many things that may exist do not do so relative to any human conceptual scheme. We can assert this fact because the philosophical context is dissimilar from other contexts in that it does not presuppose any of the ontological delimitations presupposed in the ordinary context. As a result, assertions made relative to that context don't rest on any ontological presuppositions; therefore, the truth of such assertions is dependent not on those presuppositions but on the absolute way of the world. So it is in this context, presumably, that we assert (E) and similar equivalences.

[25] Ibid., 14.
[26] Ibid., 15.
[27] Ibid., 16.

I agree that philosophy often starts with minimal, ontologically neutral truths. Yet there is quite a substantial ontological view being expressed when we say that "ontologically anything goes". That view is that the particulars of the world are objectively related and propertied in an infinite amount of ways, and in ordinary contexts humans pick some of these relations and properties while ignoring others. The resulting picture is one in which the world contains more kinds of things than ordinarily thought, not less. I submit that far from being ontologically neutral, the ontologically liberal context Sosa has in mind is itself a player, not a referee. It seems to be a conceptual scheme like any other.

Furthermore, some ontological conflicts are not about the number of objects but over how to understand the nature of one object. Consider a debate between an Aristotelian and a Spinozist. The Aristotelian will insist that a particular person is an enduring substance with certain properties. But a disciple of Spinoza will claim that a person is a mode of the one substance; Nature, as it were, is "personish here-about". The conflict between these two theories isn't additive in the manner of Putnam's mereological or Sosa's snowball and snowdiscball example. Persons are enduring, discrete particulars, or modes of the one substance. According to the advocates of these views, they cannot be both. Or consider debates over abstract objects, such as numbers, which are not concerned with issues relating to composition at all. With regard to these sorts of debate, we can't say that the philosophers involved are simply picking out different objective aspects of absolute reality while ignoring other aspects. If both views are correct, they must be so because the facts that make them true are internal to the conceptual schemes themselves.

One possibility remains. Sosa might retreat to the position that even though we can't state (either directly or indirectly) how the world is absolutely such that it can allow for distinct and equally true representations of its nature, there may still be a world independent of those representations, and absolute facts about that world. That is, Sosa may claim that BMR is still true but admit that mind-independent, absolute reality is the unknowable noumenal reality of Kantian lore.

If content relativism is true, I cannot even state that there is such a world without employing my conceptual scheme. Thus the claim that there is a world independent of my conceptual scheme is itself relative to my conceptual scheme. If it is true, then given the T-argument, it is a scheme-relative fact. Have we then contradicted ourselves? No. For even if it is a scheme-relative fact that there are some nonrelative facts, there may still be such facts. Yet the basic problem remains. Given conceptual relativity, it is utterly mysterious how we could refer to such facts, even hypothetically. We have retained absolute facts at the price of admitting they are a mystery.

IV. A SHARED REALITY

1. The lesson of the preceding section is that content relativism really does imply the radical thesis that any fact we can state—indeed, any possible state of affairs we can refer to—is relative to a conceptual scheme. Must we admit that

pluralism is thus incompatible with metaphysical realism? Put differently, is fact absolutism a necessary condition of metaphysical realism? In this section and the next I examine the prospects for fact relativism's compatibility with some form of metaphysical realism.[28]

First, let us return to Sosa's remarks. One of Sosa's underlying worries, I think, is that if we say that all facts are intrinsically perspectival, we leave no room for the obvious and clearly true thought that users of conceptual schemes inhabit a shared reality. Conceptual schemes don't make separate "worlds" (pace Goodman). But how can we allow for this from within a view that makes all facts or states of affairs relative to conceptual schemes?

Here is one way. It is frequently overlooked that nothing about content relativity rules out shared concepts and therefore shared truths. There may well be certain forms of thought and experience that are so basic to human thought in general that they are universally enjoyed in human thought at a particular time. Because we are the creatures we are, certain forms of experience and concepts will be available in every conceptual scheme. Empirical concepts stemming from perception are likely to fall into this category. And there may even be some concepts that are shared by every *conceivable* conceptual scheme, since there are some concepts that we cannot conceive of doing without. Many simple logical concepts might fall into this group.[29] In either case, the structural relationships that would exist between these universally shared concepts would entail that certain propositions would in principle be thinkable in all schemes. We could call these universally thinkable propositions *virtually absolute propositions*. And if there are virtually absolute propositions, thinkable in every conceptual scheme, there may well be propositions that are true in every scheme. (This does not follow as a matter of logic. For even if there are propositions thinkable in every scheme—because every scheme has concepts that can construct such propositions—these propositions need not have a determinate truth value.) If so, then by the T-argument, there will also be *virtually absolute facts*, or states of affairs that obtain in every conceptual scheme.

2. Some may wish to say that virtual absolutes are real absolutes. Since they are relative to every scheme, we might as well say they are relative to none.[30] And indeed there is much sense in this, since the pluralist and the absolutist can both agree that there are universal concepts and propositions involving such con-

---

[28] Alston, in *Realist Conception of Truth*, 179–87, also addresses this question. But as I read him, Alston is mainly interested in the question how far someone who does believe in at least some absolute facts or features of the world can go in accepting content and fact relativism. My own concern is whether someone who denies absolute facts altogether can hold metaphysical realism.

[29] That I cannot conceive of a scheme that does not include the minimal "sketch" concept of an object does not imply that this concept cannot be extended differently in different schemes.

[30] This is Steven Hales' position in "A Consistent Relativism," *Mind* 106, 421 (1997): 33–52.

cepts that are shared by every conceivable conceptual scheme at a particular time. Yet we need to remember two important differences between the content relativist and the content absolutist. First, according to the pluralist, the concepts we share now we may not share later. I may extend the minimal concepts I share with you in a divergent direction. Second, what is conceivable is so relative to the concepts we employ. Together with the first point this implies that it is possible that what is virtually absolute may lose that status; what we cannot help but think is universally shared may not be universally shared at all.

Hence virtual absolutes are not real absolutes, but they are absolute enough. In particular, they are helpful in understanding how a pluralist can grant that users of different conceptual schemes share a reality. For the pluralist can grant that much of what there is is picked out by our shared concepts. Put differently, we can say that our shared reality is the reality composed of the virtually absolute facts—whatever those turn out to be.

V. THE THREAT OF IDEALISM

1. So the pluralist can grant that there is a reality shared by all schemes. This goes some distance toward relieving the worry that fact relativism amounts to the view that "we make everything up". But it does not settle our question of the compatibility of metaphysical realism and metaphysical pluralism. That there is a reality shared by all schemes does not entail that this reality is mind-independent.

Recall that we earlier encountered two forms of metaphysical realism:

BMR: There is a world that exists independently of the mental

and

CMR: Tokens of most commonsense and scientific physical types objectively exist independently of the mental.

What exactly does it mean to talk of mind-dependence or mind-independence? Fred Schmitt suggests that we "identify mind-dependence with *constitution by the mind in virtue of being represented by it*".[31] On this account mind-dependent objects are those that are made or created to exist by our minds. One example Schmitt gives is Hamlet. Hamlet is a product of being represented in the play of the same name by Shakespeare. An automobile, in contrast, is not constituted by representations, even though an automobile is what it is only relative to its playing a certain role in human life.

Is pluralism—even the radical sort discussed above—committed to holding that most objects (or facts) are mind-dependent in the way that Hamlet and other fictions are mind-dependent? Clearly not, for two reasons. First, the pluralist certainly doesn't hold that minds—or conceptual schemes—constitute ob-

---

[31] Fredrick Schmitt, *Truth: A Primer* (Boulder, Colo.: Westview Press, 1995), 12.

jects or facts. Conceptual schemes are not constituents of objects or facts. Second, as Sosa has noted, to say that F's exist *relative to* a scheme is not to say that F's exist *in virtue* that scheme.[32] The pluralist's view is that a fact couldn't be the fact it is except in relation to some conceptual scheme. In the material mode this means that objects are what they are only in relation to a certain network of representation. But this means that, in line with Schmitt's examples, pluralism treats objects more like artifacts than fictional characters. Mountains don't exist because of my scheme. They exist relative to it.

2. So if we interpret "mind-independence" in Schmitt's way, fact relativism, and therefore metaphysical pluralism, is consistent with metaphysical realism. But this doesn't settle the matter. There is another way of interpreting mind dependency and independency. On this second understanding, to say that X is mind-independent is to say that if there were no minds, then X's would still exist. An idealist about X's will reject such a counterfactual. Absolutists frequently try to embarrass pluralists by appealing to the truth of similar counterfactuals concerning conceptual schemes. Thus Devitt claims that the pluralist cannot accept the following truth:

C: Were there no conceptual schemes, there would still be stars in the galaxy.[33]

For if the pluralist does accept C, then she is admitting that the state of affairs consisting of there being stars in this galaxy is not relative to conceptual schemes. For nothing can be relative to what doesn't exist. So the pluralist cannot accept that stars are mind-independent without inconsistency.

There are two ways the pluralist might respond to this question. Sosa suggests that the pluralist can handle this sort of objection by recalling the analogy between content (or concept) relativism and ordinary indexical statements. Consider the statement "The Empire State Building is 180 miles from here". The truth of this statement is relative to my position. But, Sosa says,

> despite the relativity of the truth of my statement, the Empire State Building would have been exactly where it is, 180 miles from here, even if I had not been here. Similarly, O's might have existed relative to my (our) conceptual position, even if no-one had existed to occupy this position.[34]

In response, the absolutist may point out that the two cases are dissimilar. In the spatial case, spatial locations exist independently of people or things that occupy those locations. For the analogy to work, conceptual schemes would have to exist independently of the concept users that employ them.

---

[32] Sosa originally makes this distinction in "Putnam's Pragmatic Realism."

[33] See Devitt, *Realism and Truth*, chap. 13; the specific example is mine.

[34] Ernest Sosa, "Nonabsolute Existence and Conceptual Relativity," in *Metaphysics: The Big Questions*, ed. P. van Inwagen and D. Zimmerman (Oxford: Blackwell, 1998), 410.

Whether the pluralist can handle this problem depends on what she means by "conceptual scheme". As I've argued elsewhere, many philosophers who use that term take it to mean something like "the totality of one's beliefs".[35] If that is what is meant, then clearly there could be no conceptual schemes unless there were believers. And yet even if there were no believers, there would still be stars. I don't think it best to understand schemes in this way, however. In my view conceptual schemes are best understood to be just what they sound like: schemes or networks of concepts. Depending on how one understands concepts, this understanding of conceptual schemes is compatible with their existing independently of concept users. Some philosophers believe that concepts are abstract objects, independent of the thoughts and words we use to express them. If so, then C is trivially true. For on this view conceptual schemes necessarily exist. Consequently, the antecedent of C is false, and the conditional true.[36]

This position is perfectly consistent and certainly answers the objection. But few pluralists will be attracted to it. The idea that concepts and conceptual schemes are abstract objects does not sit well with the idea that concepts are fluid and change according to our interests.

There is another answer one can make to Devitt's objection. The metaphysical pluralist relativizes the content of all statements about what exists, including those statements that express subjunctive and counterfactual propositions. So according to the pluralist, the proposition actually expressed by C is relative to a conceptual scheme. That is, relative to my conceptual scheme, it is true that were there no conceptual schemes, there would still be stars. Stars exist relative to my conceptual scheme (or so I believe), but it is not the case, relative to my scheme, that they exist because my scheme exists. They are not caused to exist by my scheme.

It is important to note that one can use similar reasoning to accept either BMR or CMR. In each case, the pluralist's position entails that these propositions, if true, are only relatively true, where the phrase "exist independently of the mental" is understood counterfactually. If she wishes, a pluralist can even grant that propositions like C are themselves virtual absolutes. That is, she can happily accept that

Relative to every scheme, if there were no minds, there would still be stars.

---

[35] Lynch, *Truth in Context*, 35–41.

[36] There is another possibility worth a brief mention. Instead of treating conceptual schemes as abstract objects, the pluralist might claim that C is true in virtue of the truth of:

C*: In every possible world w, where there are no conceptual schemes, it is still the case that were there conceptual schemes in w, there would be stars relative to those schemes.

But one wonders what facts about w would make it the case that were there conceptual schemes in w, there would be stars relative to them. The most likely explanation is that there are stars.

A pluralist needn't accept this, however. For perhaps there could be coherent conceptual schemes relative to which a loose form of Berkeley's ontological view is correct. Consider Quasi-Berkeley, who believes that everything is either a mind or an idea and that every mind only contingently exists (as opposed to Berkeley's own view, which held, of course, that God's mind necessarily existed). Relative to the Quasi-Berkeleyan scheme, it will not be the case were there no minds, there would still be stars. For similar reasons, a pluralist may be much less willing to accept that CMR is true in every scheme. CMR explicitly defines realism by reference to the concepts of our particular conceptual scheme.[37] And these concepts presumably are linked to the metaphysical criteria for object-individuation and discrimination constitutive of our conceptual scheme. A more robust pluralist will therefore allow that there may be other schemes relative to which some of these types don't exist.

Yet even though pluralists worthy of the name will limit the scope of BMR and CMR to a limited set of schemes, they can accept that an even more fundamental form of metaphysical realism is a virtual absolute. That is, they can accept

> PMR: Relative to every scheme, if there were no conceptual schemes, there would still be a world.[38]

That is, it seems a virtual absolute that were there no conceptual schemes, there would still be something. Note that acknowledging the truth of PMR entails neither that reality is noumenal nor that there are absolute facts. Strictly speaking, PMR says nothing about the knowability or unknowability of any aspect of reality. It says only that everything that is does not depend on the existence of conceptual schemes. Neither does accepting PMR require that this be an absolute fact. It is a fact relative to every scheme.

VI. PLURALISM AND NECESSARY TRUTHS
A traditional metaphysical realist like Devitt will not find the answers just given persuasive, for when he asserts metaphysical realism, he means it to be absolutely true, not simply true relative to schemes.[39] Of course, the pluralist can

---

[37] This fact is apt to make many realists unhappy with CMR as well. For surely the most robust realist allows that we could be completely mistaken about what exists, even about whether tokens of commonsense physical object types exist. So perhaps we should modify CMR to read:

> If tokens of most commonsense physical and scientific types do exist, they exist independently of the mental.

[38] Note that "If there were no conceptual schemes, there would still be a world" would seem true on a Berkeleyan conceptual scheme. For Berkeley was an absolutist of the first rank: he thought it was an absolute fact that there were only minds and ideas. And he would not have thought reference to anything like "conceptual schemes" was necessary to state this fact.

[39] See Devitt, "An Unmade World."

reply that this protest is itself unfair. She was asked if her view was consistent with BMR. According to the pluralist's understanding of her own position, it is. On pluralism's relativist account of content, these claims, like any existential claims, are true or false only relative to a scheme.

The absolutist can respond in another, less partisan way. Suppose we say it is true that relative to every conceptual scheme there is something independent of conceptual schemes. What, the absolutist may ask, explains this curious fact? Intuitively, he will say, what explains this fact is that PMR is necessarily true—it is metaphysically necessary. Surely this is the best explanation for why, relative to all viable conceptual schemes, there is a world independent of conceptual schemes. And plausibly, its necessity makes PMR an absolute fact about the way the world is.

This point raises a very general and deep problem for the pluralist. How can the pluralist account for the intuition that certain truths, including PMR, are necessary truths, without granting that there are absolute facts? For independently of our concerns about counterfactual dependence, that two and two make four seems absolutely true, true not just in every scheme but independently of all schemes whatsoever. Further, with regard to elementary mathematical or logical propositions, their necessity is plausibly a result of their *very content*— they are necessary in virtue of what they are about. Thus any attempt to ground such propositions on a contingent basis—on conceptual schemes or forms of life, for instance, may seem, as Thomas Nagel has alleged, to contradict their "true content".[40]

It is instructive to compare relativism about logical truths with Descartes's own rather infamous "voluntarism" about necessary truth, according to which the truth of every proposition, even the propositions of elementary arithmetic or logic, depends on the will of God—a will that could have been otherwise. When pressed on how this could be so, Descartes seemed to claim that although we cannot conceive of certain facts, for example that twice four makes eight, being other than what they are, we *can* conceive of being able to conceive differently than we do, since God could have easily arranged it to be so. Most philosophers interpret Descartes as claiming that although we can't understand what it would be for twice four to make nine, it is possible anyway because anything is possible for God. Thus Nagel says, "It is impossible to believe that God is responsible for the truths of arithmetic if that implies that it could have been false that twice four is eight."[41] For that would imply the absurdity that God could have made *any* statement true or false and therefore that any statement is possibly true. According to Nagel, "structurally, this argument of Descartes is precisely the same as is offered by those who want to ground logic in psychology or forms of life . . . and the same thing is wrong with it".[42] For if the propo-

[40] Thomas Nagel, *The Last Word* (Oxford: Oxford University Press, 1997), 67.
[41] Ibid., 61.
[42] Ibid.

sition that two and two must make four is relative to, for example, our conceptual scheme, then given that we could have had a different scheme, it seems like it could be false that two and two make four after all.

Nagel's argument assumes that there is only one way to understand the modal concepts employed in logical and mathematical reasoning.[43] On the absolutist reading Nagel is assuming, to say that some state of affairs is possible is to say something about the structure of ultimate reality. If either the pluralist or Descartes understood modal concepts like possibility in *this* way, then they would be committed to an absurdity. But that is not the only way to understand the modal concepts, and further, it is not, as Jonathan Bennett has persuasively argued, the best way to interpret Descartes's position on the matter. The alternative is to say that something is possible or necessary is not to say something about the way the world is in itself. Instead, "our modal concepts should be understood or analyzed in terms of what does or does not lie without the compass of our ways of thinking".[44] In short, Bennett's Descartes holds that *it is possible that p* is roughly equivalent to the claim that *humans can conceive that p*, where this means that as a matter of psychological causal fact, humans have the capacity to entertain that the proposition is true. In turn, therefore, the proposition that *it is impossible that two and two make five* means *that no human can conceive of two and two making five*. Once we understand the modal concepts in this fashion, Descartes's position begins to make more sense. The modal concepts apply as they do because of certain contingent facts about our cognitive abilities. God made us the way we are with the specific cognitive abilities we have. Yet God could have (i.e., we can conceive that he might have) made us differently than he did. If so, then the contingent facts on which the modal concepts depend would be different and the modal concepts would have applied differently.

A similar approach to modality is available to the contemporary metaphysical pluralist. The rough picture is this:

> IM: It is impossible that p if, and only if, it is inconceivable that p given our conceptual scheme.

And since our conceptual limits preclude us from conceiving that two and two make five, that proposition is rightly impossible.

In reply, the absolutist might note that the relevant instance of IM entails

> (A) Were our conceptual scheme different, then it would not be impossible that two and two equal five.

---

[43] See Jonathan Bennett, "Descartes's Theory of Modality," *Philosophical Review* 103, 4 (1994): 639–67.

[44] Ibid., 647.

Which in turn entails that

(B) Were our conceptual scheme different, then it would be possible that two and two equal five.

And since our conceptual scheme could be different,

(C) It is possible that two and two equal five.

And again, the pluralist seems convicted of absurdity.

These are deep waters. But the following remark seems relevant. The pluralist can grant that IM entails (A) but argue that *when the basis for the modal concepts is considered*, (A) does not entail (B). For where we are considering a counterfactual situation in which the elements of a conceptual scheme which ground our modal concepts are different from what they actually are, the correct inference from IM is not simply (A) but

(D) Were our conceptual scheme different, our modal concepts would be inapplicable.

And (D) clearly does not entail (B).[45] Ordinarily, inference from *it is not impossible that p* to *it is possible that p* is valid. But in this case, we are considering the basis of our modal concepts. When we consider if our scheme were different in that respect, we can say neither that p would be possible nor that it would be impossible. Rather, p is not possible and it is not impossible. Why? On the pluralist understanding of modality under consideration, what is possible or impossible is a matter of conceivability relative to our scheme. And I cannot say what would or wouldn't be conceivable relative to another scheme since any answer to that question presupposes my own.

Obviously, more needs to be said. But if this position were to be worked out, the pluralist could appeal to the same resources as the absolutist in explaining why PMR and other similar propositions are relative to every scheme. Each can say that PMR is necessarily true. But in the pluralist's case, this amounts to holding that given the concepts I have, I cannot help but believe that there is a world independent of my schemes. Yet as a pluralist, I believe that this world can be represented or conceptualized in different ways by conceptual schemes other than my own.

VII. CONCLUSION

In summary, metaphysical pluralism can account for many of the main intuitions that drive metaphysical realism. Specifically:

[45] See ibid., 655.

- The pluralist, although required by the logic of her position to accept that facts are scheme-relative, can agree that there is a reality shared by the users of different conceptual schemes. This reality is a reality not of absolute facts but of virtually absolute facts, or facts relative to every conceptual scheme.
- The pluralist can consistently assert that either BMR or CMR is true. On either understanding of "mind-independence" available, it is consistent with her position to maintain that there is a world that is independent of the mental. In particular, she can assert that relative to our common conceptual scheme, if not relative to all, BMR or CMR is true.
- The pluralist may even be able to go further and claim that a very austere form of metaphysical realism is necessarily true. It is necessary that p, on one account, just when it is inconceivable that not-p given our conceptual scheme. Assuming that this view can be maintained, the pluralist may hold that it is necessary that were there no conceptual schemes, there would still be a world. For relative to our scheme, it is inconceivable that there is nothing independent of our schemes.

Putnam once remarked that

> [according to Kant] the notion of a noumenal world is a kind of limit thought (Grenz-Begriff) rather than a clear concept. Today the notion of a noumenal world is perceived as an unnecessary metaphysical element in Kant's thought. (But perhaps Kant is right: perhaps we can't help thinking that there is somehow a mind-independent "ground" for our experiences even if attempts to talk about it lead at once to nonsense.)[46]

An upshot of our discussion is that in a very clear sense, Kant *was* right. We can and should affirm that it is a fact relative to our conceptual scheme, and indeed relative to any conceptual scheme we can imagine, that there is more to reality than conceptual schemes. What we cannot add is that this is the one and only way the world must be in itself, independently of any context. We have reached the walls of reason, walls that we make, even as they in turn make us.

[46] Putnam, *Reason, Truth, and History*, 62.

·5·

The God's I Point of View

MICHAEL J. MURRAY

Recent nonrepresentationalists and metaphysical antirealists have argued that the "Enlightenment notion" of a "God's eye" point of view of the world is unsustainable. Deployment of conceptual schemes and/or intersubjective assent both constitute the world and fix the truth value of our statements about it. Many theists, on the contrary, hold an equally extreme realist position according to which God has a view of the world as it is "in itself" which provides an exhaustive description of the world. Furthermore, on this view, God has access to this exhaustive picture because the world exists and is what it is in virtue of its being the object of divine creative intentions. For these theistic realists, truths about the world must ultimately be able to be cashed out in terms of an ontology consisting only of simple and composite substances, substances that exist in virtue of the ontological structure set out in the world via God's creative activity. As a result, on this view, the world is constituted in a way that is independent of the activity of created cognizers and their conceptualizing activity. The truth of our assertions must ultimately find its grounding in this independently constituted world.

In this chapter I will make the case that theists can and should reject both positions, arguing instead for instead for a version of moderate theistic realism inspired by Leibniz. On this moderate theistic realism, natural kinds and natural individual substances exist as they do ultimately in virtue of divine intentions and creative activity. Such substances and kinds determine what we might call the "joints of nature." But as I will further argue, the ontological stock provided by such substances and kinds is insufficient to provide truth makers for a good many claims that the theistic realist truthfully makes about the world. Claims that either treat artifacts (such as Frisbees and footballs) as subjects of predication or refer to entities (such as money and political boundaries) constitutive of what some have called social reality seem to require that the world contain things other than natural kinds and natural individual substances.

I begin with an examination of two methodological schemes that motivate a variety of ontological positions. I call these schemes bottom-up and top-down. Each of these positions is closely allied with one of the two positions I aim to critique. In Section II I outline a moderate realist position motivated by both top-down and bottom-up sentiments. This view, endorsed by Leibniz,[1] entails that in addition to divinely intended natural kinds and individual substances, an adequate ontology must countenance objects that are constituted in part by ways in which created cognizers conceptualize the world. In Section III I then examine one profoundly dissatisfying feature of the bottom-up–generated ontologies, namely, that they require either an implausible account of the propositional content of ordinary statements (if they want such statements to come out true) or a commitment to a viciously unparsimonious stock of entities. In Section IV I argue that the most satisfying way for the theistic realist to escape these bottom-up difficulties is to adopt the Leibnizian view, which permits natural "divinely constituted" kinds and substances as well as objects constituted at least in part by the cognitive activity of creatures. On this view, I claim in Section V, there are certain objective truths about the world which God is unable to know without prior access to our conceptual resources. Thus, on this view, God's first-person perspective on the world, what we might call the "God's I" point of view, provides God an awareness of some truths about the world (those having natural kinds and natural individual substances as their truth makers), leaving other truths about the world to be filled in via the cognitive activity of creatures. Thus, God would not be able to know "facts about the world" such as that "dollar bills are green" or that "Pennsylvania borders Maryland" without first, one might say, consulting creaturely conceptual resources.

I. TWO APPROACHES TO ONTOLOGY

Broadly speaking, there are two main methodological schemata that are adopted in ontology. To stick with a favored pair of phrases, let's call the two schemata "bottom-up" and "top-down." I would like to set out these two schemes here, but before I do, let me add a cautionary note. I say "broadly speaking there are two schemata" because any such talk about methodological schemes in ontology artificially focuses attention on ontological investigations as if they take place in a way divorced from the philosopher's other philosophical concerns. That, of course, never happens. Reflections on ontology from Aristotle to Russell have always gone on with an eye to how the result hangs together with one's other philosophical commitments. And thus, there is admittedly something artificial about separating out ontological methodological schemes as I propose to do here. Nonetheless, such abstractions can often point us to important underlying philosophical themes that, when brought to the surface, are philosophically informative. The distinction between rationalist and empiricist is, I suppose, an analogous case from the modern period.

On what I am calling the bottom-up scheme, one begins by settling questions about what sorts of things there must be at the ontological ground floor. One

---

[1] At least in the middle years of his career, roughly 1686–1706.

can see this bottom-up approach exemplified throughout the history of philosophy in investigations into the ontology of *nature*. Such discussions often begin by examining questions about what the ultimate entities in nature can and cannot be like. Thus, from the ancients through the moderns, questions arise first about whether ultimate reality is, for example, continuous or discrete. In addition, there is a great deal of attention focused on whether there are one or more fundamental types of continuous or discrete stuffs. Thus, on the one hand, Anaxagoras's world of homoiomerous stuffs contains ultimate constituents that are continuous but of multiple fundamental types. Descartes, on the other hand, argues that the natural world is ultimately discrete and of one fundamental type: *res extensa*.

Once these questions about the structure and types of fundamental stuffs are settled, the bottom-upper turns to thinking about whether or not these stuffs can aggregate in ways that yield composite substances, where the notion of "substance" at work here is the old-fashioned one that serves to identify those composites that exhibit an intrinsic unity such that the parts of the substance become a new ontological whole. There is a long-standing philosophical tradition in which the intrinsic unity of such composites was said to yield an *unum per se*. So Aristotle, for example, holds that the elements are such that they can be cobbled together into substances by means of substantial forms whereas Descartes regards all such composites as mere aggregates. In this way, then, the bottom-up theorist asks questions about what the fundamental structure of reality must and must not, or can and cannot, be like and then fits his philosophical scheme to the structure that emerges.

On the top-down scheme, one begins with claims in ordinary discourse that we make (a) which seem to have some ontological import and (b) to which we are firmly committed, and then argues that the world must be populated with certain sorts of entities in order to provide truth makers for these claims. Thus, if I am committed to the claims that include apparent reference to baseballs and butterflies and bananas, I am at least prima facie committed to regarding these as items in my ontology, items that serve as constituents of the truth makers of my statements. Of course, further reflection might override these prima facie considerations, but such considerations provide the starting point for ontological reflection on this scheme.

One might think a priori that the bottom-up scheme would present us with a more austere ontology whereas the top-down scheme might yield a richer ontological stock. This is so for no other reason than that the apparent ontological types represented in our ordinary stock of referring singular expressions in our language is much richer in variety than the types countenanced by most bottom-up ontological frameworks. Of course, this result does not, on its own, give us any reason to favor one framework over another. But shortly, we will see that the austerity of the bottom-up scheme creates certain difficulties.

As I have noted, these schemes are rough-edged. Still, they will not be of much use if they fail to describe procedures actually employed in ontology, so it is natural to ask if there are any paradigmatic representatives of these schemes in the tradition. I think there are. Spinoza is probably as good a representative as any of a pure bottom-upper (note the ontological austerity) whereas Aristotle is a good candidate for a pure top-downer (note, correspondingly, the ontological richness).

Better candidates for pure representatives for each scheme are in fact easier to find in the contemporary arena. The bottom up-strategy seems to predominate in the work of Peter van Inwagen, most notably in his recent book *Material Beings*.[2] According to van Inwagen, the physical world consists ultimately of material simples lacking proper parts. Some sets of them are arranged table-wise, others are arranged Frisbee-wise, and so on. Simples arranged in a table shape or Frisbee shape do not in fact compose anything, however. Being a collection of simples is not sufficient to produce an object with intrinsic unity having those simples for its parts. Other sets of simples, however, do exhibit such intrinsic unity, specifically, when those simples compose a living thing. A set of objects are caught up in a living thing when they are organized in such a way that they exhibit what van Inwagen calls a "homeodynamic stability." Simples thus organized are capable of continued existence by producing succeeding sets of simples organized in similar (living) ways. When a set of objects are caught up in a life, then there exists an object that is composed of these parts. This organism lasts just so long as the event which is its life continues. And since there is no other way of organizing a collection of objects so that they compose an object, the world contains nothing but living things and the simples from which they are made.

Van Inwagen is led to this conclusion because he is convinced that at bottom physical reality is discrete and that the view he defends is the only way of making sense of simples composing a composite substance. Bottoms up!

There are a number of candidates for contemporary top-downers. These candidates fall into roughly two categories. On the one hand are those who hand off the task of discovering the ultimate constituents of natural reality to science. These top-downers take the ordinary claims of scientific discourse as their starting point and accord the entities referred to in such descriptions prima facie ontological standing. David Armstrong is a representative of this strategy.[3] On the other hand, there are a host of metaphysical antirealists, such as Hilary Putnam. It might seem odd to put Putnam on such a continuum of ontological methodologies in light of his antirealism. Since he ends up denying the value of ontology (realistically construed), one might think that he cannot be a representative of either scheme. Despite his antirealism, however, his methodology too is top-down. Consider, for example, the following:

    [2] Peter van Inwagen, *Material Beings* (Ithaca: Cornell University Press, 1990).
    [3] See David Armstrong, *A World of States of Affairs* (New York: Cambridge University Press, 1997).

We don't have notions of the 'existence' of things or of the 'truth' of statements that are independent of the versions we construct and of the procedures and practices that give sense to talk of 'existence' and 'truth' within
those versions. Do *fields* 'exist' as physically real things? Yes, fields really
exist, relative to one scheme for describing and explaining physical phenomena; relative to another there are particles, plus 'virtual' particles. Is it true
that *brown* objects exist? Yes, relative to a common sense version of the
world: although one cannot give a necessary and sufficient condition for an
object to be brown (one that applies to all objects, under all conditions) in
the form of a finite closed formula in the language of physics. Do *dispositions* exist? Yes in our ordinary way of talking (though disposition talk is
just as recalcitrant to translation into physicalistic language as counterfactual
talk, and for similar reasons). We have many irreducibly different but legitimate ways of talking, and true 'existence' statements in all of them.

　　To postulate a set of 'ultimate' objects, the furniture of the world, or what
you will, whose 'existence' is *absolute*, not relative to our discourse at all,
and a notion of truth as 'correspondence' to these ultimate objects is simply
to revive the whole failed enterprise of traditional metaphysics.[4]

Here is, in a certain sense, an ontology as rich as you please! For Putnam, what
objects there are depends on the conceptual scheme we adopt, a conceptual
scheme reflected in both our folk and scientific descriptions of the world.

　　Notice that one of the things about which Putnam and van Inwagen disagree
is one of those issues that often separate respective advocates of the two
schemata: how to countenance what are sometimes called "conventional objects." For Putnam, the conceptual scheme we adopt determines the objects the
world contains. And in this sense, all objects are objects of convention for him.
In the preface to *Material Beings*, however, van Inwagen lays it out as one of his
axioms that there is no sense to talking about the existence of objects of convention:

　　I suppose that what there is, is never a matter of stipulation or conven-
　　tion. . . . Convention regulates behavior, including linguistic behavior, and
　　regulating behavior has no ontological implications beyond implying the ex-
　　istence of regularities in behavior.[5]

Without the details, what van Inwagen has in mind is this: either simples compose a living thing or not. If so, then we have a composite object; if not, we
don't. In any case, our establishing conventions won't make any difference to
what there is, since the simples are what they are and the composites are what

　　[4] Hilary Putnam, *Realism and Reason* (New York: Cambridge University Press, 1983),
230–31.
　　[5] Van Inwagen, *Material Beings*, 7.

they are apart from our conventions. Thus, establishing conventions can't constitute objects and so there can't be "objects by convention."

Undoubtedly, there is a sense in which this is right. If we intend to do ontology the bottom-up way and accommodate our ordinary talk to it, this is, I suppose, just what one ought to say. But this leads us back the central question: Should we opt for a bottom-up scheme? Well, why not? To see one answer to this question, we need to flesh out some motivations for the top-down scheme and see whether or not the bottom-upper can accommodate them and whether or not she should care to. To begin our thinking in this direction, let me develop the views of someone who holds out for a mixed strategy: Leibniz.

II. THE MIXED LEIBNIZIAN STRATEGY

In his middle period Leibniz endorses the following two metaphysical theses:

(a) The world of corporeal entities is infinitely divisible, and
(b) Reality must consist ultimately of atomic substances, that is, entities that could not retain their ontological integrity if further divided.[6]

Leibniz's endorsement of these two theses leads him to view corporeal reality as merely phenomenal, arising in virtue of the way God has put human perceivers in contact with ultimate monadic reality, a reality that is neither ultimately spatial nor temporal itself. With this picture we can have the potential for infinite divisibility of objects in their phenomenal presentation while recognizing that the ontological ground floor consists of atomic (monadic) substances not further divisible. Extended entities, then, have merely phenomenal existence, an existence had in virtue of the way in which God elected to have them represented to us.

This led to a tension in Leibniz's thought concerning how to think about the notion of substance generally. For the moderns, as for the pre-moderns, substance is an ontological category used to describe bits of reality that exhibit intrinsic or per se unity. If corporeal reality is merely phenomenal, then one is led to wonder whether or not anything but the rock-bottom monads exemplify unity and thus whether anything other than monads are genuine substances. If not, then none of the things that appear to us as bodies in the phenomenal manifold are phenomenal presentations of a single substance. Instead, these phenomenal presentations would be confused ideas of an infinite swarm of monads that *appear to us* as having some overarching unity. But the appearance in this case is one that arises not out of the unity of the underlying substances (the monads)

---

[6] See, for example, Leibniz's "New System of Nature," in *Philosophical Essays*, trans. Roger Ariew and Daniel Garber (Indianapolis: Hackett, 1989), 139–40.

but in virtue of perceptual "bridge principles" that God establishes, principles in virtue of which collections of monads appear to us in the way that they do.

Leibniz is not, however, quite as austere as that. Rather, he thinks that monads taken singly count as genuine substances and that some sets of monads form natural unities in virtue of certain facts about the ways in which the monads mutually represent one another. Thus, the monads that compose my body do so in virtue of a relation that each of the bodily monads bears to a rational monad that carries out the function of my soul. Leibniz called this relation of the rational monad to the monads that constitute the body the *domination relation*.[7]

For Leibniz, then, the monadic world consists of two types of real things or substances: single monads and collections of monads that constitute an *unum per se* in virtue of the domination relation of one monad over the remaining members of the collection. All this seems to represent the project of Leibnizian ontology as bottom-up.

But what do we make, then, of the ontology implied by ordinary language? Ask the folk what objects the world contains, and they will say baseballs, butter, beer, and such. What does Leibniz want to say about these things? Leibniz first wants to say that such talk is not metaphysically perspicuous. Although there are undoubtedly phenomenal presentations that we mark off as baseballs, there is no single monad or set of monads dominated by one member of the set that underlies the phenomena that we identify as the baseball. Baseballs are, in the old-fashioned sense of the phrase, mere aggregates. Nonetheless, Leibniz does not think that the folk ontology ought to be excluded from serious ontological talk altogether. We are beings that have been created by God to represent the monadic world to ourselves phenomenally by certain rules, what I earlier called the bridge principles. These principles determine the ways in which monads yield an intersubjective four-dimensional phenomenal manifold for rational creatures. Within this four-dimensional manifold, certain bits of extension seem to have a sort of unity that leads us to regard them as having ontological integrity, which they, at the monadic level, lack. Such phenomenal appearances are grounded in monadic reality, but there is no corresponding intrinsic unity among the monads that is isomorphic to the apparent unity that we take the extended phenomenal bits to have. Leibniz designates the latter "aggregates" and says that their reality is merely phenomenal.[8]

In saying this, however, Leibniz means to imply at least two things. First, like all phenomena, the phenomena constituting aggregates are grounded in monadic reality. And second, though they are so grounded, the aggregated phenomena have a unity that is less robust than per se unity. Thus, in an essay from the closing years of his life, Leibniz writes:

---

[7] See, for example, G. W. Leibniz, *Philosophical Papers and Letters*, ed. Leroy Loemker (Dordrecht: Kluwer, 1989), 604–5.

[8] Ibid., 531.

> Finally, bodies are nothing but aggregates, constituting something that is one *per accidens* or by an external denomination, and therefore they are well-founded phenomena.[9]

But despite their well-foundedness, he does not waver on the point that they are entities whose unity depends solely on convention:

> Our mind notices or conceives some genuine substances that have certain modes. These modes contain relations to other substances. From this, the mind takes occasion to join them together in thought and to put one name in the accounting for all these things together, which serves for convenience in reasoning. But one must not let oneself be deceived thereby into making of them so many substances or truly real beings. That is only for those who stop at appearances, or else for those who make realities of all abstractions of the mind.[10]

But notice that at least one of the reasons that it is "convenient" for us to reason about aggregates in this way is because God has established the bridge principles that make it appear to us, at least prima facie, that the monads underlying the baseball have a certain ontological integrity. Thus, although the monads underlying the aggregate lack genuine intrinsic unity, the fact that we perceive them as a unity is at least in part properly explained by the way in which God made them appear to us. When Leibniz, in the last year of his life, sends an "ontological chart" to DesBosses, he divides up "what there is" first by the categories "unum per se" and "unum per aggregationem." The former is further divided into "simples," that is, monadic substances, and "composites," that is, sets of monads dominated by some single monad. Concerning the latter (unum per aggregationem), he gives as examples a chorus of angels, an army, a herd of animals, a fishpond, a house, stone, and a cadaver.[11] Here we see Leibniz operating in top-down fashion.

Thus, using the word "object" in the broadest sense, we might say that the world consists of three sorts of objects for Leibniz: (a) ontological simples (monads), (b) composite entities each of which count as an *unum per se* (via the activity of a dominant monad), and (c) composites that are mere aggregates (in virtue of the way in which we represent the monads grounding the aggregated phenomena).

III. A GLOSS ON THE LEIBNIZIAN VIEW

No doubt the Leibnizian position as I have described it here represents a middle-of-the-road position. On the one hand, Leibniz argues in bottom-up fashion for the reality of monads as the ultimate constituents of nature, along

---

[9] Ariew and Garber, *Philosophical Essays*, 19.
[10] Ibid., 88–89.
[11] Leibniz, *Philosophical Papers and Letters*, 617.

with the reality of certain collections of dominated monads. On the other hand, he argues in top-down fashion that aggregates have ontological standing though their constitution depends on contingent facts about how we represent and conceptualize the world. But this does not yet tell us why we should not favor the more parsimonious bottom-up ontology instead. If we can get by with less, why not rather do so? Here is what I take to be the Leibnizian answer.

In addition to defending an *ontology* that left room for both substances and aggregates, Leibniz believed that all true assertions must be made true by occurrent states of substances. Thus, not only truths concerning the present but even truths concerning the past and future must be grounded in the "marks and traces" of present states of monadic substances (with appropriate fudging here since of course time itself is phenomenal for Leibniz as well). How might the richer ontology delivered by Leibniz's mixed strategy be preferable to the sparing bottom-up ontology when we focus on truth makers? When we think about statements such as 'The cow has a mass of 500 kg,' there is no problem for the sparing bottom-up ontology. If the statement expresses a truth, its propositional content is straightforward, and the relevant truth makers are clear. The content is: "The composite substance which is a cow has the property of having a mass of 500 kg," and the truth maker is the cow having such a mass. Here the truth makers are substances and properties of an unproblematic sort.

But what about statements of the following sorts:

(1) The table has four legs
(2) One-dollar bills are partially green
(3) The border between Pennsylvania and Maryland is 30 miles from Lancaster.

How would a bottom-up ontology of van Inwagen's sort treat claims such as these, that is, claims with apparent singular referring expressions that have no actual referent? As we saw in the description above, the favored way of treating such statements is to say that the true proposition expressed by (1) is something on the order of:

(P1): There is set of simples arranged table-wise which are also such that four nonoverlapping proper subsets of them are arranged leg-wise.

Understood in this ontologically perspicuous way, the propositional content of the statement is true, and the world contains the requisite truth makers.

There are, however, reasons to think that things may not be quite as simple as all that. The aim in the analysis above is to provide the claim with ontologically perspicuous propositional content and thus with actually existing referents. Thus, with respect to the analysis of (1), this account implies that there is an objective notion of what it means for simples to be "arranged table-wise." Yet simples being arranged in just such-and-such a way is not a sufficient condition of the simples being arranged table-wise. Two sets of simples can be arranged identically and yet be such that in one case we would correctly regard the set as a table and in another case not. To see this, imagine that I have an elaborately constructed stone table built near my pool that looks strikingly like a natural rock formation. Given our conventions, we would rightly call this "collection of simples" a table. But to stumble upon an identically arranged set of simples at the bottom of a hill after an avalanche would not license my asserting, "The avalanche has produced a table!" As a result, we might think that (P1) does not in fact represent the propositional content of (1) on this bottom-up scheme. There is still ontologically unperspicuous content in (P1). If we want to preserve the truth of ordinary claims such as (1), the propositional content of (1) will have to be much more complicated and such as to include an analysis of what table-wise arrangement consists in.

Maybe bottom-uppers would be inclined at this point to reply: "So what? When I say 'table-wise,' I just mean however it is that the ontologically unperspicuous folk think things need to be arranged in order for you rightly to apply the word 'table.'" But this reply will not suffice. The point of the example is that things being "arranged table-wise" requires (to be so arranged) an embeddedness in a system of conventions and practices in virtue of which such arrangements can come to be. So arranging simples in a certain way is a start, but for that arrangement to *constitute* a table-wise arrangement requires that certain conventions and practices be in place. *That* is part of how *such arrangements* get constituted.

Let's pass on to the next example. How might we account for the conditions that suffice as truth makers for (2) on the bottom-up account? We might begin with a similar analysis:

(P2): The simples arranged one-dollar-bill-wise are green.

But here again the available resources seem too thin for the task. The reason is that for something to count as a dollar bill in the first place requires not that any simples be arranged any "such-wise." Instead, it requires that the simples, arranged as they are, be recognized as a dollar by a certain community. And notice that a mere individual rendering of the facts is not good enough here; rather, we need recognition by either a certain group vested with authority to establish such conventions or, in some cases, by enough people in the community that, in this case at least, such an entity becomes regarded as legal tender and thus a genuine medium of exchange. In other words, we need an analysis that comes from the top down.

John Searle has offered a top-down analysis for cases such as (2) in his book *The Construction of Social Reality*. There he argues that realists need to accommodate the notion that certain facts are language-dependent. For a fact to be language-dependent requires that two conditions be met:

(A) Mental representations must be partly constitutive of the fact

(B) The representations must be language-dependent.

In the case of claim (2), the condition (A) is met in virtue of the fact that something counting as a dollar bill requires recognition that it is such, and this in turn requires prior *representation of it as such*, by a community. Showing that the second condition is met is a more difficult task but not required for our purposes since here I am making only the claim that we ought to regard some facts, and correspondingly some bits of reality, as socially constituted or at least as constituted in part by the ways in which we deploy our conceptual resources.[12]

Perhaps, however, the trouble is with the particular species of bottom-up approach I have been working with here, namely, van Inwagen's. Is there another bottom-up strategy that would avoid this unwelcome consequence? One view, defended by David Lewis, among others, holds that all mereological sums compose genuine metaphysical wholes.[13] On this bottom-up view, the ontological stock contains ultimately discrete parts of fundamentally diverse types (subatomic particles, atoms, etc.) as well as all mereological sums of those parts. Following van Inwagen, I will call this position "universalism."

On this view, the truth makers for the claims like (1) and (2) refer to actually existing things, namely, the mereological sums (tables and dollar bills) and their properties (four-leggedness and green-ness). Thus, on this view, the statements come out true without the unwieldy account of propositional content needed by the sparing bottom-up account. Further, the universalist might contend, this account is able to dispense with the unpalatable Leibnizian claim that some objects exist "by convention." This dual advantage makes the view worth considering seriously.

No doubt this view does merit serious consideration. But I think that serious consideration leaves it wanting. First, as van Inwagen points out, it rules out many common-sense claims that are hard to surrender.[14] Second, the view seems

---

[12] John Searle, *The Construction of Social Reality* (New York: Free Press, 1995), 62–69. Parenthetically, Searle makes out the case as follows: linguistic symbols have three essential features: (a) they symbolize something, (b) they do so by convention, and (c) they are public. Without some system of symbolic representation, all we can do is see pieces of green paper and people passing about such pieces of paper. We need to have the capacity for regarding the green piece of paper *as* a dollar in order for it to be constituted as one. But this *regarding as* just is to allow the representation to fill the role symbolically designated for it. Thus, there is no such thing as representing the piece of paper as a dollar bill absent the public, conventional symbol we deploy.

[13] See David Lewis, *On the Plurality of Worlds* (New York: Blackwell, 1986), 211.

[14] The reader is advised to consult van Inwagen, *Material Beings*, 75–80, for his discussion of this. Van Inwagen argues that the following claims (among others) are very plausibly true and, if true, entail the falsity of universalism: (1) I exist now and I existed ten years ago; (2) I am an organism and I have always been an organism; (3) Every organism is composed of some atoms or other at every moment of its existence; (4) Consider any organism that existed ten

viciously unparsimonious. Of course, the world may simply be overpopulated in the way the universalist suggests. But in light of the liabilities the universalist faces, the view must offer us some outweighing advantages. The advantage I have pointed to here is that it allows tables and dollar bills into an ontologically perspicuous description of reality. But it does so at the price of allowing *any* mereological sum to figure into an ontologically perspicuous description. The van Inwagen approach is stingy, but this is wildly extravagant.

IV. WHAT THE ONTOLOGY OF THE LEIBNIZIAN STRATEGY ENTAILS

What is needed is something between van Inwagen and the universalist. Specifically, what we need is an ontology that allows in certain elements of social reality, that is, reality constituted in part by convention. What results if we allow the top-downer to countenance objects constituted at least in part "by convention" in the ontology? Does the resulting conception of reality become objectionably relativistic? Far from it. Recall that the view aims to take seriously, for example, the claim that talk about "money" is talk about a publicly accessible reality—a reality that exists in a way that is independent of our individual representations of it. This is what appears to be traded away on the account that aims to render the propositional content of talk about money into talk about "simples arranged such-wise." Still, the Leibnizian strategy need not commit one to the claim that the reality of composites with intrinsic unity is *on par* with the unity exhibited by socially constituted aggregates. As Searle claims near the end of the book:

> But marriages and money, unlike mountains and atoms, do not exist independently of *all* representations, and this distinction needs to be made explicit in this account. . . . Facts about money can be epistemically objective even if the existence of money is socially constructed, and, therefore, to that extent, ontologically subjective.[15]

This seems just right. Some wholes are constituted by intrinsic states of the parts which suffice for a per se unity among those very parts whereas others are constituted by various linguistic and/or practical conventions of created language and concept users.

Does this commit the Leibnizian to the dreaded "equivocity of being"? Surely this is not entailed by the view as presented so far. Ontological wholes might have more than one principle by which they are so constituted. But this simply means there is more than one way for an ontological whole to become such. Thus, "being" is not equivocal on these grounds any more than "living"

years ago—all the atoms that compose it still exist; (5) Consider any organism that exists now and existed ten years ago—none of the atoms that now compose that organism is among those that composed it ten years ago.

[15] Searle, *Construction of Social Reality*, 190.

would be in virtue of the fact that there are a variety of ways in which molecular parts can be arranged to compose organisms.

There are, however, questions of fundamental importance and interest concerning just to what extent the reality of composites is derived from the bottom up and the top down. How many composites are such in virtue of facts independent of finite concept users, and how many depend on convention for their unity? How we answer this question will depend on more than one consideration. For the Christian at least, one might wonder whether (and how much) one might be able to glean about the ontology of composites from special revelation. Perhaps one might think, for example, that the early chapters of Genesis point to ways in which the joints of nature are structured by divine creative intentions. Perhaps not. But one might also begin to answer this question by thinking about just how the bottom-upper approaches the task when aiming to answer the question, What composites exhibit "finite mind-independent" intrinsic unity? Do we, in asking these sorts of questions, bring to the table certain "ontological conventions" that will determine the outcome of even our bottom-up metaphysical speculations?

John Haugeland, for example, has defended a more radical version of top-downism, arguing that the fundamental ontology consists entirely of objects the existence of which is to be explained in terms of our social "existential-constitutive commitments." On Haugeland's account, in determining what kinds of entities we should countenance in our ontology (i.e., which sorts of entities we might admit as real as opposed to entities whose existence we regard as merely theoretical or instrumental), we establish certain conventions that, among other things, provide necessary (and perhaps sometimes sufficient) conditions for "thing-hood." Thus, we commit ourselves to seeing and interacting with the world with an understanding that to count as a *thing*, an object must

(a) be "spatio-temporally cohesive" (no spatially or temporally noncontiguous parts),
(b) admit of regularities constitutive of the identity of the *thing* across time,
(c) have properties that are proper or intrinsic to its bearer (and thus that whether or not it exemplifies the property depends only on *it* and not on *any other* "things"),
(d) be such that its properties are determinations of its interactions with distinct *things*, and that the properties be general, and thus in principle shareable, by distinct things.[16]

Ordinary willingness to count tables and chairs as part of our ontology arises out of prior existential commitments to such constitutive principles and an acknowledgment that these objects of ordinary experience pass the test.

In contrast, the microentities hypothesized in theories of fundamental

---

[16] John Haugeland, *Having Thought: Essays in the Metaphysics of Mind* (Cambridge: Harvard University Press, 1998), 349–50.

physics—particles in superposition, photons capable of producing double-slit diffraction patterns, tachyons, and the like—are regarded as not even candidates for "the real" in virtue of their failure to meet these constitutive criteria. Could we adjust our "constitutive-existential commitments" in order to allow such deviant entities to count as "real things"? There is no reason to think not. And we might think that "deviant" metaphysics propose just such "rule changes" for our consideration (nonsubstantival ontologies of the sorts described by Peter Strawson, for example).

What does the top-downer gain by shifting the principles that constitute ontological wholes to the conventional category? The very thing I proposed above that the bottom-upper has lost: an account of propositional content or meaning that is not ungainly. The top-downer is inclined to think that the ontological parsimony of the bottom-up account comes at a price not worth paying. At best, the price is that we must take the propositional content of a great many of our ordinary assertions to be extraordinarily and unexpectedly cumbersome. The content of my assertion that the table has four legs is not that merely there is a set of simples that are arranged "table-wise" and such that four nonoverlapping proper subsets of them are arranged "leg-wise." And we have seen that this is so because "table-wise" and "leg-wise" themselves are still too convention-laden to provide the ontologically perspicuous propositional content that the bottom-upper is looking for. Every occurrence of "x-wise" is going to require some further translation along the lines of

> (P1*): simples arranged such that it accords with the conventions of a majority of English language users or the conventions established by those with the authority to determine conventional standards for what counts as an x-wise arrangement of simples.

So bottom-uppers trade ontological simplicity for complexity in their accounts of propositional content of ordinary statements.

V. THE GOD'S I POINT OF VIEW

Putnam has argued that there is no longer a place for the "God's Eye Point of View" in ontology.[17] For Putnam, the sort of metaphysical realism (MR) presupposed in the God's Eye Point of View consists of two theses:

> (MR1) Reality is what it is independent of our representations of it.
> (MR2) There is exactly one true and complete description of "the way the world is."

Arguments against this pair of theses are well known. Putnam repeatedly appeals to an example in which the reader is asked to consider some segment of

---

[17] Hilary Putnam, *Reason, Truth, and History* (New York: Cambridge University Press, 1981), 49.

the world that contains, let's say, three indivisible simples, call them A, B, and C. The question then is, How many "objects" are there in that part of the world? The answer, of course, depends on the principles that we adopt for counting. On one scheme, the one that does not admit mereological sums, there are three. But in a system of counting that permits mereological sums, the so-called Polish logician's system, there are seven (each atom, each pair, and the set of three). Through this example Putnam aims to show that there is no privileged system of counting and so no "single true and complete description" of how the world is.

Nelson Goodman makes similar claims and attempts to argue for them by appeal to an experimental situation in which subjects are shown a series of flashes on a screen that are separated by a short distance. Subjects routinely claim that they "see" the dot move from one location to another. The same sort of effect is witnessed when one looks at a message board with moving texts where the letters, composed of light bulbs flashing on and off, appear to scroll across the screen. Subjects can, however, be trained to see the flashes as distinct and immobile flashes rather than single moving flashes. Is there a privileged description of the situation? Goodman claims that there is not and thus takes himself to have undercut the plausibility of metaphysical realism as characterized above.[18]

Both these arguments against metaphysical realism have themselves been subjected to extensive critical scrutiny. But notice, for our purposes, that even if the arguments are successful, they succeed in showing only that (MR2) ought to be rejected, not (MR1). If we grant Putnam and Goodman that (MR2) is false (something I think there is no reason to grant simply on the basis of the arguments presented above), then they would have succeeded in defeating metaphysical realism so characterized. But is the characterization a straw man? Are metaphysical realists committed to (MR1) and (MR2)? And if so, ought they be so committed?

At least one self-styled metaphysical realist, Nicholas Wolterstorff, seems to think not. Wolterstorff writes:

> Reality does not come ready-made into cats and the property of being a cat or indeed, into properties generally. It is we who *decide* to count a certain segment of reality as a cat, another, as a property. In short, existence and truth are relative to conceptual schemes because *identity* is relative to conceptual schemes. And that is why the anti-realist says that "it is characteristic of this view to hold that *what objects does the world consist of?* is a question that it only makes sense to ask *within* a theory or description." Something like this, I dare say, is how the anti-realist is thinking. . . . And . . . it seems to me that this way of thinking is substantially correct.[19]

---

[18] Nelson Goodman, *Ways of Worldmaking* (Indianapolis: Hackett, 1978), 72–83.

[19] Nicholas Wolterstorff, "Are Concept-Users World-Makers?" in *Philosophical Perspectives*, ed. James E. Tomberlin (Atascadero, Calif.: Ridgeview, 1987), 260.

As I understand him, Wolterstorff thinks that the property instances that con-stitute, for example, rabbit instances must exist and be what they are indepen-dent of our abilities to cognize them. But regarding those property instances as rabbit instances and establishing identity conditions for such instances is our business. Thus, he continues:

> Apart from our decision of what shall count as *a* soandso, and what shall count as two presentations of the same soandso and what as two presenta-tions of different soandsos, there simply is no phenomenon as identity. . . . This is to be seen as a condition of our speech rather than as a reflection of reality.[20]

There is, of course, a sense in which this is trivially true. What will count as a phenomenon to which our word "rabbit" will apply is surely nothing more than our establishing a convention about how we use words. But the more re-vealing question is: Once we use a word to pick out a genuine composite sub-stance or natural kind, is there a further fact about whether or not, when we wield the word, our doing so successfully cuts nature along its own joints? I take it that this is the real question Wolterstorff is asking here, and his answer is no.

But why not rather think that this view stumbles from being too heavily top-down by allowing too much of the ontology to be determined by convention? A strong (at least prima facie) case can be made that the Christian should not go this far. For the Christian, there is a world that exists and is what it is apart from all human conceptual commitments, because this world is created by an act of God. Thus there is a world that is the way it is in part because of the di-vine creative intentions that the world contain such-and-such kinds and such-and-such substances, simple and composite. And this is going to settle at least the bottom-up ontological questions (that is, divine intentions will establish, as remarked earlier, the natural joints that distinguish both *natural kinds* and *nat-ural individual substances*). Thus, the Christian can happily engage in the bot-tom-up project assuming that these questions are settled independent of our representations of the world to ourselves. This project aims at figuring out how things are from the bottom up, or if you will, from the God's Eye Point of View.

One might say that this simply means that the Christian realist should not think about metaphysical realism in terms of (MR1) and (MR2) after all. In-stead, the Christian realist should admit that a good deal of reality is consti-tuted as it is independent of our representations of it. But segments of reality ought also to be regarded as partially constituted by our conceptual deploy-ments. As a result, (MR2) should be rejected altogether.

Nonetheless, if we think in terms of the bottom-up structure of the world, the one stamped into creation by the divine creative intentions—the world apart from any constituting activity on the part of creatures, there is a sense in which

---

[20] Ibid.

(MR2) is true. But this is so only if we exclude constituted reality from the scope of the phrase "the way the world is." We might call this divine first-person perspective on the world the "God's I Point of View."

Thus, if we buy the moderate Leibnizian line I defend above, we might think that there are a host of questions—genuinely ontological questions—which the creator cannot answer without access to our conceptual resources. We can see this by imagining what would be the case if God were, due to some divine noetic dysfunction, to find himself incapable of accessing human conceptual resources. If this were to occur, there would, first, be a number of questions that God could not answer. Questions concerning the truth or falsity of (1), (2), and (3) above are prime examples. God simply does not know where the border between Pennsylvania and Maryland lies from the "God's I Point of View." But such claims seem to be claims about "the world." If this is right, then there are a number of facts—facts about the *world*—that God cannot then know without consulting our conceptual resources.

CODA

Earlier I noted that Haugeland argues that there are certain constitutive-existential commitments we can and do make which serve to mark off what sorts of things we will allow to count as objects. Such commitments, by his lights, serve as the "principles of aggregation" that we employ when we are doing our top-down ontology. For Haugeland, these are commitments that those who share a language and a set of practices make contingently. They could commit themselves to other principles of aggregation (though not just *any* principles). But the principles are nonetheless derived from practices *we* adopt and commitments *we* make.

On the more moderate Leibnizian line, we might say that the constitutive principles we adopt serve to constitute all aspects of reality not constituted by the divine creative intentions. In this respect, at any rate, we might see in Haugeland an attempt to do without God what Leibniz attempted to do through God. For Leibniz, the principles of aggregation are in part fixed by the bridge principles that God institutes for the phenomenal presentation of monads. For Haugeland, the principles of aggregation are selected by us and are responsible for constituting much of "our world."

CONCLUSION

As Putnam was delivering his 1976 APA Eastern Presidential Address containing his forceful defense of antirealism (or "internal realism") and announcing the passing of the God's Eye View of the world, the theistic philosopher Arthur Holmes was finalizing his work *All Truth Is God's Truth*.[21] In this book Holmes defends the view that the standard for *all* truths is what I have called here the

---

[21] Arthur F. Holmes, *All Truth Is God's Truth* (Grand Rapids, Mich.: Eerdmans, 1977).

God's I Point of View: truth makers for all truths are found in the facts, and these facts are established by God via divine creative intentions.

Here I have tried to argue that the ontological choices for the theist, happily, need not be so stark. If Holmes is right, we are stuck with a stingy bottom-up scheme and are required to endorse the gerrymandered account of the meaning or propositional content of ordinary statements. But we might do well instead to help ourselves to the richer ontology of the Leibnizian, holding, pace van Inwagen, that objects can be constituted by convention and acknowledging that helping ourselves in this way provides a more intuitive understanding of truth makers and a more plausible account of propositional content.

.6.

What Metaphysical Realism Is Not

WILLIAM P. ALSTON

I

'Metaphysical realism' is used in various ways, to refer to a variety of different positions. Historically, the most prominent such positions are the medieval commitment to the objective reality of universals and the opposition to one or another metaphysical *idealism*, the view that everything is mental or an aspect of, or dependent on, the mental. Moreover, there is a plethora of "departmental realisms", in addition to the medieval realism about universals, each of which claims objective reality for the apparent objects of some field of inquiry. Thus we have realism about moral standards, values, theoretical entities in science, "abstract" objects like propositions, properties, and meanings, and so on. Such realisms are advocated in opposition both to flat denials that such entities exist and to "reductions" of entities of the type in question to something allegedly more fundamental or less problematic. Thus realism about physical objects is opposed to a reduction of physical objects to patterns of actual and possible sensory experience, and realism about propositions is opposed to their reduction to classes of synonymous sentences. Realism about values is opposed to the denial that values have any sort of objective status, and realism about meanings is opposed to the denial that there are any such things.[1]

The metaphysical realism with which I am concerned here differs from all the above. It differs from departmental realisms in being more global in character. And it differs from the anti-idealist kind of realism in the character of its principal opponent. Indeed, an initial characterization of realism is most effectively couched in terms of what it opposes. (To paraphrase a formulation of J. L. Austin's in another connection and in the old male chauvinist days, it is antirealism that "wears the trousers".) As a preliminary characterization of the kind of metaphysical realism being considered here, it is opposed to the view that whatever there is, is constituted, at least in part, by our cognitive relations thereto, by the ways we conceptualize it or construe it, by the language

[1] This is far from an exhaustive catalog. For example, there are various "realisms" in the philosophy of perception: "direct realism", "critical realism", etc.

we use to talk about it or the conceptual scheme(s) we use to think of it. In terms of major historical figures, this kind of *antirealism* stems from Kant's "Copernican revolution", according to which anything of which we can have knowledge owes at least its basic structure to the categories in terms of which we think it rather than to the way it is "in itself". In a more contemporary vein, we can think of my metaphysical realism as defined by the denial of a semi-Kantian position paradigmatically represented by the post-1980 Hilary Putnam:

> . . . *what objects does the world consist of?* is a question that it only makes sense to ask *within* a theory or description. . . . [2]

In other words, whatever there is exists and is what it is only within a certain way of "describing" or "conceptualizing" what there is. This is a relativized Kantianism in that it recognizes different ways of describing or conceptualizing reality, ways that would be incompatible if each of them were put forward as the way to characterize reality as it is in itself. Since this position avoids recognizing Kantian noumena, things as they are in themselves, it can assert the cognition or description relativity of what there is in a more unqualified way than Kant, not restricting it to what we can know.

Since the metaphysical realism I am discussing here amounts to the denial of a universal affirmative proposition (*everything* that is, is what it is, at least in part, because of the way we conceptualize it), it is not committed to the *contrary*, namely, the correlated universal negative, that *nothing* that is, is what it is, at least in part, because of the way we conceptualize it. That is, it need not deny that there is anything that is constituted, at least in part, by our cognitive relations thereto. It need only deny that all of reality is like that. In the interests of concision of formulation, let's use the Kantian term '*an sich*' ('in itself') to mark this kind of independence of our (human) modes of cognition. Thus the denial of Putnam's antirealism can be put by saying that not everything fails to exist and be what it is *in itself*. Of course, the most minimum denial, that there is *something* that exists and is what it is *an sich*, is hardly significant enough to be worth the trouble. To avoid that consequence, I will be thinking of metaphysical realism as the view that large stretches of reality enjoy that status. I won't attempt in this chapter to give a precise specification of those stretches. A rough indication will suffice. Let's say that metaphysical realism holds that the following enjoy *an sich* reality.

> (1.) Familiar macroscopic objects that we perceive in the physical environment—animal and vegetable organisms, artifacts, topographical formations . . .

---

[2] Hilary Putnam, *Reason, Truth, and History* (Cambridge: Cambridge University Press, 1981), 49.

(2.) Familiar kinds of stuff and portions thereof—water, earth, sugar, manure, snow . . .

(3.) Unperceivable entities recognized by successful scientific theories—electrons, nuclei, quanta of energy . . .

The list could be extended, but as just noted, I am not concerned here to provide a definitive list of what, according to my metaphysical realism, does and does not enjoy *an sich* reality. For present purposes it is enough that much of what we encounter in the world has that status, but that there are things that could be plausibly recognized as objectively existing that exist and are what they are only relative to a particular conceptual or theoretical choice, for which there are equally viable alternatives. Scientific theories that are equally supported by all relevant empirical data would be plausible examples of the latter.[3]

Against this background I can state the main thesis of this chapter. Many characterizations of metaphysical realism, and more to the point, many criticisms of it, involve thinking of the view as involving features that are quite different from what is contained in the characterization just given. Moreover, these additional features are not at all entailed by that characterization. To be sure, if those who introduce these features were concerned with a kind of metaphysical realism quite different from the one I have characterized, there could be no objection to their going beyond my rather lean conception. But such is not the case with the people I will be discussing. And how do I know that? By the fact that their criticisms of what they call 'metaphysical realism' are designed to support the antirealism in terms of the denial of which I introduced my conception. That is, they assume that if metaphysical realism, as they construe it, is not viable, then the only alternative is an antirealism that holds that everything exists and is what it is, in part, because of the (or a) way in which we cognize it. But insofar as their criticism is directed against something that is not necessarily involved in the denial of that kind of antirealism, it thereby fails to refute that denial, as they suppose it to do. That is what I will seek to show here.

II

I begin the survey of gratuitous accretions to metaphysical realism (hereinafter simply 'realism') with some epistemological ones. First there is the suggestion that on a realist position reality is *inaccessible* to us; we are incapable of determining what it is like. Here is a formulation from Richard Rorty:

> If one accepts the Davidson-Stroud position, then 'the world' will just be
> the stars, the people, the tables, and the grass—all those things which no-
> body except the occasional 'scientific realist' philosopher thinks might not
> exist. So in one sense of 'world'—the sense in which (except for a few

---

[3] For an attempt to go much further in distinguishing between what does and does not enjoy *an sich* reality, see William P. Alston, *A Sensible Metaphysical Realism* (Milwaukee: Marquette University Press, 2001).

fringe cases like gods, neutrinos, and natural rights) we now know perfectly well what the world is like and could not possibly be wrong about
it—there is no argument about the point that it is the world that determines truth. . . . But this is, of course, not enough for the realist. What he
wants is precisely what the Davidson-Stroud argument prevents him from
having—the notion of a world *so* "independent of our knowledge" that it
might, for all we know, prove to contain none of the things we have always
thought we were talking about. . . . The notion of 'the world' must be the
notion of something *completely* unspecified and unspecifiable—the thing in
itself, in fact.[4]

In this passage Rorty does not make explicit that he is using 'realism' to de-
nominate what I call 'metaphysical realism'. Nevertheless, he takes the only alternative to his 'realism' to be the "Davidson-Stroud" view that "the world"
just consists of what no sensible person would deny or doubt to be the case.
That is, if one is not a "realist", one takes reality to be determined by what *we*
generally agree on. And though much less sophisticated than the forms of antirealism I will be considering later, this is close enough to what my realism denies for it to be pertinent to this discussion. So to turn the direction around,
Rorty is suggesting that on the only realist alternative to the "Stroud-Davidson"
position, reality is so cognitively inaccessible to us that it is "something *completely* unspecified and unspecifiable". If these are our only alternatives, we are,
of all creatures, the most miserable.

But of course, these are not the only options. We can perfectly well be realists
in my sense and hold an epistemology on which a great deal of knowledge of reality is well within our grasp. More generally, no epistemological consequences
at all concerning the conditions under which we do or do not know (reasonably
believe) something follow from realism. Those matters are left completely open,
except for the rejection of the (bizarre) view that reality is defined by what is
generally believed. It is true that this view makes it maximally easy to acquire
knowledge. If we just go along with the crowd, we can't miss. But like most
things that easy, it is hardly worth having. A more sensible view of what is required for knowledge or reasonable belief will have the consequence that we
sometimes attain that goal and sometimes miss it. Neither outcome is guaranteed by a view as to what it takes for something to really exist or for a state of
affairs to obtain. And saddling realism with an inaccessibility clause is a much
too easy way of refuting it.

Interestingly enough, other philosophers take a diametrically opposite epistemological position to be involved in metaphysical realism.

A reasonable pretheoretical characterization of realism about, say, the external world seems to me that it is a fusion of two kinds of thoughts, one kind

---

[4] "The World Well Lost", in Richard Rorty, *Consequences of Pragmatism* (Minneapolis:
University of Minnesota Press, 1982), 14.

expressing a certain modesty, the other more presumptuous. The modest kind of thought concerns the *independence* of the external world . . . that it is as it is independently of the conceptual vocabulary in terms of which we think about it, and that it is as it is independently of the beliefs about it which we do, will, or ever would form. . . .

The presumptuous thought, by contrast, is that, while such fit as there may be between our thought and the world is determined independently of human cognitive activity, we are nevertheless, in favourable circumstances, capable of conceiving the world aright, and, often, of knowing the truth about it.[5]

In opposition to both Rorty and Wright, I take metaphysical realism to carry no assumptions whatever about our abilities to know or form true beliefs about what there is. No doubt some such assumptions are much more reasonable than others (Wright's than Rorty's, for example), and some are much more attractive to realists than others (again Wright is awarded the palm). But a distinctively metaphysical realism will not necessarily be committed to any particular estimate of human cognitive powers. A thoroughly skeptical metaphysical realism would, no doubt, be a very gloomy affair, but still neither inconsistent nor incoherent.

While discussing patently invalid attributions to realism, I should mention subtractions as well as additions. A vivid example of the former is found in Arthur Fine. He maintains that though it is perfectly sensible to accept the results of science, including those having to do with "theoretical entities" not accessible to direct observation, the "realist" is not satisfied with this but wants something more. Since Fine is, understandably, at a loss to give a sensible account of what this "more" amounts to, he has recourse to the following suggestion:

What the realist adds on is a desk-thumping, footstamping shout of "Really!". So, when the realist and antirealist agree, say, that there really are electrons and that they really carry a unit negative charge and really do have a small mass, what the realist wants to add is the emphasis that all this is really so. "There really are electrons, really!"[6]

If this is all that realism amounts to, it is certainly not worthy of serious consideration. But it appears that way only by dint of a suppression of the realist side of the realist-antirealist contrast set out in Section I; realism, as I defined it, has

[5] Crispin Wright, *Truth and Objectivity* (Cambridge: Harvard University Press, 1992), 1–2.

[6] Arthur Fine, "The Natural Ontological Attitude", in *The Shaky Game: Einstein, Realism, and the Quantum Theory* (Chicago: University of Chicago Press, 1986), 129. In fairness to Fine it must be pointed out that he clearly rejects various forms of antirealism, including the one I indicated in Section I. But when it comes to realism, he takes the strange position that it can be distinguished from his "natural ontological attitude" (electrons are real and really have certain properties) only by certain disreputable features.

disappeared from the map. Or perhaps it has been hidden in Fine's "natural on-tological attitude", a sensible-sounding (and realist-sounding) view that he is careful to distinguish from various forms of antirealism, including the kind featured in Section I. If that is what has happened, it is no wonder that he can find no significant cognitive content in what the "realist" has to add. As I intimated at the beginning of this brief discussion of Fine, we have here a misguided *subtraction* from realism rather than a gratuitous *accretion*.

Fine does try to understand why his "realist" engages in the bizarre behavior he attributes to him:

> I think the problem that makes the realist want to stamp his feet, shouting "Really!" (and invoking the external world), has to do with the stance the re-alist tries to take vis-à-vis the game of science. The realist, as it were, tries to stand outside the arena watching the ongoing game and then tries to judge (from this external point of view) what the point is. It is, he says, *about* some area external to the game.[7]

But why suppose the realist stands "outside" the game? On my understanding of this metaphor, the realist could be just as involved in the "game" of science as any antirealist and still take the (very sensible) position that scientific hy-potheses, questions, results, and so forth concern "some area external to the game". Presumably, scientists do not devote all their energies to investigating science!

III

All my further complaints about characterizations of realism are connected with Putnam's attack on what he calls "metaphysical realism" and his associ-ated defense of what he calls "internal realism", "pragmatic realism", or just "pragmatism".

Putnam's most explicit formulation of metaphysical realism, as a conjunc-tion of three theses, comes at the beginning of Chapter 3 of *Reason, Truth, and History*.

> One of these perspectives is the perspective of metaphysical realism. On this perspective, the world consists of some fixed totality of mind-independent objects. There is exactly one true and complete description of the 'the way the world is'. Truth involves some sort of correspondence relation between words or thought-signs and external things and sets of things. I shall call this perspective the *externalist* perspective, because its favorite point of view is a God's Eye point of view.[8]

"Metaphysical realism', as so characterized, is contrasted in the next paragraph with his "internal realism".

[7] Fine, "Natural Ontological Attitude", 131.
[8] Putnam, *Reason, Truth, and History*, 49.

The perspective I shall defend has no unambiguous name. . . . I shall refer to it as the *internalist* perspective, because it is characteristic of this view to hold that *what objects does the world consist of?* is a question that it only makes sense to ask *within* a theory or description. Many 'internalist' philosophers, though not all, hold further that there is more than one 'true' theory or description of the world. 'Truth', in an internalist view, is some sort of (idealized) rational acceptability—some sort of ideal coherence of our beliefs with each other and with our experiences *as those experiences are themselves represented in our belief system*—and not correspondence with mind-independent or discourse-independent 'states of affairs'. There is no God's Eye point of view that we can know or usefully imagine; there are only the various points of view of actual persons reflecting various interests and purposes that their descriptions and theories subserve.[9]

Clearly, each position is construed as made up of three theses, in such a way that for each thesis in the one position there is a contrary in the other position. Setting this out schematically (using 'M' for the metaphysical theses and 'I' for the internalist ones), we have

M1 The world consists of some fixed totality of mind-independent objects.
I1 Objects exist only relative to a certain theory or description.
M2 There is exactly one true and complete description of the way the world is.
I2 There is more than one true theory or description of the world.
M3 Truth involves a correspondence relation between words or thoughts and external things and sets of things.
I3 Truth is some sort of (idealized) rational acceptability—some sort of ideal coherence of our beliefs with one another and with our experiences.

M1 corresponds roughly with what I have called "metaphysical realism", if we understand Putnam's term 'mind-independent' as I explained 'independent of our cognitive relations thereto' and if we add that not only the objects but also what is true of them is "mind-independent". Correspondingly, I1 is the antirealism by contrast with which I explained metaphysical realism. Indeed, it was that very passage of Putnam's that I used for that purpose. The only serious qualification to this is that my metaphysical realism is more modest than M1, in that it confines itself to holding that a large segment of the world is mind-independent. As I explained earlier, it confines itself to contradicting the universally quantified I1 rather than endorsing the stronger contrary that *nothing* in the world is "mind-dependent". But M1 and my metaphysical realism are close enough to give point to the issue as to whether the latter is necessarily tied to the other components in Putnam's "metaphysical realism". One reason this is an important issue is that Putnam's polemic against metaphysical realism consists, in large part, in arguing against M2 and M3. If they are not entailed by M1,

[9] Ibid., 49–50.

then even if those arguments were successful they would fail to refute meta-physical realism as I have construed it. I will now proceed to show that no such entailment obtains and that M2 and M3, whatever is to be said for or against them in themselves, are both to be added to the list of unnecessary accretions to metaphysical realism.

It is, of course, relevant to consider what Putnam has to say in support of the view that M1 does imply the other two components. There is no doubt that he holds this. In his response to critics in a 1982 American Philosophical Association symposium on *Reason, Truth, and History*, Putnam claims that "each leans on the other", that is, each of them implies the other two.[10] This is a constant feature of his writings of the last two decades. But I have been unable to find any significant reasons for this position in Putnam's writings. Therefore I will have to examine the issue in my own way.

Begin with the question whether M2, "There is exactly one true and complete description of the 'the way the world is'", is implied by M1. This depends, in part, on how we are to understand M2, in particular on how we are to individuate descriptions. As we ordinarily count descriptions, after I describe my house and then go on to a description of my career, that would count as two descriptions. Presumably, Putnam is not using that kind of criterion of individuation when he attributes to the metaphysical realist the claim that there is one unique description of the whole world. A charitable reading would be that he is assuming that any consistent aggregate of descriptions counts as a single one. And while we are getting the bugs out, we shouldn't push 'description' and 'describe' too hard either. Presumably, the statement that Ann Arbor is forty miles from Detroit would be a component of the "unique true and complete description of the world", even though saying that would not ordinarily be thought of as *describing* anything. We need a more neutral term like 'account'.

Turning to more serious issues, is it the case that the proposition that *much of reality is what it is independently of our cognitive relations thereto* (enjoys *an sich* reality) implies, entails, or requires that it should receive a unique self-consistent and complete account? There are reasons for doubting this. First of all, there is the point that the modest realism I am presenting is prepared to recognize that some of reality is what it is only relative to one of a number of equally viable ways of conceptualizing reality. Hence those stretches of reality would be amenable to alternative descriptions, descriptions that would be incompatible if taken as describing *an sich* reality.

But there is a more substantive reason for denying the entailment from M1 to M2. Both Nicholas Wolterstorff and John Searle have argued that it is consistent with realism to hold that the world can be divided into objects in different and incompatible ways. The consistency is preserved because the bases on which each of these divisions is made is itself something that exists and is what

---

[10] Hilary Putnam, *Realism with a Human Face* (Cambridge: Harvard University Press, 1990), 31.

it is independently of our choice between those divisions. To take a favorite example of Putnam's, we are free either to recognize any set of objects as itself an object or not, without violating any constraints objective reality places on us. And so one complete account of reality would include listing such objects as the mereological sum of my computer, the Taj Mahal, and Julius Caesar, and another would lack any such component. But the "raw materials" and "principles of composition" for such mereological sums are all "there", independently of our cognitive machinations, whether we choose to use them or not. Again, it is plausible to think that we can recognize temporal parts of what are ordinarily thought of as enduring substances or not, without running into conflict with empirical or theoretical considerations. We ordinarily think of physical objects as having spatial parts but not as having temporal parts. The legs of my dining room table are spatial parts of the table. But the existence of the table through yesterday is not ordinarily thought of as a different *part* of the table from its existence through day before yesterday. Such a suggestion would naturally give rise to the response, "But the *whole* table existed both yesterday and day before yesterday". We don't ordinarily think of parts in that way. But we could if sufficiently motivated to do so. And the facts of temporal duration, succession, and order that we would use to do so are there and are what they are independently of our decision whether to make use of the notion of temporal parts of tables. If this way of thinking about the issue holds up, and I believe it does, we can be full-blooded realists without accepting Putnam's second component of his "metaphysical realism".

The supposition that metaphysical realism includes Putnam's second component often takes more outrageous forms than are found in so careful a thinker as Putnam. A fecund source of this is Michael Luntley's book *Reason, Truth, and Self*. There we find him thinking of the metaphysical realism he opposes as embracing commitments like this.

> Let us suppose that there exists a book that contains the answer to everything. . . . Let us call it the Cosmic Register. If there is such a thing as objective truth, truth independent of judgement, then we can think of the truth as what is recorded in the cosmic register.[11]

In opposition to this view he suggests the following.

> The optimism of modernity is misplaced. There is no cosmic register. The only registers are human creations for which there is no external standard. In place of the objective truth of the cosmic register, we would then have merely the local standards of truth presupposed by our different theories, religions and worldviews. Truth would not then be objective. If we cannot aspire to

[11] Michael Luntley, *Reason, Truth, and Self* (New York: Routledge, 1995), 25–26. See also 106.

the revelation of speaking the language of the world, what or who could adjudicate between our different local languages?[12]

Of course, Luntley does not seriously think that any metaphysical realist worth arguing with believes in the actual existence of any such register. It is only a picturesque way of making the same commitment as Putnam's "one true and complete description". Nevertheless, we must be alive to the dangers posed by the use of such pictures. They may lead the unwary to suppose that the position being characterized is seriously committed to the existence of such things. And an almost equally unpalatable version of the attribution is indicated by Luntley's allusion to the "language of the world" at the end of the second passage just cited. That phrase is liberally strewn about the book. Here is Luntley using this idea to throw light on the prominence of the scientific view of the world among realists.

> The idea that there is something special about the language of science that makes it ideal for a description of the world that transcends our limited points of view is important. It is the idea that there is such a thing as a unique language for describing the world as it is in itself. For such a language to be possible it must be . . . transparent. To say that the language of the cosmic register is transparent is to say that judgements found in the cosmic register must be judgements which 'stand alone'. . . . They must be truths which can be expressed in a way that is independent of anyone's particular point of view. . . . The entries . . . can be made fully explicit and recorded in full in a language that would be transparent to anyone who tried to read it. . . . A transparent language offers, if you like, a self-interpreting description of the world. It is the world's own language.[13]

Here we have the language of the world married to the cosmic register and modern science.

Putting the commitment to "one true and complete description" in these terms carries some objectionable content over and above Putnam's version. It reflects a misuse of the term 'language' that is, unfortunately, very common in philosophy. This comes out in Luntley's supposition that if we have the right language, for example, the "language of science", then we can't fail to tell it like it is. But language, in the basic sense in which languages are what linguists study, has no such magic powers. Any (real) language contains ample provisions for expressing both truths and falsehoods. That is implied by the mere fact that any language contains provisions for negating any statement that can be expressed in it. So the idea of a *language* such that just by using it you will be sure to state all and only of what is objectively true is confused. It is an idea only slightly less ridiculous than that of a cosmic register.

---

[12] Ibid., 27.
[13] Ibid., 47–48; see also 105, 114–15.

IV

Now for M3: "Truth involves some sort of correspondence relation between words or thought-signs and external things and sets of things." Although this is couched in terms of *correspondence*, what I have to say about it applies to a wider class of conceptions of truth that I term *realist*. What they all have in common is that they take the truth of, for example, a statement to be a matter of whether what the statement is about is as the statement "says" it to be. A correspondence theory, strictly speaking, goes beyond this in spelling out how the content of the statement has to be related to the fact that renders it true, in order that what I called the common feature holds. In my *Realist Conception of Truth*[14] I develop and defend a more minimalist version of this common notion, one that could be thought of as an inchoate correspondence account but does not spell out the details of a correspondence. One of the formulations I give of my minimalist account (one in terms of statements) runs as follows.

> A statement is true *iff* what the maker of the statement is attributing to what the statement is about, does actually qualify what the statement is about.[15]

In discussing Putnam's third component I will freely oscillate between speaking of correspondence and speaking of the more minimalist formulation.

The point I want to make about this part of Putnam's characterization of metaphysical realism is different from, and in a way opposite to, what I said about M2. There the point was that there is no reason a metaphysical realist should be committed to it. I don't want to say that here. I take it to be quite natural for a metaphysical realist to give a realist construal of truth. So what's my gripe about Putnam's including this in his portrayal of metaphysical realism? I have two gripes of different dimensions. The smaller one is that an account of truth is distinct from an account of the metaphysical status of objects and facts, and this difference should be respected. It would, indeed, be bizarre for a metaphysical realist in my sense to adopt an epistemic conception of truth that identifies the truth of a statement with some epistemic status of the statement (conclusively justified, member of an ideally coherent system, or whatever) rather than with its telling it as it, in fact, is. But if he should do so, he would not be contradicting himself.

The more important point is that Putnam takes a correspondence account of truth to be *distinctive* of metaphysical realism, at least to the extent of distinguishing it from his "internal realist" position.

[14] William P. Alston, *A Realist Conception of Truth* (Ithaca: Cornell University Press, 1996).
[15] Ibid., 26.

> 'Truth', in an internalist view, is some sort of (idealized) rational acceptability—some sort of ideal coherence of our beliefs with each other and with our experience *as those experiences are themselves represented in our belief system . . . .*[16]

And here is where I part company from him in an important way. As I see it, once we shake off various confusions, we will see that there is no serious alternative to a realist conception of truth, whatever our metaphysical position. In *A Realist Conception of Truth* I argued that Putnam's "internal realism" is, or can be easily made to be, quite compatible with a realist conception of truth rather than with the epistemic conception adumbrated in the passage just quoted.

Before proceeding further I should make it explicit that in later writings Putnam backed off from the explication of truth in terms of ideal epistemic status affirmed in the passage above. Here is an explicit statement of this.

> In *Reason, Truth, and History* I explained the idea thus: "truth is idealized rational acceptability". This formulation was taken by many as meaning that "rational acceptability" (and the notion of "better and worse epistemic situation", which I also employed) is supposed (by me) to be more basic than "truth"; that I was offering a reduction of truth to epistemic notions. Nothing was farther from my intention. The suggestion is simply that truth and rational acceptability are interdependent notions. Unfortunately in *Reason, Truth, and History* I gave examples of only one side of the interdependence: examples of the way truth depends on rational acceptability. But it seems clear to me that the dependence goes both ways: whether an epistemic situation is any good or not typically depends on whether many different statements are true.[17]

That, of course, changes the ball game significantly, though it still remains true that a truth-value bearer cannot be true without being ideally rationally acceptable. But for present purposes I will ignore this change in later Putnam and stick to the *Reason, Truth, and History* formulation as my target.

To return to my present concern, it is not to criticize epistemic accounts of truth, though that is done at some length in Chapter 7 of *A Realist Conception of Truth*, but to point out that Putnam's I_1, the "conceptual relativity" that is the heart of his "internal realism", does not require an epistemic account of truth but is quite compatible with a realist account.

Putnam more than once asserts that conceptual relativity leads to an epistemic conception of truth. In *Representation and Reality*, after expounding conceptual relativity, he continues:

---

[16] Putnam, *Reason, Truth, and History*, 49–50.
[17] Hilary Putnam, *Representation and Reality* (Cambridge: MIT Press, 1989), 115.

> The suggestion I am making, in short, is that *a statement is true of a situation just in case it would be correct to use the words of which the statement consists in that way in describing the situation.* . . . [We] can explain what "correct to use the words of which the statement consists in that way" means by saying that it means nothing more nor less than that a sufficiently well placed speaker who used the words in that way would be fully warranted in *counting* the statement as true of that situation.[18]

In other words, in setting out conceptual relativity, what Putnam was "suggesting" was an epistemic conception of truth.

But it is difficult to determine what Putnam's reasons are for supposing there to be this tight connection. The closest thing to an argument I have found occurs in Chapter 3 of *Reason, Truth, and History*, in which he is discussing Kant. There he suggests that Kant's view that the constitution of the physical world is dependent on our conceptually structuring our cognitions in a certain way commits him to an epistemic conception of truth, though Kant himself did not realize this.

> On Kant's view, any judgment about external or internal objects (physical things or mental entities) says that the noumenal world as a whole is such that this is the description that a rational being (one with our rational nature) given the information available to a being with our sense organs (a being with our sensible nature) would construct. . . . What then is a true judgment? . . . the only answer that one can extract from Kant's writing is this: a piece of knowledge (i.e., a 'true statement' [sic]) is a statement that a rational being would accept on sufficient experience of the kind that it is actually possible for beings with our nature to have. 'Truth' in any other sense is inaccessible to us and inconceivable by us. *Truth is ultimate goodness of fit.* (63–64)

Here Putnam is saying, in a backhanded way, that once we recognize that any reality we can cognize is partly what it is by virtue of our conceptual activity, there is nothing left for truth to be except idealized rational acceptability. Since he has given up the supposition that we can be in effective cognitive touch with a world that is what it is independently of our conceptual-cognitive doings, and so has given up the notion of correspondence to such an independent reality, there is nothing left but an epistemic conception of truth.

But this is just to assert the connection, not to argue for it. And I do not think it difficult to show that as I suggested above, Putnam's conceptual relativity is compatible with a realist conception of truth. The crucial point is this. According to I1, conceptual relativity, what objects there are is a question that can be answered only "in", relative to, a certain "conceptual scheme", a certain way of conceptually articulating the world. That does imply that relativity to a

[18] Ibid.

conceptual scheme does somehow affect whether what we say is true or not. But that influence need not come via the notion of truth, whether by construing it epistemically or otherwise. Indeed, if, as Putnam undoubtedly thinks, the conceptual scheme within which a proposition is formulated intimately affects the *content* of the proposition, that already gives us all the relativity anyone could wish for. Go back to his favorite mereological example of conceptual relativity. On one conceptual-theoretical perspective, M, any set of objects is itself an object, whereas on another, P, that is not the case. So how many objects are there in my study? Relative to P, there are, let's say, 1,473, taking only what would ordinarily be regarded as distinct physical objects as objects in the room. But according to M, there will be indefinitely many. So to avoid contradiction we must build into each proposition about the number of objects in my study an "index" specifying the conceptual scheme relative to which the counting is made. Once we have done this, we can say that each such proposition is true *iff* what one who asserts the proposition thereby takes to be the case *is* the case. And that is to employ a realist conception of truth, which may take a full-blown correspondence form. Sometimes Putnam says things that implicitly commit him to this, though he never makes it explicit. Here is a nice example.

> How we go about answering the question, 'How many objects are there?'—the method of 'counting', or the notion of what constitutes an 'object'—depends on our choice . . . but the *answer* does not thereby become a matter of convention. If I choose Carnap's language, I must say there are three objects because *that is how many there are.* If I choose the Polish logician's language, I must say there are seven objects, *because that is how many objects* (in the Polish logician's sense of 'object') *there are.* There are 'external facts', and we can *say what they are.* What we *cannot* say—because it makes no sense—is what the facts are *independent of all conceptual choices.*[19]

Relative to Carnap's "language" it is true that there are three objects because that is how many *there are*, relative to that language. Whereas relative to the Polish logician's language it is true that there are seven objects, since that is how many *there are*, relative to that language. What is true depends on *what is the case*, relative to the conceptual scheme (language) in question.

Hence we can't suppose that it is *distinctive* of metaphysical realism that it is compatible with, and even naturally associated with, a correspondence or other realist conception of truth. Because of that natural association, however, I cannot claim that M3 is associated with my realism in the wholly gratuitous way that M2 is. But the fact remains that realism *as a metaphysical thesis* does not entail any particular view on the nature of truth, and hence that M3 is not *necessarily* tied to M1.

---

[19] Hilary Putnam, *The Many Faces of Realism* (La Salle, Ill.: Open Court, 1987), 32–33.

V

There are some further liabilities that Putnam associates with metaphysical realism, though not as closely as the ones I have been discussing. He does not claim that they are part of the content of the position, but he thinks that they constitute the only form in which the position could be reasonably held today. I will discuss three such views that Putnam thinks have this status. The first two involve views in the philosophy of language.

> First, there is a position on linguistic meaning. One problem with the traditional view [of realism] is its naiveté about meaning. One tends to think that the meaning of a word is a property shared by all the things denoted by the word.[20]

Why on earth should anyone think that a realist is committed to this? No doubt, various realists have held this view, but many others have not. And in any event, I cannot imagine any reason for supposing that the view follows from realism. The existence of *an sich* reality is, I should think, obviously compatible with any view of the meaning of words, at least any that is not internally inconsistent. A refutation of this theory of meaning does not touch realism.

Next there is the causal theory of reference.

> The problem is this: there are these objects out there. Here is the mind/brain, carrying on its thinking/computing. How do the thinker's symbols (or those of the mind/brain) get into a unique correspondence with objects and sets of objects out there?[21]

Here Putnam is assuming, reasonably enough, that if our beliefs and statements are to depend for their truth value on their relations to independently existing objects and facts, they will have to contain concepts and terms that enable us to *refer* to certain objects rather than others and believe (state) certain things about them rather than others. And how is this possible, given the *an sich* reality of those objects and facts? Putnam continues as follows.

> The reply popular among externalists [realists] today is that while indeed no sign *necessarily* corresponds to one set of things rather than another, *contextual* connections between signs and external things (in particular, causal connections) will enable one to explicate the nature of reference. But this doesn't work. For example, the dominant cause of my beliefs about electrons is probably various *textbooks*. But the occurrences of the word 'electron' I pro-

---

[20] Hilary Putnam, "Sense, Nonsense, and the Senses: An Inquiry into the Powers of the Human Mind", *Journal of Philosophy* XCI, 9 (1994): 449.

[21] Putnam, *Reason, Truth, and History*, 51.

duce, though having in this sense a strong connection to textbooks, do not *refer* to textbooks.

The externalist will now reply that the word 'electron' is not connected to textbooks by a causal chain of *the appropriate type*. (But how can we have intentions which determine which causal chains are 'of the appropriate type' unless we are *already* able to *refer*?)[22]

Putnam then suggests that the only alternative account of reference that is available to the realist is one in terms of "occult rays" that connect thoughts and terms to their referents! He also alleges that the internal realist does not fall into these difficulties. For on that view " 'objects' do not exist independently of conceptual schemes. . . . Since the objects *and* the signs are alike *internal* to the scheme of description, it is possible to say what matches what."[23]

I cannot see that Putnam has succeeded in getting the internal realist off the hook by this maneuver, if hook there be. Even if the objects are "internal" to the scheme of description, we are still left with the question what connects a particular thought or term to a particular internal object rather than to others within that scheme. But that is not my present concern, which is with the supposition that the "external" realist must adopt a patently inadequate causal theory of reference or give up his realism. I agree with Putnam that the kind of causal theory of reference he has in mind is obviously inept. Indeed, so far as I am aware, no one has developed a truly illuminating account of (mental or linguistic) reference that avoids fatal difficulties, and this includes Putnam's pass at an account tailored to the "internal realist". Given that we are all in the same boat in this respect, I see no alternative to our just soldiering on with the best intuitive conception of reference we can muster and making the best of it. To reject a particular position on the realism issue on the grounds that any account of reference available to it is less than fully adequate is to be guilty of arbitrary partiality. Let him whose theory of reference is without defect cast the first stone.

The third alleged fellow traveler of realism that Putnam identifies and attacks is *physicalism*. More or less the same position is also sometimes termed "scientific realism" or, as we might say, "scientism", the view that reality is exhausted by what science can tell us. These ways of identifying the position are taken to be equivalent just because the thinkers in question take science to deal exclusively with the physical. They suppose all the results of science to be ultimately reducible to physics.

Putnam's tendency to think of metaphysical realism in these terms comes out in many ways in his writings. For example, at the beginning of *The Many Faces of Realism* he pictures realism as committed to Wilfrid Sellars's distinction between the "manifest image" of the world, the world as it appears to common

---

[22] Ibid.
[23] Ibid., 52.

sense, and the "scientific image", and committed to the position that the former is simply false, all truth residing in the second.

> Realism reminds me of the Seducer in the old-fashioned melodrama . . . the Seducer always promised various things to the Innocent Maiden which he failed to deliver when the time came. In this case the Realist (the evil Seducer) promises common sense that he will rescue her from her enemies (Idealists, Kantians and Neo-Kantians, Pragmatists) who (the Realist says) want to deprive her of her good old ice cubes and chairs. . . . But when they have traveled together for a little while the 'Scientific Realist' breaks the news that what the maiden is going to get *isn't* her ice cubes and tables and chairs. In fact, all there *really* is—the Scientific Realist tells her over breakfast—is what 'finished science' will say there is—whatever that may be.[24]

Again in *Representation and Reality* the move from "Metaphysical Realism" to "Internal Realism" is motivated by the inability of *physicalism* to account for *intentionality*.

In all this, metaphysical realism is simply assumed to appear in a physicalist, scientistic guise. This is made beautifully explicit in "A Defense of Internal Realism", in the collection *Realism with a Human Face*. After arguing that intentionality, reference, meaning, causality, explanation, knowledge, values, moral standards, and various other important items cannot be accounted for on physicalism, Putnam continues:

> I can imagine a critic who would now say, "Very well, Putnam, I will concede that what is and is not a good interpretation, what is and what is not explanatory, what is and what is not justified, are in the same boat as what is and is not *good*. But I am willing to be a metaphysical realist about goodness too." What would I say to such a critic?
>
> I would be pleased that my critic accepted my "companions in the guilt" argument. . . . There are no serious reasons in support of ethical relativism which should drive a rational man, *moved by those reasons alone*, as opposed to the sway of the Zeitgeist, to be an ethical relativist but not a total relativist. And if a rebirth of a full-bodied, red-blooded metaphysical realism were the way to get people to accept the objectivity of ethics, then I would almost be willing to pay the price of letting that happen. But I don't think the metaphysical realist picture has any content today when it is divorced from physicalism.[25]

I must say that I am staggered by this. More specifically, I am staggered by Putnam's thinking that a physicalist realism is the only game in town, while at the same time arguing that physicalism is fatally defective by reason of not taking account of various features of the world that we must recognize. I can

---

[24] Putnam, *Many Faces of Realism*, 3–4.
[25] Putnam, *Realism with a Human Face*, 37.

understand a card-carrying physicalist thinking that no other form of realism is worth taking seriously, though I don't find myself at all tempted to share that position. What I can't understand is someone's saying both "Physicalism is defunct" and "If you are going to be a realist, physicalism is the only way to go". Of course, Putnam has more fundamental criticisms of metaphysical realism than its allegedly being tied to an untenable physicalism, but that is another story.[26] Here I am concerned with his supposition that no form of metaphysical realism other than physicalism is worth taking seriously. Just what is the argument for this conclusion? I don't find Putnam explicitly proffering any such argument. One is tempted to suppose that he is simply under the influence of the Zeitgeist in a way he badmouths in another connection in the passage just quoted. It is true that physicalism is prominent among contemporary realists, and perhaps all the realists with whom Putnam has been sparring are of that persuasion. But to go from that to the supposition that no other possibilities need to be considered is to exhibit a serious deficiency of philosophical imagination that is not at all typical of Putnam. More substantively, let's ask what could possibly be out of order in supposing that various facts that cannot be accounted for in physicalist terms have *an sich* reality. There may be specific reasons for ruling this out for one or another nonphysicalist subject matter, but those would have to be presented and evaluated. A blanket dismissal of any nonphysicalist metaphysical realism simply does not cut any ice.

I want to make a parting shot here, one that involves a comparison between a metaphysical realist's and an internal realist's way of recognizing values, moral standards, intentionality, meaning, causality, and so forth. The internal realist now appears in the role of Seducer, promising the Innocent Maiden to rescue her from those wicked physicalists who seek to banish ethics, values, intentionality, and so forth from the world. Again, the Deceiver unmasks himself at breakfast, revealing to the maiden that though she can have her beloved values, moral standards, thought, reference, and meaning, what she can have is always relative to a particular conceptual scheme, one that has equally viable alternatives. Wouldn't the Innocent Maiden feel that she had been had?

VI

My aim in this chapter has been a very modest one. I have sought to identify an important form of realism, one that is at the storm center of much contemporary discussion and the target of frequent attacks by "postmodernists" of a variety of stripes. And I have pointed out ways in which the controversies over this are frequently led astray by false suppositions as to what is necessarily involved

---

[26] For reasons to take the most prominent of these criticisms not to do the job, see Alston, *Realist Conception*, chap. 5.

in this realist position. By pointing out difficulties in one or another of these alleged components of realism, opponents suppose themselves to have disposed of realism itself, when in fact they have completely failed to touch it. My aims are modest in that I have not attempted to make a positive case for metaphysical realism, nor have I sought to refute any of its antirealist competitors. Nevertheless, I believe that by getting clear as to what is and is not necessarily involved in this kind of realism, we will be much better equipped to discuss its merits and demerits without straying into deceptive and unprofitable byways.

PART II

Truth and Metaphysical Realism

On the Metaphysical Implications of Alethic Realism

RENÉ VAN WOUDENBERG

With respect to the issue of the metaphysical implications of realist theories of truth, various positions have been taken. On the one extreme there is the position according to which realist theories of truth require metaphysical realism. Richard Kirkham, for instance, defines a realist theory of truth as a theory "that says that any given proposition is true only if the very same state of affairs that the proposition says to obtain, obtains either independently of any mind or with only derivative dependence".[1] Suppose we call states of affairs that obtain 'facts'. Kirkham's definition tells us that a realist theory of truth requires that if a proposition p is true, it has to be a fact that p. It tells us furthermore that the fact at hand needs to be either independent of any mind or (at best) derivatively dependent on minds. A fact is mind-independent, according to Kirkham, if "neither its existence nor its nature depends on the existence of any mind, nor on the conceptual scheme of any mind, nor on the epistemic capacities, limitations, or achievements of any mind".[2] It is very hard to state exactly when a fact is derivatively dependent on a mind (in contrast with full-blooded dependency). But as a clue Kirkham offers the following example: the fact that a Ford Mustang is now parked on my street is derivatively dependent on a mind (or minds), since had there been no people who designed and made it (which includes mental activity), there would have been no Ford Mustang.[3] But once the car is de-

---

For comments on earlier drafts of this chapter I am especially indebted to William Alston, Terence Cuneo, Mark McLeod, Caleb Miller, and Michael Murray.

[1] Richard Kirkham, *Theories of Truth: A Critical Introduction* (Cambridge: MIT Press, 1992), 78. I have substituted 'proposition' in this definition for 'belief (statement, or whatever)'.

[2] Ibid., 73. The class of minds includes the mind of God, if such there be.

[3] Ibid., 76. Kirkham offers some other examples as well. It can be a fact of the sort required by the definition of a realist theory of truth that John has a mind. But if this is the case, that fact has to be not full-blooded dependent on a mind but at best derivatively dependent. And the fact that John has a mind is in this position, if I understand Kirkham correctly, because

signed and made, it lives, so to speak, a life of its own and is therefore not full-blown dependent on minds.

On the other extreme there is the position according to which realist theories of truth have virtually no metaphysical implications whatsoever. William Alston, for instance, holds that "the question of how truth should be construed is *not* an issue over the existence, or metaphysical status, of one or another type of entity. Alethic realism is a view about what truth is, whereas metaphysical positions . . . have to do with what *kinds of propositions* are true. And just as we must not confuse the question of what virtue *is* with the question what virtues there are . . . so we must not confuse the question of what truth *is* with the question what truths there are".[4] And the converse, he says, also holds: "Though a particular realist or antirealist metaphysical position . . . has implications for what propositions are true or false, they have no implications for what it is for a proposition to be true or false".[5]

So on the one extreme there is the position according to which realist theories of truth require some pretty robust form of metaphysical realism, and on the other extreme the position according to which such theories have no metaphysical implications and are compatible with various forms of metaphysical realism and metaphysical antirealism alike.

The burden of this chapter is to argue that we had better avoid both extremes and plump for a middle-of-the-road position, that is, a position according to which alethic realism is incompatible with at least some forms of metaphysical antirealism and requires some form of metaphysical realism (thus avoiding Alston's extreme), but not by definition (thus avoiding Kirkham's extreme). This chapter is organized as follows. In the next section I will spell out Alston's realist theory of truth and draw attention to some of its features that seem to me to depart from the officially claimed metaphysical neutrality of the theory. In the second section I will argue that there are at least two types of metaphysical antirealism that are incompatible with alethic realism. The concluding section aims to show that, contrary to what Alston argues, Putnam is right in holding that rejection of metaphysical realism goes hand in hand with a rejection of the realist conception of truth, and that acceptance of alethic realism goes hand in hand with some form of metaphysical realism.

I. ALSTON'S OFFICIAL CLAIM AND HOW IT GETS COMPROMISED (IF ONLY A LITTLE BIT)

Alston's theory of truth, named "alethic realism", is comprised of two theses: 1. The realist conception of truth is the right way to think of truth in the sense of

---

John would have a mind even if no one, not even John, believes or is warranted in asserting that John has a mind (ibid., 77).

[4] William P. Alston, *A Realist Conception of Truth* (Ithaca: Cornell University Press, 1996), 80.

[5] Ibid., 78.

'true' in which it applies in ordinary life as well as in science, to beliefs, state-ments, and propositions. 2. Truth is important (it is not a trivial notion). The realist conception of truth can be formulated in various ways. One of them is this: a proposition is true if and only if what that proposition says to be the case actually is the case.[6] Another is this: the proposition that p is true iff it is made true by the fact that p, or more minimally: the proposition that p is true iff it is a fact that p.[7] So the proposition that lemons are sour is true iff it is made true by the fact that lemons are sour (or only if it is a fact that lemons are sour). That is all. Nothing more is needed. In particular, it isn't needed that someone is jus-tified in believing that lemons are sour, or that it has been corroborated or ver-ified, or that it is rationally acceptable that they are.

Alethic realism can thus be opposed in two ways. It can be opposed by hold-ing an epistemic theory of truth, that is, a theory that identifies truth with some favorable epistemic status of the proposition, such as 'justified', 'verified', 'ra-tionally acceptable', and the like. But it can also be opposed by holding that truth is unimportant.

As I noted earlier, Alston's official claim is that alethic realism has nearly no metaphysical implications. Says Alston, "Alethic realism is neutral with respect to virtually all the controversies over the metaphysical status of this or that do-main that go under the name of 'realism vs. antirealism'".[8] More specifically, his claim is this. According to the realist conception of truth, the proposition that p is true iff it is a fact that p. The realist conception is therefore committed to the existence of facts—which is, it would seem, a weighty metaphysical com-mitment. But Alston thinks otherwise. Surely, he says, for there to be truths in the realist sense, there have to be facts;[9] but the realist conception as such carries no commitment as to the metaphysical status of facts. The proposition that that tree has no leaves is true iff it is a fact that that tree has no leaves. But whether the fact consisting in that tree's having no leaves is a congery of ideas (as Berke-ley would have it) or is in part constituted by our conceptual framework (as Kant and Putnam would hold) or is a mind-independent and mind-external state of affairs (as Reid would say) is an issue that is irrelevant for the realist conception of truth. What is relevant is that there *are* facts (truth makers); what is irrelevant is their ontological nature, their metaphysical status.

I now want to draw attention to two lines of thought in Alston's book that seem to me to compromise the official claim to metaphysical neutrality. First, in

---

[6] The realist conception can also be formulated in terms of beliefs or statements.

[7] These and other formulations can be found in Alston, *Realist Conception*, 22–26.

[8] Ibid., 84.

[9] I should indicate that Alston's most minimalist formulation of the realist conception of truth (namely, the proposition that p is true iff p) doesn't contain the word 'fact'. But Alston himself notes that even on this formulation, the realist conception of truth naturally leads into the idea that a true proposition is made true by a fact (*Realist Conception*, 32). I therefore feel justified in focusing on those formulations that explicitly have the word 'fact' on the right-hand side of the biconditional.

the epilogue of his book Alston asks for the fundamental root of the widespread opposition against alethic realism. The root of it, he maintains (remarkably enough), is "intolerance of vulnerability": "This vulnerability to the outside world, this 'subjection' to stubborn, unyielding facts beyond our thought, experience, and discourse, seems powerfully repugnant, even intolerable to many".[10] So opposition to the realist conception of truth is diagnosed as stemming from a rejection of a particular view of the nature of *facts*, namely, the view that they are 'beyond our thought, experience, and discourse'. And this, it seems to me, is a metaphysical realist characterization of facts. But if Alston's diagnosis is to be appropriate, the underlying idea must be that alethic realism is, after all, committed to metaphysical realism concerning facts, which compromises the official claim.

Second, if Alston's alethic realism is to be metaphysically neutral, it should be compatible with all sorts of metaphysical views concerning the nature of facts. But it isn't. For Alston rejects the claim, made by Peter Strawson, that facts are (in Alston's words) "mere shadows of our practice of making statements—mere pseudo entities that have no standing independent of our linguistic activity".[11] As Strawson sees it, the supposition that the proposition that grass is green is made true by the fact that grass is green is not so much false as vacuous. For facts, he holds, depend on language as much as statements do. Facts and true statements aren't two independent entities. Rather, says Strawson, "facts are what statements (when true) state; they are not what statements are about".[12] Now Alston argues against Strawson on the assumption that alethic realism would be "vacuous, completely trivial and unilluminating", if facts are what Strawson says they are. Here, I contend, in this very assumption, we encounter another point at which the official claim that alethic realism is metaphysically neutral gets compromised, if only a very little bit. For at least one view about facts is incompatible with the realist conception of truth, namely, the view that facts are "mere shadows of our practice of making statements"—entities that depend completely on our linguistic activities.

Alston criticizes Strawson's position on the grounds that it rests on the false claim that there is an intimate conceptual dependence of fact talk on statement talk (i.e., the claim that we could not have the concept of a fact unless we had the concept of a statement, or assertion, or linguistic activity). That claim, Alston argues, is false. For it seems possible that there should be a community with the ability to use "fact that _____" locutions but without the ability to talk about its own speech acts. And I think that there are even better arguments

[10] Alston, *Realist Conception*, 264.

[11] Ibid., 39.

[12] P. F. Strawson, "Truth" [1950], in *Truth*, ed. Georg Pitcher (Englewood Cliffs, N.J.: Prentice-Hall, 1964), 38. A little later Strawson says, "What could fit more perfectly the fact that it is raining than the statement that it is raining? Of course, statements and facts fit. They were made for each other. If you prise statements off the world you prise the facts off it too; but the world would be none the poorer" (38–39).

against the thesis that fact talk is conceptually dependent on statement talk, or that facts just are true statements. (1) Facts function causally in a way that statements don't. The fact that I lit the candle caused, let us say, the explosion. But it is nonsense to say that the statement that I lit the candle caused the explosion. (2) One of the constituents of the fact that I lit a candle, is the candle. But it is nonsense to say that the candle is a part of the statement "I lit the candle".

Let me round off this section by noting what I feel is a certain unclarity in Alston's rejection of Strawson. On the one hand Alston seems to reject Strawson's position *because* it is incompatible with the realist conception of truth. But on the other hand he seems to reject Strawson's position on grounds that are independent of the realist conception of truth.[13] It is my impression that the first line of thought is the driving one. If I am right about this, however, the realist conception of truth does have metaphysical bite: facts, the makers of truth, are not linguistic items.

II. ALETHIC REALISM IS INCOMPATIBLE WITH AT LEAST TWO TYPES OF ANTIREALISM

I now should like to argue that the realist conception has even more metaphysical bite than this, in that it is incompatible with at least two types of metaphysical antirealism. In order to be able to bring out these types, I must bring to mind again that one can be a metaphysical antirealist in various ways. The most obvious way is by flatly denying that items of a certain sort exist. So one can be a metaphysical antirealist about, for instance, physical objects, mental states, facts, propositions, properties, God, and so forth by flatly denying these things exist. But this is by no means the only way. One can also be an antirealist about these things not by denying that they exist but by denying that they are what we commonly think they are. One can be an antirealist in this way by, as they say, 'reducing', for example, physical objects to patterns of actual and possible sense data, or mental states to brain states. But this still does not exhaust the field. In addition to the 'flat denial' and 'reductive' ways in which one can be a metaphysical antirealist, there is yet a third way.[14] The 'flat denial' and 'reductive' forms are sometimes called 'departmental' forms of antirealism because one can be an antirealist (in one of these two ways) about, say, propositions without being an antirealist about physical objects. The third way of being an antirealist is usually called 'global'. One can be an antirealist in this way by denying that there is a way the world is independent of our representations of it. I use the word 'representation' such that sentences, thoughts, perceptions, beliefs, and so forth all count as representations. The antirealist of this type holds

---

[13] Ibid., 39; see also 52.

[14] This third type has also been classified as a subtype of reductive antirealism (see Alston, *Realist Conception*, 73). In the following way: it involves the general reduction of items that are commonly held to be nonmental to the mental. To me, however, it seems more natural to place the type I am about to introduce in a category of its own. The key word is not so much 'reduction' as 'constitution'.

that the way the world is depends, at least in part, on the conceptual schemes we employ for representing the world. Or to put it in a slightly different way, the world is constitutively dependent upon our representations.

As indicated a number of times now, Alston's official view is that the realist conception of truth is compatible with all these forms of metaphysical antirealism (as well as with the complementary forms of metaphysical realism). But I now want to bring out two version of metaphysical antirealism that are incompatible with the realist conception of truth.

FIRST. The realist conception of truth is committed to the idea that truth is a property that can be attributed to propositions, statements, beliefs, and so forth and hence to the existence of properties. Says Alston: "My minimalism . . . is firmly committed to there being a property of truth, and to apparent attributions of truth values being just what they seem".[15] This commitment constitutes a rejection of deflationary accounts of truth, such as F. P. Ramsey's 'redundancy theory'. But now consider the following. In *Reason, Truth, and History* Putnam discusses the view that all properties are secondary—a view that he ascribes to Kant.[16] If this view is right, it follows that truth too is a secondary property. I now want to argue that this view of truth is incompatible with the realist conception of truth.

We have to note first, however, that Putnam gives different meanings to the words "all properties are secondary".[17] (i) One meaning is that all properties are mind-dependent, in the sense that they depend on our minds for being instantiated. The question now before us is whether the view that truth is a mind-dependent property is compatible with alethic realism. I believe the answer is no. For if the truth property is mind-dependent, there have to be minds if there are to be true propositions. But the realist conception tells us that the only condition that has to be satisfied for the proposition p to be true is that it is a fact that p. There is no condition to the effect that there have to be minds if the property of being true is to be instantiated. (ii) Another meaning of Putnam's words "all properties are secondary" is that all properties are relational, where we, human beings, are one of the relata.[18] Generally speaking, there seems little or no reason to accept this thesis. There are evidently many properties that are not relational. Being prime is a property of the number '3', but it surely isn't a relational property. But maybe things are different with respect to the property of being true. What would it be for the truth property to be relational? It would be this: the proposition that p cannot have the property of being true unless it

---

[15] Alston, *Realist Conception*, 41.

[16] Hilary Putnam, *Reason, Truth, and History* (Cambridge: Cambridge University Press, 1981), 60–64.

[17] For a discussion of this point, see James Van Cleve, "Putnam, Kant, and Secondary Qualities", *Philosophical Papers* 24 (1995): 83–87.

[18] In the following passage Putnam stresses the relational nature of secondary properties: "Saying that something is red, or warm, or furry, is saying that it is so-and-so *in relation to us*" (*Reason, Truth, and History*, 59).

stands in some relation to us. What relation? Maybe this: being believed by us, accepted by us, asserted by us, and so on. Again, I think we can see that this way of thinking about the truth property is incompatible with alethic realism. For alethic realism doesn't require for p's being true that it stands in some relation or other (such as being believed by, etc.) to us. It doesn't even require that there are such beings as ourselves. The idea that truth is a relational property (in the way I have suggested) is in fact the idea that truth is an epistemic notion, which is the main alternative to the realist conception. (iii) The third meaning of Putnam's phrase "all properties are secondary" is that all properties are powers or dispositions to elicit certain responses in us. When it is said that truth is a secondary property, what is said is not so much that truth has the power to elicit certain responses in us (such as believing or accepting) but rather that the truth property *is* or *is identical with* the disposition to elicit certain responses, such as belief responses or acceptance responses. This way of thinking about the property of being true, it seems to me, boils down again to an epistemic conception of truth. After all, proposition p's being true consists in the disposition to elicit belief or acceptance responses in us. But the property that is picked out by the realist conception of truth is of a very different nature. For according to that conception, the proposition that p is true iff it is a fact that p. Alston explicitly intended this conception to stay clear from epistemic conceptions of truth, according to which p's truth requires something else than its being a fact that p, for example, p's being believed, or being rationally acceptable. If one accepts the realist conception, one cannot also affirm the thesis that truth is a disposition to elicit certain belief responses in us. My conclusion, therefore, is that the realist conception of truth is incompatible with the idea that truth is a dispositional property.

What I have argued in this section, then, is this. The realist conception of truth is incompatible with the view that the truth property is a secondary property (spelled out as being mind-dependent, relational, or dispositional). Alethic realism, then, requires not only that there is such a property as *being true* but also that that property is conceived of as being mind-independent as well as nonrelational (in the indicated sense)[19] and nondispositional. And these, I claim, are weighty metaphysical commitments of alethic realism.

SECOND. Putnam holds that "'objects' do not exist independently of conceptual schemes".[20] And likewise he holds that the properties objects have exist relative to conceptual schemes.[21] This last idea can be cashed out in various ways. (i) One could think that any and all properties there are, for example, *being furry* or *being taller than 180 meters*, are scheme-relative. These properties exist relative to one scheme but don't exist relative to another. If we assume that

---

[19] This qualifier is needed, for the realist conception does involve the idea that truth is some sort of relational property—it is a relation between a truth bearer and a truth maker.

[20] *Reason, Truth, and History*, 52.

[21] See Alston, *Realist Conception*, 164–68.

truth is a property, this would mean that there are schemes relative to which the property of being true exists but also that there are schemes relative to which it does not. But then these last schemes—schemes relative to which the property of being true does not exist—are incompatible with the realist conception of truth. For the realist conception of truth requires the existence of the property of being true. (ii) Another way to cash out the suggestion that properties exist relative to conceptual schemes is this. It isn't so much that one property or another exists relative to a scheme but that properties as such exist relative to conceptual schemes. The idea would then be that there are schemes relative to which properties exist and others relative to which no properties exist. And since truth is a property, it would mean that there are schemes relative to which no property of being true exists. The realist conception of truth is therefore incompatible with such schemes, for it involves commitment to the existence of the property of being true.

So again we encounter metaphysical implications of the realist conception of truth. If there is to be realist truth, there have to be schemes relative to which properties exist. The realist conception of truth, then, is incompatible with schemes relative to which no properties exist. And this, I contend, seems a weighty metaphysical implication of that conception.

III. CONCEPTUAL RELATIVITY AND THE CORRESPONDENCE THEORY

In the previous section I have tried to argue that various forms of metaphysical antirealism are incompatible with alethic realism (and hence that alethic realism has more metaphysical bite than Alston says it has). The SECOND argument involved the notion of "existence relative to a scheme". I now want to broaden the discussion considerably and reflect on the question whether the idea of conceptual relativity as such is compatible with the realist conception of truth. Having reflected on this question for quite some time now, I must confess that it still isn't quite clear to me what 'conceptual schemes' are and hence how to individuate them. So I find myself having no firm grasp on the notion of 'existence relative to a conceptual scheme'. To be sure, this makes the argument in both this section and the second part of the previous one a hazardous undertaking. Still, I am not completely wandering in the dark.[22] For one thing about it is relatively clear, namely, that Putnam uses it to deny, or formulate an alternative to, what he calls 'metaphysical realism', which he describes as follows:

> On [the 'metaphysical realist'] perspective, (1) the world consists of some
> fixed totality of mind-independent objects. (2) There is exactly one true and

[22] For an explication and defense of the notion of 'existence relative to a scheme', see Michael Lynch, *Truth in Context: An Essay on Pluralism and Objectivity* (Cambridge: MIT Press, 1998), chaps. 2, 3. Like Alston, Lynch maintains that the realist conception of truth is compatible with what he calls 'metaphysical pluralism' (which is the thesis that facts exist relative to conceptual schemes).

complete description of 'the way the world is'. (3) Truth involves some sort of correspondence relation between words and thought-signs and external things and sets of things.[23]

How are the three theses (let us call them MR1,[24] MR2, and MR3,[25] respectively) that make up metaphysical realism (as portrayed by Putnam) related? Hartry Field has suggested that they are logically independent of one another. Someone who accepts the idea that the world consists of some fixed totality of mind-independent objects isn't by that token committed to the idea that there is only one true description of the way the world is or to a correspondence theory of truth (which is an elaboration of the realist conception of truth).[26] And if this is true, Putnam's denials of these theses too are logically independent of one another. But Putnam does not accept that. The theses that go into metaphysical realism, he claims, "do not have content standing on their own, one by one; each leans on the others and on a variety of further assumptions and notions".[27] The idea, then, is that MR1, MR2, and MR3 form a tightly knit whole, that one can't deny one of them without denying the others as well. And the same, of course, must hold for the theses that constitute Putnam's 'internal realism': they too form a tightly knit whole; none of them can be rejected without the rejection of the others as well.

For the purposes of this chapter I am especially interested in the relationship between MR1 (metaphysical realism, or one type thereof) and MR3 (the realist conception of truth). Putnam and Field differ over that issue. And so do Alston and Searle. Alston holds that alethic realism is compatible with the view that facts exist relative to schemes (which is the denial of MR1).[28] Searle, however, says, "On a normal interpretation, the correspondence theory [or alethic realism] implies realism since it implies that there is a reality to which statements

---

[23] *Reason, Truth, and History*, 49. The parenthetical numbers are my own addition.

[24] This thesis could also be formulated as: the world exists independent of our representations of it.

[25] In the discussion that follows I assume that MR3 is the realist conception of truth.

[26] Hartry Field, "Realism and Relativism", *Journal of Philosophy* 79 (1982): 553 ff. Field himself, for instance, accepts the first thesis of metaphysical realism but rejects the correspondence theory of truth (he embraces a redundancy theory).

[27] Hilary Putnam, "A Defense of Internal Realism", in *Realism with a Human Face* (Cambridge: Harvard University Press, 1990), 33.

[28] Says Alston: "There is a prima facie case for the compatibility of alethic realism even with a view that holds that everything is constitutively dependent on human cognition. For doesn't this view simply amount to a certain view as to the mode of reality of what makes our beliefs and statements true, not as to what truth consists in? Isn't Putnam free to recognize that even though the statement that that tree has no leaves is one that can be true (indeed, can only exist) in a certain 'conceptual scheme', still the statement is true if and only if *that tree does have no leaves* (in that conceptual scheme)? That is not Putnam's position on truth, but why couldn't it be?" (*Realist Conception*, 83).

correspond if they are true".[29] The notion of 'realism' that Searle uses here is the same notion he elsewhere calls 'external realism', which is the thesis that there is a way the world is independent of our representations of it. Is there a way to decide this controversy between Putnam/Searle on the one hand and Field/Alston on the other? I propose first to summarize Putnam's reason for holding that the denial of MR1 (what Searle calls 'external realism') somehow commits one to the denial of MR3 and then to discuss Alston's reasons for holding that Putnam is wrong here.

Here is my reconstruction of Putnam's reason for taking the line he does. Putnam holds that if there isn't a way the world is independent of our representations of it, truth cannot consist in the correspondence between statements and the way the world is independent of our representations of it. He holds that the correspondence theory of truth (or, in Alston's terminology, the realist conception of truth) requires correspondence with objects (or facts) that are what they are independent of our representations of them.[30] But since MR1 is false, that is, since there isn't a way the world is independent of our representations of it, correspondence with (parts of) that world (facts) is impossible. If truth requires such a correspondence, none of our statements will then be true. But Putnam wants to maintain some use for some notion of truth. Hence he has to reject the realist conception of truth. His alternative to it is this: a statement is true not if it corresponds with mind-independent or discourse-independent 'states of affairs' but if it displays ideal coherence with one's beliefs "and with our experiences *as those experiences are themselves represented in our belief system*".[31] A true statement, he holds, is "a statement that a rational being would accept on sufficient experience of the kind that it is actually possible for beings with our nature to have".[32] Putnam, then, operates on the assumption that correspondence truth requires facts to have a certain metaphysical status, namely, mind-independence.

Alston's view, by contrast, is this. Alethic realism requires that there be truth makers, facts. But it does not require that facts be of a certain nature. Facts may be 'constitutively dependent' upon our representations and be good truth makers all the same. So alethic realism is compatible with Putnam's antirealism. Rejection of MR1 need not commit one to the rejection of MR3.

My view of the matter is that what has historically been called the correspondence theory of truth, the heart of which is the realist conception of truth, is, as Searle says, most naturally interpreted as implying (or requiring) mind-independent status for facts. Let me try to clarify this point by considering Alice. Alice has read, or tried to read, Kant. I should make it clear from the outset that I don't claim that Alice's reading of Kant is correct (it is, for one thing,

---

[29] John Searle, *The Construction of Social Reality* (New York: Free Press, 1995), 154.
[30] *Reason, Truth, and History*, 63.
[31] Ibid., 50.
[32] Ibid., 64.

much too subjectivist—she hasn't paid proper attention to the "empirically real" part of Kant's famous conjunction). Alice's thought, nevertheless, is somewhat influenced by various things Kant has written. I introduce Alice only for the reason that she can help clarify why it is counterintuitive to strip realist truth from metaphysical realism. So Alice has read Kant. As a result she has come to think that what we call 'the world' isn't really THE WORLD. 'The world' ('the natural world'), she thinks, displays the features of being spatially, temporally, and causally structured, but THE WORLD does not. 'The world' has these features thanks to our cognitive dealings with THE WORLD; it is, so to say, constitutively dependent on human cognizers. Let us now suppose Alice considers the following propositions:

(1) The kettle started whistling because the water started boiling,
(2) Amsterdam is south of Oslo,
(3) Wordsworth was born well after Chaucer,

and asks herself whether any of these are true, assuming the realist conception of truth is the correct one. Alice's thoughts, I suggest, might take the following turns:

For all the world it would seem that that kettle started whistling because the water started boiling, and likewise it would seem that Amsterdam is south of Oslo and that Wordsworth was born well after Chaucer. This is the way æthe world' seems to me. But THE WORLD isn't such that the kettle started whistling because the water started boiling. Nor is THE WORLD such that Amsterdam is south of Oslo and that Wordsworth was born well after Chaucer. For, as I believe is the case, the causal, spatial, and temporal features or attributes the world displays are due to my own conceptual constitutive activities. The attributes of 'the world' are my own attribu*tions* to THE WORLD. If, on the realist conception, (1), (2), and (3) are to be true, there have to be facts that make them true. After all, according to that conception the proposition that the kettle started whistling because the water started boiling is true if and only if it is a fact that the kettle started whistling because the water started boiling. But I don't believe this is a fact and hence am in no position to say that (1) is true. All I am in a position to claim is that my cognitive dealings with THE WORLD are such that due to those dealings it *seems* to me that the kettle started whistling because the water started boiling. But I cannot claim that what seems to me to be the case due to my cognitive dealings with THE WORLD actually is the case. I cannot claim that what seems to me to be the case are facts, that is, makers of truth. Hence I cannot claim that (1) as well as (2) and (3) are true in the realist sense. The realist conception therefore has no use for me. If I am to use a notion of truth, it will have to be a nonrealist one. It will have to be something like this: proposition p is true, if and only if what that proposition says to be the case, due to my cognitive dealings with THE WORLD, *seems or appears* to be the case. And this conception of truth differs from the realist one in two respects. (i) for p to be true, various things have to *seem or appear* to be the case. (ii) for (1), (2), and (3) to be true in this sense, there has to be *me*, or other persons. And the realist conception requires neither (i) nor (ii).

Alice's line of thought, I suggest, is a perfectly natural one. That is, her interpretation of the correspondence theory is a natural one. And thus it casts more doubt on the idea that the realist conception of truth is without metaphysical implications. What it shows at the very least is that that idea isn't very natural—given those positions that have traditionally been called 'correspondence theories'.

CONCLUSION

I have aimed to show, first, that Alston's official position that the realist conception of truth is metaphysically neutral on some points gets (mildly) compromised, in that he holds (i) that opposition to the realist conception of truth stems from intolerance to the idea that facts, *truth makers*, are mind-dependent, and (ii) that facts need to have a more robust status than being mere shadows of our practice of making statements. Second, I have tried to show that there are at least two versions of metaphysical antirealism that are incompatible with alethic realism. First, those versions according to which truth is a secondary property (which can be explained as 'being mind-dependent', or 'being relational', or 'being dispositional') and, second, those versions that allow for conceptual schemes relative to which properties don't exist. Finally, I have suggested that the most natural interpretation of correspondence theories is that they require mind-independent and conceptual scheme nonrelative status for truth makers.

.8.

Why God Is Not a Semantic Realist

DAVID LEECH ANDERSON

What is the proper interpretation of statements about the external world—that is, statements about trees, planets, tables, and other of the objects that constitute the world we inhabit? On the contemporary philosophical scene, traditional theists are among the most vocal defenders of a *realist* interpretation of such statements. And this for good reason. There seem to be compelling reasons for a theist to think that the truth about the world is to be determined *not* by how things seem from the human perspective (as those who reject realism typically argue) but by how an omniscient mind knows things to be in themselves, in their brute objectivity. According to this view, if there is such a God, then our claims about the world are properly judged (true or false) by how the world is in itself, not by how things seem to us from our finite epistemic perspective.

It is not surprising, then, that traditional theists are, with few exceptions, *global semantic realists* about the interpretation of external world statements, interpreting *all* such statements realistically.[1] Realism of this kind is treated by many as a shibboleth of traditional Christianity, a sine qua non of theological orthodoxy. Yet this love affair between theists and semantic realism is a poor match. I suggest that everyone (theist or no) has compelling evidence drawn from everyday linguistic practice to reject a realist interpretation of most external world statements. But theists have further reason to forswear this view because those who insist on global semantic realism open themselves to the charge of hubris of a theologically inappropriate kind. If the arguments in this chapter

Many people provided help on this chapter: Ann Baker, Larry BonJour, Thom Carlson, Paul Tidman, Hilary Putnam, Mark Timmons, Harry Deutsch, Pat Francken, Kent Machina, Mark Siderits, Liane Stillwell, and William Alston, to name just a few.
[1] Alvin Plantinga is one theist who defends a certain kind of antirealism. He claims that there could be no propositions, and thus no truths or falsehoods, if there were no mind as the creative source of those propositions. The source he has in mind here is God. And though this is indeed a kind of antirealism, once God has populated the universe with all possible propositions, things then can go on (I think) pretty much as the traditional realist would have imagined it. Alvin Plantinga, "How to Be an Anti-Realist," Presidential Address, 80th Annual Western Division Meeting of the American Philosophical Association, Columbus, Ohio, April 29, 1982.

are sound, then neither God nor any of us has reason to apply a realist interpretation to all or even most statements about the external world.

THE REALISM-ANTIREALISM DEBATE

What is the proper interpretation of statements about the external world? Should they be given a *realist* or an *antirealist* interpretation? Consider the statement "There is a walnut tree in the quad." According to the realist, this statement makes a claim about how things are in-and-of-themselves, quite apart from what any human being (or other cognitive agent) says, thinks, or believes about the matter. According to semantic realism, the statement will be true only if there exists a mind-independent walnut tree located in a mind-independent quad. On the alternative antirealist interpretation, these statements are essentially claims about the world-as-experienced, the world-as-knowable by humans. If the most scrupulous human investigation of the "quad" consistently produces coherent evidence of the presence of a 'walnut tree' (i.e., if people with normal faculties see, feel, hear, etc., the "tree") and these experiences continue in the sufficiently long run, then according to semantic antirealism *it is true* that there is a walnut tree in the quad.

It is important, at this juncture, to recognize the distinction between semantic realism and metaphysical realism. *Semantic* realism is a theory about how to interpret a certain set of sentences; it is a theory about the *meaning* of our words. *Metaphysical* realism is a theory about the ultimate nature of reality; it is a theory about our *ontological* commitments. Let's define the theories as follows:

> *Metaphysical Realism* =$_{DEF}$ Mind-independent objects are the immediate cause of human experiences of the external world. Objects in the external world exist in-themselves, independent of the cognitive activity of any agent, and they genuinely possess most of the properties that we attribute to them.
>
> *Global Semantic Realism* =$_{DEF}$ All statements about the external world express claims about mind-independent objects and the properties they possess. All external world statements will be determined as true or false in virtue of how things stand with respect to independently existing objects and irrespective of what any cognitive agent thinks, believes, or experiences.

Obviously, the truth of metaphysical realism does not entail semantic realism, nor does the converse hold. It might turn out that metaphysically real objects exist but that the statements that we utter about the external world do not in fact express a commitment to these objects. Alternatively, it might turn out that although all our statements about the external world assert the existence of mind-independent objects, we are somehow being deceived and none of the objects to which we are committed does in fact exist.

The purpose of this chapter is not to debunk metaphysical realism. Far from it. I am a staunch defender of that theory. Nor am I suggesting that *no* external world statements should receive a realist interpretation. Some such statements clearly require a realist interpretation. The only view I am disputing is *global* semantic realism, the view that *all* external world statements must be interpreted realistically. I shall argue that human language is far more pluralistic than simple, one-note semantic theories like global realism would have us believe. Though I suspect that a thorough semantic theory may multiply semantic types even further, I am presently advancing only a *dualistic* theory, which suggests that two distinct theories govern the interpretation of external world statements:

> *Limited Semantic Realism* $=_{DEF}$ Some statements about the external world express claims with realist truth conditions, claims about mind-independent objects and the properties they possess. These statements will be determined as true or false in virtue of how things stand with respect to mind-independent objects.
>
> *Limited Semantic Antirealism* $=_{DEF}$ Some statements about the external world express claims with antirealist truth conditions, claims about (and only about) empirical conditions that are accessible from the perspective of human beings. These statements will be determined as true or false in virtue of how things stand with respect to the epistemic perspective of human beings.

Although each of these theories is limited in scope, they can be joined to create a theory that governs the entire domain of external world statements. So joined and with a little further elaboration, they form a new theory, semantic dualism:

> *Semantic Dualism* $=_{DEF}$ Statements about the external world uttered in some contexts (e.g., in normal, everyday contexts) express antirealist claims and will be determined as true or false in virtue of how things stand with respect to the epistemic perspective of human beings. Statements about the external world uttered in other contexts (e.g., in contexts where the central purpose of the speech act is to express a commitment to metaphysical realism) will be determined as true or false in virtue of how things stand with respect to mind-independent reality.

The arguments advanced from this point on will support the claim that all speakers have reasons to embrace semantic dualism and that theists have even more reasons than nontheists for holding this position. It will follow from this that neither theists nor anyone else should accept *global semantic realism for external world statements*.

Before moving to the arguments in defense of semantic dualism, I want to clarify certain aspects of the theory. The view combines two distinct semantic theories. The difference between the two can be cashed out in two quite different ways. On one account, the semantic difference is to be found in conflicting analyses of the nature of truth. If this view is correct, then there are two different kinds of truth requiring two distinct truth predicates. Realist statements would be governed by one notion of truth (e.g., the correspondence theory), and antirealist statements would be governed by another notion of truth (e.g., the coherence theory). On this analysis, semantic dualism would consist in the claim that the predicate "true" is systematically ambiguous, expressing one property in some contexts, another property in other contexts. Though there are those who have argued for multiple truth predicates,[2] I believe that there is only one coherent notion of truth. It is a primitive notion that admits of very little in the way of analysis (although it is probably closer to "correspondence" than to any other popular alternative). If this is true, then the semantic differences between realism and antirealism must reside somewhere other than in the truth predicate itself.

Assuming that "truth" is a univocal notion, the difference between semantic realism and semantic antirealism will simply reflect a difference in the type of truth *conditions* (mind-independent vs. mind-dependent) expressed by a particular class of statements. On this view, to say that an external world statement, p, has mind-*independent* truth conditions is just to say that the truth value of p is wholly insensitive to the activity of any actual (or possible) cognitive agent.[3] Thus, in surveying a world, W, to determine if p (realistically interpreted) is true in that world, no account need be taken of the cognitive states, capacities, or activities of any knower(s) in W or in any other possible world because the conditions asserted to obtain by the external world statement are wholly independent of any mind.[4] Likewise, the mind-*dependence* that is the central feature of antirealism is also located in the *conditions* that make a statement true. To claim that p has mind-*dependent* truth conditions is to say that the truth value of p is sensitive to the cognitive states, activities, or general epistemic perspective of some actual (or possible) cognitive agent. Thus, it is impossible to determine the truth value of p in W (antirealistically interpreted) without reference to the epistemic perspective of the relevant cognitive agents—which in our case are human beings. By "epistemic perspective" here, I mean both what the agents do in actual fact experience, think, and believe as well as what they would experience, think, and believe under certain epistemically relevant circumstances.

One final caveat. The account of semantic antirealism just offered should not be conflated with *phenomenalism*, the justifiably discredited semantic theory

---

[2] Terry Horgan has defended a view that treats the truth predicate itself as multiply ambiguous, resulting in a version of semantic pluralism. See "Metaphysical Realism and Psychologistic Semantics," *Erkenntnis* 36 (1991): 297–322.

[3] This account of "mind-independent truth conditions" can be stated in such simple terms because the theory is intended to apply only to statements about the external world. A more complicated account is required for an analysis of "mind-independent truth conditions" as applied to statements about an individual's mental states.

[4] This characterization purposely qualifies human artifacts as "mind-independent" in the relevant sense. The existence of this table is *causally* dependent upon the mind that conceived and built it. But to determine the truth value of a realist utterance of the statement 'the book is on the table' (uttered at time t in world W), we need to survey only the nonmental objects that exist in W. Every mind that exists in W can simply be ignored, including the mind of the carpenter who built the table.

advanced in the first half of the twentieth century. Semantic dualism escapes the famous criticisms that ultimately doomed phenomenalism because semantic dualism does not include phenomenalism's two most dubious claims. First, semantic dualism does not attempt to reduce the whole of language to talk of epistemic conditions (since realist talk of objects is available, if necessary, to explain how speakers can cash out talk of epistemic conditions). Second, it does not pretend to offer an exhaustive account of the specific conditions that make any particular statement true; it asserts only that the conditions to which the statements are truth-functionally sensitive must be conditions of a certain broad *type* (the "epistemic" type). This avoids the need for an implausible commitment to speakers' ability to grasp the meaning of statements that consist of infinite disjunctions of "phenomenalistic" truth conditions.

TRADITIONAL THEISM AND SEMANTIC REALISM

What reasons do theists have for rejecting semantic antirealism in favor of an unqualified semantic realism? One possible reason is the rather obvious difficulty that arises when one attempts to render an antirealist interpretation of the doctrine of theism. To be a traditional theist is, let us say, to believe at least the following:

(T) There exists a divine moral agent who is unlimited in knowledge, power, and goodness and who created the universe.

It is hard to know what (T) would mean, interpreted antirealistically. How are we to understand the claim that there exists a being of unlimited knowledge and power given that we must understand it as a claim about conditions that obtain only from the perspective of beings woefully limited in knowledge and power? What could the antirealist truth conditions for such a statement conceivably be?[5] At best the statement will be reduced to a claim that no longer entails the truth of traditional theism and at worst it will be incoherent. Thus, it seems that a necessary condition for the very possibility of being a traditional theist is being able to grasp (T), *realistically* interpreted, and then to be able to believe that (T), so interpreted, is true.

If this is correct, and I believe it is, then to be a traditional theist, one must reject any semantic theory that has a universal prohibition against a realist interpretation of any statement whatsoever. Yet many people are convinced that

---

[5] It might be suggested that theologians like Gordon Kaufman actually defend a kind of "antirealist theism" and that they are in the business of providing idealist truth conditions for traditional theistic doctrines. This I think would be a confusion. Kaufman is not simply advancing a semantic idealist interpretation of (T). For Kaufman, "God" functions as a regulative idea and not as the name for an entity in the universe (idealistically construed or otherwise). He holds what I consider to be a coherent worldview that is a challenge to traditional theism, but that view can hardly be captured by attempting (per impossibile) an "antirealist" interpretation of the Apostles' Creed.

the only good arguments for antirealism are principled arguments, like those from Michael Dummett[6] and Hilary Putnam,[7] that claim that humans do indeed lack the capacity to grasp realist truth conditions. This leads people to think that the only real options are the two dominant *monistic* theories: *global semantic realism* or *global semantic antirealism.* Theists rightly judge that global antirealism cannot be reconciled with theism, and so global realism seems to be the only game in town.

It is also popular to believe that arguments in defense of semantic antirealism are fundamentally arguments against a correspondence theory of truth and in favor of an epistemic theory of truth. Theists have rightly judged that an "epistemic" theory of truth will again threaten the very intelligibility of theism, and so they seem justified in rejecting all forms of antirealism. As a matter of fact, though, semantic antirealism does not commit one to a coherence theory of truth but is perfectly consistent with the correspondence theory, as William Alston has judiciously shown.[8]

Given this tendency to accord antirealism universal scope, whether in the form of an epistemic theory of truth or a global commitment to antirealist truth conditions, it should come as no surprise that theists often have an immediate and negative knee-jerk reaction against all forms of the view. As I have explained, however, the semantic dualism that I propose does not have any such "global" consequences. Not only can all theological discourse be interpreted realistically (meeting the condition necessary for the very possibility of being a theist), but there can be statements from *every* domain of discourse that receive a realist interpretation. My claim is only that *some* statements from *one* domain of discourse (viz., external world statements) receive an antirealist interpretation—and that is no direct threat to theism.

But this doesn't tell the whole story. The threat of global antirealism isn't the only reason that theists are suspicious of antirealism. Even for the limited domain of discourse that concerns us here (statements about the external world), theists think they have good reason to assume that a globally realist semantics is required. After all, if metaphysical realism is true (as I concede), then God has created mind-independent physical objects and has given us cognitive and sensible faculties that provide us with reliable information about those mind-independent objects. Surely, the theist would argue, one is justified in believing that when we *speak* about the "physical objects" in our environment, we are speaking about those very mind-independent objects and not merely the objects "as experienced from our own epistemic perspective," as antirealism would re-

---

[6] Michael Dummett, "Realism" and "The Reality of the Past," in *Truth and Other Enigmas* (Cambridge: Harvard University Press, 1978), 145–65, 358–74.

[7] Hilary Putnam, "Realism and Reason," in *Meaning and the Moral Sciences* (Boston: Routledge & Kegan Paul, 1978), 123–38; and *Reason, Truth, and History* (Cambridge: Cambridge University Press, 1981), 1–74.

[8] William P. Alston, *A Realist Conception of Truth* (Ithaca: Cornell University Press, 1996).

quire. Surely the default position for the theist is that *all* external world state-ments are governed by a realist semantics. The burden would fall on the naysayer to show otherwise. And so it does.

WHERE THE RUBBER MEETS THE ROAD

As I am prepared to concede, the burden falls on me to show that *some* state-ments about the external world are properly interpreted antirealistically. In fact, I shall claim that *most* such statements are expressed with antirealist, rather than with realist, force. But how could such a claim be supported, especially in the face of the prima facie evidence against the view already articulated? To see how the argument will go, let us consider the difference between interpreting the 'walnut tree' statement realistically rather than antirealistically. One way to give intuitive force to the distinction between the two interpretations is to con-sider the role played by what we shall call *ultimate ontology*. We have a rich and complex set of experiences of an "external world," and there is, obviously enough, some ultimate explanation for why we have the experiences that we do. Most of us believe that mind-independent objects provide the ontological ex-planation, and so we are committed to metaphysical realism.

(A) *Metaphysical Realism* $=_{DEF}$ Mind-independent objects are the immediate cause of human experiences of an external world. These objects exist in-themselves, independent of the cognitive activity of any agent, and they gen-uinely possess most of the properties that we attribute to them.

But what if metaphysical realism is false? Consider two alternative explanations for our experiences of the external world, two scenarios with which you are probably familiar.

(B) *Theocentric Idealism* $=_{DEF}$ The interaction of God's mind with human minds is the immediate cause of present and future human experiences of an external world. (This is, roughly, Berkeley's view that objects in the environ-ment are mental entities created by God's mental activity.)

(C) *The BIV Hypothesis* $=_{DEF}$ We all are and always have been brains in a vat, à la Putnam's famous description.[9] Our present and future experiences of an external world are caused by a computer that is stimulating our disembodied brains and giving us mutually consistent experiences of a shared environment.

If either of these hypotheses is true, then human experiences of objects (past, present, and future) are caused by Berkeley's God or a supercomputer rather than by mind-independent objects. In all three worlds, (A)–(C), human beings are having exactly the same subjective experiences (of "walnut trees," "tables and chairs," "planets," and the like).

[9] Putnam, *Reason, Truth, and History*, 1–21.

We are now in a position to see how realist and antirealist interpretations will diverge in actual linguistic practice. Consider again our statement:

(1) There is a walnut tree in the quad.

We need only track the truth value of our 'walnut tree' statement in the possible worlds just described. If either of scenarios (B) or (C) is true, then (1) will be false on a realist interpretation because there exist no mind-independent trees in those worlds to make it true. Yet the statement will be true on an antirealist in-terpretation because, by stipulation, these are worlds in which people are hav-ing the very same kinds of experiences that people have in world (A). That is, people in worlds (B) and (C) have "visual," "tactile," "auditory," and the like, experiences sufficient to meet the empirical demands of an antirealist claim that there is a "walnut tree" in the "quad"—thus making (1) true in those worlds, when (1) is interpreted antirealistically.

This brings us to the central question under consideration: When (1) is ut-tered in normal, everyday contexts, is it uttered with realist or antirealist force? If you ask me the location of the walnut tree and I answer you by asserting (1), am I making a strictly empirical claim that is neutral with respect to *ultimate ontology* or am I making a robust metaphysical assertion that will be true only if (A) is true? The global semantic realist insists that a robust affirmation of metaphysical realism is a part of the very *meaning* of every statement we utter about trees. I disagree. It is this disagreement that I hope to settle in the argu-ments that follow.

Before going any further, I wish to be clear about what exactly it is that would make one semantic theory true and another false. In saying that most statements about the external world have antirealist truth conditions, I am not offering a *prescription;* I am not saying that we *ought* to utter these statements with antirealist force. I am saying that we already do. Most traditional theists, I shall assume, disagree. What evidence could either side give to support their claim?

Let's say that we ask a college student the location of the famous walnut tree on campus, and she utters our statement:

(1) There is a walnut tree in the quad.

Does this particular utterance have realist or antirealist truth conditions? We might think that the speaker herself can settle the question. We might ask her if she believes in the existence of a mind-independent walnut tree. Of course, from the fact that she *believes* in a mind-independent tree it doesn't necessarily follow that she has, just now, expressed that belief. If it isn't her metaphysical beliefs that matter when she utters the sentence, maybe it is her linguistic intentions. After all, surely she knows what she means. Thus, we might ask her, "In assert-ing (1), are you thereby asserting the existence of a mind-independent tree and quad?" If this were a reliable method for discovering the meaning of our utterances, then I would surely lose my battle with the global semantic realist. Anyone who holds that theory will most likely give an affirmative answer to that question. Happily for me, this methodology has come under widespread attack. The difficulty is that even competent speakers are notoriously unreliable in the answers they give to such questions. Speakers frequently misrepresent their own semantic intentions. What we say about our semantic intentions in discussion is often little more than a rehearsal of our metaphysical commitments and may be quite incompatible with what I shall call our "considered semantic intentions," which can be identified only by careful examination of our actual linguistic practice. "How can that be?" you ask.

Consider the case of natural kind terms. Locke believed that the word 'gold' referred to all and only those things that fit a particular description (shiny, yellow, malleable, etc.). A majority of contemporary philosophers disagree (I think) and now hold that 'gold' has an ineliminable indexical component, that it rigidly designates that deep explanatory property (probably, atomic number 79) that science will ultimately determine is the fundamental nature of gold. In making that claim, we are not, of course, saying that Locke invested the term with descriptive content whereas we now invest it with directly referential content. That would not be to disagree with Locke but merely to have effected a change in the meaning of the term 'gold.' No, Putnam's claim is that the term had an indexical character *even when Locke used it.* And it doesn't matter that Locke had a penchant for associating (in his mind's eye) the concepts "yellow," "shiny," and "malleable" with the term 'gold.' Such facts about Locke's psychology are not sufficient for making 'gold' a definite description. But on what grounds do we claim to know what Locke's words really meant? The grounds must ultimately derive from the nature of his linguistic competence.

Our competence as language speakers is primarily a practical knowledge that we exercise, not a propositional knowledge that we can readily express in a theory. We are interested in how Locke the English speaker did use (and would have used) the English language in actual practice, not in what Locke the philosopher did or did not believe about semantic theories. What, then, would make it the case that Locke meant the same thing by 'gold' that we do? In short, the answer is: his linguistic dispositions as a competent speaker of English. Putnam and Kripke suggest that we test our own linguistic dispositions by considering the truth value of certain claims in carefully chosen counterfactual situations. If 'gold' were indeed a definite description meaning "yellow, shiny, and malleable, etc.," then competent speakers would be disposed to call anything with those properties 'gold' and would refuse to apply that term to anything that lacked those features. To test the dispositions of speakers with respect to the 'gold' case, we must ask them to make a judgment about objects (or hypothetical objects) that separate the deep explanatory property (atomic number 79) from the superficial properties (yellow, shiny, malleable), thus forcing the speaker to choose that characteristic to which the term is semantically tied. We might imagine that we've found a piece of metal that has all the superficial properties of gold (yellow, shiny, malleable, etc.) but fails to have the same atomic structure (let's say its fundamental nature is XYZ, a heretofore unknown physical structure). Alternatively, we might consider a piece of atomic number 79 that is green, dull, and brittle and thus lacks the familiar superficial properties that characterize gold on our planet while maintaining its essential atomic structure.

We now have the means to test a speaker's linguistic dispositions with respect to her use of the term 'gold.' Simply ask a competent speaker whether these hypothetical substances do or do not fall within the extension of the term 'gold.' Most speakers are willing to call anything that is atomic number 79 'gold,' no matter what superficial properties it has, and they are not willing to call anything that lacks atomic number 79 'gold,' no matter how much it resembles our gold in superficial properties. Therefore, if we have reason to believe that Locke (and his compatriots) would, upon learning all the relevant facts about our atomic theories, have called green atomic number 79 'gold,' and would have withheld that label from yellow, shiny, malleable XYZ, then we have grounds for saying that Locke's linguistic competence was consistent with the new (indexical) theory of natural kind terms and inconsistent with his own definite description theory. We would, in short, have reason to say that 'gold' functioned for Locke as a rigid designator and thus that the definite description theory that he championed failed to capture the meaning *of his own words*.

Likewise, it is my contention that contemporary speakers who believe that all external world statements have realist truth conditions hold a theory that is not consistent with their own linguistic practice. To substantiate this claim, I must set up the right kind of thought experiment that will elicit the relevant linguistic performance. Let us begin with the traditional realist who holds that every utterance of

(1) There is a walnut tree in the quad.

has realist truth conditions and thus will be false in every possible world that lacks a mind-independent tree and quad. Thus we get the familiar conditional used to raise the specter of radical skepticism:

S_1: If I am being deceived by a malevolent demon, then (1) is false.

We can substitute any world in the antecedent, so long as it lacks mind-independent trees. Since the demon's malevolency is not semantically relevant and since the claim of deception begs the question against my theory, let's use Berkeley's world instead.

S_2: If Berkeleyan idealism is true, then (1) is false.

Since on my view, two utterances of (1) may vary in meaning, it is important to specify a particular utterance. Assume, as before, that (1) is what a passerby says when I ask about the location of the famous walnut tree. Thus, we get:

S_3: If Berkeleyan idealism is true, then the passerby's utterance of (1) is false.

Now the semantic dispute between myself and the global realist is very simple. She says that S_3 is true, and I say that it is false. I do not believe that statements about the external world, like (1), when uttered in normal, everyday contexts, entail the truth of any metaphysical theory. Yes, there probably exists a mind-independent walnut tree, and yes, I am justified in believing as much. But it does not follow that every time I speak of a "tree," my utterance entails the truth of a deep theory of ultimate ontology.

When it comes to determining the meaning of our language, everything hinges on what we as competent speakers are prepared to say about certain outcomes. The global semantic realist insists that every statement we make about the world is asserting a popular, but still controversial, metaphysical theory. They insist that if it turns out that the world we inhabit is a mental one (Berkeleyan idealism) rather than a physical one and, thus, that we were wrong about the ultimate nature of reality, then every affirmative external world statement we ever uttered is *false*. What that means is that when I tell my father, "Yes, I am the one who cleaned the garage for you and threw out the old paint cans," I say something false. Why? Not because I didn't do what my father wanted me to do. I did! The garage is as clean as any human has a right to demand. It is false because the "paint cans" turned out to be Berkeleyan, mind-dependent paint cans rather than mind-independent ones. But surely, when I am talking with my dad about paint cans, I have no interest in taking a stand on deep metaphysical disputes. I have no interest in asserting that Berkeleyan idealism is false.

Granted, there are occasions when I do assert that metaphysical realism is true and that Berkeleyan idealism is false. In my epistemology classes, for example. But I did *not* assert its falsity in the conversation with my father. Realism, in that context, isn't bad metaphysics; it is simply bad semantics. It misrepresents the meaning and function of our utterances. Statements about the external world, uttered in normal (nonphilosophical) contexts do not make claims about *ultimate ontology*. Their truth value is sensitive only to how things stand with respect to the epistemic perspective of human beings (viz., the antirealist truth conditions), not to how things stand with respect to ultimate ontology (viz., the realist truth conditions).

This same line of argument is even more compelling when applied to moral discourse. If we *were* to discover (or even if we were wrongly to *believe* that we had discovered) that the objects of common sense are mind-dependent as Berkeley thought, would we judge that that fact falsified my daughter's utterance of the following sentence?

m: I kept my promise to you, Dad, by making my bed and cleaning my room.

I say, no. God has ordained that we live out our moral and spiritual lives in this environment (whatever its nature). If I am *wrong* about ultimate ontology and Berkeley is right, my daughter's action will be no less an instance of bed-making and promise-keeping than if I am *right* about metaphysical realism. It seems to exhibit altogether the wrong spirit to say what the global semantic realist must say about the Berkeleyan scenario. She must say that my daughter (i) promised to make a mind-independent bed, (ii) did not (and could not) make a mind-independent bed (because they don't exist), and thus (iii) didn't keep her promise. But why say that? God is responsible for our present epistemic situation, whatever it is. If my daughter sleeps in a Berkeleyan bed, that bed is real enough to be the referent of her 'bed' statements and it is real enough to be the occasion of her promise-keeping. What possible grounds would we have for saying otherwise?

The arguments just offered ought to be compelling to everyone, theist and atheist alike. But theism brings an added dimension to the discussion. To make the point, let us assume, for the sake of argument, that Christian theism is true and that we find ourselves in heaven. Saint Peter informs us, "Yes, indeed, Berkeley was right all along. God created a mental, not a physical, universe." Now the global semantic realist must insist that when the Bible says that Jesus fed the five thousand with five loaves and two fishes, the Bible says what is false. Because on her account what it *means* to say that "there are loaves and fishes" is to say that there are mind-independent objects of a certain kind. Surely this result is unacceptable. The theist cannot really be so presumptuous as to say, in effect, the following:

> If God chose to create a mental world instead of a physical world, then Jesus uttered countless falsehoods because *we humans* insist upon speaking a language that entails the truth of our favorite metaphysical theory. God may have the power to create any kind of world that God wants, but we hold the power to make God's own words false because we refuse to speak about any "trees" except mind-independent trees or any "fish" other than mind-independent fish.

This exhibits a kind of hubris not consistent with the spirit of theism.

How, then, should the theist understand the place of metaphysical realism in her worldview? As I've said, I think it is rational for everyone to believe that metaphysical realism is true. Nor do any of the semantic arguments just offered require anything like an attack on the *truth* of metaphysical realism. When we appeal to the possibility of Berkeleyan idealism, it functions just as well for semantic purposes if we simply stipulate that it is a *counterfactual* conditional and ignore the possibility that it might actually be true. But having said all that, I believe it is possible for the theist to be *too* dogmatic about her commitment to metaphysical realism. For naturalist realists of a certain stripe, it may well be that the mind-independent existence of the external world is a ground-level, all but unrevisable commitment. But it shouldn't be so for the theist. The Bible is full of admonitions against the presumptuousness of human beings who privilege themselves as knowing more of the deep facts about the universe than it is their station to know. Paul observes that "we see through a glass darkly," and there are numerous places in Psalms, Proverbs, Ecclesiastes, and many other books that speak of the extreme limits of human understanding. I do not mean to suggest that these biblical passages uncontroversially apply to the issue of the mind-independent existence of objects in the external world. I do believe, however, that the Bible as a whole prescribes a certain self-understanding concerning our epistemic and doxastic perspective. We know for certain *whose* we are, we know that our present epistemic situation (whatever it is) is ordained by God, and we know that the objects around us (whatever their nature) are "real enough" to constitute the arena in which God requires that we lead lives worthy of our high calling. But do we know as certainly the fundamental nature of the "physical" universe? Might it not be *hubris* to pound the table and insist that our language will countenance only one kind of metaphysical stuff? Semantic dualism is guilty of no such hubris and is also supported by independent arguments. It is the semantic theory most congenial to traditional theism.

A LITTLE HAND-WAVING ABOUT THE EXTERNALIST OBJECTION

There is one obvious objection to semantic dualism that has not yet been mentioned. All the arguments offered thus far against global semantic realism have assumed that the semantic realism in question is of a Cartesian, or internalist, variety. Put simply, this means that the content expressed by a particular utterance is determined by the internal mental states of speakers. It is only when we make this assumption that we can take for granted (as we have) that our 'walnut tree' sentence:

(1) There is a walnut tree in the quad.

expresses the same proposition (and thus has the same truth conditions) in both the metaphysical realist world and the nonstandard worlds of brains-in-a-vat and Berkeleyan idealism. Since the internal mental states of human beings (the sensations, the cognitive activity, etc.) are stipulated to be the same in each of these possible worlds, the propositions expressed by a particular utterance will be the same as well.

Although internalist semantic realism continues to be defended by many, an externalist version of semantic realism has garnered many adherents. According to externalism, traditional semantic realists go wrong by assuming that meanings are fundamentally "in the head" and that our statements about the external world will have the same truth conditions regardless of which possible ontology,

(A)–(C), is true of the actual world.[10] It is this last assumption that the externalist denies. According to externalism, an object term like 'tree' refers to whatever is causally responsible for (and thus is causally regulating) our use of that term. Thus, in the possible world in which my 'tree' experience is caused by a mind-independent physical object, the word 'tree' will refer to the relevant mind-independent object; in the world in which I am a brain in a vat, the word 'tree' will (probably) refer to the relevant subroutine in the computer's software;[11] and in the possible world in which my 'tree' experiences are caused by Berkeley's God, the word 'tree' will refer to certain causally efficacious thoughts in the mind of God.

The reason that externalism seems to offer a way out for the global semantic realist is that externalism agrees with antirealism in determining that our walnut tree statement, (1), will come out true even if it turns out that we live in a brains-in-vat (BIV) world or in a Berkeleyan world. In a BIV world, 'tree' statements will express (largely) true claims about the states of the governing computer software; in a Berkeleyan world, 'tree' statements will express (largely) true claims about God's thoughts. The upshot is that semantic externalism of this type will agree with semantic antirealism in determining that most 'tree' statements uttered in normal speech contexts will come out true even if there exist no mind-independent "trees" (of the standard type) to make them true. This makes it seem like semantic externalism is a natural way for the theist to concede the claims made in this chapter about the linguistic dispositions of competent speakers, at the same time resisting the conclusion that this points toward an antirealist element in our semantics.

Externalism is a serious and increasingly popular semantic theory that cannot be adequately addressed in a brief postscript. All I can offer is a bit of handwaving that points to the deficiencies of externalism that should make it hard for the theist (or anyone else) to love. Semantic externalism has counterintuitive consequences that I think most philosophers have yet to fully appreciate. One such consequence is that it raises a rather serious skeptical worry about any

---

[10] We know that Descartes did assume that our statements about the external world would have the same truth conditions regardless of which possible ontology is true of the actual world because the threat of radical skepticism that he took so seriously simply doesn't arise without this assumption. The only reason for thinking that my present 'table' beliefs will be threatened by the demon ontology is if my 'table' statements make the *same* realist assertion whether the actual world is a demon world or a mind-independent world.

[11] Putnam suggested two other possible alternatives for what brains in the vat might be talking about. He says: "Given what 'tree' refers to in vat-English and what 'in front of' refers to, assuming one of these theories is correct, then the truth conditions for 'There is a tree in front of me' when it occurs in vat-English are simply that a tree in the image be 'in front of' the 'me' in question—in the image—or, perhaps, that the kind of electronic impulse that normally produces this experience be coming from the automatic machinery, or, perhaps, that the feature of the machinery that is supposed to produce the 'tree in front of one' experience be operating" (*Reason, Truth, and History*, 14). The first option seems an unlikely one for the typical externalist realist; the second option will produce results very like the one I have in fact used (i.e., states of the software program).

speaker's ability to know the content of his own beliefs and utterances. The problem arises because the content expressed by an utterance is determined by facts about the external environment, facts that may well be epistemically inaccessible to the speaker. Theists are not likely to be happy with a semantic theory if it makes it impossible for speakers to know what they are talking or thinking about.

A second, more pressing worry is that semantic externalism is incompatible with radical skepticism and, as a consequence, may threaten metaphysical realism itself. If this is the case, as I believe it is, externalism has the ironic consequence of taking a semantic theory that seems to be initially realist in its commitments yet that ultimately undermines the very intelligibility of metaphysical realism. This feature of externalism has been exploited by people like Putnam and Gary Ebbs,[12] who have used semantic externalism to defend the truth of metaphysical antirealism. Since metaphysical antirealism cannot, in my opinion, be reconciled with traditional theism, this will not likely be a popular position for theists.[13]

Although this bit of hand-waving may not satisfy the theist genuinely drawn to semantic externalism, complete versions of these arguments against externalism, as well as others, can be found elsewhere.[14] When externalism is fully understood, I am convinced that very few people will find it easily reconcilable with traditional theism.

SUMMARY

I have offered general arguments to show that *global semantic realism* is false and more specific arguments to show that it is an especially problematic theory for traditional theists. As an alternative I've defended *semantic dualism*. According to this theory, the English sentence 'This is a hand' is ambiguous. If I am teaching an epistemology class and speak as a metaphysical realist using a G. E. Moore–type strategy to refute the skeptic, and I say, "This is a hand and thus I refute the skeptic," this utterance demands a realist interpretation. It makes no sense otherwise. But in a normal everyday context, if I am playing a word game with my two-year-old and say "this is a foot," "this is a hand," I suggest that the very same English sentence would express an antirealist claim. The linguistic ability accorded by the first interpretation gives me the resources necessary to express my commitment to metaphysical realism. The linguistic ability accorded by the second interpretation gives me the resources necessary

---

[12] Gary Ebbs, *Rule-Following and Realism* (Cambridge: Harvard University Press, 1997).

[13] Hilary Putnam is one person who does not see a conflict between metaphysical antirealism (what he used to call "internal realism") and theism. Although I have never been clear about how he thinks the two can be reconciled, he has never been persuaded by my arguments that the two are incompatible.

[14] David Leech Anderson, "A Dogma of Metaphysical Realism," *American Philosophical Quarterly* 32 (January 1995): 1–11; "What Is Realist about Putnam's Internal Realism?" *Philosophical Topics* 20 (Spring 1992): 49–83; and "The Truth in Antirealism" (typescript).

to make claims about the empirical environment in which we live, independent of considerations of ultimate ontology. This latter ability is one that is underappreciated. It allows me to express the significance of "the world-as-experienced," a world of moral, spiritual, and aesthetic value *regardless of* its ultimate ontological nature.

PART III

Realism and Epistemology

9

Cooperative, Coordinative, and Coercive Epistemologies

CHRISTOPHER TOLLEFSEN

In the introduction to her recent book *Virtues of the Mind*, Linda Zagzebski writes, "The deepest disputes in epistemology focus on concepts that are quite obviously ethical and often borrowed directly from theoretical moral discourse."[1] Zagzebski has in mind here concepts such as 'good,' 'duty,' 'right,' and 'virtue,' the last of which she articulates with great care, showing its relation to various epistemic difficulties.

In this chapter I want to discuss a cluster of concepts from moral discourse—cooperation, coordination, and coercion—which overlap with many if not all of these notions from Zagzebski's list, in an effort to articulate different ways of conceptualizing the relation between persons and the world. Two of these concepts—coercion and coordination—do not, I think, enable us to see enough of, or the right kind of, relation between persons and the world. So I shall introduce a third notion, cooperation. If this notion is viable for the understanding of the relations in question, then I think it will allow us to see through to a broadly realist position; indeed, I will claim that such a notion is necessary for a genuinely realist position. But the notion of cooperation comes with its costs. On the one hand, a cooperative epistemology is possible only if the world is a suitable partner in our cooperative knowing venture. On the other hand, as the contrast with coercion, especially, will make clear, cooperation is an irredeemably voluntarist notion; that is, there is cooperation only where action is subject to the will. A cooperative epistemology is therefore a voluntarist epistemology. Here I do not argue directly for either the necessary ontology or voluntarism about belief, but both are required to the extent that my overall position is accepted.

This chapter would have been impossible but for the time spent during the summer of 1999 in William Alston's seminar Realism and Antirealism, as part of Calvin College's Summer Seminars in Christian Scholarship. Thanks are due to Alston especially, to the participants, and to the Calvin College Summer Seminar staff and administrators.

[1] Linda Zagzebski, *Virtues of the Mind* (Cambridge: Cambridge University Press, 1996), xiii.

I begin in ethics, the natural home of these concepts. Coercion, coordination, and cooperation represent, intuitively, different forms of relationships agents may have with or to one another. Coercion, obviously enough, involves some degree of force; at the limit, enough force to eliminate entirely responsibility or culpability on the part of the agent so coerced. There are, of course, degrees here: Aristotle suggests, rightly, I think, that genuine coercion is such that the agent absolutely could not do otherwise. The famous example of the ship captain who throws the cargo overboard in a storm is, Aristotle says, an example of action that is involuntary in itself but voluntary on the occasion.[2]

In cases in which one agent is coerced by another agent, there are two important points. First, coercion in no way respects the freedom of the agent coerced. Second, although the coerced agent in some sense acts in concert with the coercing agent, one necessary condition for saying that they act together is absent: they do not share a common will concerning what is to be done. So really, there is only one agent in a genuine case of coercion.

The distinction between coordination and cooperation is more difficult to draw, but I think it is crucial to the foundations of ethics and politics. The distinction may be understood as follows. Two agents coordinate their actions when (a) both have different ends, but (b) the ends in question may be more easily or efficiently achieved if the agents each act in awareness of the way the other agent will act, and both expect to benefit, and to be benefited, from acting on this mutual awareness. Two builders working for the same company, and thus building the same house, coordinate their actions if their reasons for working on the house are different—each, say, *only* wants to be paid—but their different reasons can be best satisfied by work done in awareness of the way the other agent will work. Coordination in this sense will prevent, for example, workplace collisions. Colloquially, both agents may be said to be doing the same thing—working on the house—but as long as their ends are not shared, they may not, in a different sense, be said to be doing the same thing. We could say that their respective intentions do not share any content, although they might coincide in content.

Joint action for the same end, in which condition (b) for coordination is also met, is cooperative action. Agents who cooperate may be doing quite different things by way of their performance and yet still be cooperating, even as agents who are engaged in precisely the same performance may be only coordinating their performances. With agents who cooperate, they must be said to do the same thing under a description that refers to their ends. Two builders who share a love for work, or who are committed to the ends of Habitat for Humanity, cooperate in performing different tasks—indeed, they may cooperate with people who do not directly work on the house itself.

More needs to be said about the ends in question: not all ends admit of being

---

[2] Aristotle, *Nicomachean Ethics*, trans. Terence Irwin (Indianapolis: Hackett, 1985), 1110a10–20.

shared in the way required for genuine cooperation. For example, the relation between means and end cannot simply be that of part to whole; if it is, each agent pursues a different part of the whole, and thus not the same end. What I mean by this may perhaps be understood by analogy with the difference between knowing and eating: if two knowers both know that X, then they both know the same thing: X. But two eaters who both eat the same pie have not eaten the same thing. Each has eaten a part of the pie. Similarly, ends may not be set by desire, for then each agent's end would be subjective, in a sense identified by Kant. Even if those ends are in some sense 'the same,' they would still, Kant says, be only subjectively universal. By this I mean that their ends only coincide. If it is knowledge of X that motivates me and you, we are both motivated by the same end. But if it is a desire for knowledge of X that motivates me, and a similar desire that motivates you, then the end that motivates each of us is indexed to our individual desires and hence is not shared.[3]

A strong condition thus emerges for ends that are to be the basis for mutual cooperation: such ends must be objective. Among the various implications of this are the following two. First, the relationship between means to objective ends, not being part to whole, is better understood as constitutive, or participatory. Second, since ends motivate, objective ends motivate impersonally, that is, without reference to any particular agent motivated by those ends.

It is a consequence of these claims that genuine community is possible only under conditions of cooperation—that is, if there are objective ends. Following up a Kantian thought, we can also see that genuine community is a community of a kind of shared freedom: rational responsiveness to shared reasons. Conditions of coercion—that is, tyranny—and of mere coordination—that is, a nonperfectionist liberal state—are not genuine conditions of community.

These claims are contentious and have been but briefly made, but my aim here is to see what role distinctions like these could play in accounts of knowing. I want to suggest that the notion of cooperation should shape our understanding of knowing along two axes: knowing is a cooperative venture with other knowing agents, and knowing involves something very like cooperation between agents and their world. By contrast, if either of these relations is dominated by coercion or coordination, then genuine knowing, like genuine community, disappears.

Clearly, three possible relations on two axes leaves eight possibilities, and indeed, even more since a view of knowing might eliminate one of the axes: purely social accounts of knowledge eliminate the world, and highly individualistic accounts of knowing eliminate any relationship of the knower to other knowing agents. Rather than discuss each possibility, I want to make a case for a natural progression from thinking about knowing in terms of coercion, to thinking in

[3] For an elaboration of these claims, see my "Sidgwickian Objectivity and Ordinary Morality," *The Journal of Value Inquiry* 33 (1999): 57–70. See also Thomas Nagel, *The Possibility of Altruism* (Princeton: Princeton University Press, 1978).

terms of coordination, to thinking in terms of cooperation. I'll then outline what possible advantages might be had by a cooperative account and what conditions would need to be met for this approach to be possible.

Richard Rorty has, more than once, drawn attention to a strand of epistemology that takes coercion by the world as its dominant image: "the desire for a theory of knowledge is a desire for constraint—a desire to find 'foundations' to which one might cling, frameworks beyond which one must not stray, objects which impose themselves, representations which cannot be gainsaid."[4] Following Rorty, Donald Davidson, and especially Wilfrid Sellars, John McDowell has in turn linked this notion to a Kantian notion of freedom. Knowing is a normative activity, but seeking some 'Given' that exerts this form of constraint or coercion substitutes mere exculpation for justification. Being forced, by the brute impact of world, would mean that we were not to blame for our beliefs, but it would be insufficient to say that our knowings and thinkings were rationally responsive to the world.[5]

I think a similar point would be made if we viewed our relation to the rest of the knowing community along similar lines. On this sort of a picture, our conceptual resources would be brutely given by our linguistic peers, for example. More obvious cases of socially coerced belief could likewise be imagined. No matter what one's relationship to the world really was, it would be vitiated by an inescapable Foucauldian 'regime of truth.'[6] So viewing our relationship to the world and our knowing peers as forced, constrained, or coercive is destructive of the notion that we know—McDowell would even say "think"—at all.

McDowell's paradigm for such a coercive relationship of world to mind is any account in which the world's impact upon us is brutely causal *and* that brute causal relationship is taken to have epistemic significance. Such a relationship is, in Sellars's words, a kind of 'mongrel conflation,' a conflation between justification and explanation.[7] McDowell argues that one recoil from the realization that the mongrel conception cannot do its job is a move to a pure coherentism, in which one's conceptual capacities are "unconstrained" by the deliverances of sense.

I think there are, in fact, a number of ways that this recoil can be manifest. In particular, I will address three, all of which are, in my sense, coordinative accounts of the mind-world relationship. Interestingly, they do not all have the same aspirations. The three forms of coordinative relationship I will discuss are (1) a BonJour-type coherentist epistemology, (2) Rortian pragmatism, and (3) epistemological forms of externalism.

[4] Richard Rorty, *Philosophy and the Mirror of Nature* (Princeton: Princeton University Press, 1979), 315.

[5] John McDowell, *Mind and World* (Cambridge: Harvard University Press, 1994).

[6] Michel Foucault, "Truth and Power," in *The Foucault Reader*, ed. Paul Rabinow (New York: Pantheon, 1984), 51–75.

[7] Wilfrid Sellars, *Empiricism and the Philosophy of Mind* (Cambridge: Harvard University Press, 1997), sec. 7.

A coherentist epistemology must be distinguished from a coherentist account of truth; I am concerned with the view which has it that what we want is truth, nonepistemically construed, but which also holds that our justificatory practices are entirely coherentist. The basic idea behind this is likely to be, as it is for BonJour, the thought that beliefs are justified only by their relation to other beliefs and that all knowings are believings. So even at what McDowell calls the periphery of our scheme of beliefs, it is not sense experience that justifies beliefs, or aspects of the world, but judgments or beliefs about experience or aspects of the world.[8]

I call this a coordinative picture because, as with coordination in the moral sphere, it puts the activities of two things—here the world and the knowing agent—at a distance from each other. Should a coherent set of beliefs accurately mirror the world, it will not be by way of the shared activity of the knower and the world; rather, the world will do its thing and the knower hers. Put another way, and in keeping with BonJour's (and Sellars's) objections to the Given, the way knowers operate—justification of beliefs by beliefs—and the way the world operates—particulars having causal consequences on other particulars—are intrinsically different, even if their activities overlap with one another, or even make one another in some way possible. This parallels the moral case in which two agents do not share an end, even though their activities might overlap with one another and even, in some way, make one another possible. The notion of coordination seems, in particular, to describe well BonJour's attempts to get experience in the picture. His so-called Observational Requirement is precisely an attempt to coordinate the causal effect the world has on our beliefs with our justificatory practices.[9]

Rorty's Sellarianism is likewise coordinative, although without the same aspirations as BonJour's coherentism. For Rorty, truth is not to be construed in a realist fashion but is simply a term of commendation for beliefs approved by one's linguistic community. For members of such a community, the space of reasons is normative, a space of asking for and giving reasons for beliefs, and is guided by community norms. The world, by contrast, exerts only a causal agency over speakers. This limits, in some obvious ways, what people can go on saying—a culture that claims it can fly like birds won't last long—but the world exists in no rational relationship with the linguistic community. At best there is forced coordination, as the world exerts its causality and linguistic communities decide whether and how to shift their norms.

I will return to Rorty in a moment. Consider first, however, the basic claim of an epistemological externalist. Internalists claim that what justifies a cognitive agent in holding a belief must be available to the agent as a reason for her to assent to the claim in question; externalists deny this. We can see two forms

---

[8] Laurence BonJour, *The Structure of Empirical Knowledge* (Cambridge: Harvard University Press, 1985).
[9] Ibid., 141–44.

of externalism here. One takes it that everything by which a belief could be said to be justified is external to an agent's point of view; a more limited externalism distinguishes, as Plantinga does, between justification and warrant. What justifies is that an agent meets her epistemic obligations, and this is internal; but what makes the belief true, and thus provides warrant, is the presence of a reliable and properly functioning belief-producing mechanism in an appropriate environment, and this is external. Thus, that her belief has been so produced is often not something available from the first-person perspective of a believing agent.[10]

Externalism is both unintuitive and, as BonJour points out, relatively recent; I think its intuitive unsatisfactoriness comes precisely again from its being one form of a purely coordinative account of knowing. The believing agent, taken precisely as an agent, does one thing: fulfills her epistemic duties, for example. But then whatever is responsible for providing warrant does its thing. The second cause may be a causal relationship between sense faculties and the world; it might be an act of God. But it acts only in coordination with the activity of the believer: the world and the believer do not cooperate to constitute a veridical belief, they coordinate.

I think the consequences of such an account are more severe than are ordinarily realized, and I will attempt to sketch why in relation to Rorty's work. In an important essay, Rorty writes:

> There are two principal ways in which reflective human beings try, by placing their lives in a larger context, to give sense to those lives. The first is by telling the story of their contribution to a community. This community may be the actual historical one in which they live, or another actual one, distant in time or place, or a quite imaginary one. . . . The second way is to describe themselves as standing in immediate relation to a nonhuman reality. . . . I shall say that stories of the former kind exemplify the desire for solidarity, and that stories of the latter kind exemplify the desire for objectivity. Insofar as a person is seeking solidarity, he or she does not ask about the relation between the practices of the chosen community and something outside that community. Insofar as he seeks objectivity, he distances himself from the actual persons around him by not thinking of himself as a member of some other real or imaginary group, but rather by attaching himself to something that can be described without reference to any particular human beings.[11]

Rorty describes the solidarity model precisely in terms of cooperation—"cooperative human inquiry" is what characterizes a community. But I shall argue

---

[10] Alvin Plantinga, *Warrant and Proper Function* (New York: Oxford University Press, 1993). For a criticism of Plantinga similar to mine, see Patrick Lee, "Evidentialism, Plantinga, and Faith and Reason," in *Rational Faith: Catholic Responses to Reformed Epistemology*, ed. Linda Zagzebski (Notre Dame: University of Notre Dame Press, 1993), 140–67.

[11] Richard Rorty, "Solidarity and Objectivity," in *Objectivity, Relativism, and Truth: Philosophical Papers*, vol. 1 (Cambridge: Cambridge University Press, 1991), 21.

that there is no social cooperation without mind-world cooperation. The converse is true also, however. There is no mind-world cooperation without social cooperation. The notions of a linguistic *community* and of a knowing agent are inextricably tied.

What would it take for a group of people to have a community? One plausible, if incomplete, answer would stress the need for a shared set of norms. A group of agents operating according to entirely different normative standards would fail to constitute a community. But recent work in the philosophy of law has indicated that a mere convergence of accepted norms is insufficient for community: the norms must be shared because of a shared acceptance of the *point* of the norms. This reflects what I earlier said about the conditions for cooperation requiring shared ends.[12]

Now Rorty's idea of a linguistic community can be glossed in similar fashion around the notion of norms. A linguistic community just is a group of language users who share a set of norms for what counts as appropriate and inappropriate, justified and unjustified language use. And the extension of a community, for Rorty, just is the extension of intersubjective agreement as to which norms are in play. The question is, What force can be given to the notion of 'agreement' here sufficient to ground genuine community? Can the norms of the linguistic community be shared, possess the same content, be accepted for the same reasons from agent to agent within the community?

They could, if the point of accepting the norms was that they enabled the members of a linguistic community to grasp and communicate aspects of non-human reality. That is, if the forms of rational responsiveness shared by members of a community were such as to place members in a cognitive relation to the world, then there would be a shared content to their utterances which could be mutually understood by members of the community and a shared, rather than merely convergent, acceptance of the norms in question. By virtue of a shared connection to the world, members of the community would have the basis for genuine linguistic cooperation.

But linking language use to the world is not what Rorty thinks grounds linguistic community. We are to think of language users as engaged in mutually understanding one another, not mutually understanding the world. Rorty explicitly denies the form of objectivity I have just described:

> To sum up the 'existentialist' view of objectivity, then: objectivity should be seen as conformity to the norms of justification (for assertions and for actions) we find about us. Such conformity becomes dubious and self-deceptive only when seen as something more than this—namely, as a way of obtaining

---

[12] For the development of this thought, see, in order, H. L. A. Hart, *The Concept of Law* (Oxford: Oxford University Press, 1961); Joseph Raz, *Practical Reason and Norms* (Oxford: Oxford University Press, 1975); and John Finnis, *Natural Law and Natural Rights* (Oxford: Clarendon Press, 1980).

access to something which 'grounds' current practices of justification in something else.[13]

But what is involved in this conformity to the local norms of justification? What grasp do we have of them? For those norms, and the language used by adherents to these norms, are parts of our world—indeed, among the parts of our world with which we are earliest made acquainted. If the world lies beyond my current practices of justification, so too do the current practices of justification of anybody else.

Consider the metaphor of the space of reasons, introduced by Sellars and taken over by Rorty. How many such spaces are there among a group of individuals using the same language? Rorty and Sellars assume without qualm that there is one, into which language users are initiated, but it is difficult to see how this could be. There is nothing, neither the world nor the language, to which teacher and learner could both be attuned in such a way as to share the same cognitive content.

Here is an analogy. Suppose that there are two species, developing in a shared environment, both of which adapt in such a way as to be able to take advantage of the adaptations of the other species. The respective adaptations are merely coordinated—the two species don't share a plan, a goal, or a purpose, but the way things work out may make it seem as if they do.

But what about members of a species that all possess the same adaptive features? It looks like this must be different, but I don't see how it could be: each member of the species stands in the same sort of relationship to other members of its species that the species stands in with respect to other co-adapted species. There is no cooperation among members of the species.

Rorty's view of language, however, makes it out to be one more sort of adaptation, this time of the human species, and on this view, it seems to me that every individual who possesses a language is merely co-adapted to other individuals who possess that same language. But now the very notion of 'the same language' begins to seem out of place. If at the age of six everyone picked up a hammer in his or her right hand and held and used it throughout the rest of his or her life, these people wouldn't possess the same hammer. The point is this: we get the notion of same language only by recognizing the sameness of the contents of the language, and any argument that cuts the world out of the language works equally against anything that could constitute the notion of sameness of content.

By way of a last stab at making my objection clearer and bringing it into line with the metaphor of coordination, consider Rorty's discussion, in "Pragmatism, Davidson, and Truth," of two different standpoints. The first is that of the field linguist, who sees verbal utterances "from outside . . . as causal interactions with the environment." The second is that of the "pre-epistemological na-

---

[13] Rorty, *Philosophy and the Mirror of Nature*, 361.

tive," who sees them "as rules for action."[14] Rorty writes: "To abjure *tertia* is to abjure the possibility of a third way of seeing them—one which somehow combines the outside view and the inside view, the descriptive and the normative attitudes. To see language in the same way as we see beliefs—not as a 'conceptual framework' but as the causal interaction with the environment described by the field linguist, makes it impossible to think of language as something which may or may not (how could we ever tell?) 'fit the world.' "[15]

Two points. First, it seems to me that Rorty is here drawing the proper moral from a coordinative picture of the mind-world relationship, more adequately than does BonJour. If the world is doing its causal thing, and we are doing our normative thing, then the stories are different and can't be integrated into a practical standpoint that assigns world and mind the same end of producing true beliefs. Rather, we will want to coordinate our normative schemes to the world so as to ensure survival—no beliefs that we can fly—and beyond that, work within our language game in either progressive or conservative ways, depending on our tastes.

Second, McDowell's criticism of this two-standpoint picture is similar to mine: "It is the whole point," he writes, "of the idea of norms of inquiry that following them ought to improve our chances of being right about 'the way the world is.' "[16] So McDowell thinks Rorty's normative standpoint fails precisely with respect to the world if it is not connected to that world in an appropriate way. My further argument is that this failure with respect to the world cannot but be destructive of the whole notion of shared norms itself. The argument can't be avoided by saying that linguistic norms have some *other* point, for your language, with its norms and their 'point,' stands in a world-to-language relationship with my language, and hence itself can't be grasped *an sich*. So there can be, on this picture, no such thing as a linguistic or normative community.

So now to cooperation. The picture I want to offer is of cooperative relationships between persons and other persons, and between persons and the world. The picture is in various ways indebted to McDowell's recent work, so I will spend a bit of time at the end indicating where it departs from McDowell.

Suppose we thought that the relationship between the mind and the world was best understood by analogy with human cooperation. We would do well, then, I think, to accept McDowell's rejection of the Given—something standing outside the space of reasons, and hence outside our rational freedom, exerting a brutely causal influence over us. But we would also need to establish some rational connection with the world, in virtue of which we could make sense of the notion of a shared, not simply coordinated, activity. Further, the rational connection would have to be understood in terms of a shared content.

---

[14] Richard Rorty, "Pragmatism, Davidson, and Truth," in *Objectivity, Relativism, and Truth*, 139.

[15] Ibid.

[16] McDowell, *Mind and World*, 151.

Nevertheless, cooperation allows for multiplicity of roles, so mind and world would not need to be the same thing or be playing the same role in the sharing of content.

Consider, then, four aspects of the knowing relation between mind and world. There is the world of things, events, and facts; there is experience; there is the formation and consideration of propositions; and there is judgment of the proposition. Each stage or aspect of knowing is clearly different in some respects from the others; but if at any stage there is a radical enough difference, then knowledge will be impossible. So I think that it is one of McDowell's great innovations to make it possible, following Kant, to see experience as continuous in the right ways with the expression and judgments of propositions. If, in particular, experience was at some point nonconceptual, it would not be within the same logical space in which formation and judgment of propositions reside, for propositions and judgments are certainly conceptual.

McDowell introduces the possibility that experience can have a kind of propositional shape: just as one judges that things are thus and so, so at a different stage of cognition, "that things are thus and so is the conceptual content of an experience."[17] But whereas judging is paradigmatically active, on the part of the knowing agent, experience is paradigmatically passive: "In 'outer experience', a subject is passively saddled with conceptual contents, drawing into operation capacities seamlessly integrated into a conceptual repertoire that she employs in the continuing activity of adjusting her world-view."[18]

Still, the picture would not be cooperative with respect to mind and world if it were not the world itself that acts on the agent in such a way as for her to be saddled with conceptual content in experience. So the same propositional locution, that things are thus and so, becomes available to characterize the way the world is: "if the subject of an experience is not misled, that very same thing, that things are thus and so, is also a perceptible fact, an aspect of the perceptible world."[19]

Something along these lines may be found, as Michael Lynch has suggested, in William Alston's *Realist Conception of Truth*. In formulating his minimalist account of truth, Alston writes:

(p)(the proposition that p is true *iff* it is a fact that p).[20]

He continues:

That this marks out the right sort of correspondence between proposition and fact is guaranteed by the requirement for instantiations of the schema,

[17] Ibid., 26.
[18] Ibid., 31.
[19] Ibid., 26.
[20] William Alston, *A Realist Conception of Truth* (Ithaca: Cornell University Press, 1996), 38.

that the same substitution be made for '*p*' in its two occurrences. This guarantees that the proposition and the fact that makes it true share the same propositional content. What the fact is a fact *that*, is the same as what the proposition is a proposition *that*.[21]

As with McDowell's view, this seems to go some distance toward making possible the kind of cooperation I have in mind. In particular, we have the requisite sameness of content across mind and world. There are some problems, as Lynch points out, with saying that it is *propositional* content that is shared by propositions and the world.[22] So I would stick with just the notion of sameness of content and hold that this content is propositional when entertained by a mind but not when instantiated in the world. I should say as well that Alston's view here articulates only the fact-proposition relationship and, as he has noted, "nothing about how to think of experience. On the latter I am strongly opposed to the view of McDowell, and others, that perceptual experience is essentially propositionally structured."[23]

What is crucial to this type of picture is that there not be a boundary within which thought is enclosed and outside which is the world. The independence of the world from thought is not the same as the opacity of the world to thought, an opacity that would result if we saw the meeting of mind and world as at an interface. This also fits well within the metaphor of cooperation. When two agents cooperate, they do not meet at an interface, as they do in mere coordination. Rather, my awareness of the other extends right out to take in her reasons for action and make them my own. The content of my reasons and the content of her reasons are the same. And this is, again, compatible with our playing different roles in the cooperative venture.

In particular, it is compatible with the mix of activity and passivity which characterizes experience. McDowell briefly acknowledges in a footnote the ways in which experience is an activity of the cognitive agent: we move ourselves into position, we engage with the world, and so on. But, and this is a traditional scholastic point, the activation of our sense capacities is not under our control. We are passive with respect to the world in this regard. But this is no different from cooperation with other agents. My cooperation with my doctor, when we share the same ends, is passive in large part, although I actively seek him out, question him, and so on.

This cooperative relation with the world both helps explain, and is partially explained by, our cooperative relations with other members of our linguistic community. It is by way of a shared access to the world that our attempts at mutual understanding and communication are possible; yet clearly, McDowell's

[21] Ibid.

[22] Michael Lynch, "Minimal Realism or Realistic Minimalism?" *Philosophical Quarterly* 47(1997): 516.

[23] William Alston, personal communication, April 2000.

conceptualized view of experience and awareness requires that we come into possession of the concepts by which we cooperate with the world by being initiated into our linguistic community. We learn cooperation with the world by learning cooperatively with others.

As a side note, I would here point out two troubling aspects of this picture, especially as they figure in Sellars and Rorty. First, Sellars and Rorty tend to equate initiation into the linguistic community with initiation into personhood. But of course, most animals cannot be so initiated at all; so there is some reason to reserve the notion of 'person' for membership in a species the individuals of which are capable of being initiated into the space of reasons.

Second, and following on the first aspect, it is an acknowledged consequence of McDowell's view that animals do not have experience—spontaneity is a necessary condition for something's being able to have that. So there is not something that nonhuman animals and mature human animals share in the same way—perceptual experience, to which is added conceptual capacities in our case. But what about small children? On the one hand, they do not have experience in the robust sense until initiated fully into the space of reasons. But does this mean that they have the same thing that nonhuman animals have, at least at early stages of their lives, until so initiated? I do not see how this could be the case: although their mode of responsiveness to their environment is not ours, it cannot, if it is to become ours, be entirely like that of nonhuman animals either; the gap between the two would simply be too large to be bridged. So some room needs to be made, as Sellars, for instance, seems to deny, for a kind of prelinguistic awareness in human children. Among other things, such a form of awareness would provide some discriminating form of orientation toward members of our species which guides our initial attempts at cooperation. I can't say more about this here, however.

What further advantages may be eked out of the cooperative metaphor, and what obligations are undertaken by use of that metaphor? The remainder of the chapter addresses these questions.

As regards the advantages, I wish to discuss two. The first concerns the actual norms of knowing. The second concerns Gettier-style difficulties.

That the activity of inquiry is normatively guided is, for most epistemologists, old news. But work is still done in trying to articulate both the nature and the explanation of the norms in question. Happily, the notion of cooperation is, as they say, fraught with ought, and I think in two helpful ways. First, there are distinct and well-articulated norms for cooperation, including straightforward deontological norms such as requirements of respect for the other. There are also requirements of fairness: genuine cooperation, precisely because of the role shared reasons play, is vitiated by subsumption of the shared reasons under self-interested or biased motives. Laziness is incompatible with genuine cooperation, as is uncritical acceptance of the results of cooperation—genuinely cooperating agents will not rest with the easily available or the mere appearance of success.

Another normative dimension of cooperation is the way in which it begs integration into wider spheres of practical activity, including wider spheres of cooperation, both through time and across persons. The goods that may be achieved in cooperation are rarely, if ever, achieved all at once, and broader cooperative schemes than two- or three-person schemes are often necessary for the achievement of significant and difficult goods. So cooperation brings with it a standing need for temporal and interpersonal extension.

A second normative aspect of cooperation is the respect in which the notion underdetermines what specific applications of its norms must be utilized. Because cooperation is highly dependent on the nature of the goods sought and the circumstances of the cooperative activity, it is a norm of cooperation that the application of norms must be sensitive to these particulars; hence there can be no final articulation of all the norms necessary to cooperation; rather, narrow casuistic reasoning and virtues such as prudence must be available for success in the particular.

Many of these normative dimensions seem applicable in the knowing context across both axes: mind-world relationships and person-person relationships, where those persons are engaged in knowing the world together. There are clear parallels in inquiry, for example, to the requirements of fairness and unbiasedness in interpersonal cooperation. Likewise, laziness, uncritical acceptance of results, or willingness to rest with mere appearance is ruled out.

Also important are the parallels to the norms demanding that inquiry be integrated into wider cooperative spheres, across both time and persons. Genuine inquiry cannot be carried out all at once, and the more committed one is to knowledge, the more one's commitment takes shape as a vocation for knowledge, to be carried out across a lifetime. Nor can significant inquiry be carried on in a vacuum: the notion of an intellectual or knowing community is not an accidental rider to the notion of genuine inquiry but a necessary component.

Moreover, these norms are then applicable as well to the relations between persons *in* the communities of inquiry and knowledge, so the metaphor of cooperation has normative implications for both axes of inquiry and knowledge. (I do not think I have here fully articulated those implications.)

Of course, when we are dealing with cooperation in a straightforward sense between persons, we have available to us not only a conception of norms to which *we* are responsible but also norms to which the cooperating agent is responsible. So, for example, we can blame our cooperating partner when cooperation breaks down. And it will seem highly suspect to think that similar opportunities are available in the case of inquiry into the world—can we blame the world for our failures? I'll postpone addressing this question; I promised early in the chapter that the metaphor of cooperation would have to bear much weight, and this is clearly part of the burden.

Let me first, though, say something quickly about Gettier-style problems. In Gettier-style cases, the three conditions traditionally thought sufficient for knowledge—belief, justification, and truth—are all met, but the agent does not have knowledge because of some sort of accidental relationship obtaining between the justifying conditions and the truth of the belief. We seem stuck between two desiderata: leaving room between the notions of justification and belief, and providing a set of sufficient conditions for knowledge.

I think the notion of mind-world cooperation I have been exploring would get around Gettier-style difficulties, in a way that parallels Zagzebski's virtue solution to Gettier cases. Zagzebski proposes that knowledge is "a state of belief arising out of acts of intellectual virtue."[24] She then distinguishes between acts arising from virtues and acts of virtue, reserving the latter notion as a 'success' term:

> An act of intellectual virtue A is an act that arises from the motivational component of A, is something a person with virtue A would (probably) do in the circumstances, is successful in achieving the end of the A motivation, and is such that the agent acquires a true belief (cognitive contact with reality) through the features of the act.[25]

Because success is built into the notion of an act of virtue—unlike the notion of an act arising out of a virtue—it follows that the definition just given provides a sufficient condition for knowledge while leaving the required gap between justification and belief.

But the mind-world cooperation metaphor, if it could be carried off, would provide exactly this benefit, and more. It would, first, solve Gettier problems.[26] Although Zagzebski thinks that there can be Gettier-style difficulties in ethics—someone performs an act from the virtue of justice, but due to accidents it is just only accidentally—it seems impossible that there should be Gettier-style cases of cooperation. Two agents cooperate *only* when they share a common intention, and although the intention might or might not miscarry, they cannot *share* an intention by accident.

The analogue to Gettier cases in cooperation would have to run like this: A intends to cooperate with B in Φing and takes B to have the same intention. But B does not have that intention. Nonetheless, B, by accident of some other intention, does what A expected she would do from a shared intention, so A and B jointly Φ, and A thinks they have cooperated in Φing. For this to be a Gettier case, we would have to say that A is correct that A and B have cooperated but that they have done so by accident. By analogy with Gettier cases in knowing, we would say: in knowing, the goal is truth, and A has gotten it, although by accident. Likewise, in cooperating, the goal is shared action, and A has gotten it, although by accident. But this is clearly false—the goal of genuine cooperation

---

[24] Zagzebski, *Virtues of the Mind,* 271.

[25] Ibid., 270.

[26] The original "Gettier problem" is in Edmund Gettier, "Is Justified True Belief Knowledge?" *Analysis* 23(1963): 121–23. I found Zagzebski's discussion, in *Virtues of the Mind,* and Plantinga's, in *Warrant and Proper Function,* to be extremely helpful.

is not a shared performance but a shared intention. Without this, no amount of fortune will provide that the goal of cooperation has been met.

Suppose, then, that knowers should be thought of as cooperating with the world in such a way as to share content. Such sharing of content is to be distinguished from the mere convergence of content that can come about by accident—a lucky guess, for example. So if there are cases of true belief arising out of genuine cooperation, then those beliefs will be instances of knowledge; and any belief that arises by fortuitous accident will not be a case of genuine cooperation and hence not genuine knowledge. The conditions are sufficient, but since it is possible to *think*, with good reason, that one is cooperating, when in fact one's partner is recalcitrant, there is in the case of inquiry the requisite gap between justification and knowledge.

What further advantage over Zagzebski's virtue account does this account offer? The answer, I think, is that cooperation is a notion more fundamental to ethics than is virtue: the virtues of cooperation are understood only in light (a) of cooperation and (b) of the ends of the cooperation. So although a virtue account will work in dissolving Gettier cases, a cooperative account gets more to the root of the issue. In a related way, I think we are led to wonder why intellectual virtues should be conducive to the right kind of cognitive contact with reality and what the nature of the contact is. Understanding experience and inquiry in terms of cooperation between mind and world gives us some answers to these questions.

I said earlier that I would indicate the ways in which my account differed from McDowell's. In one way, the attention I have just given to the norms of mind-world cooperation and to Gettier-style cases is one difference: McDowell does not have much interest in epistemology conceived in such a way as to make one worry about these problems. In the final part of this chapter I suggest a second possible difference. At issue is whether McDowell offers a robust enough ontology to make his view sufficiently realist.

Consider McDowell's worries about idealism in *Mind and World*. Because the world does not lie outside the realm of the thinkable, or alternately, because thought can extend all the way out to its object, McDowell acknowledges the worry that this leaves thought insufficiently constrained by reality. A typically worrisome passage might be the following: "There is no ontological gap between the sort of thing one can mean, or generally the sort of thing one can think, and the sort of thing that can be the case. When one thinks truly, what one thinks *is* the case."[27]

McDowell wants to insist, however, that we can effect the deletion of a boundary between thought and thinkable content "without slighting the independence of reality." But it seems to me that he addresses only one form of this worry. For we should distinguish between a concern for the independence of reality and a concern for the independence of the nature of reality. McDow-

[27] McDowell, *Mind and World*, 27.

ell's focus on the constraint that the world exerts in experience does not seem to go deep enough toward alleviating the worry that the rest of the world—the world of our 'worldview'—may be characterized in any number of ways consistent with the minimal constraint exerted upon us in experience.

McDowell's account of the relationship between our worldview and the world is fascinating. For example, when we have a visual experience, we take that experience to be "fraught with implications for the subject's cognitive situation in the world."[28] Because we draw upon our entire network of cognitive capacities in the visual experience, and because this wider network constitutes a worldview, we can understand our visual experience as a "glimpse" of a wider reality and as integrated into that wider reality "in a way that mirrors how the relevant concepts are integrated into the repertoire of spontaneity at large."[29] Further, spontaneity at large carries with it a "standing obligation" for continuous critical reflection, as the worldview is adjusted in response to experience. We want to get our worldview right, to share content with the world at large.

McDowell's empiricism, though, rightly has it that this broader sharing of content between worldview and world is made possible only through experience—it is in experience that the world, as it were, communicates itself to us. But what is communicated must be taken as significantly wider in scope than the details of experience, if our worldview is to be responsive to the world by being responsive to experience.

What must the world be like for this to be possible? Two needs, I think, must be met, which might be very difficult to swallow—these are the burdens of the cooperative metaphor. First, the world must be of a definite sort, and the way the world is must bear an appropriate relation to the way the world appears. McDowell does not like the idea of a state of affairs that could be called "the end of inquiry," a state in which the worldview would need no further revision—even as a mere ideal of reason, he seems to think it suspect. Well, fair enough, as an expression of reason's limited nature, perhaps, but some counter is needed to the possibility of endless revision of our worldview as well if we want to hold on to the notion of thought taking in how the world is through experiential glimpses. For mind and world successfully to cooperate in knowledge requires that the world be definite enough to be known, in some respects and at some points, and *when* known in these respects and points, there will be no need for further revision. So I think the tendency of some, like Hilary Putnam, who have been impressed by McDowell's account of experience, still to hold on to the notion that an endless number of descriptions of the world is possible must be resisted.[30]

---

[28] Ibid., 32.
[29] Ibid.
[30] Hilary Putnam, *The Threefold Cord: The John Dewey Lectures in Philosophy* (New York: Columbia University Press, 2000).

Second, not only must the world be of a definite sort, but the sort of thing it is must be such as to be knowable by us—it must be not only definite but intelligible for us. This, I think, is why in recent years John Haldane, who is, like me, impressed with McDowell's work, has stressed the importance of a return to Aristotelian form.[31] Form just is a kind of intelligibility, and as variably manifest in things and in thought, it is available to play exactly the right sort of role in the sharing of content between mind and world.

I don't want to argue that form is a necessary condition for the success of the cooperative picture. For example, some sort of ontology might be provided to go along with Alston's suggestion that facts and propositions have the same content. One could, perhaps, claim that the world is propositionally, or pre-propositionally, shaped in some way. But the cooperation metaphor's twin, and related, burdens of essentialism and intelligibility for us make, I think, ontological demands.[32]

Nor are these the only demands. If the cooperative picture makes ontological demands of the world, it also makes demands of the agent, demands many epistemologists have been unwilling to countenance. For cooperation is a richly normative notion, as are the surrounding concepts that I have drawn from in elaborating that notion. Central to the cooperative view is a picture of epistemological *agents*, responsible to the world in their acts of knowing. Such a picture simply cannot work in the absence of a high degree of doxastic control. This chapter has not provided a direct argument for the existence of such control. But if such control stands as a necessary condition for the cooperative account's truth, then if the cooperative account *is* true, there is modus ponens demonstrating the truth of voluntarism. And I hope to have given *some* reason for thinking the cooperative account is true.

I here add a word to any theistic readers. The cooperation metaphor grows stronger in a theistic context. First, the notion that there is a definite way the world is seems necessary in a theistic view. If there is a creator God, he must create in something like an analogous way to us: by way of a plan. And if God has such a plan, then there is, as it were, a way the world and the things of the world ought to be. Some form of essentialism is on the theistic horizon.

Second, I think it is no stretch, within the Judeo-Christian theistic worldview, to see the world as there for our contemplation. God himself contem-

---

[31] John Haldane, "Insight, Inference, and Intellection," *Proceedings of the American Catholic Philosophical Association* 73 (1999): 31–45; and "A Return to Form in the Philosophy of Mind," *Ratio* 11 (1998): 253–77.

[32] Since writing this chapter I have read David Braine's magnificent book *The Human Person: Animal and Spirit* (Notre Dame: University of Notre Dame Press, 1992). Braine also is concerned with providing an account of persons, nature, and knowledge that is more akin to cooperation than coordination. Any further work I do on this subject will certainly need to take account of Braine's approach, which follows up on both Saint Thomas Aquinas and the ordinary-language philosophy of the middle part of the twentieth century.

plates what he has done, and God gives the world to human beings; so a reasonable expectation is that we ought to do with the world in part what God has done: consider it and know it. On this view, our knowing the world can, in turn, be thought of as perfecting the world—it exists in part for our contemplation. So it fails itself when it fails us. And thus is it given reason to get involved in the mixed-up knowings of our benighted species.

10

"In Your Light, We See Light": The Continuing Viability of a Christocentric Epistemology

LAURA A. SMIT

I discovered the thirteenth-century Franciscan thinker Bonaventure in 1995, and soon after I started reading him I decided to take him as my teacher. He has been the focus of my study since then, and I expect that he will continue to be the focus of my study for the rest of my academic life. It is not that I agree with everything Bonaventure says, but when I approach Bonaventure I come to him with a certain presumption of wisdom. I read him with a hermeneutic of trust. I understand that he is the teacher and I am the student in our relationship, that I need to have a teachable spirit when reading what he has to say.

Therefore, when I realized that Bonaventure's approach to epistemology was radically different from what I'd been taught in philosophy class, I was intrigued. Bonaventure's epistemology is consistently Trinitarian and pervasively Christocentric. Whenever a human being knows anything true, Christ is at the center of that act of knowing, and the other two persons of the Trinity are also taking part in that act. The person of Christ is the key both to knowing ourselves and to knowing the external, sensible world. This approach is not unique to Bonaventure—he himself would say that he's simply learning from Augustine—but he does articulate this approach more systematically and fully than anyone else I've encountered. As I read what he had to say about epistemology, I found it deeply compelling, particularly because it is an approach to epistemology that emphasizes our radical dependence on God at every moment of our lives. When I started sharing this approach with other Christians, they almost always reacted as I had, by finding it deeply compelling, even moving . . . with the significant exception of my colleagues in analytic philosophy. They, for the most part, found this approach incompatible with the ways they were used to thinking about epistemology, and their first response was to dismiss Bonaventure's approach as theology rather than philosophy. The focus of this chapter is therefore on bridging this comprehension gap.

It has become clear to me that the major difficulty for contemporary philosophers in understanding Bonaventure is that within the big jigsaw puzzle that is epistemology, the pieces he is focusing on are different from those on which most contemporary philosophers focus. This is a problem if one listens to Bonaventure with the thought that he is addressing the same questions contemporary epistemology always addresses; then his answers simply don't make sense. But once the listener gets oriented in the right part of the puzzle, things becomes much more clear, and at that point this difference of focus is revealed not as a problem but as a strength. Since Bonaventure is addressing questions that very few people address today, he may be able to help us fill a gap in our understanding of epistemology.

When Bonaventure talks about knowing something true, he is speaking of a very specific range of things. He lives in the expectation that someday God is going to shake the heavens and the earth, and everything that is ephemeral or inessential will fall away, revealing the city with firm foundations, *a kingdom that cannot be shaken.*[1] He wants to be invested in that kingdom. We can't know how to invest our time, our resources, our attention, or our love unless we can distinguish what is essential from what is not. As Bonaventure sees the world, it's as if everything is camouflaged, or covered with trompe-l'oeil paintings. If we're taken in by that, then we have no true knowledge. Somehow we need to find a way to penetrate the camouflage and see the true, essential, lasting nature of things. That is what Bonaventure is seeking. Notice that he is not focused only on what's *necessary*. Since only God is necessary and everything else is contingent, that would be a very restricted realm for knowledge. Rather, Bonaventure is concerned only with what is *essential*.

Bonaventure starts with the assumption that we may call something true only if it is essential, because only things that are essential are lasting. Things that are changeable and ephemeral can't be true since truth by its very nature is lasting and essential. Clearly, Bonaventure is standing in the long, venerable tradition of Christian Neoplatonism. But as it happens, in this instance I think Bonaventure has another reason for making his assumption about the nature of truth, a reason that I believe should carry weight with Christian philosophers, even those who reject the framework of Neoplatonism.

The reason he makes this assumption is scriptural. In the Gospel of John, Jesus explicitly identifies himself as the Truth (John 14:6), saying "I am the way, and the truth, and the life." This self-identification seems intrinsically different from most of the other "I am" sayings in the Gospel of John, such as "I am the good shepherd" or "I am the vine." Those are clearly metaphorical sayings, in which terms that apply primarily to human life are being metaphorically or analogically applied to Christ. In the context of John 14, however, the claim to be "the way, the truth, and the life" seems quite different. Jesus has just said that no one can reach the Father except through him; he really is the only point of

[1] Hebrews 12:27, 28 NRSV.

access, the only way. This is quite literally true. It is the incarnation that establishes a point of contact between God and humanity, so Jesus in his body is the contact point, the way to God. Similarly, if we take seriously the sustaining role of the second person of the Trinity in the creation, he really is the life. Anything that is living is necessarily participating in God. In the same way, when Jesus claims to be truth, he is saying something more than that he is a truthful person. He is truth in a preeminent sense, just as he is the preeminent source of life and the preeminent point of access to the Father. This statement in John 14 is thus in a different rhetorical category than statements about being a vine, or a door, or a shepherd. These terms in John 14 are properly primarily applied to God and only analogically applied to anything or anyone else.

The Gospel of John puts this claim of Jesus to be the truth in the context of an understanding of Jesus as the Word, or Logos, who reveals God and sustains life. David Crump writes about the concept of truth in the Gospel of John:

> The incarnation of God in the Logos is presented as the supreme disclosure of the Lord who revealed himself to Moses in the giving of the Law at Sinai (1:17). Jesus shows us God as he really is. This assertion sets the stage for John's use of "truth." Contrary to Greek background, truth is personal, not merely intellectual; truth is acquired through the revelation of God, not through mental application; truth is not abstract, but has been individually revealed in history. It is also reminiscent of the Jewish view of both Torah and Wisdom.
>
> *God Is Truth.* As the revealer of truth, Jesus only teaches what the Father has given to him (3:33; 8:40; 18:37). The Father *is* the truth. His eternal reality is ultimate reality. There are no external standards to evaluate his reality; according to John, his truth can only be accepted through faith in Jesus as the one who comes down from heaven. . . . By perfectly testifying to the Father, [Jesus] also testifies to himself (8:18), because he and his Father are one (10:30). To know Jesus is to know the Father (14:9). Consequently, Jesus can say that he, too, *is* the truth (14:6). Of course, this is commensurate with the prologue's claim that the Logos is God (1:1, 18). John presents Jesus as the final revelation of God, who is himself God; the one against whom all claims to meaning and reality are to be evaluated.[2]

To those who would understand Jesus' claim to be the truth in what is often seen as a more "Hebrew" way, in terms of faithfulness or "troth," Crump points out that "the common distinction made between Greek and Hebrew meanings for truth simply does not work linguistically." Such contemporary biblical scholarship supports rather than denies Bonaventure's understanding of Jesus as the truth.

The Gospel of John is not the only place in Scripture in which Christ is identi-

---

[2] "Truth," *Dictionary of Jesus and the Gospels*, ed. Joel B. Green, Scott McKnight, and I. Howard Marshall (Downers Grove, Ill.: InterVarsity Press, 1992), 861.

fied with truth and knowledge. In the Letter to the Colossians, Jesus is identified as the one "in whom all things hold together." Colossians 2:3 says that "in him are hidden all the treasures of wisdom and of knowledge." Later in that same chapter we read that we are not to be captured by worldly philosophy but instead are to understand everything in light of Christ. We are to fix our minds on the things that are above, hidden in him. For Bonaventure, as for Augustine and Anselm before him, and indeed as for the vast majority of Christians throughout most of Christian history, passages such as these suggest that when we are talking about the human act of knowing the truth, the person of Christ is relevant to such conversation. For Bonaventure, as for Augustine and Anselm, the identification of Christ with the Truth suggests that all other experiences of truth that I have in life must somehow relate back to Christ, must somehow be participating in Christ. *That* is why it seems inappropriate to talk about things that are ephemeral, inessential, or not lasting as if they are true. How can something inessential participate in Christ? Bonaventure's assumptions about truth are based not first and foremost on his Neoplatonism but on his understanding of the Bible.

Of course, this raises a few other questions. Bonaventure assumes that Scripture and the tradition of Christian faith should play a role in the work of philosophy, not just in the work of theology. Is he right about this? Should a Christian philosopher be obliged to take scriptural statements into account? Should a Christian philosopher who is discussing issues of truth and knowing have to discuss the person of Jesus Christ? Some Christian philosophers would say no, saying that considering how the person of Christ is relevant to issues of truth and knowing is not a philosophical project but a theological one and that therefore philosophers are free to disregard such questions. Alvin Plantinga summarizes this objection in his article "Augustinian Christian Philosophy":

> The objector claims that if, as a scholar, you start from what you know by way of faith, if you employ as premises in your arguments propositions that you know by faith (rather than by way of reason), then your results will really be theology rather than philosophy or psychology or sociology or whatever. If you start from theological convictions in a given area—in understanding love, or humor, or aggression, or knowledge, or abstract objects, for example—then any conclusions you come to will be dependent upon theological convictions and will themselves, in consequence, be theology. Theology in, theology out, as the computer literati say. And while a theological understanding of these phenomena may indeed be desirable or necessary, it is still theology; it isn't philosophy. . . . To have the latter, we must keep ourselves pure and unspotted from theology.[3]

Such insistence on disciplinary boundaries seems to me (and to Plantinga) to be profoundly wrongheaded. If it should happen that the second person of the Trinity really *is* relevant to our perceptions of reality, our knowledge of truth,

---

[3] "Augustinian Christian Philosophy," *The Monist* 75 (July 1992): 304.

and our epistemic functioning, then any theories about those issues which fail to take him into account will not simply be incomplete; they will be wrong.

In the face of the scriptural claims about Jesus Christ being the Truth, it seems to me that Christian philosophers have three options. First, it is possible to discount those claims either by taking a low view of scriptural authority or by demythologizing it in some way. Second, it is possible to take the claims of Scripture seriously and therefore to conclude that philosophy may not speak to epistemological questions. Philosophers may choose to turn over all epistemological questions to the theologians. Third, a philosopher may join Bonaventure—and Plantinga, and me—in being more concerned with the question at hand than with disciplinary boundaries. Again quoting from Plantinga:

> According to the Augustinian tradition . . . what we need and want, in studying a given area, is the best total understanding we can get, using all the resources at our command; the question whether that best understanding should be called 'theology' on the one hand, or 'philosophy' (or 'sociology', or 'psychology' or whatever) on the other is of secondary interest.[4]

Bonaventure was nothing if not an Augustinian and believed that Christians who do philosophy should do Christian philosophy. The starting point for Christian philosophy is faith, without which we can have no understanding. This means—among other things—that the data of revelation are relevant to philosophical reasoning and that the person of Christ has claims on that process.

Bonaventure considers it obvious "that a beginning should be made from the center (medium), that is, from Christ. For He Himself is the Mediator between God and [people], holding the central position in all things. . . . Hence it is necessary to start from Him if [anyone] wants to reach Christian wisdom." He makes that statement in his *Commentary on the Six Days of Creation*, a commentary known as the *Hexaemeron*, in which he explores the nature of created reality.[5] He begins that commentary by quoting one of his favorite verses from Colossians, a verse to which I referred earlier. He says, "Our intent [in this work] is to show that in Christ are hidden all the treasures of wisdom and knowledge, and that He Himself is the central point of all understanding" (*Hex*, I.10.11). He bases this claim on an assumption that he makes explicit in the preceding sentence: "It is impossible to understand a creature except through that by which it was made." For this reason, "it is necessary that the true Word go before thee." It is because God made us and everything that exists that we cannot understand ourselves or anything that exists without reference to God. Although all three persons of the Trinity are involved in the illumination of our

---

[4] Ibid.

[5] *Collations on the Six Days (Hexaemeron)*, trans. José de Vinck, Vol. V of *The Works of Bonaventure* (Paterson, N.J.: St. Anthony Guild Press, 1970). Cited hereafter as *Hex*.

minds that is necessary to penetrate the camouflage of the world, it is Christ the Son who focuses that illumination. The Father is the source of everything that is, but it is the Word who communicates and articulates the essential nature of every creature. All the ideas that are conceived by the Father are made concrete in the Son, who is the Exemplar of the Father's nature. In the person of the Son, the Father has expressed the fullness of his potency. Every idea that exists in the Father is expressed in the Son, who "so to speak is His Art" (*Hex*, I.13). It is the Word who speaks everything into existence.

To have certain, true knowledge of something, I must penetrate the illusion with which it is surrounded and see its essential nature. That is possible only if my intellect has illuminating contact with what Bonaventure calls the eternal reason of what I am trying to know, that is, its likeness as expressed in Christ. This is true for all certain knowledge, not just when we get to heaven someday, but already now, in our fallen state; and this is true not just for Christians but for any people who know anything true, whether or not they realize that they are having such contact. Bonaventure does not claim that such illumination is the only complete cause of knowledge, nor does he think that our access to God's mind is direct and unimpeded. If it were, there would be no appreciable difference between seeing that $2 + 2 = 4$ and the beatific vision. No, for us eternal reasons are "known obscurely and as in a mirror" (1 Corinthians 13:12). Bonaventure insists, however, that divine illumination is more than a general effect of God's creating work. As I understand him, Aquinas would say that God gives us this illumination all at once up front as part of our created nature. Bonaventure thinks that illumination requires a constant relationship of dependency. Just as we are constantly dependent on the existence of light in order to see anything with our eyes, so too we are constantly dependent on the presence of Christ in order to understand anything with our minds. Such illumination is necessary in order for us to know anything with certainty.

Bonaventure's epistemology has four tiers, or levels. The first level is symbolic or sensory knowledge, by which we know the sensible world. The second is speculative or rational knowledge, by which we know our own inner life. The third is direct knowledge of God, and finally, there is the possibility of ecstatic union with God as the highest form of knowing. Bonaventure himself recognizes a methodological shift within level two, the knowledge of ourselves. Knowledge of the external world and the lowest form of self-knowledge are forms of knowing available to philosophy, whereas knowing oneself as the image of God and knowing God directly transcend the limits of natural knowledge and depend on special revelation. For now, we will consider the very first level: that is, symbolic or sensory knowing of the external world.

In the Son is contained the essential likeness of all that is. This essential likeness is not the same as the likeness of things that we perceive and hold in our minds. Bonaventure says:

There is one kind of likeness caused by the truth of the thing outside the knower, and about this likeness it is true that it never as perfectly expresses the thing as the thing itself would, were the thing present within the soul; and God does not know by means of this kind of likeness. But there is another kind of likeness which is the very expressive truth of the thing known and is precisely a likeness because it is the truth of the thing. Such a likeness expresses the thing more perfectly than the thing can express itself, since the thing receives its structure of expression from that truth and likeness; and according to such a likeness the most perfect knowledge is obtained and God does know by means of such a likeness.[6]

God's knowledge of an object is more expressive of that object than the object is expressive of itself. When God knows a tree, the true "treeness" of that tree is fully expressed, as it could not be without God's knowledge. The likeness that is "the truth of" every created thing, of every creature, is fully expressed and fully known in the Son.

Through illumination, we may also glimpse the likeness that is "the truth of the thing"; we may come to have true knowledge of the external world. As Wordsworth says: "with an eye made quiet by the power / Of harmony, and the deep power of joy, / We see into the life of things."[7] Bonaventure gives a name to that "power of harmony" by which we are able to "see into the life of things"; he calls that power the Word, or the Logos. Christ is "the power of harmony and the deep power of joy" who illuminates our sense perceptions and our imaginations so that we may "see into the life of things."

Bonaventure teaches that we are the world in microcosm, or—seen the other way round—that the world is a macrocosm that corresponds to us.[8] Because a medieval person saw the world as a macrocosm of his own being, he would have experienced himself not as isolated or fully distinct from that world but rather as intimately and literally connected to it. As Owen Barfield puts it, "In his relation to his environment, the man of the middle ages was rather less like an island, rather more like an embryo, than we are."[9] If there were no correspondence between ourselves and the world, there could be no communication, but as it is, our senses operate through the medium of light to apprehend the world. The exterior world is a manifestation of the interior world. When we understand the world of sense perception, it reveals to us the inner world of other beings. Without illumination, however, that connection we have with the external world is lifeless, like an electrical wire that has no current running through it.

The perceptible world enters us through our senses. In some way, we receive within ourselves those things that we experience. Bonaventure con-

---

[6] *Commentary on the Sentences*, Vol. I of *Opera Omnia*, Quaracchi edition (Florence: College of St. Bonaventure, 1882), I.35.q1, ad. 3, translation courtesy of Tim Noone.

[7] William Wordsworth, "Lines Above Tintern Abbey."

[8] *Journey of the Mind to God (Itinerarium)*, trans. Philotheus Boehner, ed. Stephen Brown (Indianapolis: Hackett, 1993), II.2. Cited hereafter as *Itin.*

[9] *Saving the Appearances: A Study in Idolatry*, 2d ed. (Middletown, Conn.: Wesleyan University Press, 1988), 78.

ceives of human beings not as autonomous centers of sense perception but rather as created beings among beings, receiving sensory input in the form of particles of light and smell and taste, all of which enable us to interact with the world around us. He observes, "The whole of this visible world . . . enters the human soul through apprehension. These visible and external things are what first enter the soul through the doors of the five senses" (*Itin*, II.4). Through sense perception, the external world is united with our soul's inner world.

Through the imagination, our mind then converts these sense perceptions to an image of the thing perceived. As Bonaventure uses the word, imagination does not create a subjective response to sense perception but rather sets aside one's preconceptions in order to receive the message of the perception. He calls imagination the mind's "primary collating power."[10] Imagination brings the object into focus so that it may be perceived with greater clarity. Imagination is a matter not of creativity but rather of recognition or discovery, which should result in epiphany, not in invention. This recognition is possible because of the presence of Christ illuminating the eye of the mind, enabling us to arrive at true knowledge of what we perceive rather than illusions. As Zachary Hayes says, "One sees the objects of experience," that is, these images based on sense perceptions, "in the light shed on them by the eternal reasons," which are contained in Christ, the Word.[11]

In the act of illuminated imagination, when the soul pays loving attention to an object, that object is then offered back to God as known. Our knowing is a priestly act. Bonaventure teaches that "the human intellect was made to grasp great things and many things in a grand and manifold way, like some noble mirror made to reflect the whole complex of the created world, not only naturally, but also supernaturally" (*Brev*, Pro. 3). The soul becomes a mirror in which known objects are received and reflected. The virtuous soul is able to receive sense perceptions and process them in a way that reveals the splendor of the objects being observed. This is also true for perceptions of concepts, or "intelligible things," and for self-knowledge, though for the purposes of this chapter, we are considering only sense perception. God's design for human beings is that we will understand, will grasp the truth of the things around us. In doing this, we reflect the image of Christ, who, as the Exemplar, contains or grasps the essential forms of all that exists. In perceiving the world, we are able to reflect and understand what we perceive in the same way that we are reflected and understood by Christ, and so in our knowing we are being like Christ.

For Bonaventure, it is when objects are known by a human knower that their

---

[10] *Breviloquium*, trans. José de Vinck, Vol. II of *The Works of Bonaventure* (Paterson, N.J.: St. Anthony Guild Press, 1963), 2.9.5. Cited hereafter as *Brev*.

[11] Zachary Hayes, *The Hidden Center: Spirituality and Speculative Christology in St. Bonaventure*, ed. Cyprian J. Lynch, O.F.M., *Franciscan Pathways* (St. Bonaventure, N.Y.: Franciscan Institute, 1992), 58.

nature as traces or vestiges (*vestigia*) of God is revealed. This knowing and reflecting of objects is the proper function of art in the symbolist tradition. Human artistic expression, when it responds to and attempts to express an object of nature, may be—indeed should be—closer to the truth of that object than is the phenomenon itself. It is in this sense that the Son is the art of the Father, for in the Son the objects' essences are themselves expressed. All our knowing is meant to be "artistic" in this way, though obviously we may fail to bring our knowing to this level much of the time.

Like many Augustinian thinkers who preceded him, Bonaventure thus teaches that all true knowledge is rooted in Christ and that Christ, the incarnate Word, is the solution to two ongoing epistemological problems. First, there is the problem of how finite humans are able to know an infinite God. Jesus, the incarnate Son, bridges the gap between the supernatural and incorporeal essence of God and our temporal and corporeal nature, because in him "the fullness of God" was contained in physical human form and incarnate within time. Second, there is the problem of how human mental faculties are able to interact with the physical, sensory world. This knowledge is also channeled through Christ, even for those who are unaware of his presence or his work, because the Son is Truth "immutable, undisturbed, and unconfined" (*Hex*, I.13). In the incarnation, this immutable and timeless Truth enters time and becomes accessible. This does not just mean that now we can know God; it explains how we can know anything at all. Through the incarnation, God, as it were, charges the human timeline with epistemic current, creating connections between mind and body, spiritual and physical, and even finite and infinite.

It is in the power of the incarnate Christ that sinful human beings are equipped with the ability to know the external, sensory world and see the traces of God that are there. Sin has left us "bent over" so that we "sit in darkness," the mind blinded by ignorance and the flesh blinded by concupiscence, so that we are incapable of seeing the light of God's emanating presence

> unless grace comes to [our] aid—with justice to fight concupiscence, and with knowledge and wisdom to oppose ignorance. These effects are brought about through Jesus Christ, who has become for us God-given wisdom, and justice, and sanctification, and redemption. . . . He has taught the knowledge of truth . . . so that . . . we may rightly use [both] sensible things [and] intelligible things. (*Itin*, I.7)

In order, then, that we may "rightly use" both concrete objects and intelligible concepts, we must experience the grace of Christ, so that we may avoid sin and share in his wisdom. Otherwise, we will not be able to see the traces of God in the world around us. But grace is not just necessary for such God-directed right use. All true knowledge depends on receiving some measure of gracious illumination, for as Stephen Clark has observed, "knowledge is only possible, and only obligatory, if we have already got the Truth, our Master, deep within our selves."[12] Certain knowing is possible only in the context of this experience of grace. Bonaventure teaches that even the scientific mode of investigation, which requires using the senses and the imagination to observe "things in themselves" in terms of their "weight, number, and measure" categorized by "mode, species, and order, as well as substance, power, and activity" (*Itin*, I.11), presupposes illumination in order to reach truth.

Part of the intellect's "proper condition" is to be illuminated by God. The defect of will that results in ignorance consists of the willful rejection of this illumination. All that we know is courtesy of God's gracious revelation through the illuminating work of Christ. This work may be resisted by the intellect, just as the illuminating work of the sun may be resisted if we close our eyes. But our nature is to receive illumination, just as it is our nature to live in a sunlit world. We have been made with the capacity to receive light from God, to receive the impress of God's nature on ourselves and be formed by it. This capacity is not based on reason or analysis. It is the knowing of recognition, of insight, of intuition. It is the experience of desire that itself is knowledge. What Stephen Brown calls the "ideal and necessary aspects" of things, the deeper realities that we grasp behind the sense perception, "shine forth beyond any doubt as infallibly true," and so they clearly transcend not only the temporal world but even our reason.[13] In order for us to know anything, then, there must be an intersection of concrete reality, divine illumination, and our own light of reason.

We are able to perceive the sensible world and make coherent judgments about it only because we have an eternal standard against which to compare the temporal. We may not be consciously aware of that standard or light, but without it we would be able to see nothing. Brown uses the analogy of looking at stained-glass windows from within a church on a sunny day. The colors of the windows are visible only because the sun is shining through the glass, even though the viewer does not see the sun directly and may not even think about the need for the sun's illumination for the colors to be seen. In the same way, our perception of any truth is possible only because we see it in the illumination of the absolute standard of Christ's emanation. As T. S. Eliot says in "Choruses from the Rock," his hymn to the "Light invisible," which is "too bright for mortal vision":

Our gaze is submarine, our eyes look upward
And see the light that fractures through unquiet water.
We see the light but see not whence it comes.[14]

We see the light in that all our vision is really a vision of the light, by virtue of the light, but we cannot see the source of the light itself.

[12] *A Parliament of Souls: Limits and Renewals 2* (Oxford: Clarendon Press, 1990), 111.
[13] Notes to *Itin*, II.9.
[14] T. S. Eliot, *The Complete Poems and Plays, 1909–1950* (New York: Harcourt, Brace and World, 1962).

Bonaventure believes that there are three particular mental acts that require divine illumination in order to function properly, and it is at this point that his discussion becomes more Trinitarian and less Christocentric. The first is the act of memory. Bonaventure points out that most knowing is of particular beings, which the understanding must then judge and categorize. But such judgments presuppose a standard against which the particular may be compared. That standard is Being-in-itself, a standard that we hold in memory. He asks, "For how could the intellect know that a specific being is defective and incomplete if it had no knowledge of the Being that is free from all defect?" (*Itin*, III.3). For Bonaventure, this is clearly a rhetorical question. The intellect could know nothing if the connection were severed to Being per se, "this first Being which all creatures represent. But This name is written in all Things: and it is upon these conditions of being that the most certain reasonings are founded" (*Hex*, 10.17). Bonaventure uses the word *memory* to talk about our ability to retain an image or concept over time, and he should not be understood as if referring to some past life or some pre-conception existence. We are born with certain knowledge already present to us, knowledge that we access through the work of memory. The power of memory is seen in our ability to process events from the past, present, and future simultaneously, albeit not with the true simultaneity that characterizes God's perspective.[15] The power of memory is seen in our immediate apprehension of basic geometric figures and principles. The power of memory is seen in our direct apprehension of other a priori knowledge, such as the first principles that are the foundation of all sciences. Knowing God, knowing ourselves, and knowing the world around us—all these forms of knowing are in some sense simply recognizing what I already know implicitly through participation in the mind of God. Even though we now live in shadows, we are still illumined by enough light that there are truths we may recognize. As Xavier Seubert says, for Bonaventure, "the enemy of light is thus not darkness, but forgetfulness."[16]

The second act of the mind is understanding. Illumination assists our natural power of understanding by connecting the intellect directly to the Truth. Bonaventure says:

Our understanding is joined to eternal Truth Itself, and if this light does not teach, no truth can be grasped with certitude. You are able, then, to see within yourself the Truth that teaches you, if desires and sensory images do not hinder you and become as clouds between you and the ray of Truth. (*Itin*, III.3)

Since Bonaventure assumes that Truth is changeless, only those things that are lasting may accurately be described as true. But our mind is not unchanging and

---

[15] *Disputed Questions on the Mystery of the Trinity*, trans. Zachary Hayes, ed. George Marcil, O.F.M., Vol. III of *The Works of St. Bonaventure* (St. Bonaventure, N.Y.: Franciscan Institute, 1979), q5, a1.

[16] Lecture notes, "Bonaventure's Aesthetics," Saint Bonaventure University, July 14, 1997.

can know that which is unchanging only when assisted by divine illumination. Bonaventure teaches this clearly in the *Hexaemeron*:

> For from all eternity the Father begets a Son similar to Himself and expresses Himself and a likeness similar to Himself, and in so doing He expresses the sum total of His [active] potency; He expresses what He can do, and most of all, what He wills to do, and He expresses everything in Him, that is, in the Son or in that very center, which so to speak is His Art. Hence this Center is Truth; and it is proved by Augustine and other saints that "Christ having His chair in heaven teaches inwardly"; nor can any truth be known in any way whatsoever except through this Truth. For the same is the principle both of being and of knowing. If, then, as the Philosopher says, the knowable is eternal as such, it necessarily follows that nothing can be known except through a truth that is immutable, undisturbed, and unconfined. (1.13)

Christ himself is the "immutable, undisturbed, and unconfined" Truth. He, "by necessity, must be the central one of the Persons" (*Hex*, 1.14). As the Art of the Father, Christ contains within himself the essence of all that is. If we are to understand anything that is, to have any real knowledge of lasting truth, we must apprehend the essence of what we are trying to know, not just its accidental instantiation. Since our understanding is limited, the only way we can apprehend an eternal essence is to see it within the person of Christ. It is our connection to Christ that makes it possible for the power of the understanding to function, even in the case of those people who are unaware of Christ's presence. How this works has already been discussed.

Finally, Bonaventure turns to the third act of the mind: love. Bonaventure points out that the mind not only makes judgments and distinctions of description and categorization, which are dependent on memory, but also makes judgments of value and of ethical behavior. Such judgments are possible only because we have an intrinsic love of goodness. This presupposition of a standard of judgment has sometimes been used as a proof for the existence if not of God then at least of a reality beyond the material. But Bonaventure would find the attacks of materialism counterintuitive and would not have thought to defend against them. He is concerned with moving in the opposite direction—explaining the human ability to make valid judgments and distinctions on the basis of a shared perception of some standard of Goodness that we all naturally desire. It is also because we desire, or love, the Good that we desire to be happy. Our innate desire for Good is seen in all our desires for happiness, even though in practice those desires may be misplaced. The problem is that our happiness is to be found in surrender to one who is unchanging, in being possessed by the Goodness we desire, but we persist in seeking happiness through acquisition, through the act of possessing. "This is the death of men: they desire indeed to possess and retain" (*Hex*, 5.3). Knowing is meant to be enjoyment not use, or *frui* not *uti* (to use Augustine's distinction), concerned with attention not consumption.

In his analysis of these three acts, Bonaventure establishes a typology by which the natural soul, even if unredeemed, is ineluctably connected to each person of the Godhead. "See, therefore, how close the soul is to God, and how, through their activity, memory leads us to Eternity, intelligence to Truth, and the elective faculty to the highest Good" (*Itin*, III.4). The innate memory of Being per se, such as accounts for the existence of a priori knowledge, connects the soul to the Father. The innate understanding of Truth, such that we may come to know things and other people in terms of their essence, is a direct perception of the mind of Christ, in whom all forms are hid. The innate love for Goodness is expressed in every soul as a desire to be happy, a desire animated by the Holy Spirit, who—as love—is the bond uniting us to God.

Bonaventure wants his readers to become attentive to a dynamic in knowledge which is operating even when we are unaware of it: all our knowledge is dependent on our contact with God as Being, as Truth, and as Goodness. We can know no other being; we cannot even know nonbeing except by presupposing that something exists, which is to presuppose Being. Whether or not we realize it, this is to presuppose God. Every epistemic act is an act of radical dependency on God, who is the ground of Reality. Being is self-evident, undeniable, present, and open to intuition and direct apprehension. It does not need to be reached by reason but can be seen directly through the threefold illuminating work of God.

To see that all existing things coincide in Christ is to be open to the Logos that structures creation, to see into the nature of reality. Sin results in the distracting of our attention whereas the power of illumination refocuses us on Christ. Clark affirms this same idea: "If we wish to see things clearly and to see them whole we must believe that there is a divine Logos that is also human. Without that belief we may as well despair."[17] It is only through the illuminating presence of the Word, or Logos, within us that any understanding is possible. It is only through a love for Goodness that such understanding may be rightly ordered and directed.

It is easy not to pay attention to our dependence on God's illuminating presence. Bonaventure speaks of "the blindness of the intellect which does not consider that which it sees before all others and without which it can recognize nothing" (*Itin*, V.4). It is not that the intellect doesn't see Being, or Truth, or Goodness, but that it sees without awareness. God may easily become part of the taken-for-granted reality to which we fail to pay attention.

But just as the eye, intent on the various differences of color, does not see the light through which it sees other things, or if it does see, does not notice it, so our mind's eye, intent on particular and universal beings, does not notice that Being which is beyond all categories, even though it comes first to the mind, and through it, all other things. . . . Thus our mind, accustomed as it is

[17] *God's World and the Great Awakening: Limits and Renewals 3* (Oxford: Clarendon Press, 1991), 221.

to the opaqueness in beings and the phantasms of visible things, seems to itself to be seeing nothing when it gazes upon the light of the highest being. It
does not understand that this very darkness is the supreme illumination of
our mind, just as when the eye sees pure light, it seems to be seeing nothing.
(*Itin*, V.4)

This is the darkness of weak eyes, which are not accustomed to perceiving much
light directly and which find that light blinding. If we wish to strengthen our
eyes and to know things truly, we must start by accepting the work of Christ,
the Truth. Through him we may eventually come to a clearer vision of everything else.

PART IV
Departmental Realisms and Antirealisms

11

Thomism with a Realist Face:
A Response to Hilary Putnam

GAVIN T. COLVERT

Hilary Putnam's essay "Thoughts Addressed to an Analytical Thomist" seeks to engage analytically inclined Thomists in a dialogue about the status of religious discourse, specifically claims concerning the existence and nature of God.[1] Although his presentation is sympathetic to Aquinas's thought, including the acknowledgment of the possibility of formally valid causal arguments for God's existence, Putnam offers some serious challenges to the Thomistic position. The purpose of this chapter is to offer a coherent response, from a Thomistic viewpoint, to Putnam's invitation to dialogue. Put succinctly, it will demonstrate the thesis that Aquinas can simultaneously retain a commitment to metaphysical realism and accommodate much of Putnam's concern that recognition of the truth conditions of religious discourse must occur within religious practice. Indeed, the analytical Thomist can even accept a version of Putnam's more generalized claim, upon which his view of religious discourse is based, that description of the world is to a certain extent 'interest-relative.' Given the limits of space, the extent of this inquiry must be circumscribed within certain well-defined limits. The latter part of Putnam's article adds a brief interpretation and discussion of the theory of analogical predication. Significantly, Putnam suggests that Aquinas's attempts to explain analogical predication may ultimately collapse into a kind of Maimonidean equivocation and that theological language is "*sui generis.*"[2] A full account of the Thomistic position concerning the nature of religious language would require a thorough study of Aquinas's doctrine of analogy showing that analogical predication is consistent with Aquinas's metaphysical realism. Since it is beyond the scope of the present consideration to undertake that task, this chapter will concentrate upon laying the groundwork for such an interpretation by arguing that more general considerations about

---

[1] Hilary Putnam, "Thoughts Addressed to an Analytical Thomist," *The Monist* 80 (October 1997): 487–99.

[2] Ibid., 496–97.

the nature of religious language can be integrated into a coherent version of Thomistic metaphysical realism.

A CENTRAL TERMINOLOGICAL ISSUE: INCOMMENSURABILITY

Although this analysis will have occasion to disagree with elements of Putnam's account of religious language, it will also conclude that the gap between Putnam and Thomists is not as wide as it might at first appear to be. To borrow a phrase from Donald Davidson, we may be 'words' rather than 'worlds' apart.[3] A central tenet of Putnam's interpretation of religious language is that it is meaningful but "incommensurable" with ordinary empirical descriptions and scientific discourse.[4] This character of theological discourse is substantiated for Putnam by the claim that the meaning of theological concepts can be established only from within the context of religious practice, a line of thought that is deeply indebted to his reading of Wittgenstein.[5] There is bound to be a difference of opinion with Thomists concerning Putnam's thesis that religious discourse is incommensurable with ordinary empirical language. After all, this thesis is closely related to his more general internal realist program. But the extent of this disagreement is very difficult to establish without a clear understanding of the term 'incommensurability' itself. To complicate matters further, what precisely Putnam means by incommensurability is difficult to ascertain, since he explicitly distinguishes his use of the term from its typical application in theories of scientific discourse.[6] Furthermore, he rejects the notion that a *theory* of the incommensurability of religious and ordinary discourse can be given apart from an understanding of religious discourse itself.[7] This view in turn is based upon a more general claim about the nature of all language, inspired by Wittgenstein, which holds that the meaning of terms in a language cannot be established except by a grasp of the use of those terms in the context of the particular language game in which they are deployed.[8]

Fortunately, despite these theoretical obstacles, Putnam does offer some insight into the relationship between religious and ordinary discourse, which he views as essentially threefold. First, the meaningfulness of religious language is internal to the practice of religious forms of life. Although nonbelievers are not automatically excluded from recognizing the truth conditions for religious

---

[3] Donald Davidson, *Inquiries into Truth and Interpretation* (Oxford: Oxford University Press, 1984), 189.

[4] Putnam, "Thoughts," 491.

[5] Ibid., 498, also 492–93. Putnam is deeply influenced in this regard by a short work containing the hand-recorded notes of a series of lectures given by Wittgenstein on the nature of religious belief: see Ludwig Wittgenstein, *Lectures and Conversations on Aesthetics, Psychology, and Religious Belief*, ed. Cyril Barrett (Berkeley: University of California Press, 1966).

[6] Putnam, "Thoughts," 499 n. 9.

[7] Ibid.

[8] Hilary Putnam, "God and the Philosophers," in *Midwest Studies in Philosophy, Vol. XXI: Philosophy of Religion*, ed. Peter French et al. (Notre Dame: University of Notre Dame Press, 1997), 177.

statements, they must be able to enter the language game as "engaged players" in order to evaluate truth claims.[9] He stresses that although the potentiality for such imaginative engagement is available to every human being, for some it is not a genuine possibility given their circumstances in life.[10] Second, religious language cannot be translated into a neutral descriptive language that does not make use of religious terms. That is, it is nonreducible. His target here is a version of reductive naturalism, such as that of Bernard Williams's 'absolute conception of the world', which dismisses religious discourse as meaningless because it cannot be reduced by translation to empirical science.[11] As Putnam observes, "*Understanding a language game is sharing a form of life*. And forms of life cannot be described in a fixed positivistic metalanguage, whether they be scientific or religious."[12] We should note that this does not entail that religious language is completely isolated from ordinary discourse, such as the notion of two mutually exclusive conceptual schemes would entail. Whatever Putnam may have said about conceptual relativity elsewhere, he is careful to deny that the religious and nonreligious language games are strictly self-enclosed.[13]

This point is strengthened by his articulation of a third characteristic of religious discourse: despite the incommensurability of religious and ordinary language, we should not regard the two as incompatible or as entailing contradictory descriptions. Putnam repeatedly stresses Wittgenstein's point that religious and scientific statements do not contradict or refute each other directly.[14] There are, however, stronger and weaker ways of interpreting this claim.[15] In a weaker sense, two discourses may not be intertranslatable or strictly reducible, but one may be made relevant to the evaluation of the other through the introduction of certain bridging premises. The bridge premises themselves do not entail a reduction because their terms are constituted by elements in the two underlying languages. In a stronger sense, religious and other forms of discourse may be incommensurable not only because they fail to be reducible but also because bridging premises are, in principle, unavailable.

The weaker interpretation of the denial of incompatibility and intertranslatability is more consonant with our ordinary understanding of religious language and with Aquinas's program in philosophical theology, which notoriously holds that philosophical rationality and religious faith are complemen-

---

[9] Ibid., 178.

[10] Putnam, "Thoughts," 491–92.

[11] Putnam, "God and the Philosophers," 176.

[12] Ibid., 178.

[13] Putnam, "Thoughts," 492.

[14] See, e.g., Putnam, "God and the Philosophers," 179: "Although the language games of science and of religion do not (that is to say, should not) contradict one another, it is important to notice that what Wittgenstein said does *not* have the tone of 'it's true in his language game but not in mine.'"

[15] I am indebted to William Alston for suggesting the importance of making this distinction.

tary.[16] Thus, for example, Christianity's claims about the incarnation, death, resurrection, and second coming of Christ are more than merely empirical historical claims, but they are not immune from historical criticism. Putnam rightly stresses that religious belief cannot be reduced to a series of theoretical or observational fact claims.[17] He also holds that the potentiality for meaningful use of religious language is available to all and continuous with our other discourses.[18] Furthermore, he denies that religious language is immune from criticism.[19]

Nevertheless, certain features of his account suggest the stronger reading of antireductionism. While discussing fruitful dialogue between religious and non-religious thinkers, for instance, Putnam restricts his examples to cases of internal criticism.[20] No mention is made of the possibility of bridging premises. Furthermore, following Wittgenstein, he stresses that religious and empirical discourse cannot refute each other.[21] Putnam does assert that Wittgenstein's program has important shortcomings with regard to the question of religious language and the entailment of conflicting ethical judgments.[22] In response to this difficulty, he introduces a series of pragmatist criteria for handling the problem of incompatible moral attitudes. These criteria suggest the possibility of dialogue and external criticism, but they leave the reader without a definitive understanding of Putnam's concept of incommensurability. For the purpose of the present argument, it will therefore be necessary to stipulate that the analytical Thomist can accommodate the denial of intertranslatability and antireductionism in the weaker sense mentioned above. It will be argued that this sense of incommensurability captures enough of Putnam's concerns in order to be viable. At any rate, Aquinas's view of the relation between reason and faith, as well as our common understanding of religious language, cannot be squared easily with the stronger thesis. Without minimizing the importance of remaining points of dispute, this chapter will therefore attempt to show that when properly understood, Aquinas can accommodate many of Putnam's concerns, including the view that recognition of the truth conditions of much religious discourse must occur within religious practice. The Thomistic commitment to 'metaphysical realism' can thus avoid Putnam's sharper criticisms of the tradition.

Not surprisingly, the size of the intellectual gap between Putnam and Thomists on the nature of religious language will depend to a significant degree upon the interpretation of certain background concepts that inform Putnam's

[16] See, e.g., Thomas Aquinas, *Summa theologiae*, 5 vols. (Ottawa: Instituti Studiorum Medievalium Ottaviensis, 1941), I.1.1–2 (hereafter cited as *ST*), and *Summa contra gentiles* (Rome: Desclée & Herder, 1934), I.7–9 (hereafter cited as *SCG*).

[17] See, e.g., Putnam, "Thoughts," 492; also Putnam, "God and the Philosophers," 179.

[18] Putnam, "Thoughts," 492.

[19] Ibid., 491.

[20] Ibid., 492.

[21] Ibid., 491; Putnam, "God and the Philosophers," 179.

[22] Putnam, "God and the Philosophers," 180–82.

view, such as the status of his commitment to a form of pragmatic or 'internal' realism. The interpretation of this background is complicated by the fact that his thought has undergone a subtle but progressive shift over a twenty-five-year period, from a self-described sort of scientific realism, to a moderate form of antirealism, and back to what he now calls the natural realism of the ordinary man.[23] To make matters worse, not only is his thought rich, deep, and wide-ranging, but the shift in his doctrine is, by his own admission, somewhat ambiguous. In his 1994 Dewey Lectures, for instance, commenting upon whether he has given up his internal realist doctrine of the mid-1980s, he remarks, "Whether I am still, to some extent, an 'internal realist' is, I guess, as unclear as how much I was including under that unhappy label."[24] Furthermore, though Putnam still unequivocally resists embracing a position he labels 'metaphysical realism', as William Alston has observed, it is increasingly unclear whether genuine metaphysical realists must commit themselves to precisely the sort of position Putnam envisions they must endorse.[25] This analysis will conclude that there are substantive differences remaining between the parties to the dialogue but that there is hope for a meeting of the minds upon conceptual common ground.

THOMISM AN ANALOGOUS TERM

Up to this point, we have been speaking of "Thomists" as if they constituted a sort of natural philosophical kind, admitting of a single invariable description. The fact is that the term 'Thomist' is itself susceptible of analogous predication. This is partially true because the richness of Aquinas's thought, like that of Putnam, leaves room for interpretive disagreement. More significantly, if Aquinas himself can serve as a primary reference point for the term 'Thomist', then the measure of a Thomist cannot merely be the degree of similarity of one's views to Aquinas's stated position on any given topic. After all, Aquinas himself held that in philosophy the argument from authority is the weakest and, like Aristotle, that we should love the truth more than a friend.[26] To be authentically Thomistic, then, is not a matter of slavish adherence to a particular text, even though Thomists regard Aquinas's work as seminal and substantially correct.

In addition, Putnam's thoughts are addressed specifically to 'analytical Thomists'. John Haldane defines this species of the genus as follows: "Analyti-

---

[23] See Hilary Putnam, "Sense, Nonsense, and the Senses: An Inquiry into the Powers of the Human Mind," *Journal of Philosophy* 91 (September 1994): 454; also Hilary Putnam, "The Question of Realism," in *Words and Life*, ed. James Conant (Cambridge: Harvard University Press, 1994), 303.

[24] See Putnam, "Sense, Nonsense," 463 n. 41.

[25] William Alston, *A Realist Conception of Truth* (Ithaca: Cornell University Press, 1996), 148. For an interesting example of this point, see the discussion of John Haldane's work below.

[26] See Aquinas, *ST* I.1.8. ad. 2, and S. Thomae Aquinatis, *In decem libros Ethicorum Aristoteles ad Nicomachum expositio*, ed. Fr. Raymundi M. Spiazzi, O.P. (Rome: Marietti, 1949), I Lec. 6.

cal Thomism . . . seeks to deploy the methods and ideas of twentieth-century philosophy—of the sort dominant within the English-speaking world—in connection with the broad framework of ideas introduced and developed by Aquinas."[27] Although Haldane is, no doubt, correct that such a position bears analogous resemblance to Aquinas and is worthy of the designation 'Thomistic' for certain intents and purposes, it is clear that this viewpoint will not constitute a suitably well defined description of Putnam's interlocutor. After all, a contemporary proponent of Scotistic realism, Ockhamistic nominalism, or even Cartesian indirect realism might well be in the class of 'analytical Thomists' as Haldane has described it. For the purposes of this analysis it will therefore be necessary to interpret 'analytical Thomism' more narrowly than Haldane's definition. In particular, use of the term will imply a substantive commitment to Aquinas's realist metaphysics and the epistemological implications that accompany it.[28] More specific details will be made clear as they are deployed in the course of this chapter. Free use will therefore be made of Aquinas's works as a model of the view in question. It should be borne in mind, however, that this implies neither a naive understanding of the range of possible interpretations of his thought nor a commitment to the letter of his position on every individual occasion.

POINT OF DEPARTURE: PROOFS FOR THE EXISTENCE OF GOD

Putnam takes as his point of departure for the dialogue the subject of proofs for the existence of God. He articulates three central areas of concern: (1) the formal validity of so-called causal arguments like those given by Aquinas in his two *Summae*, (2) the notion of proof and the idea of universal assent, and (3) the value of the project of natural theology as an enterprise. There is little need for dispute between the parties about the first point. Putnam dismisses the critique of traditional causal arguments, which holds that they require fallacious inferential steps. In fact, he points out that a common criticism of Aquinas's arguments, namely, that they are predicated upon the denial of the possibility of infinite temporal regress, is simply misconceived.[29]

---

[27] John Haldane, "Analytical Thomism: A Prefatory Note," *The Monist* 80 (October 1997): 486.

[28] We must grant that the precise nature of these commitments and their implications are themselves controversial matters within Aquinas scholarship, matters that fall outside the range of what can be treated here. Consider, for example, Robert Pasnau's recent critique of Aquinas's theory of cognition as a successful form of direct realism (Pasnau, *Theories of Cognition in the Later Middle Ages* [Cambridge: Cambridge University Press, 1997]).

[29] Putnam, "Thoughts," 488. On this point in Aquinas, see *ST* I.46.2; see also Elizabeth Anscombe and P.T. Geach, *Three Philosophers* (Ithaca: Cornell University Press, 1961), 111 ff.; Patterson Brown, "Infinite Causal Regression," in *Aquinas: A Collection of Critical Essays*, ed. Anthony Kenny (Notre Dame: University of Notre Dame Press, 1969), 214–36; and David Braine, "Cosmological Arguments," in *Philosophy of Religion: A Guide to the Subject*, ed. Brian Davies (Washington, D.C.: Georgetown University Press, 1998), 52. Putnam maintains that some work is required in order to bring the traditional arguments into a suitably precise form, but this point should not disturb most Thomists. Many of them recognize that

The second and third points present a more complicated set of challenges. Though Putnam concedes that traditional causal arguments can be stated in a formally valid manner, he also holds that the truth or falsity of their premises remains controversial, depending upon an intuition that is not in fact available to every rational agent, even if religious discourse is potentially available to every human being. Thus the soundness of such arguments can be called into question. Aquinas grants that the existence of God is rationally dubitable and that many are unable to grasp the premises necessary for a demonstration.[30] Hence Thomists can agree with Putnam that the premises of causal arguments remain controversial. The sense in which Putnam thinks that the grasp of these premises is unavailable, however, depends upon his Wittgensteinian reading of the nature of theological discourse, which requires that the intuition in question can be made intelligible only within the context of religious practice. Most significantly, Putnam concludes that the project of natural theology is of dubious value, since assent to the premises of theological arguments can be made only from within a religious form of life. Those who are outside will not find causal arguments compelling, and many of those who share a religious form of life will not find such arguments useful or necessary.[31] Clearly, the Thomist cannot accept the inference from the controversial nature of the premises to the dubious value of natural theology. But the latter is assumed to follow from the former and from the idea that the meaningfulness of religious discourse is internal to practice. Aquinas, for his part, has certain resources for explaining the role of religious practice in the understanding of theological language which do not render the project of natural theology moot. We must therefore compare Aquinas's position on this point with that of Putnam.

AQUINAS: THEOLOGICAL DISCOURSE

We can begin with an important measure of agreement. Putnam dismisses as too simplistic the idea that arguments for God's existence should provide demonstrations that compel universal assent. He rejects the notion that "a sound proof ought to be able to convince any rational person who sees it."[32] When the notion is considered in this general way, Thomists should certainly have no trouble agreeing with Putnam's point. There is a distinction to be made between a sound argument and one that is rhetorically persuasive because it begins from premises that are evident to all reasonable persons. Aquinas is very clear about the fact that natural theology, as a *scientia* offering demonstrative conclusions, is not accessible to many individuals. His discussion of the ques-

---

Aquinas's proofs need restatement in light of apparent inconsistencies with developments in contemporary science and philosophy, as well as certain ambiguities in the language of the proofs themselves. See, for example, Anthony Kenny, *The Five Ways: St. Thomas Aquinas' Proofs of God's Existence* (New York: Schocken, 1969), 27–33, and John Haldane and J. J. C. Smart, *Atheism and Theism: A Philosophy of Religion* (Oxford: Blackwell, 1996), 132.

[30] See Aquinas, *ST* I.2.1–2, *SCG* I.4.

[31] Putnam, "Thoughts," 490.

[32] Ibid., 489.

tion whether truths accessible to natural reason should be objects of assent by faith in the *Summa contra gentiles* is perhaps his most lucid treatment of the subject.[33] In addition to acknowledging the fact that demonstrative arguments can fail to produce universal assent, he makes two important points. First, he admits that some are not temperamentally disposed to acquire natural theological knowledge and, second, that attainment of knowledge in this domain depends upon understanding a wide array of premises from other fields of inquiry. A satisfactory grasp of the truth of the premises in natural theology therefore requires a wide range of cognitive and affective abilities, which few rational agents may possess.

There is another point to be made, however, to which Thomists may well have been less than sensitive in the past. For Putnam, the grasp of such theoretical premises cannot be abstracted from our praxis.[34] In her recent book on virtue epistemology, Linda Zagzebski has pointed out that there are resources available in the tradition for recognizing the parallelism between moral and intellectual virtue, as well as the important element of practice in the acquisition of the 'intellectual virtues'.[35] Zagzebski faults the Aristotelian tradition, however, for sharply distinguishing the moral and intellectual virtues, and stresses that we should attend more to the similarities. As John McDowell has observed, for Aristotle (and we may add for Aquinas) the acquisition of the moral virtues through practice induces not only dispositions to act but also understanding of practical truth. Virtuous dispositions are simultaneously cognitive and affective.[36] For the Aristotelian and Thomistic traditions the cognitive dimension of moral virtue thus cannot easily be separated from the practice within which it is generated. For Putnam the role of practice is equally important in the explanation of our grasp of the truth conditions of theological discourse. We must therefore ask, Can Aquinas understand the role that practice, self-discipline, and participation in an epistemic community must have for the grasp of theoretical premises in natural theology?

In light of these considerations it is significant that in the passage from the *Summa contra gentiles* just mentioned, Aquinas recognizes the affective or tem-

---

[33] Aquinas, *SCG* I.4.

[34] See the discussion of religious discourse and 'forms of life' below.

[35] Linda Zagzebski, *Virtues of the Mind: An Inquiry into the Nature of Virtue and the Ethical Foundations of Knowledge* (Cambridge: Cambridge University Press, 1996). See especially sec. 3.1–2, on the connection between 'moral' and 'intellectual' virtues, 137–65.

[36] See John McDowell, "Values and Secondary Qualities," in *Essays on Moral Realism*, ed. Kenneth Sayre-McCord (Ithaca: Cornell University Press, 1988), and John McDowell, "Virtue and Reason," in *Virtue Ethics*, ed. Roger Crisp and Michael Slote (Oxford: Oxford University Press, 1998). Careful treatment of the matter is beyond the scope of the present analysis, but it should be noted that although Aquinas recognizes the dispositive role of practice in the acquisition of the intellectual virtues, he continues to distinguish them from the moral virtues in terms of the latter's tendency to confer the "right use of a power or habit" (Aquinas, *ST* I-II.57.1c). Significantly, though, he also notes that the right use of intellectual virtues requires moral virtue.

peramental component behind our cognitive grasp of these premises. Successful attainment of the knowledge of divine things requires the cultivation of the intellectual virtues of wisdom, science, and prudence to a high degree, which is not possible for many people, because of their circumstances in life, their natural abilities, or even their openness to the truths in question. We may fail to understand the significance of this point if we focus only upon Aquinas's formal treatment of the intellectual virtues in question. So, for instance, in the *Summa theologiae* he asks whether the moral and intellectual virtues are connected to each other. His answer, briefly, is that whereas prudence and the moral virtues are mutually connected, the intellectual virtues of wisdom, science, and understanding may exist without the moral virtues and vice versa.[37]

But if we recall that Aquinas considered the Dominican life to be an ideal sort of preparation for engaging in the activity of philosophical theology, then we must temper his former remarks by his treatment of the relation between the active and contemplative lives. Doing so requires us to recognize, as Pierre Hadot has observed about ancient and medieval philosophy, that its practitioners were well aware of the fact that the attainment of wisdom requires participation in a certain form of life.[38] Aquinas remarks that although the essential nature of contemplation consists in the intellect's grasp of truth, the will must dispose the agent to the act of contemplation. Appetite moves the agent to observe or attend to certain things more carefully, effectively guiding cognition through love.[39] This training of the mind for contemplation of truth is further accomplished through the possession of the moral virtues.

To these strictly human preconditions for the grasp of the premises of our reasoning in natural theology, Aquinas adds an acute awareness for what we might call our 'cognitive fallenness' as persons and the need for divine grace. On the one hand, our intellectual capacities are sometimes truncated because pride and other faults stand in the way of acknowledging truth that is available to us. On the other, grasp of divine things requires the assistance of a transcendent source, which even Aristotle recognized was above the ordinary capacities of nature.[40] Indeed, one cannot live the contemplative life without meditation and prayer, which are essential for disposing the mind to receive truth and for the acceptance of divine grace.[41]

Thus, for a variety of reasons an analytical Thomist should not be surprised or discouraged by the failure of something like the 'five ways' to produce an in-

---

[37] See Aquinas, *ST* I-II.58.4–5.

[38] See Pierre Hadot, *Philosophy as a Way of Life: Spiritual Exercises from Socrates to Foucault* (Oxford: Blackwell, 1995). It is especially worth noting the debt Hadot acknowledges to Wittgenstein's conception of "forms of life" as instrumental for his own understanding of the practice of philosophy, given Putnam's Wittgensteinian arguments considered below (ibid., 280).

[39] Aquinas, *ST* II-II.180.1c.

[40] See, e.g., Aquinas, *ST* II-II.180.3. ad. 4.

[41] Ibid., II-II.180.3. ad. 4.

stant change of mind among all the rational unbelievers who encounter them. Furthermore, he or she should not hold the view that such failure is merely a product of not having thought the matter through or having failed to consider some important detail. Possession of the virtues of wisdom, science, and understanding, which enable one to grasp the truth of the relevant premises, comes primarily as the fruit of a certain way of life, from which grasp of those truths cannot be separated.

We may add one additional point. A proof like one of those offered at the beginning of the *Summa theologiae* serves as an entry point into treating the question of the existence of God. Aquinas is well aware of the fact that the proof of an uncaused cause or self-necessary being is hardly a demonstration of the Christian God or even what might constitute an adequate object of worship.[42] Furthermore, it does not purport to offer solutions for the most significant counterexamples or apparent paradoxes of religious belief, such as the problem of evil.[43] Thus, even if it were granted that someone had a demonstrative grasp of the truth of the conclusion offered by one of Aquinas's 'five ways', Aquinas would not have assumed that this would induce in him or her a religious way of life.

We cannot therefore understand the full significance of religious discourse for Aquinas merely in terms of what natural reason delivers to us in the form of a causal argument, even if we grant that such an argument is sound in principle. Speaking of his intellectual background, in addition to his later interest in Wittgenstein's idea that 'language games' constitute 'forms of life', Hadot mentions the early importance of Cardinal Newman's distinction between real and notional assent:

> Newman shows in this work that it's not the same thing to give one's assent
> to an affirmation which one understands in a purely abstract way, and to
> give one's assent while engaging one's entire being, and "realizing"—in the
> English sense of the word—with one's heart and one's imagination, just what
> this affirmation means for us.[44]

---

[42] For example, Aquinas ends each of his proofs for the existence of a first self-necessary cause in the *ST* with a statement such as "and this we call God" (*ST* I.2.3). On this point, see Haldane and Smart, *Atheism and Theism*, 140–41; also Germain Grisez, *Beyond the New Theism: A Philosophy of Religion* (Notre Dame: University of Notre Dame Press, 1975), 36–37; and Braine, "Cosmological Arguments," 52, 53 n. 7.

[43] See Grisez, *Beyond the New Theism*, 28–29.

[44] Hadot, *Philosophy*, 276. See John Henry Newman, *An Essay in Aid of a Grammar of Assent* (Notre Dame: University of Notre Dame Press, 1979), 86–92: "It appears that, though Real Assent is not intrinsically operative, it accidentally and indirectly affects practice. It is in itself an intellectual act, of which the object is presented to it by the imagination . . . the imagination has the means, which pure intellect has not, of stimulating those powers of the mind from which action proceeds . . . no religion yet has been a religion of physics or of philosophy. It never has been a deduction from what we know; it has ever been an assertion of what we are to believe."

In his own way, Aquinas is cognizant of this point. Speaking of the virtue of faith, he cites with approbation Augustine's definition of faith as "to think with assent."[45] Faith is a mean between science and opinion because although it lacks the certainty of knowledge, it shares firmness of assent with knowing. He adds that the act of faith consists of three components: (1) "believing God," (2) "believing in a God," and (3) "believing in God."[46] The third of these components is not superfluous because it signals that the intellect's assent to what it accepts as true is strengthened by the will's tendency toward what is believed as good or lovable.[47] The conclusion that there is something that exists as a first self-necessary cause is only a very small part of what gives meaning to religious discourse and practice for Aquinas.

PUTNAM'S VIEW

We must now compare this more detailed account of Aquinas's view of the nature of theological discourse with that of Putnam in order to see how the latter's concerns can be addressed. Putnam's rejection of the idea of universal assent to proofs for God's existence goes well beyond the acknowledgment of a distinction between sound argumentation and rhetorically persuasive premises, to the idea that religious discourse can be understood only from within a 'form of life'. According to his view, there are domain-specific reasons why religious discourse constitutes a special case in which the premises of our arguments are available only to certain rational interlocutors. Here the Wittgensteinian dimension of his position not only comes to the fore but appears to apply more vigorously to the case of religious discourse.

The precise nature of this position can be illustrated by considering the related case of proofs in mathematics. It is, of course, true that for one who does not understand the reasoning behind the postulation of non-Euclidean geometry, the rejection of the parallel-lines postulate can seem highly controversial and quite unreasonable. But for anyone who understands the principles of non-Euclidean geometry, it is reasonable to reject this postulate within those geometrical systems. Thus, among "those who understand them," mathematical proofs seem to produce universal assent.[48] Putnam contends that the same situation is not the case with theological proofs.[49]

The problem according to him rests with the fact that 'understanding' relevant theological concepts such as 'God' in the theological case is not analogous to the case of understanding mathematical concepts such as the nature of parallel lines.[50] There are senses in which rational agents may 'understand' theolog-

---

[45] Aquinas, *ST* II-II.2.1.

[46] Ibid., II-II.2.2. For a useful commentary on this point, see Josef Pieper, *Faith, Hope, Love* (San Francisco: Ignatius Press, 1986), 57.

[47] Aquinas, *ST* II-II.2.2.

[48] Putnam, "Thoughts," 489.

[49] Ibid., 489–90.

[50] Ibid., 490.

ical concepts without finding causal arguments compelling. Hence, we should not expect universal assent as we do in the case of mathematics. Putnam offers two examples of these cases, which serve to illustrate his point that recognition of the meaning of religious discourse is embedded within a particular form of life. In the first place, there are rational unbelievers who have a conception of God not unlike that of their theist counterparts but who do not share with theists the requisite intuition about the causal ground of contingent existence.[51] In addition, there are deeply religious persons who have a profound sense of God's existence but who do not share with Thomists the theoretical underpinnings of the projects of ancient and medieval philosophy.[52] Both types of agents may be said to understand the relevant theological concepts even though they do not find causal arguments compelling. It is not that the causal arguments are fallacious or question begging in themselves; rather, certain obstacles that have no analogue in the case of mathematics stand in the way. These obstacles fuel Putnam's doubts about the usefulness of natural theology.

Theoretical Obstacles

Putnam gives two sorts of explanations for the resistance to acceptance of the premises of causal arguments: (1) certain theoretical obstacles and (2) the irreducibly practical nature of religious forms of life. A full treatment of the theoretical obstacles is beyond the scope of the present analysis. Since Putnam's attitude toward the surmountability of these obstacles is closely bound to the latter explanation, however, it is necessary to examine them together briefly.

The theoretical obstacles come from Kant and Hume, respectively. Typically, causal arguments, such as those found in Aquinas's 'five ways', depend upon an inference from the existence of particular contingent existents to the radical contingence of the world and its dependence upon a first cause. Kant rejected such a move as transcending the proper limits within which human reason may speak about causal relationships. Putnam notes, "But (as Immanuel Kant recognized), even if it goes beyond what we have come to call 'scientific thinking' to apply this [the notion of contingence] to the world as a whole, there is something in the human mind itself that makes us want to think that there is a cause for anything whose existence is contingent."[53] Kant's objection is not simply rejected here but accepted insofar as it points to the special sense in which the grasp of theological premises transcends the ordinary capacity of reason. This point is strengthened by Putnam's appeal to the second obstacle, that is, Hume's rejection of the idea that contingent existence requires an explanation.[54]

---

[51] Ibid., 489.

[52] Ibid., 490.

[53] Ibid., 488.

[54] Ibid., 489: "It was the triumph (at least in secular thought) after David Hume of the idea that there is nothing problematic about the idea that the universe as a whole should exist contingently that represented a fundamental break with what was long taken to be a fundamental principle of human reason as such."

The premises of causal arguments remain controversial, therefore, because they require the transcendent use of reason and because they depend upon something like Leibniz's principle of sufficient reason. Putnam grants that these ideas are very basic human "intuitions" or "intellectual urges" that belong to a "natural conception of reason itself."[55] But ultimately, unlike certain mathematical truths, they can be grasped only by participation in a certain form of life, which gives them meaning. Indeed, they cannot be shown apart from the context of religious practice.[56] He thus neither unequivocally rejects nor affirms the theoretical obstacles. He is also elusive about the accessibility of a religious form of life to all rational agents, describing it as we have noted as a universal "potentiality" but not a "real possibility" for all persons.[57] Thus, the status of these theoretical obstacles is tied closely to his account of the experiential dimension of a religious form of life.

A Preliminary Thomistic Response

Before considering that second explanation, we should note that it is far from clear that Thomists should concede the status Putnam wishes to attribute to these theoretical obstacles outside the context of a religious form of life. There have been a number of vigorous critiques of both Kant's prohibition of the transcendent use of reason and Hume's rejection of the causal principle.[58] There are, of course, different strands of opinion among the proponents of causal arguments, but some would also reject explicit dependence of such arguments upon the principle of sufficient reason.[59] Thomists should certainly avoid a naive understanding of the accessibility of the premises of these arguments. Indeed, Aquinas has a whole array of tools concerning the acquisition of the intellectual virtues which can explain why the doctrine of universal assent is mistaken. But there is hope that such premises can be made intelligible to suitably disposed philosophical minds who remain outside the community of believers. As we have suggested, the antireductionist account of religious language need not entail the denial of the view that bridge premises are in principle available. Indeed, where Jewish and Christian religious belief is concerned, the fundamentally historical nature of their doctrinal commitments virtually requires such premises. Some of what Putnam says about the incommensurability of religious

---

[55] Putnam, "Thoughts," 489.

[56] Ibid., 498.

[57] Ibid., 492.

[58] For a critique of Kant, see, e.g., David Braine, *The Reality of Time and the Existence of God* (Oxford: Oxford University Press, 1988); Grisez, *Beyond the New Theism*; and Anscombe and Geach, *Three Philosophers*. For a critique of Hume, see, e.g., Anscombe, " 'Whatever Has a Beginning of Existence Must Have a Cause': Hume's Argument Exposed," in Elizabeth Anscombe, *From Parmenides to Wittgenstein: Collected Philosophical Papers, Volume 1* (Minneapolis: University of Minnesota Press, 1981).

[59] See, e.g., Grisez, *Beyond the New Theism*, 69–70; and Braine, "Cosmological Arguments," 47–48.

discourse, in contrast, tends toward the view that one cannot, in principle, make a substantive response to the foregoing theoretical obstacles from a point of view accessible to rational unbelievers.[60] In other words, the intelligibility of theological discourse would be isolated in the stronger sense discussed earlier within the context of religious practice. We must examine the motivation for this more radical viewpoint.

The Role of the Concept 'God'

Putnam offers two observations in this regard: (1) in order to engage in theological discourse, we must have an understanding of the concept 'God', and (2) in order to grasp the meaning of the traditional causal arguments, we need to connect this concept to a set of "highly theoretical philosophical principles" that lie in the background.[61] With regard to the first point, we should bear in mind Aquinas's general dissatisfaction with the strategy of ontological arguments. One cannot deny the truism that it is impossible to argue to and about a conclusion for which one has no conceptual grasp whatsoever. But this is not the point of the distinction Aquinas makes between *propter quid* and *quia* methods of demonstration in the course of laying out his strategy for proving God's existence.[62] In the former, one argues from the properties of a cause to its effects, and in the latter, one argues from a given state of affairs to the existence of a cause of that state. There are very good reasons why Aquinas thinks we should begin argumentation in natural theology from a very inadequate conception of God, not the least of which is that inquiry must proceed from what is more known to us to what is more knowable in itself. As we have noted, the causal proof is for Aquinas merely an opening salvo. It is hardly the source of an adequate conception of God, let alone a sufficient foundation upon which one could build a seriously religious attitude toward life. For Aquinas this process cannot be completed within natural theology at all. One must bring faith into the picture, where both intellect and will operate together in order to make the transition from notional to real assent.

Putnam appears to conflate the significance of various different conceptions of the term 'God' here. He points out that many "profound religious thinkers" have had a concept of God that is completely unrelated to the ancient and medieval philosophical idea of a self-necessary first cause. The latter notion does not appear to be a necessary condition for a fulfilling religious attitude toward life, nor could it serve as the sufficient condition to ground one's religious life.[63]

---

[60] See, e.g., Putnam, "Thoughts," 498: "And neither can I explain what I mean by 'God', except by showing how my use of the term figures in my religious life—and that is not something I can do at just any time or to any person. Of course, this disbars me from claiming that I can 'prove' that God exists to an atheist. But I have already indicated that that is not a claim that I think a religious person should make."

[61] Putnam, "Thoughts," 490.

[62] See Aquinas, *ST* I.2.2.

[63] Putnam, "Thoughts," 490.

With appropriate qualifications, there is no reason why Aquinas could not agree with both these points. Why, then, should we undertake the exercise of formulating such an inadequate conception? One reason for Aquinas is precisely that this conception can, in principle, be made intelligible to those who do not share fully in the form of life of the religious believer. It is, so to speak, a real possibility for a suitably reflective rational agent. To be sure, Aquinas does not have a naive conception of what is required for one to grasp the truth of the premises of a causal argument, nor does he have unrealistic expectations that such an argument can produce the sort of real assent of which Newman spoke. Rather, it is an entry point, albeit a very sophisticated one, for a conversation.

The Irreducibly Practical Nature of Religious Discourse

These observations point to a subtle but important difference between the more extreme view of incommensurability Putnam may wish to endorse and the Thomist position. For the stronger view of incommensurability there is a wall of separation between the nonbeliever and access to the meaning of theological discourse, a wall that one can scale only by beginning to inhabit a religious form of life. For Aquinas the possibility of such a shift has stronger roots in nontheological discourse. The reason for taking up the more extreme position depends, in turn, upon Putnam's adoption of Wittgenstein's idea that different forms of discourse constitute language games and that the meaning of the terms used can be understood only from within the game. Putnam carefully distinguishes his position from the noncognitivist interpretation of Wittgensteinian language games and the view that such games are completely self-enclosed.[64] Nevertheless, it is difficult for those of his remarks that tend to endorse the stronger sense of incommensurability to avoid the implications of these more relativistic views. Significantly, Putnam holds that the language-game model applies to all forms of discourse:

> *The use of the words in a language game cannot be described without employing concepts which are internally related to the concepts used in the game.* This point has been made in connection with the language games of preliterate peoples, and also the case of religious utterances in our society, but I believe the same point applies to all language games.[65]

It is therefore indicative of his tendency toward the stronger view of incommensurability that his description of the nature of theological language emphasizes, as we have seen, a disanalogy between it and other ordinary uses of language. We might wonder what makes the religious case so special. Talk of electrons and quarks, for example, surely involves a highly theoretical context within which that talk is embedded. Nor can we begin to talk about entities in

---

[64] Putnam, "God and the Philosophers," 177, 179.
[65] Ibid., 177–78.

the field of particle physics without having certain important concepts as a pre-condition for doing so. Furthermore, Putnam himself rejects the various crude and sophisticated versions of verificationism.[66] Yet he cautions the reader that talk about God requires us to understand the concept 'God' in some way for which there is no analogue in the mathematical case.[67] Even if we grant this point, shall we not have to say the same thing about many other kinds of dis-course, including particle physics, in which the relevant terms depend signifi-cantly upon a set of highly theoretical contexts?

In one sense, Putnam is bound to agree with this argument, since he explic-itly rejects Bernard Williams's idea that science constitutes a privileged absolute conception of the way the world is.[68] Putnam can thus concur with the claim that theological language is not unique in regard to its being embedded within a language game. Nevertheless, it is impossible to avoid concluding that for him theological language is still different. The Wittgensteinian model of language games seems to apply to religious discourse in a more isolating way because of the disanalogy between proofs in its domain and in others. This is a subtle but important point. On the one hand, Putnam quotes with approval Cora Dia-mond's remark that fundamental religious questioning "belongs to language it-self, and not to any particular language game."[69] At the same time, he argues that religious discourse is not a "real possibility" for certain persons.[70] He offers an illustration of his position in terms of an image borrowed from Elizabeth Anscombe: the religious believer sees the stained-glass windows from inside and the atheist sees them from outside.[71] This image is meant to capture for Putnam the sense in which religious discourse is incommensurable with ordinary empir-ical and scientific discourse. Of course, this image can be interpreted in a multi-tude of ways. In one sense it may be consistent with the weaker version of in-commensurability mentioned earlier. That is, the believer and nonbeliever see the same phenomena (the windows) in different ways. Perhaps a dialogue is possible in which bridging premises can be given, allowing for movement across the divide between the believer and nonbeliever. Putnam's stress upon the idea that we should not identify incommensurability with a noncognitivist interpre-tation of religious discourse, or with the idea of a "self-enclosed language game," tends to support this reading.[72] Yet he also asserts that theological lan-guage is "*sui generis*" and that the natural theological project of making proofs intelligible to nonbelievers is futile and pointless.[73]

The Thomist should understand and sympathize with the Wittgensteinian

---

[66] For his latest view on this point, see, e.g., Putnam, "Sense, Nonsense," 500–505.

[67] Putnam, "Thoughts," 490.

[68] Putnam, "God and the Philosophers," 176.

[69] Cora Diamond in Putnam, "Thoughts," 491–92.

[70] Putnam, "Thoughts," 492.

[71] Ibid., 491.

[72] See, e.g., ibid., 491; also Putnam, "God and the Philosophers," 184.

[73] Putnam, "God and the Philosophers," 497–98.

point that is made here about all language, namely, that the meanings of our terms are often discovered in use. Aristotle and Aquinas were particularly well aware of this point with regard to practical reason, but as we have seen, this insight can be extended to the acquisition of the intellectual virtues as well. What should be of concern, however, is that despite Putnam's assertions about the nature of incommensurability and the claim that religious belief is not immune from criticism, one cannot avoid the conclusion that religious discourse does turn out to be isolated in the stronger sense suggested by Putnam's use of the term '*sui generis*'. The examples of critical dialogue between theists and nontheists which Putnam gives are cases of internal criticism, in which the interlocutors can only point to internal inconsistencies within each other's conceptual systems.[74] One cannot, so to speak, engage in a conversation at the doorway to the cathedral where the windows can be glimpsed from a distance. This must be a real possibility for Aquinas, who begins with what he takes to be a wholly inadequate but broadly intelligible conception of God as his starting point. To be sure, we cannot reduce the meanings of theological terms to a neutral nonreligious metalanguage. But nonreligious discourse can be made relevant to religious discourse through the employment of bridging premises, which though they contain irreducible theological terms, also answer to certain canons of consistency and coherence from the point of view of the nonbeliever.

Perhaps the more extreme sketch of Putnam's view is mistaken and he can envision a conversation in which the view from outside somehow constitutes the intellectual possibility of imagining what it is like from inside. We might hasten to add that it is not *merely* an intellectual possibility and that Thomists should acknowledge the correctness of Putnam's stress upon the role of practice in understanding. But if the possibility is not *at least* intellectual, then it is purely volitional or noncognitive.[75] If such a conversation were intellectually possible, then Putnam and the analytical Thomist would be only 'words apart', struggling together with the very real phenomenon of a lack of universal assent. The problem with Putnam's line of argument is that it is very difficult to identify how he can sustain his perch on the fence between denying Kuhnian incommensurability and his de facto isolation of the believer in a sort of private or semiprivate language game.

The solution to this problem is supposed to be the Wittgensteinian notion of a practice embedded within a form of life. According to Putnam, this notion will allow him to negotiate a middle path between noncognitivism or a form of

---

[74] Ibid., 492: "It is appropriate for a secular thinker to try to convince a religious thinker that some of his or her views are indefensible in the thinker's own terms. But that is a very different thing from trying to explain what it means to be religious in a purely intellectual way." The use of *intellectual* here suggests a distinction between thought and practice which runs through Wittgenstein's remarks on religion and, though not strictly a form of noncognitivism, strongly bifurcates the cognitive and affective. See, e.g., Wittgenstein in Anthony Kenny, ed., *The Wittgenstein Reader* (Oxford: Blackwell, 1994), 300.

[75] See the discussion of Wittgenstein on 'faith' vs. 'wisdom' below.

strict conceptual relativism and naive realism about the meaning of religious discourse:

> Like the atheist, such a theologian [the naive one] thinks of "literally" believing that God is personal, or "literally" believing that God loves individuals as a matter of "believing a proposition." If Wittgenstein or Kirkegaard suggest that what is involved is not a belief in a form of words but rather a form of life they are not saying that *all* that is involved is a form of life; they are saying that *what it is to believe that God is personal and loves individuals depends on who one is all the way down and how one lives all the way down.*[76]

There is no question that for Aquinas, believing *in* God is not *merely* propositional.[77] It is much more, but it is also propositional in part. Even the act of faith, which transcends the efforts of natural theology unaided by grace, has both a propositional content and the movement of will toward an *understood* good (*bonum intellectum*). Aquinas could therefore agree with the notion that religious belief involves the totality of one's being in a way that mere assent to the truth of a proposition cannot capture. Moreover, he conceptualized the living out of this form of life in terms of the natural virtue of religion and the supernatural virtues of faith, hope, and charity. But Aquinas would certainly take issue with the dichotomy between 'a form of words' and 'a form of life'. For Aquinas, as we have indicated, the acquisition of the virtues is both cognitive and affective.

Perhaps Putnam can also avoid this problem by not treating this dichotomy as mutually exclusive. He has suggested as much. But if so, why then resist the analogy between speaking of God and speaking of quarks and neutrinos? Presumably, although quarks and neutrinos involve a highly theoretical background context, Putnam would not say that they are isolated from the language of 'ordinary description' in the way that he has suggested theological discourse is. Certainly religious belief is much more, but is it also much less?

There is another reason for concern that a satisfactory explanation of the cognitive character of religious discourse is not forthcoming. Putnam's argument rests upon Wittgenstein's remarks about religious discourse as being embedded in a form of life. Although it is very difficult to say just what sort of rational status Wittgenstein accorded religious belief, there are signs that he would not give a cognitive account of its nature. Speaking of ethics and religious belief together, Wittgenstein explains that the sense in which such discourse is, as Diamond has suggested, part of the very fabric of language itself is also the sense in which it threatens to become unintelligible.[78] Speech concerning the absolute is a potentiality in language, but it is a potentiality for language to attempt an impossible transcendence of itself:

[76] Putnam, "God and the Philosophers," 184.
[77] See the discussion of Aquinas's *ST* II-II.2 above.
[78] Wittgenstein, in Kenny, *Wittgenstein Reader*, 291–96.

The tendency of all men who ever tried to write or talk Ethics or Religion was to run against the boundaries of language. This running against the walls of our cage is perfectly, absolutely hopeless. What it [Ethics or Religion] says does not add to our knowledge in any sense. But it is a document of a tendency in the human mind which I personally cannot help respecting deeply.[79]

We should not, of course, require Putnam to endorse fully Wittgenstein's remarks, since Putnam recognizes Wittgenstein as someone who examined the stained-glass windows from outside. But we should then expect some qualification of them, which is apparently not forthcoming. We might attribute the absence of such an account to Putnam's antitheoretical insistence upon the idea that whatever can be said in response to Wittgenstein's concerns can be articulated only from a point of view internal to religious practice. We are then faced with a problem. We must wonder how we are to judge when a credible answer to Wittgenstein's worry has been given and when we are in the right language game or conceptual scheme to recognize it. For it seems that we could be in a position to judge Putnam's response only if it did in fact make sense to us. Can the identity conditions be given for the scheme, even to one who now inhabits the form of life that embodies it, in such a way that we may be able to know that we are inhabiting Putnam's scheme while judging his attempt a success or failure? I do not mean to insist that there should be some language-neutral point from which to judge all our language games, but rather I want to query how it is possible for us to distinguish between what looks like a falsehood and what is unavailable to us because we do not yet properly inhabit a form of life.

Perhaps the answer to this concern also can be given only through practice and cannot be specified cognitively, even for one who now inhabits the given form of life. Then it appears religious believers will inhabit a form of life that they cannot integrate with their own ordinary empirical language, since they presumably share the latter with Wittgenstein. This would entail the unacceptable stronger form of incommensurability discussed earlier and require Putnam to deny the theoretical possibility of finding bridge premises. In addition, religious believers would be unable to be confident when they were inhabiting the scheme and could also not be confident from one part of their life that another part made any rational sense. A similar way of putting this question is, In what sense does the religious believer continue to inhabit the world in which Wittgenstein thinks that religious language attempts to say the unsayable? If we endorse the stronger sense of incommensurability, then he or she would end up on the outside of Wittgenstein's world looking in. Looking in from outside the believer's world, Wittgenstein cannot see the reasonableness of faith:

What I need is *certainty*—not wisdom, dreams or speculation—and this certainty is faith. And faith is faith in what is needed by my *heart*, my *soul*, not

[79] Ibid., 296.

my speculative intelligence. . . . Wisdom is cold and to that extent stupid. (Faith on the other hand is passion.)[80]

The believer should want to say, yes, passion but also wisdom. Once we inhabit that conceptual scheme, what shall we say of the old conception of wisdom? Will we cease to understand it? Surely this is not a tenable viewpoint. If we do not cease to understand it, then we must say that for the believer the schemes of religious and nonreligious discourse are not reducible because the terms of the former cannot merely be translated into those of the latter without remainder, but there is also not a complete disjunction between the two spheres. We should therefore not want to endorse the stronger sense of incommensurability because rational standards for the evaluation of our beliefs in one if not both spheres will break down. That is, agents will be faced internally with multiple schemes of description, which they can neither integrate nor adjudicate between.

On Aquinas's view certain dispositional changes are required before one can have a grasp of the truth of religious discourse. But those dispositional changes, which it would be reasonable to call 'participating in a form of life', enable the cognitive integration of new beliefs into one's interpretation of the world. Moreover, they are clearly governed by principles of consistency and revision in light of contradictions. In the absence of some other compelling reason for postulating the stronger sense of incommensurability, we should favor Aquinas's position, which can accommodate much of what Putnam wants from the notions of 'incommensurability' and 'forms of life' without these puzzles. There is evidence to indicate that for Putnam the compelling reason to move in the direction of endorsing the stronger sense of incommensurability lies in what he sees as an untenable commitment to metaphysical realism undergirding Aquinas's view of the relation between religious and nonreligious discourse. We must therefore briefly turn to that subject.

METAPHYSICAL REALISM

In addition to Putnam's Wittgensteinian reluctance to offer a theory of religious discourse by which the theist and the agnostic can find a common intellectual space for dialogue about the meaning of religious language, there is another concern lying in the background of his reservations about the Thomistic position. One can see this in his hypothetical example of an implausible view he hopes the Thomist will wish to repudiate. Putting together some of the elements of this view, we can see that it entails thinking of theological discourse as in some sense testable by or reducible to scientific discourse.[81] This point comes out explicitly in Putnam's parallel treatment of religious language from the

[80] Ibid., 300–301.
[81] Putnam, "Thoughts," 491.

same time period as his response to analytical Thomism. In that piece Putnam criticizes both scientism and a certain kind of theological literalism:

> Of course, it is not only the scientistic intellectual who confuses scientific and religious language games; the literalistic fundamentalist who deduces the age of the earth, or the falsity of the theory of evolution, or whatever, from his reading of scripture also confuses the spheres, and to the detriment of both.[82]

The Thomist can certainly agree with Putnam that the religious believer does not take himself or herself to be "engaged in the prediction of empirical phenomena."[83] The Thomist can also agree that religious and scientific questions about, for instance, the origin of things are of a different kind, and that answers in one domain do not necessarily refute answers in the other.[84] That having been said, Aquinas cannot agree that scientific discourse is not in principle susceptible to being contradicted by religious discourse and vice versa, since he holds the compatibility of reason and religious faith.[85] Putnam is very cautious to avoid asserting that the two spheres are immune from each other's criticism. He is nevertheless reluctant to countenance much critical interaction between them. At most we are given examples of internal criticism in the piece in question.[86] Fortunately, we have a very clear indication of Aquinas's views on the subject in his small treatise against the Averroist theory of the unicity of the agent intellect. In a display of unmitigated passion, which is quite rare for Aquinas, he attacks the theory of the so-called double truth, namely, that something can be true according to religious faith but false according to natural reason.[87] It is not possible for Aquinas to maintain the linkage between these two sorts of truth and continue to support the stronger sense of incommensurability between the two spheres, which Putnam often appears to endorse. What, then, is the reason for embracing the stronger view of incommensurability?

Recall that for Putnam the naive view of proofs for the existence of God is that they should be accessible to all rational agents because there is some grand single language for describing the world into which the meaningfulness of all our statements can be reduced. For Putnam this view, which he calls "metaphysical realism," constitutes a generally mistaken conception of how language

---

[82] Putnam, "God and the Philosophers," 179.

[83] Putnam, "Thoughts," 491.

[84] See ibid., 491, and Putnam, "God and the Philosophers," 179.

[85] See, e.g., Aquinas, *SCG* I.7.

[86] Wittgenstein is also elusive about this point, arguing, "The historical accounts in the Gospels might, historically speaking, be demonstrably false and yet belief would lose nothing by this: *not*, however, because it concerns 'universal truths of reason' Rather, because historical proof (the historical proof-game) is irrelevant to belief" (Kenny, *Wittgenstein Reader*, 299–300).

[87] Thomas Aquinas, *Aquinas Against the Averroists: On There Being Only One Intellect*, trans. Ralph McInerny (West Lafayette: Purdue University Press, 1993), V par. 123–24.

hooks onto the world. Furthermore, he thinks the Thomist must fall into the unfortunate position of being a "metaphysical realist," a position he continues to repudiate even from the point of view of commonsense realism.[88] We must therefore briefly examine how his concerns about the pitfalls of metaphysical realism can be accommodated within the Thomistic view and especially whether the "metaphysical realist" must hold as odd a view as Putnam thinks he or she must. This subject matter merits a treatise in itself, so it is necessary to confine our consideration to a few key points.

The Many Faces of Putnam's Realism

Putnam has come a long way back down the road toward realism over the years, so much so that he has recently described his position as "Aristotelian Realism without Aristotelian metaphysics."[89] He has also described the very same position as "Deweyan Realism," and so one must be cautious about interpreting his self-characterizations. In an essay published in his 1994 collection *Words and Life*, for instance, he suggests that he has left behind the view he once called "internal realism."[90] But in a curious footnote to his 1994 Dewey Lectures Putnam offers an ambiguous answer to the same question, reaffirming the core of his older view. The answer merits careful scrutiny since it offers a concise but somewhat elusive account of his position:

> Am I then giving up "internal realism"? Well, while in *Reason, Truth, and History* I identified "internal realism" with what I am here calling "moderate verificationism," in *The Many Faces of Realism* I identified it with the rejection of the traditional realist assumptions of 1) a fixed totality of all objects; 2) a fixed totality of all properties; 3) a sharp line between properties we "discover" in the world and properties we "project" onto the world; 4) a fixed relation of "correspondence" in terms of which truth is supposed to be defined. I rejected those assumptions . . . as unintelligible. . . . I still regard each and every one of those assumptions as unintelligible, although I would argue for that conclusion in a different way. So whether I am still, to some extent, an "internal realist" is, I guess, as unclear as how much I was including under that unhappy label.[91]

Recognition-Transcendence

When we overcome a certain sense of vertigo about this typically Putnamian response to his critics, it is possible to identify several views that he has given up and several that he has held onto. Significantly, he has repudiated any epistemic conception of truth, for instance that truth is "an idealization of rational acceptability," as he had argued in *Reason, Truth, and History*.[92] But he has gone

---

[88] See Putnam, "Sense, Nonsense."
[89] Ibid., 447.
[90] Putnam, *Words and Life*, 306.
[91] Putnam, "Sense, Nonsense," 463 n. 41.
[92] Hilary Putnam, *Reason, Truth, and History* (Cambridge: Cambridge University Press, 1981), 55–56.

even further and is willing to speak of a sense in which truth is recognition-transcendent. Yet he maintains that this new view of recognition-transcendence is still incompatible with metaphysical realism, principally because the latter cannot accommodate interest-relativity.[93] This point proves to be of great importance, since the Thomist can go a significant distance toward agreement with Putnam's position on this subject. That is, in maintaining that Putnam should move toward 'Aristotelian realism with Aristotelian metaphysics', the Thomist will wish to grant partial acceptance and partial denial of interest-relativity.

The impetus to accept a moderately recognition-transcendent view of truth comes from Putnam's sense of dissatisfaction with Dummettian verificationism's need to revise drastically our commonsense understanding of language and logic, for instance the classical principle of bivalence and the reality of the past.[94] Putnam wishes to avoid what he views as metaphysical realism's commitment to a mysterious "substantive property" of truth, lurking in the background.[95] But he wants at the same time to maintain a commitment to the mind-independence of truth. Put simply, what guarantees the truth of a statement is ultimately the fact that things are as they are, and that is so whether we can conceive of it or not. Speaking of the past-tense assertion "Lizzie Borden killed her parents with an axe," he notes:

> What makes it true, if it is, is simply that Lizzie Borden killed her parents with an axe. The recognition transcendence of truth comes, in this case, to no more than the "recognition transcendence" of some killings.[96]

What, then, is the mysterious substantive property of truth that we must repudiate? Putnam offers an illustration: "It is true that the sky would still have been blue even if language users had not evolved, it is not true that *true propositions* would still have existed."[97] The offensive view of truth to which the metaphysical realist must essentially be committed is a sort of Platonic account of the eternality of propositions, not merely the claim that truth is recognition-transcendent.

Although there are some metaphysical realists who would be committed to this view, it is clear that the Thomist need have no such commitment to the nature of truth. In his explicit treatment of the subject of truth in the *Summa theologiae* Aquinas argues that truth is found principally in the intellect, insofar as there is a conformity between the intellect and the thing known.[98] More provocatively, he grants that some truth is eternal, but only because God is an

---

[93] Putnam, "Sense, Nonsense," 494.
[94] Ibid.
[95] Ibid., 500.
[96] Ibid., 511.
[97] Putnam, *Words and Life*, 302.
[98] Aquinas, *ST* I.16.1.

eternal intellect. Hence, if per impossibile God did not exist, there would be no eternal truth.[99] Furthermore, although Aquinas certainly argues that truth and being are convertible terms, it seems fair to conclude that the Thomist need say no more about this than Putnam has said about the sky being what it is and Lizzie Borden's actions being what they were whether or not we could form judgments about them. Truth is founded on being, but it is not a mysterious, elusive, Platonic entity. With regard to this point, at least, Putnam and the Thomist have much about which to agree.

The Crucial Point of Contention

Before we rest in the conclusion that Putnam is merely shadowboxing, we must consider briefly what he has not repudiated from his earlier internal realist view. We might capture the key tenets of this position under three headings: (1) interest-relativity, (2) the denial of privileged descriptions, and (3) incommensurability in the stronger sense (including incompatible descriptions). For Putnam, all three of these are tightly bound together. With his continued commitment to these theses, we have reached a point where, it seems, Putnam and the Thomist must part ways. The problem of interest-relativity arises from the putative failure of the metaphysical realist to reject hyperrealism about the property of truth. This commitment leads to the idea that nature has "its very own language which it is waiting for us to discover and use."[100] In Putnam's own case, before 1975 the language of choice was that of science.[101] His rejection of scientific reductionism was therefore also the rejection of the project of seeking one true absolutely privileged metaphysical description of the world as it is in itself.[102] He appears to have generalized this idea, however, arguing that metaphysical realism must in all cases be committed to the denial of interest-relativity or to the denial of variant descriptions and antireductionism. As he puts it, "Traditional forms of realism are committed to the claim that it makes sense to speak of a fixed totality of all 'objects' that our propositions can be about."[103] The progress of science in the form of modern particle physics has shown us that the quest for the ultimate particle or basic physical object in terms of which everything can be counted is a pipe dream.[104] Likewise, he argues, traditional attempts to carve nature at the joints are bound to fail. He gives as an example the case of an ordinary table lamp. If we grant the traditional notion that a single object is one whose parts move with it, then the lamp and its shade cannot be an object if the shade falls off while it is in motion.[105] From the interest-relativity of

[99]   Ibid., I.16.7.
[100] Putnam, *Words and Life*, 302.
[101] Ibid., 303.
[102] Ibid., 302.
[103] Putnam, "Sense, Nonsense," 449.
[104] Ibid., 451.
[105] Ibid., 450. As we shall see later, this example represents a caricature of Aquinas's view of the nature of the term 'object', which is an analogous term admitting of variant descriptions. Although Aquinas is committed to the existence of certain privileged descriptions, referring to

the notion of an object and the futility of the search for the absolute language of description, Putnam infers his second point concerning conceptual relativity: that there are no metaphysically privileged descriptions of things.[106]

We are compelled to postulate that he infers the third point, incommensurable languages of description, at least in part from the first two, since as we have seen, incommensurability continues to figure in his most recent work on religious language. Moreover, given his previous interest in ontological relativity and incompatible descriptions during his earlier internal realist phase, that would appear to include incommensurability in the stronger sense already mentioned. But this conclusion must be drawn with some caution because it would appear that Putnam's understanding of incommensurability may itself be undergoing some shift. This shift, in turn, opens up the possibility that Putnam and the Thomists need not remain so far apart concerning their views of religious discourse. In another footnote to his *Dewey Lectures* he takes up the question of one of his most frequently used examples of incommensurable languages, the quantum-mechanical description of the particle/wave duality.[107] According to his previous view, the incommensurable languages of description in this case implied a form of conceptual and ontological relativity, argued for on pragmatist grounds.[108] Along with his rejection of an epistemic conception of truth in the *Dewey Lectures*, Putnam is much more cautious about reading ontological implications into the particle/wave duality:

> My current view on the interpretation of quantum mechanics is that the quantum theories are best thought of as describing real physical things—not just the behavior of measuring instruments. . . . How quantum-mechanical "particles," "fields," etc., act when they are not being measured can be "pictured" in various incompatible ways . . . all of them paradoxical and none of them compelling.[109]

The sense in which this constitutes a shift in Putnam's thinking is not entirely clear, but it seems to indicate movement away from the notion that variant descriptions can be conceptually and ontologically incompatible.

---

organic natural kinds, he would have no problem granting that the sortal term 'object' may be fixed relative to certain interests, especially with respect to artifacts such as lamps and their shades. He can even admit a certain amount of interest-relativity with regard to sortal terms for natural entities.

[106] Putnam, *Words and Life*, 302.

[107] For a discussion of this example illustrating his earlier view, see, e.g., Hilary Putnam, "Realism with a Human Face," in *Realism with a Human Face*, ed. James Conant (Cambridge: Harvard University Press, 1990), 3–11. See also Hilary Putnam, "A Defense of Internal Realism," in *Realism with a Human Face*, 38–39, for a critique of antireductionist metaphysical realism and a defense of a pragmatist form of ontological relativity.

[108] See Putnam, "Defense of Internal Realism," 41–42.

[109] Putnam, "Sense, Nonsense," 506.

A Thomist Response

What, then, can the Thomist say in response to these three central tenets of Putnam's position? Two crucial points can be made. First, in supporting Aristotelian/Thomistic realism, it is simply not the case that we need to deny every kind of interest-relativity. Second, the Thomist will want to maintain that although interest-relativity entails variant descriptions, it entails neither the denial of all metaphysically privileged descriptions nor that we should concede such descriptions can be incommensurable in the stronger sense of affirming ontological and epistemic incompatibility and denying the possibility of bridge premises between discourses.

With regard to the first point, Aquinas provides numerous examples of interest-relative classifications of objects, some of them quite pertinent to the present discussion. Two useful examples are the cases of moral acts and the classification of objects in logic and natural philosophy.[110] With regard to moral acts, two important kinds of interest-relativity arise: (1) with respect to the classification of different types of moral acts and (2) with respect to the individuation of different moral acts. Aquinas grants that a single kind of natural act, say an instance of human procreative sexual activity, can be placed in two differing moral species. Thus, the same kind of natural sexual activity within marriage is virtuous and outside it is vicious.[111] Furthermore, whereas from the natural viewpoint they cause the same effect, from the moral point of view they cause different effects. More significant, Aquinas also grants that numerically the same natural act can be placed in different moral species depending upon the change of the intention of the agent. Thus there is, for Aquinas, no absolutely neutral point from which to ask the question, 'How many human actions did you undertake today?' even though he certainly thinks there are correct and incorrect answers to this question depending upon the moral theoretical context.

A similar example occurs in the case of the classification of various types of substances in logic and natural philosophy. This example is most interesting because it illustrates how a naive interpretation of the medieval conception of genera and species of objects in the world must be avoided. Aquinas notes that according to logic we have a general concept 'substance' that constitutes a single genus of things into which fall both material and immaterial entities, but according to natural philosophy, material and immaterial entities fall into different genera.[112] Thus, he is quite accustomed to the idea that the classification and individuation of different stretches of reality can vary according to different interests and points of view.

It is, of course, true that unlike Putnam, Aquinas does think there are various sorts of metaphysically privileged descriptions. In particular, Aquinas would

---

[110] I am indebted to Chris Tollefsen for suggesting the first-mentioned class of examples.

[111] See Aquinas, *ST* I-II.18.5.

[112] See ibid., I-II.88.2, and Thomas Aquinas, *Expositio super librum Boethii De Trinitate*, ed. B. Decker (Leiden: Brill, 1955), 6.3c.

deny Putnam's antiessentialism and assert an ontology of natural kinds, which individuates certain stretches of reality into natural organic substances. Haldane has offered the argument that such a theory of natural kinds not only would be consistent but would do important explanatory work in showing how Putnam's newfound commitment to direct or commonsense realism can succeed.[113] That is, according to Haldane, we can make sense of immediate realism only if we accept the notion that there are mind-independent structures of reality that are formally identical with our conceptual grasp of them. Putnam has seen the force of this argument and in fact grants that it provides a prima facie attractive alternative to causal theories of reference, which he has rejected on the grounds of semantic permutation arguments.[114]

In the final analysis, Putnam rejects the possibility of such natural kinds on two accounts, first that we have been frequently wrong in the past about the metaphysically deep structure of various kinds of things, and second that examples can be given of various incompatible descriptions of natural kinds from different scientific points of view.[115] It is beyond the scope of the present analysis to offer a full response to these arguments, so we must content ourselves with two observations that render the case for such natural kinds plausible. First, contrary to an overly simple caricature of Aquinas's theory of knowledge, it is perfectly consistent with his view that the metaphysically deep structure of reality will become clear to us only over time and that in consequence we may have to revise our conceptual account of reality as it becomes so. Second, Haldane has offered a compelling argument for thinking that the various biological and biochemical descriptions of natural kinds that Putnam cites can be viewed as variant but not incompatible descriptions that contribute to moving us toward a metaphysically deeper understanding of the structure of reality.[116]

CONCLUSION

How, then, shall we characterize the Thomist response to Putnam's invitation to dialogue about the nature of religious discourse? There is manifest disagreement about substantive issues, including Putnam's continued resistance to metaphysical realism and the nature of the incommensurability between religious and nonreligious language. It is premature, however, to conclude that such disagreement is intractable. Putnam's resistance to metaphysical realism no longer seems to be predicated upon the sort of conceptual and ontological relativity he previously endorsed. Having rejected an epistemic account of truth and having even endorsed a moderate thesis concerning recognition-transcendence, he remains opposed only to realism's putative commitment to a single absolute de-

---

[113] John Haldane, "On Coming Home to (Metaphysical) Realism," *Philosophy* 71 (1996): 291.

[114] Putnam, *Words and Life*, 69–71.

[115] Ibid., 73–79.

[116] Haldane, "On Coming Home," 288–91.

scription of reality. He thinks that this denial of interest-relativity and a hyper-realist conception of truth as a 'substantive property' is required by the Thomist metaphysical realist's commitment to essentialism, or an ontology of natural kinds.

But we have seen that Aquinas's realism does not require these consequences. Furthermore, despite his postulation of metaphysically privileged schemes of description, we have seen that Aquinas's account of religious discourse can be responsive to Putnam's concern that our grasp of the meaning of theological terms must be embedded in a form of life. It would appear that substantive room for disagreement remains about the sense in which religious discourse is incommensurable with nonreligious discourse, but Putnam himself wishes to avoid a noncognitive or relativistic interpretation of the relation between the two. With his enhanced commitment to the recognition-transcendence of truth, there is hope that we can find the *words* and the *practices* to bridge that gap.

12

Realist Reference to God:
Analogy or Univocity?

PHILIP A. ROLNICK

Since the times of Thomas Aquinas and John Duns Scotus, the most exalted short list of predicates for reference to God, the 'transcendentals' or 'pure perfection terms,' such as 'being,' 'good,' and 'true,' have been construed either analogically or univocally. Since it has been rightly said, "To understand a philosopher you must understand what he is afraid of,"[1] how might the particular fears of these competing claimants for realist reference to God be summarized? On the one hand, those who favor univocity over analogy fear that analogical predication is knowingly or unknowingly agnostic—that the presuppositions of Thomist or neo-Thomist analogy actually prevent our knowledge of God. On the other hand, those who favor analogy fear that univocal predication about God and humans is impossible—that ignoring the ontological distinctiveness of God as the referent, univocity deforms theological inquiry. By examining (1) Aquinas's arguments, (2) William P. Alston's substantive criticisms of those arguments, and (3) Alston's own counterproposal for univocity, this chapter will attempt to outline the basic case for the superiority of analogy.

"TWO PATHS DIVERGED"

In his study of Duns Scotus, Etienne Gilson tries to make sense of the univocity or analogy preference in relating God and humans. According to Gilson, Duns Scotus attempts to relate the different subjects strictly through a *concept*

I am indebted to several people who read earlier drafts of this chapter, including William Alston. Although I have argued from the other side of the net from Alston, he has raised issues and criticisms that have improved my own understanding. Also, I would like to thank Gavin Colvert, Richard McClelland, W. Norris Clarke, David B. Burrell, and Reinhard Hütter for their suggestions.

[1] Martin Simon, "Identity and Analogy: Balthasar's Hölderlin and Hamann," in *The Analogy of Beauty: The Theology of Hans Urs von Balthasar*, ed. John Riches (Edinburgh: T & T Clark, 1986), 34.

whereas Aquinas insists that relating such different subjects as God and humans requires the additional exercise of *compositio* (judgment).[2]

> St. Thomas distinguishes between two operations of the understanding. The first is that which Aristotle calls the intellection of simple objects (*intelligentia indivisibilium*), which consists in apprehending essence as something indivisible. The second is that which combines essences among themselves or separates them, forming propositions. This second operation, which St. Thomas calls *compositio*, is called today 'judgment.' These two distinct operations both concern the real, but they do not penetrate it equally far. Intellection reaches the essence which the definition formulates. The judgment reaches the very act-of-being: *Prima operatio respicit quidditatem rei, secunda respicit esse ipsius* [*In I Sent.*, I, 19, 5, I ad 7]. . . . To be is to exercise an act. It requires therefore an act to express it. To the static character of the essence corresponds that of the definition simply presented to the intuition of the intellect. To the dynamic character of the act of existing corresponds that of the judgment. . . . This is why, moreover, the active spring of the judgment, its copula, is always a verb, the verb 'is.' The judgment puts all its relations in terms of existence because its proper function is to signify the act of existing.[3]

Although both approaches require conceptual understanding, judgment further attempts to grasp the *esse* (the act of being). It is doubtful that Aquinas can be understood without this second operation, for the semantics is largely determined by the metaphysics.

Even at the level of defining the basic options for referring to God, disagreements arise. Alston defines the terms and sets out the categorial boundaries as follows:

> A term is *univocal* in two or more uses when it bears the same sense (meaning) in those uses. A term is *equivocal* in two or more uses when it bears different senses in those uses. Analogy, in the semantic sense that is in question here, is a species of equivocity. A term is used analogically in two or more employments when it is used in different senses, but those senses are related to each other in appropriate ways.[4]

Several problems emerge at this point. First, Alston's complete attention to the *semantic* sense of the terms already leaves out Aquinas's ontological focus on

---

[2] Etienne Gilson, *Jean Duns Scot: Introduction à ses positions fondamentales* (Paris: J. Vrin, 1952), 101 ff.

[3] Gilson, *The Christian Philosophy of St. Thomas Aquinas*, trans. L. K. Shook, C.S.B. (New York: Random House, 1956), 40–41.

[4] William P. Alston, "Aquinas on Theological Predication: A Look Backward and a Look Forward," in *Reasoned Faith: Essays in Philosophical Theology in Honor of Norman Kretzmann*, ed. Eleonore Stump (Ithaca: Cornell University Press, 1993), 148. Henceforth, this work, which contains Alston's most extended criticisms of Aquinas, is cited parenthetically within the text, e.g., "(Alston, 160)."

existing things, whether those existents be creatures or God, whom Aquinas often refers to as *ipsum esse subsistens* (subsistent act of being).[5] In terms of Gilson's distinction, we can see already that Alston is heading down the strictly conceptual path of Scotus.

Furthermore, Alston's definition of univocity significantly differs from Aquinas's, where "whatever is predicated of many things univocally is either a genus, a species, a difference, an accident, or a property."[6] Since God is not in any genus and has neither accidents nor intrinsic differentiation, no term can be predicated univocally of God and creatures.

Yet although Aquinas rules out univocity because of the ontological distinction of God from all else that is (divine simplicity), he offers multiple arguments why more than purely equivocal predication between God and creatures can be accomplished. First, when God and creatures, especially humans, share a property such as 'good,' the property is ordered by cause and effect. Thus creation is the causal bond that transmits properties from God to humans, but for Aquinas, God not only is the cause of human perfections but also possesses those perfections in an eminent manner (*via eminentiae*).[7] Hence, both parties, God and humans, possess the given perfection *intrinsically*. Second, whereas pure equivocation has likeness in name only but not in the things themselves, by contrast, "there is a certain mode of likeness of things to God." Third, purely equivocal predication about different things gives no knowledge of how the things are related. Because of shared meaning, however, "from what we find in other things, we do arrive at a knowledge of divine things." Fourth, since equivocation "impedes the process of reasoning," then "no reasoning proceeding from creatures to God could take place. But, the contrary is evident from all those who have spoken about God." Fifth, "a name is predicated of some being uselessly unless through that name we understand something of the being." Yet Aquinas thinks that we can say some things and prove some things about God. Sixth, in reply to those who claim that the names for God tell us only what God is not, Aquinas argues that more than pure equivocation takes place because "it will at least have to be the case that *living* said of God and creatures agrees in the denial of the lifeless" (*SCG* I.33.2–7). Moreover, since God possesses all

[5] For a treatment of the focus on existing things, see David B. Burrell, C.S.C., "Aquinas and Scotus: Contrary Patterns for Philosophical Theology," in *Theology and Dialogue: Essays in Conversation with George Lindbeck*, ed. Bruce D. Marshall (Notre Dame: University of Notre Dame Press, 1990), 105–29.

[6] St. Thomas Aquinas, *On the Truth of the Catholic Faith (Summa contra Gentiles)*, trans. Anton C. Pegis, F.R.S.C. (Garden City, N.Y.: Image Books, 1955), I.32.4. Further citations appear parenthetically in the text as *SCG*.

[7] Although creation provides a certain kind of causal bond between God and creatures, because creation is to be understood as *creatio ex nihilo*, God cannot be understood as part of a causal chain within space-time. The ex nihilo aspect of creation actually reinforces the distinction between God and all else that is; hence, it reinforces the reasons for preferring analogy over univocity.

perfections and is the cause of all genera, a certain resemblance of the creature to God (as well as the possibility of expressing that resemblance) is given.

Given these arguments, Alston's claim that "analogy . . . is a species of equivocation" unreasonably conflates Aquinas's categories in which analogy is developed as an alternative to both univocity and equivocation. Alston might argue that if univocity is using a term for God and humans in exactly the same sense, then analogy, like pure equivocation, is other than univocal usage. He cannot, however, justifiably conclude from this merely negative commonality (that is, neither analogy nor equivocation is univocity) that analogy is a "species of equivocation." Instead, given Aquinas's arguments above for why more than equivocation is present in our (analogical) reference to God, analogy must be categorized as different from *both* univocity and equivocation. The categorial independence of analogy functions as a theological golden mean in which the uniqueness of the divine-human relationship is expressed and both the excess of univocity and the deficiency of equivocation are averted.

SIMPLICITY, PARTICIPATION, AND JUDGMENT

At least in part, Aquinas's argument for the venerable doctrine of simplicity (no real distinctions in God or intrinsic accidental properties) is based on the insight that the origin of all things cannot come from nothing and that it is impossible for the first being to compose itself ex nihilo. Furthermore, if any thing, being, or principle composed the parts of God, it would have to be prior and superior to God. Hence, Aquinas argues that God must be simple, must be fully, infinitely actualized, and must lack nothing on the intrinsic level of the divine being.[8] Simplicity forces us to recognize that reference to God is reference to a *unique* being, a salutary reminder for those who undertake the tasks of philosophical theology. Simplicity is a way of saying that God is distinct from all else that is. Analogical discourse incorporates this distinction. Univocal discourse would incorporate its de facto denial. Yet both discourse formations variously seek to relate God and human through the shared transcendentals.

To assert simplicity is an intensely positive affirmation of divine unity. Indeed, simplicity functions as an *infinite* unity of existence and essence. What is sewn in a virtuous mortal (see Plato's *Protagoras* 329d, where Socrates argues for the unity of the virtues) is seamless in the divine being. In fact, we could say that in Aquinas's terms, what Socrates seeks is possible only in God. What God is and the way God is are perfectly, infinitely, seamlessly unified. In metaphysical terms, God's essence is identical to God's existence. In religious terms, God is so fully alive, existent, and active that there is nothing that can be added to God's infinite perfection. Simplicity implies that there is no way to improve

---

[8] St. Thomas Aquinas, *Summa Theologica*, trans. Fathers of the English Dominican Province (London: Burns, Oates and Washburn, 1920), I.3. Further citations appear parenthetically in the text as *ST*.

God. But note that what is excluded is a higher level of intrinsic being, not the existence of other, finite beings.[9]

The proper effect of the God who is the infinite act of being is to make other beings actual (*ST* I.8.1; I.45.5). Thus human life and thought is first and foremost to be understood as creaturely life, as life that bears the birthmark of created, composed status. Where God is the unique, infinite, simple being whose existence and essence are the same, finite essence limits finite existence. The development of the act/potency and essence/existence distinctions are metaphysical counterparts to the uniqueness and originality of creation ex nihilo. The freshness of creation implies something new, something other than God. Creation ex nihilo implies that in all that is created, act is distinguished from potency, essence from existence.

Throughout Aquinas's corpus analogical predication linguistically expresses participation metaphysics, which in turn is an expression of his doctrine of creation.[10] As Aquinas states it:

> Now nothing is predicated of God and creatures as though they were in the same order, but, rather, according to priority and posteriority. For all things are predicated of God essentially. For God is called being as being entity itself, and He is called good as being goodness itself. But in other beings predications are made by participation, as Socrates is said to be a man, not because he is humanity itself, but because he possesses humanity. It is impossible, therefore, that anything be predicated univocally of God and other things. (*SCG* I.32.7)

> Likeness of creatures to God is not affirmed on account of agreement in form according to the formality of the same genus or species, but solely according to analogy, inasmuch as God is essential being, whereas other things are beings by participation. (*ST* I.4.3.ad. 3)

So where God infinitely actualizes a given property, the human participates it. Even though the property in question is shared, because of the simple/composed, infinite/finite, Creator/creature, eternal/time-sequential distinction, the attribution cannot be univocal. To participate is to have a share of, to actualize to some degree. The participation of the creature is given to it by the creator, who thereby gives its potential, its telos, in its relation to the infinite actuality of the divine being; for the closer a creature approaches God, the more fully it exists (*ST* I.5.3. ad. 2).

---

[9] A point elaborated by W. Norris Clarke, S.J., *The Philosophical Approach to God: A Contemporary Neo-Thomist Perspective* (Winston-Salem: Wake University Press, 1979), 98.

[10] For a chronological analysis of analogy in Aquinas's corpus, see George P. Klubertanz, *St. Thomas Aquinas on Analogy: A Textual Analysis and Systematic Synthesis* (Chicago: Loyola University Press, 1960). Klubertanz shows that although other types of analogy are used in early works, participation metaphysics is predominant in the corpus, especially in the more mature works.

God's being is not participated directly. Were direct participation the case, the independence of the finite would be compromised by God's total domination. Creatures would be mere components of the divine rather than independent beings. Creation would not be *other* to God. If, *per impossibile*, the independence of creation could be removed, then the objections to univocity would also be removed, but doing so would compromise the integrity of creation, the integrity that is its most precious characteristic. In avoiding a necessary relation to the creation, God has evidently enabled an even greater possibility: being related to the creation by personal and mutual prerogatives of intellect and will.[11] Thus God, understood as *ipsum esse subsistens* (subsistent act of being), remains distinct from, but related by intellect and will to, *esse commune* (being in general). Freedom is evidently part of the plan, for not only is God the cause of goodness in others, God also gives others the power to cause goodness (*ST* I.103.4; *SCG* III.21). In this understanding of creation (and participation) as non-necessary, a noetic and ontological possibility is given with the creation so that humans can respond to the creator and creation through knowledge and love.

As a philosophical shorthand for distinguishing between God and all else that is, simplicity functions as a constant caveat in our reference to God, but Aquinas takes pain to show that it does not falsify our conceptual attributions. Our finite, composed nature prevents any one term from being univocally applied to God's infinite act of being, but what we say can nonetheless be true:

> The proposition, *The intellect understanding anything otherwise than it is, is false*, can be taken in two senses, accordingly as this adverb *otherwise* determines the word *understanding* on the part of the thing understood, or on the part of the one who understands. Taken as referring to the thing understood, the proposition is true, and the meaning is: Any intellect which understands that the thing is otherwise than it is, is false. But this does not hold in the present case; because our intellect, when forming a proposition about God, does not affirm that He is composite, but that He is simple. But taken as referring to the one who understands, the proposition is false. For the mode of the intellect in understanding is different than the mode of the thing in its essence. Since it is clear that our intellect understands material things below itself in an immaterial manner; not that it understands them to be immaterial things; but its manner of understanding is immaterial. Likewise, when it understands simple things above itself, it understands them according to its own mode, which is in a composite manner; yet not so as to understand them to be composite things. And thus our intellect is not false in forming composition in its ideas concerning God. (*ST* I.13.12. ad. 3)

---

[11] This point arises from the debate about whether God has "real relations," i.e., necessary relations, with the creation. See Aquinas, *ST* I.28.1–3; David B. Burrell, *Aquinas: God and Action* (Notre Dame: University of Notre Dame Press, 1979), 85–87; and my *Analogical Possibilities: How Words Refer to God* (Atlanta: Scholars Press, 1993; New York: Oxford University Press, 1999), 145–51.

The status of creaturely composition does not prevent understanding a material rock in an immaterial way below us, nor does it prevent forming a compound proposition about God, who is above us and simple (*ST* I.13.12. ad. 3). We can speak about God accurately or inaccurately, wisely or foolishly. We just cannot speak univocally. And yet the encouragement to speak in humility should not be understood as apophatic agnosticism, for successful reference to God is possible. Any such success would not complete our task, however, but only propel us forward. We are thus led to the necessity of joining concept to concept to speak about God; and so we form judgments, where we recognize unity in God and diversity in our way of knowing. As Gilson defines it: "To judge is always to affirm unity by a complex act."[12]

While Aquinas's portrayal of God is served with a philosophical warning that God is always more than human understanding, *more than* does not secretly mean *less than*, unrelated to, or no understanding at all. The openness of analogical terms corresponds to the ongoing nature of the task of relating to and understanding God. Rather than end a given inquiry, say, of the good, true discoveries and affirmations open up further possibilities of discovering more of the infinite good that is actualized in God.

By contrast, univocity has a settled, on/off, right/wrong, algorithmic quality. Comparing analogical predicates with metaphorical ones reveals something similar. Where metaphorical terms begin with a kind of wildness, even verbal violence, over time they settle down into fixed, specific, virtually univocal meanings.[13] By contrast, the short list of transcendental predicates never settles down into reified definitions. What 'good' means is never a settled affair for us. The moving nature of human understanding is yet another argument against univocity in our reference to God. We may and should increase our participation and understanding of what God already perfectly, infinitely, eternally actualizes. The theological/religious goal is progress.

ALSTON'S CRITIQUE OF AQUINAS

Much of Alston's dissatisfaction with Aquinas stems from the claim that Aquinas cannot specify an analogically related sense of perfection terms that adequately fit the divine application, that is, how God possesses a given perfection or how divine knowledge and will function:

> Aquinas makes no pretense of giving a positive account of what this higher way is in which the perfection exists in God. (Alston, 158)

> But we never find him explaining what it is for a creature to have knowledge or the like in terms of what it is for God to have knowledge. (Alston, 160)

---

[12] Gilson, *St. Thomas Aquinas*, 108.

[13] Thus, "to run a red light," or as the French would say, "*brûler le feu*" ("burn the light," or even more literally, "burn the fire"), has come to mean something quite fixed.

Now Aquinas actually does give an account of how perfections exist in God (divine simplicity infinitely unifies all perfections) as well as how creaturely knowledge and other perfections are related to God's (by creaturely participation). Furthermore, Aquinas's calling God "a universally perfect being" and defining universally perfect as "that to which the excellence of no genus is lacking" (*SCG* I.28.1) would seem to answer Alston's first criticism. Alston's concern is more pointed, however: he doubts that Aquinas's simplicity doctrine allows us to make *any* truth claims about God, because

> a condition of truth is that there is a distinction between [an agent] and [his] action. . . . But then that means that none of the statements we make about God can be wholly true. For a necessary condition of the truth of each is that what we are asserting of God is related to Him in a certain way, and hence is distinguishable from Him. And that condition contradicts divine simplicity. Precisely what makes all our terms for God defective in their *modi significandi* prevents anything we say of God from being true. And if truth goes, the game is up with theology. (Alston, 168–69)

So how might this rather sweeping charge be answered?

In "Whether Names Applied to God Are Synonymous" (*ST* I.13.4) Aquinas takes on something like the objection that Alston raises. To the assertion that all names of God are synonymous, Aquinas begins the *Responsio* with a flat counterassertion: "These names spoken of God are not synonymous." He then suggests that these nonsynonymous names (attributes) would be easy to understand if we simply focused on remotion from creatures or used them to express divine causal relation to creatures: "for thus it would follow that there are different ideas as regards the diverse things denied of God, or as regards diverse effects connoted." But Aquinas makes a much stronger claim, namely, that our terms used for God actually do "signify the divine substance, although in an imperfect manner." As always, the doctrine of simplicity, with its concomitants of the essence/existence distinction in all else but God and the notion of creaturely participation, is being invoked. On one level, Alston's criticism amounts to an assertion of nonsimplicity as a prerequisite for *all* truth, whether human, divine, or their interrelationship: "a condition of truth is that there is a distinction between [an agent] and [his] action." This criterion is of course applicable to things human, but whether and how it might apply to God and the divine-human relation is a far more complex matter.

Through creation, that is, divine causality, we receive the transcendentals in a divided and multiplex manner. These same qualities, however, preexist in God "unitedly and simply" (*ST* I.13.4) Our concepts of these transcendentals will naturally correspond to our received, divided, multiple manner of possessing them. Nonetheless, we can conceive that God possesses these qualities simply, perfectly, infinitely, unifiedly. Such a conception, as already mentioned, amounts to the complete and virtuous unity of the most noble qualities, that is, the divine character itself. This conception prevents univocity, but it need not prevent truth claims about the divine nature. As Aquinas argues:

> As, therefore, to the different perfections of creatures there corresponds one simple principle represented by different perfections of creatures in a various and manifold manner, so also to the various and multiplied conceptions of our intellect there corresponds one altogether simple principle, according to these conceptions, imperfectly understood. Therefore, although the names applied to God signify one thing, still because they signify that thing under many and different aspects, they are not synonymous. (*ST* I.13.4)

Aquinas further clarifies that because terms signify through the medium of their conception, "words which signify different aspects of one thing, do not signify primarily and absolutely one thing" (*ST* I.13.4. ad. 1).

Although I think that Alston's criticism correctly identifies the Achilles' heel of analogical discourse and restates the general fear of univocal theorists, I also think that the arguments above adequately defend Aquinas on this point. In short, the properties that we may distinguish in human affairs do not disappear when applied to God. They are, from our perspective, transformed in the simplicity of the divine being but hardly wiped out so that truth claims become impossible. Truth claims are, I would concede, qualified in analogical discourse; but authentic univocal reference would require God's point of view; and this impossible requirement restates the fear of analogical advocates about univocity.

In a related demand for a more positive account, Alston contends:

> Understanding the divine sense [Aquinas's account for how God wills] does not give us as much as we might like to have by way of a detailed conception of what it is for God to will that *P*, for example. (Alston, 161)

Once again to the contrary, Aquinas actually does provide a quite detailed conception of how God wills, including a thirteenth-century version of how God wills that *P*, "That the Divine Will Extends to Singular Goods" (*SCG* I.78). Aquinas begins with an account of how the will, both divine and human, is free but neither independent nor neutral. Instead, the will is inclined toward the good in close association with the intellect that is aware of the good.[14] Now since the divine being is the highest good, and God is omniscient, God thus necessarily wills himself as that highest good:

> Moreover, will accompanies intellect. But by His intellect God principally understands Himself, and He understands other things in Himself. In the same way, therefore, He principally wills Himself, and wills all other things in willing Himself. (*SCG* I.75.7)

---

[14] See Eleonore Stump and Norman Kretzmann, "Absolute Simplicity," *Faith and Philosophy* 2 (October 1985): 353–82.

So where simplicity entails that God is goodness essentially, creatures are good by participation, which participation is derived from God's creating and ordering the creature to the divine being:

> Again, the will of God is related to other things in so far as they participate in goodness in virtue of their order to the divine goodness, which is for God the reason of His willing. But not only the totality of goods, but even each one of them derives its goodness from the divine goodness, as well as its being. Therefore, the will of God extends to singular goods. (*SCG* I. 78.3)

Aquinas further argues that since God is "best and first in relation to singulars," divine simplicity "does not forbid its being related even to many particulars" (*SCG* I.78.2). Simplicity, which distinguishes God from all else, is intended to depict the limitlessness and fullness of God, not to limit God or close God off from the creation, "for a power that can do great things can likewise do small ones" (*SCG* I.70.6).

But Alston repeatedly demands more specific information about how God's knowledge is related to ours:

> The perfection signified is not fully specified; instead we simply indicate that it is a higher form of a creaturely perfection but without being able to say just what the higher form is. (Alston, 171)

> But if we can't *spell out* the ways in which this higher version is like and unlike the lower analogue, how can we even address the question of whether principles that hold of the lower form also hold of the higher form? (Alston, 173; emphasis added)

> By his own admission [Aquinas] is in no position *to spell out* the respects of similarity and dissimilarity between divine and human causal agency, willing, and so on. (Alston, 173; emphasis added)

These criticisms I find puzzling for two reasons. First, as we have seen, Aquinas has given an account of how God is both like and unlike creaturely perfection. Second, since Alston would agree that God's ways are higher than our ways, God's thoughts higher than ours, then what is the point of asking a (human) philosopher for a full account of something higher than her own possibility?

Aquinas rejects univocal predication between God and creatures because of the different way that we have our being, but he likewise rejects the notion, as we have seen, that our truth has nothing to do with God's truth (equivocation). Here again may be seen the wisdom of Aquinas's development of analogy as the middle way. And of course this middle way cannot be quite as clear cut as the extremes of univocity or pure equivocation. Hence, though Aquinas may not satisfy Alston when Alston demands that Aquinas "spell out" how the higher analogue is like and unlike the lower human one, it cannot be said that Aquinas does not give an account that relates the two.

Actually, Aquinas does say quite a bit about God's knowledge, more than alternative accounts can credibly provide. For instance, Aquinas tells us that God's knowledge, as implied by God's simplicity, is not discursive. But this higher, nondiscursive way of knowing does not keep God from knowing and understanding our lower, discursive way of knowledge: "God does not consider one thing after the other as it were in succession, but all together. His knowledge, therefore, is not ratiocinative or discursive, although He knows all discourse and ratiocination" (*SCG* I.57.2).[15] Here again we must caution against tacitly or explicitly holding that anything but discursive knowledge is somehow inferior. Rather than God's having a piecemeal kind of discursive knowledge, Aquinas (1) argues that God comprehends all at once; (2) presents a philosophical admonition about the limited status and methodology of human knowledge; and (3) proposes how the two can be related, that is, through analogy based on participation metaphysics.

In another important criticism of Aquinas, Alston proposes a distinction between 'property' and 'concept' that alleges a range of univocal predication between God and humans. First, he characterizes Aquinas's argument as going from, "God and creatures do not share exactly the same forms," to the conclusion, "No terms can be predicated univocally of God and creatures" (Alston, 174). He then observes that "because for Aquinas terms signify immediately our concepts, and through them what these are concepts of, this claim is based on the assumption that our concepts reflect precisely the ontological character of their objects" (Alston, 174). So as Alston understands Aquinas, since 'wills' for God differs ontologically from 'wills' for humans, the meaning of 'wills' is "correspondingly different" (Alston, 174). Having thus framed the issue, Alston then proposes that a concept need not be so closely conformed to the nature of the thing conceived: "Why suppose that our conceptual operations are so closely tied to the character of what is conceived that we cannot form concepts that prescind from some of those features?" (Alston, 175). Alston then cites part of a passage from the *Commentary on the Sentences* in which he thinks Aquinas is allowing his point. Finally, Alston concludes that if Aquinas can allow this sort of abstraction, then we should likewise be able "to form a concept of willing, knowing, forgiving, or loving that abstracts from the differences in the ways in which these forms are realized in God and creatures, and hence can be predicated univocally of both" (Alston, 175).

Unfortunately, Alston's argument is at least in part based on a misunderstanding of the *Commentary on the Sentences*. What Alston has apparently done is to take the argument of the *Objection* and present it as Aquinas's position. Tellingly, the objection is based on how a logician, who worked without

---

[15] See *SCG* I.55–59 for a fuller account.

considering the element of *being*, might conclude that univocity was possible. As Alston cites the passage:

> The second mode of analogical predication is in effect when several things are put on an equal footing under one and the same common concept, although the nature that they share in common exists diversely in them. Thus all bodies [however diverse they may be in their actual existence] are on a par so far as the concept of corporeity is concerned. Thus the logician, who considers intentions only, says that the term body is predicated univocally of all bodies, and yet corporeity does not exist in corruptible and in incorruptible bodies in the same mode.[16]

However, Alston stops his citation just where Aquinas opposes the metaphysician's and natural philosopher's understanding to the logician's position: "From which according to the metaphysician and the natural philosopher, who consider the thing according to its being, neither this term 'body' nor any other is said univocally of corruptible and incorruptible things."[17] Yet Aquinas's own position goes even further, as he embraces a third option that holds together diverse truths that differ according to both concept and being (*secundum intentionem et secundum esse*):

> And this is when there is equality neither in terms of a common concept nor in terms of being; as being is said of substance and of accident; and in such things, it is necessary that the common nature have some being in each of the things about which it is said, but understood as differing according to a greater or lesser perfection. And similarly I say that truth, and the good, and all such things are said analogously of God and creatures. From which it is appropriate that all these things are in God with respect to his being, and that they are in creatures according to a greater or lesser manner of perfection; from which it follows that they differ in truth, since the two cases cannot exist according to a single act of being.[18]

---

[16] Alston, 175, citing from James F. Anderson's translation, *An Introduction to the Metaphysics of St. Thomas Aquinas* (Chicago: Regnery, 1953), 37.

[17] Aquinas, *Commentum in Primum Librum Sententiarum Magistri Petri Lombardi*, d. XIX, q. 5, a. 2, ad. 1, my translation. "Unde quantum ad metaphysicum et naturalem, qui considerant res secundum suum esse, nec hoc nomen, corpus, nec aliquid aliud dicitur univoce de corruptibilibus et incorruptibilibus, ut patet, X *Met.*, text. 5, ex Philosopho et Commentatore."

[18] Ibid. "Et hoc est quando neque parificatur in intentione communi, neque in esse; sicut ens dicitur de substantia et accidente; et de talibus oportet quod natura communis habeat aliquod esse in unoquoque eorum de quibus dicitur, sed differens secundum rationem majoris vel minoris perfectionis. Et similiter dico, quod veritas, et bonitas, et omnia hujusmodi dicuntur analogice de Deo et creaturis. Unde oportet quod secundum suum esse omnia haec in Deo sint, et in creaturis secundum rationem majoris perfectionis et minoris; ex quo sequitur, cum non possint esse secundum unum esse utrobique, quod sint diversae veritates."

Although Aquinas adjusted his position on this issue over the years,[19] he never advocated anything like the univocity that Alston attributes to him. It is clear that Aquinas understood how someone might advocate such a position ("the logician"), but it is equally clear that he considered it inadequate.

Alston's distinction between 'property' and 'concept' can be helpful when applied (as Aquinas would also) to the concept of finite things. However, when Alston attempts to apply the distinction to how God and humans might share a given property, he once again ignores *being* and takes the purely conceptual path of which Gilson warned. Concept is adequate to grasp form, or at least some part of form. But when Alston summarizes Aquinas thusly, "God and creatures do not share exactly the same forms," he has entered upon a slippery slope; for not sharing exactly the same form would be problematic, but perhaps not overly so. However, Aquinas's position is not that God and humans do not share exactly the same form, but that God is not in *any* form, genus, or species. Hence abstracting from creaturely limitations en route to attribution to God requires more than logic. It requires the recognition that God's simplicity, the infinite unity of *esse* and *essentia* in the divine character, which is not available to discursive reasoning alone, requires a second operation of the mind, one that "considers being itself."[20] Aquinas would agree with Alston that a common property is shared, but he would deny that the sharing was univocal because for Aquinas 'univocal' is restricted to use within the same genus or species, a difference, accident, or property (*SCG* I.32.4). Reference to God is unique because the divine being is not limited, not *formed*, not finite. Therefore, something more than concept and property is required, something that enlivens the concept through attention to the act of being.

ALSTON'S *RES/MODUS* CRITICISM

Much of Alston's critique of Aquinas and analogy is centered upon Aquinas's *modus significandi/res significata* (way of signifying/thing signified) distinction (Alston, 161–67). As is his wont, in his critique of the *res/modus* distinction Alston attempts to abstract the semantic treatment from the doctrine of creation that guides Aquinas's semantics: "I must confess that I can't see why Aquinas thinks that the first order [causal or ontological priority] is an order that has to do with words" (Alston, 160). Given our subject matter, this implied separation of the ontological from the logical is itself puzzling. As David Burrell comments:

> The medievals were no strangers, certainly, to the paradigms of formal logic. They assumed that no proposed argument could contravene these paradigms. This test alone, however, was not regarded as a sufficient one. For besides

---

[19] See Klubertanz, *Aquinas on Analogy*, for an account of such adjustments.

[20] See notes 2 and 3.

the universal principles of logic there remain the principles proper to the domain under consideration.[21]

Undertaking philosophical theology, why must we divorce Aquinas's doctrinal commitment to creation from his semantic treatment of the relation between creatures and the creator? Understanding Aquinas's use of analogy requires holding the "ontological communication" of creation together with our subsequent semantic communication about, and perhaps to, God.[22]

Addressing the titular question "Whether Any Name Can Be Applied to God in Its Literal Sense," Aquinas explicates the *res/modus* distinction as follows:

> Our knowledge of God is derived from the perfections which flow from Him to creatures, which perfections are in God in a more eminent way than in creatures. Now our intellect apprehends them as they are in creatures, and as it apprehends them it signifies them by names. Therefore as to the names applied to God, there are two things to be considered—viz., the perfections which they signify, such as goodness, life, and the like, and their mode of signification. As regards what is signified by these names, they belong properly to God, and more properly than they belong to creatures, and are applied primarily to Him. But as regards their mode of signification, they do not properly and strictly apply to God; for their mode of signification applies to creatures. (*ST* I.13.3 Responsio)

Given the intrinsic composition of creatures, the creaturely mode of signification has to reflect our synthetic activity of joining subject to verb, even when we are referring to the intrinsic simplicity of God.

Where Alston interprets emptiness of meaning due to a perceived lack of determinateness (Alston, 172), an excess of meaning can equally well be asserted.[23] For in the *res/modus* distinction, Aquinas portrays properties that appear to begin with human naming but in fact begin with eminent actuality in the divine being and are subsequently communicated to humans through divine causality. In the *res/modus* distinction such predicates as 'good' and 'wise' do not become equivocal or lose their meaning when applied to God; instead, they retain all their human force and understanding and are *intensified* in the ana-

---

[21] Burrell, *Aquinas*, 3. Also, see Alvin Plantinga, "Advice to Christian Philosophers" *Faith and Philosophy* 1 (July 1984): 253–71, which argues that Christian philosophers may and should bring certain presuppositions to their work. In fact, the insistence that each science has its own first principle goes back at least to Aristotle, *Nicomachean Ethics*, 1098b.

[22] "Ontological communication" is from Jean Richard, "Analogie et symbolism chez saint Thomas," *Laval Théologique et Philosophique* (October 1974): 392.

[23] The complaint about 'indeterminateness' may be a bit tendentious, given Alston's recognition that "most or all predicate terms have meanings that are vague, exhibit 'open texture', or suffer from indeterminacy in other ways." See William P. Alston, "Can We Speak Literally of God?" in *Divine Nature and Human Language: Essays in Philosophical Theology* (Ithaca: Cornell University Press, 1989), 43 n. 4.

logical act of applying such terms to God. In the act of recognizing God as infinite exemplar and original source of the property in question, our human understanding of the property is reoriented to God, who makes shared possession of the property possible. In the conceptual reversal realized in the *res/modus* distinction, the meaning of shared properties is grounded in the prior ontological communication of creation, affirmed in its creaturely use, and drawn forward toward greater imitation of the divine manner in which the perfection is held. Were the meaning so firmly fixed that it could be univocally stated once and for all, the need to express analogically this forward motion toward God would be obviated. Any property worthy of *literal* predication of both God and humans, that is, the transcendentals, must have sufficient flexibility (a concomitant of 'indeterminateness') to be attributed to both finite and infinite, complex and simple, human and God. Without such flexibility, the term could not allow for growth of understanding as we approach God.

Overlooking (or, at least, dismissing) the analogical unity that Aquinas's account offers, Alston's understanding of Aquinas bifurcates the shared predicates between God and humans. This problematic understanding is generated when Alston conflates Aquinas's claim of *literal* reference with univocity. Alston claims that Aquinas "certainly gives the impression that all is clear sailing, *univocity*-wise, with the perfection signified" (Alston, 164; my emphasis) and then in the next sentence illicitly substitutes "literal" to support this claim. Thus citing Aquinas, Alston writes: " 'So far as the perfections signified are concerned the words are used *literally* of God' (*ST* I, 13, 3, R)" (Alston, 164; my emphasis). The substitution is especially surprising since Alston carefully differentiates 'univocal' from 'literal' in other writings, where 'univocal' means "the application to God of the terms in question in just the same sense as that in which they are applied to us (straight univocity). . . . Now we must not confuse 'univocal' and 'literal.' "[24] The apparent misrepresentation of Aquinas and analogical theory is reiterated when Alston (correctly) states that "an opponent of literal theological talk is denying that any *intrinsic* predicate can be literally true of God"[25] but unwarrantedly links analogy to such denial: "those who deny that any terms (concepts) we can form can be literally applied to God: the alternatives of analogy, metaphor, symbolism, etc."[26] He then seems to overlook both Aquinas's explicit differentiation of metaphor from analogy due to *intrinsic* possession of the property signified (*ST* I.13.6) as well as Aquinas's explicit affirmation that some terms can be literally predicated of God, as he addresses the question cited above, "Whether Any Name Can Be Applied to God in Its Literal Sense" (*ST* I.13.3).

Aquinas consistently differentiates 'literal' from 'equivocation,' where a given predicate intrinsically belongs to one subject but not to the other in the

---

[24] Alston, *Divine Nature*, 14.
[25] See Alston, "Can We Speak Literally," 39–63, particularly 40.
[26] Alston, "Divine and Human Action," in *Divine Nature*, 81–102, particularly 102.

comparison. So if we were to say, "God is our rock," the literal meaning of 'rock' cannot be applied to God because 'rock' primarily designates a material object and the materiality of the rock must be denied in referring to God; therefore, the reference remains purely extrinsic. (See, for example, *ST* I.13.6. Responsio.) By contrast, Alston himself recognizes that for Aquinas,

> some terms can be used literally (*proprie*) of God, namely, those that do not include in their meaning the imperfect mode in which a perfection is realized in creatures, for example, such terms as 'being', 'good', and 'living'. (Alston, 147)

Note especially the etymological sense of Aquinas's *proprie*, in which something *intrinsically* belongs to the nature of the subject in question, that is, it is *appropriate*. Applying terms literally, in the sense of *proprie*, means that the subject in question intrinsically possesses the attribute. The case for successful analogical predication about God rests on an account of how God and creatures can intrinsically share the transcendental predicates. This sharing, however, will never settle into a defined, univocal core. The ontological dependence upon God as infinite exemplar, source, and final goal presents the human subject with the possibility of acknowledging and actualizing a dynamic, moving state caused by being in relation to God, a relation and an orientation in which the very being of the creature is constituted (*ST* I.45.3).

Alston's critique, fueled by the substitution of 'univocal' for 'literal,' strangely tears asunder what analogy has joined together: "There is no hint in these passages that the *res significata* side of the matter forces a change in the meaning of pure perfection terms when applied to God" (164). Once again to the contrary, Aquinas's doctrine of simplicity forces a different kind of discussion. It is not just the epistemological problem that the *modus significandi* is different between God and human. It is first and foremost the case that the varying ways that God and humans *possess* shared qualities constitutes a seeming ontological divide—but one that has been bridged by divine causality (creation), which makes possible human participation, and the analogical discourse that expresses such participation. Hence Aquinas never attempts a separate discourse about the *res* or *modus* side of the distinction. The point is to hold them together.

Yet Alston argues that (1) the lack of univocity "would seem" to apply only to the *modus significandi* side, and then concludes, (2) "But if the lack of univocity attaches only to the *modus significandi* side of the matter, there is no room for analogically related senses" (165). Alston's argument seems to be that because Aquinas thinks that "the words are used literally of God" (*ST* I.13.3. R), we really have univocity in referring to God, except that the creaturely way of signifying is defective:

> Hence it appears that the doctrine of an analogical meaning of theological terms has been frozen out; there is no place for it. Instead of analogically related crea-

turely and divine senses, what we have are creaturely senses all up and down the line, together with the recognition that one aspect of each sense is ineluctably *inappropriate* for application to the divine. (Alston, 165; my emphasis)

The flaw in Alston's interpretation is that Aquinas, as Alston himself cites him, does think that the transcendentals can be used literally (*proprie*) of both God and humans. As we have seen, the status of the creaturely intellect does not prevent understanding a material rock in an immaterial way below us, nor does it prevent forming a compound proposition about God, who is above us and simple (*ST* I.13.12. ad. 3). The flexibility of analogical discourse makes it suitable to express recognized ontological differences.

Alston's claim that Aquinas "is not in a position to map, delimit, or demarcate that area of indeterminacy" in the higher way that God possesses a given perfection (172) is refuted by human participation in the perfection, wherein we already resemble God and may increase such resemblance by moving toward God in intellect and will. The mapped out, limited, demarcated, determined, defined, and the like can be applied to human accomplishments as a sort of lower limit. What humans know, discover, or accomplish is not nothing; but neither, given the incompleteness and dynamic of our relation to the fullness of God, is it forever settled in a "univocal core." For though all human knowledge is relative, it is meaningfully relative in relation to the absolute *perfectio* of the divine being (*ST* I.4). As Rudi te Velde puts it, "The human mind in its philosophical inquiry into reality passes through a dialectical process of experience in which each next phase is born from a reflection on the inadequacy of the previous one."[27] Recognizing the finite inability to comprehend the infinity of the divine being, analogy incorporates an epistemological humility that may serve as a heuristic device for further discovery.

ALSTON'S ALTERNATIVE: FUNCTIONALISM AND UNIVOCITY

Having addressed much of Alston's criticism of Aquinas, let us now examine Alston's claims to have demonstrated a successful account of univocity. Seeking "a concept that is . . . common to divine and human knowing, willing, or whatever," Alston suggests: "If the question is merely whether one can form *any* concept that applies equally to God and human beings, that is easily answered. Try *not identical with Richard Nixon* or *possible object of thought*" (Alston, 176 n. 41). Both suggestions fail for the same reason: they are purely *extrinsic* attributions (something that Alston elsewhere recognizes). Whether our best candidate for realist reference to God ends up being univocity or analogy, a retreat into purely extrinsic attribution is more akin to the reason for which both Alston and I dismiss panmetaphoricism. Hence, these first examples have no bearing on the matter at hand.

[27] Rudy A. te Velde, *Participation and Substantiality in Thomas Aquinas* (Leiden: Brill, 1995), 134.

Attempting to forge a new category that he calls "modified univocity" or "partial univocity,"[28] Alston more seriously claims that "it may be possible to devise more abstract terms that capture something strictly in common between God and creature, as briefly adumbrated by my functionalist account of knowledge" (178). Alston's *strategy* is to use functionalism to show univocal commonality between human and divine psychology. His *motivation*, which I applaud, is to show that God is not so utterly transcendent that we must remain agnostic about the most important religious concerns, such as whether God can communicate to mortals, take action in the world, and so forth. Alston is particularly concerned about personal predicates, and here again, I fully share his concern.

Alston attempts to show that incorporeality does not prevent God from being a personal agent, nor does it prevent univocal predication about God. He employs Logical Connectionism (LC) for its idea that "there is a logical (conceptual) connection between a mental state and its manifestation,"[29] and he sees functionalism as a more subtle form of LC. Likening the concept of functionalism to a mousetrap, he says that the device need only catch mice. The method and the effectiveness can vary, so that he can be "neutral as to the composition and structure."[30] Alston contends that "functionalism can help us to reconcile a degree of univocity with the radical otherness of the divine" and that "a *functional* concept of X is noncommittal as to the intrinsic nature, character, composition or structure of X."[31] Thus "in conceiving of a Φ in functional terms," we can conceive of it "in terms of the job(s) it is fitted to do" and not bother ourselves unduly about "whatever it is like in itself."[32]

The problem here is that Alston appears to have adopted a complicated, contemporary form of the analogy of proportionality. Thus even if he were to deliver on his functionalist claims, he would have achieved no more than

God's psychology:God's action :: human psychology:human action.

Critics of this sort of analogy have long pointed out that it harbors an agnosticism about the God side of the relation. The suspicion that we are dealing with no more than an analogy of proportionality (a:b :: c:d) in Alston's functionalism-en-route-to-univocity scheme is corroborated by his explicitly agnostic claims about "whatever it is like in itself" or being "noncommittal as to the in-

---

[28] Alston's positions are developed in the following chapters of *Divine Nature and Human Language*: "Can We Speak Literally of God?" 39–63; "Functionalism and Theological Language," 64–80; "Divine and Human Action," 81–102; and "Referring to God," 103–17. "Modified univocity" is taken from "Functionalism," 65; "partial univocity," his preferred term, appears in many of the articles listed.

[29] Alston, "Can We Speak Literally," 49.

[30] Ibid., 50.

[31] Alston, "Functionalism," 70–71.

[32] Ibid., 71.

trinsic nature, character, composition." Now Aquinas did use an analogy of proportionality in an early work:

> As the infinite is to the infinite, so the finite is . . . to the finite. In this way there is a likeness between the creature and God, because as He is related to the things which belong to Him, so the creature is related to what is proper to it.[33]

But evidently, Aquinas perceived the problem of a hidden agnosticism because he drops proportionality from this time forward in his published works.[34]

But what Aquinas came to see as a fatal problem of realist reference to God, Alston asks us to exclude from the question:

> The concepts I have been adumbrating are very thin, to say the least.

> We have laid out a certain structure of what depends on what in what way, but as to what it is that stands in these relations of dependence we have said virtually nothing.

> But we can hardly pretend to any such insight into what it is like to be God, or even to have purposes, intentions, and the like in the way God does.[35]

However, we cannot exclude whether or not a given predicate *intrinsically* refers to God; for the issue of shared, intrinsic predicates is determinative for our question, and Alston not only embraces this criterion when critiquing Aquinas but also demands that Aquinas "spell out" the relation of the higher and lower in God and humans.

Alston's functionalism takes a detour from univocal reference to God when Alston (correctly) notices that a function requires a temporal duration but that in order to speak about God, whom Alston agrees is atemporal, "we shall have to abandon the term 'function' in its strictest sense, but that does not mean that we shall have to give up the project of applying to God what functionalism calls 'functional concepts.' "[36] At best, Alston is now working with an analogy of re-motion, clearly not a univocal reference to both God and humans.

By his own admission Alston does not tell us very much about the univocal content. His argument runs more to the effect that nothing rules out what he is saying about univocity.[37] Of course, Aquinas's doctrine of simplicity does rule out what he is saying. And where Aquinas presents arguments for divine sim-

---

[33] *Truth (De Veritate)*, trans. Robert Mulligan, S.J. (Chicago: Regnery, 1952), XXIII, 7, ad. 9.

[34] See Klubertanz, *Aquinas on Analogy*, 98–99.

[35] Alston, "Functionalism," 98 (first quotation), 99.

[36] Ibid., 72.

[37] Alston, "Can We Speak Literally," 60; "Divine and Human Action," 88.

plicity, Alston, at least in the works under discussion here, presents either what might best be characterized as *speculation* regarding the divine nature or, as we have seen, agnosticism or something close to it. Applying functionalism to the divine and human contexts, Alston contends:

> But at the very least the position will hold that the difference between know-ing that *p* and having a pro-attitude toward *p* is unanalyzable in terms of anything else.

He then excludes intrinsic attribution:

> In particular, a positive attitude toward a state of affairs—taking it to be desir-able, gratifying, attractive, worth while, a good thing, or whatever—is a basic underivative feature of our mental life. No doubt such attitudes, in conjunction with other facts, have various consequences for behavior, thought, and feeling; but it would be a grave mistake to suppose that the *intrinsic nature* of attitudes can be specified in terms of such consequences. (my emphasis)

He then concludes:

> On this view there would seem to be no bar to the univocal predication of some intentional concepts to God and to us. If *taking a state of affairs to be a good thing* is a basic, unanalyzable relation of an intelligent agent to a (possible) state of affairs, there is nothing in the concept to limit it to an em-bodied, finite, imperfect, or temporal agent. Why shouldn't God, as we are thinking of Him here, relate Himself in such a manner to possible states of affairs? There would seem to be no basis for a negative answer.[38]

What Alston seems to have done amounts to an analogy of relations to an ex-trinsic set of possibles. And as Eleonore Stump and Norman Kretzmann have ar-gued, "But no entity, not even a mathematical or a divine entity, can be ex-empted from having extrinsic accidental properties."[39] Granting that God and all entities have extrinsic, accidental properties, we are left wondering what pre-cisely is being predicated univocally of God and humans in Alston's account. By his own definition of 'univocal,' "the application to God of the terms in question in just the same sense as they apply to us,"[40] Alston's alternative comes up short. Instead, he seems to provide an analogy of relations to something extrinsic to both subjects, divine and human, without delivering the promised univocity.

SIMPLICITY (ALMOST)
As Alston defends theistic positions, he often tends to revert to, or at the least strongly approach, positions that Aquinas has already developed. Thus Alston

---

[38] Alston, "Divine and Human Action," 87–88.
[39] Stump and Kretzmann, "Absolute Simplicity," 354.
[40] Alston, *Divine Nature*, 14.

addresses the "problem of finding something that could play the same basic role for incorporeal basic actions that bodily movements play for corporeal basic actions."[41] He then adds: "We can conceive of agents, corporeal or otherwise, such that things other than their bodies (if any) are under their direct voluntary control."[42] Alston then surmises that "all God's actions might be basic actions."[43] So what begins as an argument by analogy and remotion (removing bodily movement as we conceive of divine causality) ends up as a speculation (*"might be* basic actions") that all God's actions are basic. Interestingly, Alston's conclusion fits rather well with Aquinas's claim that God is *actus purus* (pure act). Aquinas might agree that all God's actions are basic action but would add that God *is* basic action, understood as the infinite act of being.

Alston's concern, that is, that God be able to bring about a change in the world, is easily met when we consider an important but often overlooked passage of Aquinas. In it God has brought about the very world itself, knows all that is, and is eternally, actively present to all that is, in the way an agent exerts power in its sphere of influence:

> God is in all things; not, indeed, as part of their essence, nor as an accident; but as an agent is present to that upon which it works. For an agent must be joined to that wherein it acts immediately, and touch it by its power. . . .
> Now since God is very being by His own essence, created being must be His proper effect; as to ignite is the proper effect of fire. Now God causes this effect in things not only when they first begin to be, but as long as they are preserved in being. . . . Therefore, as long as a thing has being, God must be present to it, according to its mode of being. But being is innermost in each thing and most fundamentally inherent in all things since it is formal in respect of everything found in a thing. . . . Hence, it must be that God is in all things, and innermostly. (*ST* I.8.1)

So while Aquinas's interlocking doctrines of simplicity, infinity, and God's essence being identical to God's existence mark a great distinction between God and all else that is, Aquinas synthesizes his commitment to divine simplicity with his doctrine of creation, so that in creation God is most "immediately," "innermostly," *intimately* present to all that God has created. This divine power-to-be-present as an agent is related to the same power that constitutes simplicity: the infinite actuality.

Similarly, in addressing Charles Hartshorne's concerns on this point, concerns shared by Alston, W. Norris Clarke has demonstrated how Aquinas's position does not make God into a "metaphysical iceberg."[44] The basic point is that a distinction must be drawn between the simplicity of God's intrinsic being

[41] Alston, "Can We Speak Literally," 60.

[42] Ibid., 61.

[43] Ibid.

[44] W. Norris Clarke, "A New Look at the Immutability of God," in *Explorations in Metaphysics* (Notre Dame: University of Notre Dame Press), 185.

and God's intentional consciousness which can recognize the finite for what it is and lovingly relate to its multiplicity. In terms of a realist epistemology and metaphysics, Clarke illustrates the necessity of something like the Thomist distinction with the following scenario. When a real fire is raging outside me, if there were no distinction between my perception and knowledge of the fire and the fire itself, there would in effect be a second real fire within my consciousness—an absurdity that would vitiate the purpose of the act of knowledge and litter the ontological realm with cognitional and propositional *realia*. A second real world is not created by knowledge, only knowledge of an existing world. This distinction between the knower and what is known

> is required for any act of knowledge where what is known is other in its real being than the knower itself; hence it holds even in the case of God, as knowing and loving a real world other than himself.[45]

This kind of contingency and determinate differentiation no more alters the simplicity and infinity of the divine being itself than my knowledge of the fire changes my essence.

Relating God's knowledge to creation, Clarke adds:

> Were we, however, to know something we had totally thought up and totally produced in all its being from our own preexisting plenitude, then knowledge of such a being would not add to our real perfection, though it would add a new determination to our field of intentional consciousness. This is precisely the case with God.[46]

Thus upholding the distinction between the order of being and the order of knowledge avoids the ontological clutter brought on by an exaggerated realism. Furthermore, the religious possibility of God's loving relations to the world is preserved, something that all involved want to uphold. By awareness of the multiplicity of the world, God does not become less than simple; likewise, we who contemplate God's infinity and simplicity do not become infinite or simple.

Even though he rejects it when addressing Aquinas, Alston not surprisingly moves toward simplicity in order to defend theistic claims:

> The divine psyche is much simpler than the human psyche in the variety of its constituents. Assuming God to be atemporal, it involves no processes or activities, no sequences of events. . . . There is only one kind of goal-setting state, which could perhaps best be characterized as the recognition that something is good or right.[47]

---

[45] Ibid., 192.

[46] Ibid., 210 n. 16.

[47] Alston, "Functionalism," 78, and similarly, 75, 79; also see "Divine and Human Action," 100.

First we must ask, once Alston rejects simplicity simpliciter, why should he assume that "the divine psyche is much simpler than the human"? If the arguments for simplicity fail, then how can Alston assert "no processes or activities,
no sequences or events"? Alston's own positions would actually be strengthened
and clarified were he to adopt simplicity instead of using it ad hoc. By way of
contrast, in Aquinas's account of simplicity God knows God's being infinitely
and all at once, without composition; and God knows all else that exists—that
is, the composed—through perfect and infinite knowledge of the divine being.
Thus Aquinas cites Dionysius with favor:

> "In knowing itself, the divine wisdom knows all things—the material imma-
> terially, the divisible indivisibly, and the many unitedly." (*SCG* I.58.10)

God's simplicity refers to the intrinsic divine being; it does not prevent God's
creating, knowing, and relating to a finite realm of things and persons.

ANALOGY OR UNIVOCITY?
The basic religious intuition that Alston and many others share, namely, that
some core of common meaning must be present in our reference to God, has
prima facie merit. However, giving an account of such a common core remains
deeply problematic. In his attempt to overcome this problem, Alston's strongest
argument for univocity, in the "project of identifying psychological commonal-
ities in God and human beings,"[48] is probably his case for "tendency terms"
shared by God and humans:

> But despite all these differences there is a basic commonality in the way in
> which attitudes combine with cognitions to determine action tendencies, and
> the way in which action tendencies are related to the final active volition or
> executive intention. There will be crucial conditionals in common, of the sort
> listed earlier. In both cases, e.g., if the agent has a pro-attitude toward G and
> a cognition that doing A is a way to realize G, then the agent will have a ten-
> dency to do A.[49]

The point seems to be that if doing G requires doing A first, then both God and
humans who may want to accomplish G will tend to do A. Although this scenario asserts a common purpose, how does having a common purpose or even a
somewhat common route to achieving the purpose amount to univocity? The
issue is not whether there is any similitude between God and humans in extrin-

[48] Alston, "Functionalism," 78.
[49] Alston, "Divine and Human Action," 97.

sic relations. Rather, as Alston himself sometimes puts it, the issue is whether terms refer to both God and humans *intrinsically*:

> Hence our language can contain terms that stand for intrinsic properties of God *iff* we can form concepts of intrinsic properties of God. And since we can make true literal predications of God *iff* our language contains terms that stand for properties exemplified by God, we say, finally, that we can speak literally of God (in the relevant sense of true literal predication) *iff* we can form concepts of intrinsic divine properties.[50]

But in the light of his own definition of univocal—"A term is *univocal* in two or more uses when it bears the same sense (meaning) in those uses" (Alston, 148)—it is strange that Alston frequently denies the kind of knowledge of intrinsic properties of God that would yield a univocal account. Thus, comparing the functional concept of God's knowledge of a possible state of affairs p to human knowledge, he writes: "They do not apply just as they stand, because of the human limitations."[51] Univocity is not achieved here because nothing intrinsic between God and humans is pointed out; in fact, it is denied. In the same article Alston again limits the claims being made:

> Our ordinary concepts of human psychological states cannot be applied in their entirety to a timeless being. But I have already disavowed any intention to show that any of the psychological terms we commonly apply to creatures can, in precisely the same sense, be applied to God. I am seeking only to show that terms for psychological functions can be devised that apply in just the same sense to God and creature.[52]

As I understand him, Alston denies intrinsic commonality of psychological states but claims univocity of "terms for psychological functions." Yet a few pages later he claims:

> This [commonality of tendency] brings out a significant commonality of meaning between psychological terms applicable to God and to man. Even though there is no carry-over of the complete package from one side of the divide to the other, there is a core of meaning in common. And the distinctive features on the divine side simply consist in the dropping out of creaturely limitations.[53]

Unless Alston is prepared to specify what the meaning is to God, he can hardly claim to have depicted "a core of common meaning." By contrast, the "dropping out of creaturely limitation" and the failure to have a "carry-over of the complete package" are the very sort of reasons that lead Aquinas to declare the

---

[50] Alston, "Can We Speak Literally," 44–45.
[51] Alston, "Functionalism," 79.
[52] Ibid., 73.
[53] Ibid., 79–80.

impossibility of univocity between God and humans. Alston, who recognizes "an abstract core of predicates that are true of God,"[54] does not differ from Aquinas in that affirmation. The difference is that Aquinas recognizes that a univocal proposition relating God and creatures could be achieved only if that aspect of our knowledge were fully equivalent to God's knowledge. And for reasons discussed above, reasons that Alston also recognizes—"we have no right to expect a satisfactory theoretical grasp of the divine nature and doings"[55]— claims to univocity should be avoided.

If univocity has a settled, on/off, right/wrong, algorithmic quality, then "partial univocity" is an oxymoron. Either we have said the whole truth in a given proposition about God (univocity), or there is always a "leftover" that remains to be said. To the degree that univocity is achieved, there is no leftover, at least on the matter at hand. In the participation metaphysics that analogy expresses, there is always a leftover because human achievement and expression is open to increasing participation and thus reinterpretation through the operation of intellect and will that responds to God in freedom.

SOMETHING BEYOND CONCEPT

In what I take as a more fruitful approach, Alston's essay "Referring to God" suggests a way in which he is not all that far from a neo-Thomist position.[56] This essay manages both erudition and piety as Alston uses Saul Kripke's objections to a descriptivist account of proper name reference in order to advocate something beyond mere conceptual reference to God. In doing so, Alston argues that "direct reference" is more fundamental[57] as he moves to *experience* in something like the neo-Thomist insistence on joining concept to *existence* in acts of judgment: "But on the direct reference view we start with a being presented in individual and community experience, not with a set of attributes."[58] Alston's preferential turn to *being* over *attributes* is highly significant, for in it he has come quite close to the account of judgment above.

Alston's notion of 'direct reference' arises out of contact with God, and these "real contacts"[59] democratize and universalize the enterprise of referring to God:

> First, the primacy of direct reference provides a reassurance that God can be
> successfully referred to by the weak and foolish as well as by the wise and
> proud. . . . If one's referent in religious worship and discourse is determined
> by what one takes God to be like, then we [Christians, Jews, and Muslims],
> the Hindus, and the ancient Greeks and Romans cannot be credited with

---

[54] Alston, "Divine and Human Action," 102.
[55] Ibid., 100.
[56] See Alston, "Referring to God," in *Divine Nature*, 103–17.
[57] Ibid., 103.
[58] Ibid., 116.
[59] Ibid., 115.

worshipping the same being. But if reference is determined rather by the real contacts from which a referential practice stems, then there may indeed be a common referent, in case these traditions, including their referential traditions, all stemmed from experiential contacts with the one God.[60]

Given this rapprochement among seemingly incompatible religious understandings, the meaning of Alston's "modified univocity,"[61] once purged of its oxymoron and coupled with reference based on experience, might likewise be harmonized with an analogy theory based on participation metaphysics.

CONCLUSION

Because he thought it falsely and arrogantly brought God and humankind together, Karl Barth once infamously railed against *analogia entis*, calling it the doctrine of the Antichrist.[62] At the other extreme, Alston has misunderstood analogy as keeping God and humankind too far separated. Either univocity or a "species of equivocation" is a false dichotomy. The argument of this chapter is how best to locate and describe a third option.

I have argued that analogical predication is that superior third option, a middle ground that is our only ground; for it holds together conceptual reference, where terms are used "substantially" and "properly" of both God and humans (*ST* I.13.2–3), and the concomitant awareness that the divine referent is unique. Thus, analogical predication is the one most fitting to the unique human situation between structure and change, certainty and contingency, reason and faith, known and unknown, humanity and divinity. The task of analogy is not to create a connection between God and humanity but to express one that has already been discovered in creation or revealed in Christ. Analogy attempts to express a dynamic ontological differential in which our entire being is transcendently oriented and repeatedly reoriented toward God. Analogy, as a function of our ongoing incompleteness, has dialectical implications of both present understanding and achievement as well as 'not fully,' 'not yet.' The relationship with God provides an inexhaustible depth of semantic meaning for analogical predicates, but as John Milbank argues, this same relationship forbids "any semantic resting place."[63] We should, however, consider that virtually all human religious communities tend to construct such "resting places," indeed, to reify them.

The profundity of divine simplicity and the ontological communication of God's creation provide ascending possibilities for all aspects of human develop-

---

[60] Ibid.

[61] Alston, "Functionalism," 65.

[62] Karl Barth, *Church Dogmatics* I/1, trans. Geoffrey Bromiley (Edinburgh: T & T Clark, 1975), xiii.

[63] John Milbank, " 'Between Purgation and Illumination': A Critique of the Theology of Right," in *Christ, Ethics, and Tragedy: Essays in Honour of Donald MacKinnon*, ed. Kenneth Surin (Cambridge: Cambridge University Press, 1989), 172.

ment, both individual and communal. So for example, humanity will always be in the business of redefining the good, and those redefinitions, especially the most radical ones, are rarely welcomed by the rest of the "cave dwellers," as can be seen in the experiences of both Socrates and Jesus. We cave dwellers are innately conservative and tend to be especially so about religious matters. Although the list of transcendentals, the predicates that qualify for analogical predication about God, is not long, the mark of each of those terms is that it is sufficiently expansile to express a certain achievement and yet point to the ongoing task of actualizing further potential in our orientation toward God. Unlike metaphorical or univocal terms, analogical terms never settle down. Hence their use is self-involving, requiring conceptual grasp and responsible application to actual conditions, that is, judgment.

Alston's work, both in his preference for "direct reference" of the believer over "descriptivism" and in his search for *personal* predicates, comes dressed for this same party, since the *person* has increasingly been recognized as the primary analogate in recent neo-Thomist writing.[64] So although I do not think that Alston has created a viable category of "partial univocity," what he wants to accomplish—literal and personal predication between God and humans—has been delivered by current understandings of analogy. Alston refers to his own account of God's attributes as "very thin," "austere," "sparse," and so on. He is perhaps untroubled by these admissions because he understands that the task of a Christian philosophical theology at some point involves a handoff to overtly religious, theological enterprises that begin with revelation. Although revelation does not end the work of philosophy, it redirects it and reminds us that we are not the only thinkers and communicators. As Eberhard Jüngel once remarked, the God of whom we write is not the only one in the universe who is deaf and dumb. Hence, part of the choice between analogy and univocity depends upon which one better handles the transition to listening, to revelation. As Aquinas, citing Hilary, puts it:

> "Enter these truths by believing, press forward, persevere. And though I may know that you will not arrive at an end, yet I will congratulate you in your progress." (*SCG* I.8.2)

[64] The work of Clarke and Burrell particularly insists on *person* as primary. I have commented at length on their turn to the *person* in *Analogical Possibilities*, 82–94, 116–26. Also see Clarke, *Person and Being*, The Aquinas Lecture, 1993 (Milwaukee: Marquette University Press, 1993).

·13·

Van Fraassen's Constructive Empiricist Philosophy of Science and Religious Belief: Prospects for a Unified Epistemology

ANNE L. HISKES

"Constructive empiricism" is the name given by Bas Van Fraassen to the philosophy of science that he first articulated and defended in his 1980 book *The Scientific Image*.[1] In many respects constructive empiricism is the heir of seventeenth- and eighteenth-century British empiricism and early-twentieth-century logical positivist/empiricist philosophy of science. In common with these earlier empiricisms, constructive empiricism is inspired by the empirical character of science and its apparent success in producing knowledge. This success is attributed to a set of intellectual values which includes a critical attitude, humility, antidogmatism, and tolerance.

Epistemologies inspired by the empirical character and achievements of science sometimes tend to regard religious belief either as unwarranted and perhaps irrational or else as of no cognitive value. Because constructive empiricist philosophy of science advocates an agnostic attitude about the existence of unobservable entities postulated by scientific theories, one may well wonder whether constructive empiricism is compatible with cognitive attitudes toward religious claims acceptable to mainstream devout Christians. In other words, must there be an inconsistency between being a good constructive empiricist and a good Christian? As a first step in answering these questions, I will explore what it means to be a constructive empiricist by focusing on the neglected concept of an epistemic community. This concept will be useful in showing how constructive empiricism provides a distinctive framework for accommodating both religious and scientific inquiry as noncompetitive, complementary truth-seeking activities that may even interact imaginatively.

[1] Bas C. Van Fraassen, *Scientific Image* (New York: Oxford University Press, 1980).

I. CONSTRUCTIVE EMPIRICISM AND THE IDEAL
EPISTEMIC COMMUNITY OF SCIENCE

Van Fraassen has argued extensively that constructive empiricism is not in the business of making substantive claims about the world, for example, about the sources or scope of human experience, but should instead be regarded as a "stance".[2] It is an intellectual perspective or orientation that includes the values of a critical attitude and tolerance and the celebration of the imagination in the pursuit of knowledge. In common with earlier forms of empiricism, constructive empiricism regards scientific inquiry as representing the epitome of human rationality and what it can achieve.[3] By looking at the actual achievements of science, and the methods and practices used by scientists in producing these achievements, the constructive empiricist extracts certain operative values and practices and then constructs an idealized model of the scientific community as an epistemic community of rational inquirers. The resulting model is, of course, only one possible interpretation of science which nonetheless claims to be true to the observable features of scientific practice and its successes. The claim is not that all good scientists have been constructive empiricists or that scientists always act ideally. Rather, the claim is that the successes of science, as we find them, could have been the results of applying constructive empiricist principles. I will also suggest that strict adherence to constructive empiricist principles may even enhance scientific inquiry.

The constructive empiricist and his rival the scientific realist agree that science is tremendously successful in producing knowledge. Both agree that science is a truth-seeking enterprise at some level. It has been tremendously successful in developing theoretical models that enable us to predict observable events, lead us to discoveries of new phenomena, and in general provide us with accurate maps of the observable world. These empirical successes would not be possible without the invention and use of theories whose claims extend beyond the domain of what has been observed and even beyond the domain of what can be observed. Theories are indispensable as tools for the discovery of experiential truths. They direct our attention to new patterns of experience, give access to new kinds of experiences, and provide us with new vocabularies for understanding experience.

Scientific inquiry is also impressive in its dynamical and progressive character. As a group, scientists are constantly inventing new theoretical approaches and hypotheses or revising and extending old ones. Through the invention of increasingly powerful theories, the history of science seems to show a clear direction of progress in both the accuracy and scope of our knowledge of the observable world.

Although the constructive empiricist and the scientific realist agree on the

---

[2] Bas C. Van Fraassen, "Against Transcendental Empiricism", in *The Questions of Hermeneutics*, ed. T.J. Stapledon (Dordrecht: Kluwer, 1994), 309–35.

[3] Ibid., 313.

empirical successes of science, they disagree on the nature of its actual and possible theoretical successes. Van Fraassen characterizes scientific realism as the view that the aim of science, namely, what defines recognizable, achievable success in science, is the production of theories that provide "literally true stories of what the world is like". Furthermore, when a scientific realist accepts a theory as fully meeting the aims of science, he or she believes (with some degree of confidence) that the theory is true in what it says about both the observable and unobservable aspects of the world.[4] The constructive empiricist, in contrast, identifies the recognizable, achievable successes of science as the production of theories that provide true descriptions of all the phenomena in their domain. When a constructive empiricist accepts a theory as fully meeting the aims of science, he or she believes with some degree of confidence only that part of the theory that describes the phenomena and remains agnostic about those claims of the theory that describe unobservable objects and events.

A constructive empiricist, and probably most scientific realists as well, attributes the successes of modern science to a commitment on the part of scientists qua members of a scientific community to a certain set of empirically oriented epistemic policies. These epistemic principles include commitments to constrain theorizing by experience; to actively seek out potential negative evidence and criticism for hypotheses and to adjust theories accordingly; to keep in mind the fallibility of all empirical beliefs; to be undogmatic in both one's theorizing and descriptions of experience; and to be open and creative in exploring new ways of understanding the phenomena. The points of disagreement between constructive empiricists and scientific realists concern the relevance for truth of superempirical criteria of theory evaluation such as explanatory plausibility and simplicity and the extent to which good scientific inferences can go beyond the level of observable objects.

In my view the community of science has an important epistemic role to play in rendering these commitments effective in generating scientific knowledge and progress. One role of the scientific community is to provide a collective pool of experience that members can use as evidence in their theorizing. The community serves to define standards of evidence by setting the criteria for the kinds and circumstances of experiences that generate evidence. Clearly, the community also plays an important critical function by subjecting theories and hypotheses to open discussion and scrutiny by the group. In addition, group interactions should ideally stimulate the creative imagination in developing alternative solutions to problems or alternative explanatory models of the same phenomena. Juxtaposition of these alternative theories furthers the goal of criticism by providing points of comparison between theories and forcing one to acknowledge the limits of empirical evidence in dictating a unique choice of theory. The community also serves to remind individual members of their epistemic commitments should they become lax.

---

[4] Van Fraassen, *Scientific Image*, 8.

Both the empiricist and the scientific realist would agree that the success of science, which is due to the empirical and critical policies of its practitioners, is enhanced by its communal nature. In light of the fallibility of all human knowledge claims and the acknowledged incursion of personal interests and biases into science, the process of peer review and open discussion is essential to the function of science as a truth-seeking enterprise. It seems to me that the value of open, critical discussion is best served by an epistemic community constituted by individuals with diverse perspectives who also respect one another's rationality. Consequently, the promotion of such a community should also be seen as part of the stance of constructive empiricism. Yet open and critical discussion can be productive only if there is some common ground that provides a basis for producing consensus, if not on opinion then consensus on when it is rational and legitimate to disagree. The ideal epistemic community must achieve a delicate balance between being open in promoting intellectual diversity and drawing boundaries to avoid the "anything goes" phenomena associated with epistemic or metaphysical relativism.

The constructive empiricist sees the practices of science as revealing the key to building an optimal epistemic community. In what follows I take an epistemic community to be constituted by a set of individuals who for the most part agree on what would count as evidence at the level of basic beliefs and whose epistemic policies and aims are close enough that they can engage in fruitful critical discussion. Members of the same epistemic community are disposed to regard one another's observation reports as evidence because they trust the competence and integrity of their members in making sound judgments.

Although specific disciplines in science form the most closely knit epistemic communities, there is also cross-disciplinary communication and theory building. This is possible from the empiricist perspective because these individuals can, perhaps through training and discipline, have access to the same world of theory-independent observable objects which provides the basis for members of different subcommunities to learn one another's languages and share a level of basic evidence in the service of their common goal of understanding the empirical world. What functioned perhaps as two separate epistemic communities can be joined to form a larger, more diverse community. For similar reasons the empiricist regards all human beings as potentially constituting a single epistemic community whose members, in virtue of shared perceptual and cognitive capacities, all have epistemic access in principle to the same world of experience.

My aim in this chapter is not to critically examine constructive empiricist views about observation or epistemology but to explore the picture of religious inquiry and belief that could emerge from a constructive empiricist framework. I will argue that the empirical orientation and critical attitudes of constructive empiricism are prima facie religion-friendly and could in principle provide a framework that can support and encourage an epistemic community that includes both committed Christians and committed scientists.

II. CONSTRUCTIVE EMPIRICIST EPISTEMOLOGY

Here I will explore those distinctive features of constructive empiricism that provide a foundation for an open and inclusive epistemic community. I will postpone until the next section a detailed discussion of the nature of experience and its role in drawing the boundaries of an epistemic community.

II.1. Truth and Language

Constructive empiricism provides a framework that can potentially include the epistemic aim of truth-seeking among the aims of both religious and scientific communities because it adopts a standard, commonsensical philosophy of language and concept of truth. Constructive empiricism differs from early-twentieth-century positivistic versions of empiricism in that it does not subscribe to any version of the verificationist theory of meaning, in which either a linguistic form has no representational content or representational content is translatable into some special observation language. In the verificationist framework, putative claims about electrons and God either have no cognitive meaning or are really just about some observable, natural phenomena. Constructive empiricism interprets putatively descriptive discourse as literally providing a picture of reality that is either true or false, and it makes no distinction between theoretical and observational vocabulary.[5]

In addition, constructive empiricism eschews a relativistic or epistemic concept of truth that makes the truth of a proposition depend on human values, attitudes, or cognition. By adopting a "realist" or alethic concept of truth according to which the truth of a proposition depends only on its content and the world,[6] constructive empiricism regards the truth of putative claims about God to depend only on God's nature and not on human attitudes, beliefs, or needs. Constructive empiricism is therefore immune to certain kinds of objections that might be raised against metaphysical antirealists by those with traditional understandings of the Christian faith.[7]

II.2 Inference to the Best Explanation, and Pragmatic versus Epistemic Criteria

A crucial point of divergence between the scientific realist and the constructive empiricist concerns the epistemic status of an ampliative inference pattern typically called "inference to the best explanation" (hereafter abbreviated IBE). Scientific realists generally accept this type of inference pattern as a basis for assessments of the relative probable truth or falsity of theoretical claims about un-

---

[5] See ibid., 10–12, 53–56, for Van Fraassen's positions on literal interpretation and the distinction between observational and theoretical terms, respectively.

[6] The alethic theory can be characterized simply as: the proposition that q is true iff q. See William P. Alston, *A Realist Conception of Truth* (Ithaca: Cornell University Press, 1996), 27, and "Realism and the Christian Faith", *International Journal for Philosophy of Religion* 38 (1995): 37–60.

[7] See Alston, "Realism".

observable objects or events. IBE is also the pattern of inference used in traditional a posteriori arguments for God's existence. When IBE is used, the truth or falsity of claims about unobservable objects, properties, or events is evaluated in terms of how well these claims explain the facts described by some set of beliefs about observable objects or events. Truth values of claims about unobservable objects such as quarks or perhaps God are evaluated not just in terms of their logical or formal relations to a selected set of experiential data but also in terms of superempirical criteria such as intuitive plausibility, simplicity, and coherence with some preferred underlying ontology or metaphysical system. Out of all the possible explanations of the phenomena, the *best* overall explanation merits and demands the greatest degree of belief.

The constructive empiricist contends that the scientific realist has no alternative but to use some kind of superempirical criteria in trying to epistemically justify claims about unobservables. Their use is unavoidable, according to the constructive empiricist, because of the underdetermination of theory by data. For any given set of true observation reports, even the set of all true observation reports, there are in principle indefinitely many different explanations of the data which bear the same logical, formal relations to the data. In other words, there are many alternative ways the world could be, all of which could produce the same set of phenomena. Assigning degrees of belief or truth assessments to different but empirically equivalent world-pictures clearly requires superempirical criteria. Even the assumption that the phenomena need an explanation cannot come from the phenomena themselves.

A consistent empiricist has only one option for justifying a rule or principle for assessing truth, and this is to show a priori an inherent conceptual connection between that rule and truth or probable truth.[8] Empirical justifications must be ruled out on pain of circularity. Within the constructive empiricist framework developed by Van Fraassen, the only justified rules of inference are those whose conceptual links with truth are provided by the formal systems of deduction and the probability calculus. These rules simply constrain the rational change of opinion about the truth of propositions in light of new evidence and prior beliefs. Violation of these rules is irrational in that it results in an inconsistent or incoherent set of opinions regarding truth values, necessarily defeating the purpose of engaging in epistemic evaluation in the first place.[9]

The constructive empiricist rejects the epistemic relevance of IBE and any rule that uses superempirical virtues, thus in effect cutting off claims about unobservables from epistemic evaluation. One reason for rejecting IBE and its attendant superempirical virtues of simplicity, coherence with a preferred meta-

---

[8] See Van Fraassen, "Transcendental Empiricism", for a discussion of this point. Note also that we are here talking about adopting rules of inference that are codified and context-independent, in contrast to engaging in a practice that isn't codified and may be highly context-dependent.

[9] These claims are developed and supported in Bas C. Van Fraassen, *Laws and Symmetries* (New York: Oxford University Press, 1989), chaps. 6, 7, 13.

physical picture, and intuitive "explanatory satisfactoriness" is their lack of any inherent conceptual or otherwise demonstrable connection to the accepted alethic conception of truth.

Superempirical criteria of evaluation in the context of IBE are considered by the constructive empiricist to be purely pragmatic and not epistemic. Criteria of evaluation are pragmatic insofar as they depend on and reflect properties of the user of the propositions, such as his interests, values, or historical-cultural context.[10] Epistemic criteria are those relevant to the assessment of truth and falsity. Criteria relating to the explanatory character of a theory which go beyond predictive accuracy pertain to the usefulness of that theory in meeting the human desire to construct a world that exhibits a certain kind of order rather than the desire of just obtaining a true picture of the world. The claim here is not that pragmatic criteria necessarily lead one astray from truth but rather that the user-dependent character of pragmatic virtues renders them incapable of being justified as criteria for assessing user-independent truth. Indeed, the fact that some people require a trans-experiential entity or process in order to render the phenomena intelligible or meaningful is highly contingent and variable and should carry no epistemic weight.

The problem with using some version of IBE as an epistemic rule is not limited to its status as an unjustified rule. According to Van Fraassen, a commitment to the systematic use of any nonempirical criterion as a rule in assigning probabilities to claims about unobservables will yield incoherence in one's body of opinions.[11] Thus the constructive empiricist regards elevating IBE to the status of an obligatory epistemic rule not only to lack justification but also to be forbidden by the constraints of rationality.

II.3 Acceptance, Belief, and the Epistemic Community

The distinction between epistemic and pragmatic criteria of evaluation provides a basis for the constructive empiricist's distinction between accepting a theory or proposition and having some degree of belief in it. Belief in this context is an intentional, and in some sense voluntary, judgment about the likely truth or falsity of a proposition,[12] and those who adopt a constructive empiricist stance will bestow degrees of belief only on statements whose truth values can be assessed and updated in light of experience. In contrast, acceptance of a proposition is a decision to act in some way as if the proposition is true with

---

[10] See Van Fraassen, *Scientific Image*, 87–92.

[11] See Van Fraassen, *Laws and Symmetries*, 155–70.

[12] See Bas C. Van Fraassen, "Belief and the Will", *Journal of Philosophy* 81 (1984): 235–56, for an account and defense of his voluntarist view of belief as a kind of mental act. This is in contrast to the concept of belief as an involuntary feeling that is discussed by Alston in "Belief, Acceptance, and Religious Faith", in *Faith, Freedom, and Rationality*, ed. J. Jordan and D. Howard-Snyder (Lanham, Md.: Rowman & Littlefield, 1996), 3–27. See also Jonathan L. Cohen, *An Essay on Belief and Acceptance* (New York: Oxford University Press, 1992).

some degree of confidence, and acceptance differs from belief to the extent that it is based on considerations that go beyond just the assessment of truth.[13] Pragmatic criteria legitimately give reasons for accepting a proposition but, when possible, should not be used in assigning degrees of belief.

The topic of the logical relations and psychological interactions between belief and acceptance could easily generate a book-length discussion, but I hope a few comments will suffice. A theory or proposition can be accepted with different degrees of commitment for many different purposes that vary in scope and importance. Even scientific realists accept a theory such as Newtonian mechanics for the purposes of solving some practical problems without believing that the theory is true or even true at just the empirical level. In fact, they probably judge the theory to be false. Here the acceptance of Newtonian mechanics has a rather limited scope as a basis for inference and action.

In contrast, when a constructive empiricist fully accepts a scientific theory, he commits himself to using the entire theory as a basis for research and problem solving. While judging the likely truth of the empirical claims of the theory to be high, a constructive empiricist remains agnostic about the theory's claims regarding unobservable objects or events. To be an agnostic about a proposition is not to assign a confidence level to it in the neighborhood of one-half but instead to refrain from assigning a confidence level. From the constructive empiricist's point of view, a claim about unobservables is cut off in principle from epistemic evaluation in light of experience, and on that supposition there is no possibility that the confidence level of that proposition will increase or fluctuate in relation to a changing body of empirical evidence. In contrast, even a proposition that is initially assigned a low confidence level on the basis of experience might later be assigned a high probability in light of new evidence. From the perspective of constructive empiricism there is something not quite right about believing propositions whose credibility cannot be constrained by experience.

Although propositions clearly may be accepted without belief, it is doubtful whether as a matter of psychological fact belief ever occurs without some accompanying pragmatic dimension since, from the start, people attend to those facts that for some reason are deemed noteworthy. But the presence of pragmatic desires in the context of making epistemic judgments implies neither that those desires play a role in the epistemic assessment nor that there is no conceptual distinction between epistemic and nonepistemic grounds for the appraisal of propositions and theories. There indeed seems to be a logical and conceptual distinction between belief and acceptance since they are subject to different kinds of normative criteria. Beliefs can be justified in terms of their relations with empirical evidence or other beliefs. In contrast, acceptance is vindicated

---

[13] See Bas C. Van Fraassen, "Empiricism in the Philosophy of Science", in *Images of Science: Essays on Realism and Empiricism*, ed. P. M. Churchland and C. A. Hooker (Chicago: Chicago University Press, 1985), 276–81, and Van Fraassen, *Laws and Symmetries*, 192–210, for discussions of the distinction between belief and acceptance.

after the fact by success in meeting the purposes for which acceptance was intended.

One may well wonder, however, whether there are any behavioral differences between a scientific realist who fully believes a theory and a constructive empiricist who fully accepts but does not believe that theory. Van Fraassen points out that these two individuals will probably exhibit the same first-order linguistic behavior in that they equally use the language of the theory in doing their scientific work.[14] But these two individuals differ in the intentions that give rise to their linguistic behavior, and they are in fact engaged in different speech acts. The realist asserts the claims of the theory whereas the empiricist "displays" the claims of the theory.

It seems to me that there would be dispositional differences in the attitudes of the realist versus the empiricist toward rival theories for the same phenomena and toward proposals for new theories in other domains. One would expect a realist who believes a given theory to be more dismissive and more prone to a negative attitude toward rival approaches than an empiricist who only accepts that theory. An empiricist can acknowledge the equal merit of different theoretical approaches for the same phenomena by relativizing the evaluation to different values. This approach is not open to the realist, who takes the primary aim of theorizing to be truth and whose attitudes toward new theories are constrained by the probabilities assigned to prior theories.

Furthermore, since explanatory power is linked to truth for a realist but not for an empiricist, one would analogously expect a realist who believes a theory to be more disposed to projecting the ontology of an accepted theory to new domains and more committed to the project of reducing all phenomena to one fundamental ontology. In fact, the realist seems to be rationally compelled to this behavior given his aims and beliefs. Thus one would expect scientific realists who embrace inference to the best explanation as an epistemic principle to be more disposed than empiricists toward regarding a religious ontology and a scientific ontology as rivals in a competition for the best ultimate explanation.

In contrast, it's axiomatic that an empiricist can fully and rationally accept any given theological theory and fully and rationally accept any given scientific theory as long as they don't make contradictory claims about the world of experience and are accepted for different purposes. They might, for example, point the way to different patterns or kinds of experiences or provide different ways of thinking about the same experiences. The perspective of the constructive empiricist thus creates a predisposition to think of a science-religion dialogue not as a competition for the truth but as an opportunity to enrich one's understanding and knowledge of the epistemically accessible world of experience. This possibility is open to the scientific realist too, but only to the extent that she adopts the empiricist's stance of suspending belief. Before we can draw any further conclusions about the implications of constructive empiricism for

[14] See Van Fraassen, *Scientific Image*, 14.

an epistemology of religion, we must look at the constructive empiricist view of experience.

III. EXPERIENCE AND THE EPISTEMIC COMMUNITY

The core of the empiricist approach is the policy to let experience and only experience be the guide in assessing the truth values of propositions. A committed constructive empiricist assigns degrees of belief only to claims about the observable world in light of claims about actual experience. Thus for the sake of consistency, empiricism cannot stipulate a priori answers to questions of what kinds of objects can be experienced and what the sources of experience can be. These are questions that can be answered only by reference to actual experience. In answering these questions, the constructive empiricist begins exactly where everyone else begins, namely, as a member of a specific linguistic and epistemic community who learns to describe the content of experience in terms of the vocabulary and practices of the community.[15]

Experience provides evidence for use in inferences only in the form of observation reports. Observation reports are formulated in immediate response to some experience, and their very utterance is taken to be symptomatic of their probable truth within the community.[16] The constructive empiricist accepts the now familiar claims supported by Thomas Kuhn and others of the theory-dependent and interest-relative nature of concepts that we all must use in understanding and describing perceptual experience. The vocabulary of observation reports varies with area of inquiry and also over time as worldviews change.

Furthermore, observation reports are fallible and subject to scrutiny by the community in light of community standards of reliability and earlier accepted accounts of experience. Clearly, the observational beliefs of an individual and a community are constrained by pragmatic factors that reflect historically and culturally variable features of the epistemic agents.

Although the particular linguistic forms used as observation reports are context- and user-dependent, it is important to keep in mind that the truth or falsity of observation reports is not regarded as user-dependent or community-dependent within the constructive empiricist perspective. Whether the actual use of a linguistic form tracks any object at all, and what object it tracks, is not determined just by human interests and concepts. In other words, although the content and credibility of observation reports is strongly influenced by pragmatic factors, the objects observable to humans and actually observed by them are not constituted just by pragmatic factors. Furthermore, the fact that a lin-

---

[15] On Van Fraassen's view of observation reports and his pragmatic theory of observation, see Bas C. Van Fraassen, "From Vicious Circle to Infinite Regress, and Back Again", in *PSA 1992*, *Vol. 2*, ed. D. Hull, M. Forbes, and K. Ohkruhlik (Chicago: Northwestern University Press, 1993), 13–21.

[16] Ibid., 16.

guistic form functions as an observation report within a linguistic community is accessible even to people who are not members of that community.

The constructive empiricist pragmatic view of observation reports has some interesting implications that are problematic for the coherence of constructive empiricist epistemology; I will address this topic shortly. I regard a group of people as forming an epistemic community to the extent that they share standards for assessing observation reports should the need arise and under normal conditions are disposed to accept one another's observation reports as evidence, as if they were grounded in their own personal experience. From the pragmatic point of view, a religious community determines its own vocabulary for describing religious experience and sets its own standards for judging the acceptability of descriptions of that experience. Furthermore, on the constructive empiricist view, objective standards of rational belief require only consistency and coherence in one's body of opinion and cannot require the humanly impossible task of justifying every opinion in terms of methods that can themselves be shown to be reliable.[17] Indeed, a consistent empiricist has to admit that there is no noncircular a priori or a posteriori justification of the reliability of experience as a source of information about an external reality. Therefore, members of a religious community, or any community, are perfectly rational in believing those propositions that are regarded by their community as reliable observation reports and in taking them to describe features of an external reality.

The admittedly pragmatic aspect of observation reports implies that a consistent constructive empiricist who is not a member of the religious community cannot dismiss descriptions of religious experience on the grounds that they are alien or strange. This is not to say that the outsider must himself take these claims as evidence. He must either remain agnostic or attempt to enter into the life of the religious community and see for himself how those reports function. Only if he successfully learns the language and engages in the practices of the community will the outsider be in a position to form judgments about the status of the community's claims about experience. Furthermore, the empiricist's presumption that the objects that are experienced are theory-independent and epistemically accessible to humanity in general suggests that given enough effort, our outsider will be in a position to either agree or disagree with the judgments of the religious community.

The pragmatic and yet privileged epistemic character of observation reports may seem to pose a fatal problem for constructive empiricist epistemology. Inferences to hidden causes or structures operating behind the phenomena carry no epistemic weight because of their epistemically unjustified and pragmatic character, yet these same characteristics seem to permeate any human description of experience.[18] The constructive empiricist's policy of believing only claims

---

[17] This point can also be made by saying that there are no rules that dictate the assignment of prior probabilities.

[18] This problematic feature of constructive empiricism is discussed in Paul Churchland, "The Ontological Status of Observables: In Praise of the Superempirical Virtues", in *Images of*

about the observable world, that is, those claims whose truth values can in principle be assessed in light of experience, begins to look arbitrary, and the accompanying distinction between believing a proposition and only accepting it starts to look pretty foggy.

I believe that the constructive empiricist can construct a plausible defense against the charge of arbitrariness. To construct and understand this defense, we have to return to the view that constructive empiricism is presented as a possible stance or orientation applicable to life in general and cannot be characterized in terms of factual propositions or beliefs or even a codified set of rules. As a possible life stance, constructive empiricism sees our epistemic practices intertwined in a network of epistemic and nonepistemic values that guide our actions. By their nature, epistemic practices are taken to serve the value of truth and thus should be subject to the constraints of logic and probability theory, but beyond that they can be evaluated only as other life choices or practices are evaluated, that is, in terms of their fruits assessed in light of some broader set of values. And so it is for the epistemic choices of the constructive empiricist, which are deeply intertwined with the values of tolerance, humility, open-mindedness, and creative imagination.[19] These choices are neither forced nor prohibited by objective standards of rationality.

Even though the constructive empiricist acknowledges no ultimate logical justification for the probable truth of observation reports, and openly acknowledges that their content and credibility is mediated by cultural factors, this hardly renders arbitrary the epistemic distinction between claims about observables and claims about unobservables. It is not arbitrary from either a psychological or logical point of view. From a logical point of view, the observable/unobservable distinction mirrors the logical distinction between premises whose truth is assumed and conclusions that are inferred from those premises. The conflict between realists and empiricists is not about the initial premises but about admissible inference rules.

From a psychological point of view, we have no choice but to describe and perhaps even to literally experience the world through our own inherited biological and social cognitive structures. We also seem to have no real psychological option but to initially believe descriptions of our own experience since that is the way the world actually seems to be presented to us. In contrast to the framework we inherit at birth, we seem to have a range of options from which to choose concerning the postulation or not of objects and facts that go beyond

---

Science, ed. Churchland and Hooker, 35–47. See also John O'Leary-Hawthorne, "What Does Van Fraassen's Critique of Scientific Realism Show?" *The Monist* 77 (1994): 128–45, and Jaap Van Brakel, "Empiricism and the Manifest Image", in *Realism in the Sciences*, ed. Igor Douven and Leon Horsten (Leuven: Leuven University Press, 1996), 147–64.

[19] See Bas C. Van Fraassen, "The False Hopes of Traditional Epistemology", *Philosophy and Phenomenological Research* 60 (2000): 253–80, on the roles of luck and courage in epistemology. In my view, understanding the role of luck in our epistemic successes, i.e., the role of factors beyond our control, fosters the virtue of humility. Courage is necessary once we acknowledge the role of luck in epistemic success.

the domain of anything that has been experienced or ever could be experienced by our lights. We also seem to have a genuine choice in this case between believing (to some degree) that these claims actually represent reality and accepting them as useful representations for other purposes. Although we may be unable to avoid widespread systematic error in belief due to mistaken presuppositions at a fundamental level of our observational framework, such error seems avoidable at the level of postulated superempirical facts via the suspension of any degree of belief. Since Van Fraassen adopts the perspective that "ought implies can" in epistemology, we are absolved from epistemic guilt at the observational level for reasons and to a degree that simply do not apply at the superobservational level.[20]

IV. CONSTRUCTIVE EMPIRICISM AND THE RELIGIOUS COMMUNITY

How a constructive empiricist stance plays out as a religious epistemology depends in part on the nature and scope of religious experience.[21] Within the Christian tradition it is plausible to assume that individuals can directly experience the presence and love of God through prayer and meditation. For example, some individuals have claimed to be directly aware of the presence of a divine being and that being's love or concern. For these individuals, utterances of "God loves me" or "God is going to see me through this difficulty", together with the implied claim that God exists, would function as observation reports in that they describe what seems to be the content of their immediate experience. These reports would be genuine and true observation reports if their utterance was prompted by an experience of the described external state of affairs.

A direct experience of God should not to be confused, for example, with "seeing" the order of the observed natural world as evidence for the existence and providence of a divine creator, since that is exactly the kind of inference ruled out by constructive empiricism. This inference is analogous to "seeing" the solidity of ordinary objects as evidence for the existence of atoms and their interatomic forces. Furthermore, the direct experience of God described here should not be confused with a kind of spiritual halo that might accompany, for example, our everyday interactions with loved ones when we see love between humans as a reflection of God's love for us. A special appreciation and understanding of the order of nature and interpersonal relations may be consequences of both believing and accepting without belief certain religious claims, but these consequences are of pragmatic value and not epistemic value.

Just as the epistemic community of science extends back in time in that the observational judgments of previous generations often retain their status as evi-

---

[20] See Van Fraassen, "Empiricism", 247. This line of defense is suggested in Van Fraassen, "Vicious Circle", 20–27. It should be noted that Van Fraassen does not regard belief in unobservables as irrational. Such belief is simply never required by the dictates of reason and is incompatible with the value choices of the constructive empiricist.

[21] This section is not intended to represent any claims explicitly endorsed by Van Fraassen.

dence, so too the Christian epistemic community may be thought of as extending back in time to encompass religious experiences over thousands of years. This raises the possibility of accepting Scripture as descriptions of religious experience. Thus it is possible that a Christian constructive empiricist actually has a rich pool of experiential claims that are candidates for belief.

If we put aside the question of the content and scope of religious experience, a constructive empiricist would naturally think of the members of a religious community as engaged in the search for personal and communal experiential knowledge of God. Rival theological doctrines and models that equally agree with the community's account of experiences of God but disagree over claims on which experience is silent may be accepted on the basis of nonepistemic values as guides for personal or communal action. Such doctrines or models derive value not from providing correct pictures of the nature of God but from their function in enriching and extending our personal and communal experiences of God. Religious experience need not serve as confirmation of some theistic doctrine to be of value but has value in its own right.

A constructive empiricist who fully accepts a given system of Christian propositions may be virtually indistinguishable in behavior from a religious realist who fully believes those propositions. They will use the same language in describing both religious and ordinary experiences. They may equally be committed to incorporating these propositions into every aspect of their lives. The defining difference between a realist and a constructive empiricist rests with their epistemic policies concerning the nature of evidence and legitimate inferences. It could even be that a realist and a constructive empiricist believe exactly the same religious propositions if belief is construed in terms of a high degree of confidence. In such a case the relevant difference between the realist and empiricist would concern a class of propositions, namely, those describing facts not accessible via religious experience, which the realist currently does not believe but which according to her current opinion she might believe later should the evidence improve. In contrast, it is the opinion of the constructive empiricist that these claims are not even candidates for future belief since they are in principle not epistemically accessible through experience. The constructive empiricist, as a matter of personal integrity, refrains from assigning any probability values to those propositions because those probabilities would float free from correction in light of experience.

Finally, because a constructive empiricist regards shared experience to be a potentially unifying factor that can serve to broaden an epistemic community, and because he is committed to fostering as diverse and inclusive a community as possible in the interest of enriching and broadening the class of truths that are learned from experience, he will not be silent about the good news he has discovered. He will seek to unite epistemic communities, both religious and secular, not in the interests of proselytizing but in the interests of expanding our understanding of the world that is accessible to us. Thus I see the constructive empiricist stance as providing a framework for a noncompetitive, complemen-

252 Anne L. Hiskes

tary partnership between science and religion in which each seeks to illuminate a specific domain of experience that is in principle accessible to all humans. So can one be a good empiricist and a good Christian? I think so. But even if in the final analysis constructive empiricism fails as an adequate epistemology for either science or religion, we should welcome the constructive empiricists into our epistemic communities because of the reminders they provide that in epistemology there are always other values at work besides the value of being correct.

Truth in Fiction: The Whole Story

FRANCES HOWARD-SNYDER

Does Macbeth meet three witches? Does he see or merely imagine a dagger? These questions and answers to them must be understood as containing an implicit sentential operator such as, "In the fiction *Macbeth* . . ." Otherwise, such seemingly mundane claims would commit the speaker to the existence of witches.[1] Responses to these questions can be divided into three kinds: relativism, which says the answers will depend on the viewer or the time at which the play is read;[2] nihilism, which says there is no answer; and realism, which says there are objective or determinate answers to some or all of them, answers that don't depend on the viewer or the time at which the work is read.[3] Realism

I am grateful to William P. Alston and Daniel Howard-Snyder for helpful comments on an earlier draft of this chapter.

[1] "Macbeth" is so immediately recognizable as the name of a fictional character that the operator needn't be made explicit. Contrast this with the claim that "Richard III killed the little princes." As it stands, this is ambiguous between a controversial historical claim about the actual historical Richard and a less controversial claim about the play *Richard III*. To ensure that one is interpreted as making the latter claim, it is obviously necessary to add the sentential operator, "In the fiction *Richard III*, . . ." or some variant on that phrase.

[2] Hans-Georg Gadamer expresses relativism when he writes: "What is fixed in writing has detached itself from the contingency of its origin and its author and made itself free for new relationships." The text can be understood "only if it is understood in a different way every time." "The real meaning of a text does not depend on the contingencies of the author . . . for it is always partly determined by the historical situation of the interpreter and hence by the totality of the objective course of history." *Truth and Method*, trans. and ed. Garrett Barden and John Cumming (New York: Continuum, 1975), 357, 276, 263.

[3] Realists allow that sometimes the answer is that the story is ambiguous or vague on some point. "A vague or ambiguous text is just as determinate as a logical proposition; it means what it means and nothing else. This is true even if one argues that a text could display shifting emphases like those magic squares which first seem to jut out and then to jut in. With texts of this character (if any exist), one need only say that the emphases shift and must not, therefore, be construed statically. Any static construction would be wrong." E. D. Hirsch, Jr., "In Defense of the Author," in *Intention and Interpretation*, ed. Gary Iseminger (Philadelphia: Temple University Press, 1992). Note, moreover, that a realist is not committed to the claim that either P is true or ~P is true in every fiction.

is the most natural position to take. We may have to give it up in the end, but it certainly looks like a good starting point. If realism is correct, if these questions do have answers that aren't simply a matter of whatever the viewer or reader happens to think about the matter, what makes it correct? In other words, how do we fill in the blanks in the following:

"In fiction F, Φ" is true if and only if . . ."

If this can be completed in a brief, accurate, and plausible way, then realism about truth in fiction will be bolstered. If it cannot be completed in a brief, accurate, and plausible way, that won't mean that realism is false, but it will be forced on the defensive.[4]

Fiction is a kind of make-believe. An author imaginatively explores what things would be like if animals could talk, if we could travel back in time, if there were a girl named Alice who fell down a rabbit hole and talked to the Queen of Hearts; and we, the reader, imagine along with him. This account of fiction suggests a simple and natural account of *truth* in fiction. A proposition, Φ, is true in fiction F if and only if Φ would be true if the fiction F were true. That's objectionably circular, since the definiens must contain the notion "truth in F" that it purports to analyze. What would it be for the fiction F to be true? It would be for all the propositions *true in F* to be true. And that leaves us with our initial puzzlement: what is it for a proposition to be true in F?

To escape this circularity, let us distinguish aspects of the story that are true explicitly or primarily, aspects that are given on the page, so to speak, from aspects that require extrapolation. If the text says, "In a land far, far away, lived a very tall and irritable princess", it is true at the first level that a princess exists in the story; and it is true at another level (unless the text proceeds to make this or its denial explicit) that the princess had a mother and father and kidneys and a spine in the story. The problem of truth in fiction can be seen as two problems: that of accounting for truth in fiction at the first level and that of accounting for truth in fiction at the other level or levels. David Lewis suggests the Reality Principle (RP, for short):[5]

"In the fiction F, Φ" is true if and only if were the story told as known fact Φ would be true.

---

[4] See Kendall Walton, *Mimesis as Make-Believe* (Cambridge: Harvard University Press, 1990), 183–87, on this point.

[5] The name "the Reality Principle" is Walton's, as is the explicit distinction between first and second levels of truth in fiction. The principle is a slightly modified version of David Lewis's. See his "Truth in Fiction," in *Philosophical Papers I* (New York: Oxford University Press, 1983), 261–80, first published in *American Philosophical Quarterly* 15 (1978): 37–46. Nicholas Wolterstorff has a very similar principle, the *a*-principle. See his *Works and Worlds of Art* (Oxford: Clarendon Press, 1980), 126.

Or if the Lewis/Stalnaker analysis of counterfactuals is correct:

> "In the fiction F, Φ" is . . . true if and only if some world where F is told as known fact and Φ is true differs less from our actual world, on balance, than does any world where F is told as known fact and Φ is not true.[6]

We are asked to imagine the words of the text being uttered by someone who speaks the same language as the author and who knows them to be true.[7] That is, we are directed to the set of closest worlds where the words of the text are uttered as known fact. Whatever is true in all of them is true in the fiction. The sentences of the text determine what is true at the first level;[8] what they counterfactually imply determines what is true at higher levels. This avoids the circularity above since instead of defining truth in F in terms of truth in F, we define truth at higher levels in F in terms of truth at the primary level in F.

Although most philosophers who discuss the issue consider the Reality Principle a good starting point, I know of no one who defends it as uniquely correct, as I shall attempt to do: first by discussing and refuting four competitor principles and then by defending the Reality Principle or a modified version of it against objections.

I. AUTHORIAL INTENTION PRINCIPLE

The author creates the fiction. Surely her intentions have a significant, even decisive, bearing on what is true in it. This suggests a simple account of truth in fiction:

> "In the fiction F, Φ" is true if and only if the author of F intends that in the fiction F, Φ.

The role of authorial intention is a much-debated issue that has spawned a vast literature. Some critics have denied authorial intention any role in fixing the content of fiction, calling any appeal to such intentions a fallacy. I believe they have gone too far. The author's intentions are certainly one factor. For example,

---

[6] David Lewis, *Counterfactuals* (Oxford: Blackwell, 1973), and Robert Stalnaker, "A Theory of Conditionals," in *Studies in Logical Theory*, edited by Nicholas Rescher (Oxford: Blackwell, 1968).

[7] That is how I—following Lewis—shall use the phrase "told as known fact". To some ears, the phrase suggests something weaker, such as "told and *believed* to be known fact".

[8] Lewis does not make this distinction between first and second levels explicit. I think this way of doing things is a fair interpretation of his views. He does, however, discuss a difficulty for (what amounts to) this account of first-level truth in fiction. See the discussion of the Flash Stockman example in Section XII below.

when Hart Crane wrote "Thy Nazarene and tender eyes", a printer's error transformed it into "Thy Nazarene and tinder eyes".[9] Suppose that Crane had noticed the error and had asked the press to correct it. In that case, it seems obvious that Crane's intention would determine that the text really said 'tender' rather than 'tinder' and hence that in the fiction the eyes were tender rather than tinder. If he had decided (as he did) that he preferred the 'tinder' version, however, then that would have been the correct version.[10] Either way, his intention seems decisive. Shakespeare includes a song in one of his plays with the lines:

> Golden lads and girls all must,
> As chimney-sweepers, come to dust.
>   (*Cymbeline* IV, ii, 262–63)

A critic has pointed out that "golden lads" and "chimney-sweepers" are Warwickshire dialect terms for dandelions in various stages.[11] Is this an element in the poem? Well, surely that depends on whether Shakespeare used (or at least was aware of) those dialect terms. And that, arguably, is because if he were unaware of them, he couldn't (at any level of his mind) have *intended* them to be part of the poem. The original British edition of Anthony Burgess's *A Clockwork Orange* includes a chapter in which Alex reforms, but the first American edition did not include that chapter. Does Alex reform in *A Clockwork Orange*? Unless we want to say that there are two different stories here, we should surely say that it depends on whether Burgess intended the last chapter to be included (as he did).

Suppose, however, that Jane Austen wrote *Pride and Prejudice* exactly as she did but intended Mrs. Bennet to be a great wit. The Authorial Intention Principle, or AIP, implies that Mrs. Bennet would be a great wit, which obviously she would not be. Or suppose that Austen had intended the behavior of Wickham to be morally exemplary. Again AIP implies that, in that case, Wickham's behavior would be morally exemplary, which it obviously wasn't. John F. Phillips imagines that Coleridge wrote "The Rime of the Ancient Mariner" intending it to be about a botched attempt to steal the crown jewels and not to be about an ancient mariner accosting a man on his way to a wedding to tell him a tragic tale. If AIP were correct, then "The Rime of the Ancient Mariner", in the imagined scenario, would be about a botched attempt to steal the crown jewels and would not be about an ancient mariner telling a tragic tale. "This, of course, is absurd", says Phillips. I agree.[12]

---

[9] Monroe Beardsley, "The Authority of the Text," in *Intention and Interpretation*, ed. Iseminger, 26, is the source of this example. He makes a different point with it, however.

[10] When do the eyes change from being tender to being tinder? This is an interesting question that I shall not pursue here.

[11] Jonathan Bate, "Golden Lads and Chimney-Sweepers," *Harper's*, April 1999, 60–62.

[12] John F. Phillips, "Truth and Inference in Fiction," *Philosophical Studies* 94 (1999): 276–77.

Attractively simple as it is, the Authorial Intention Principle is inadequate as it stands. Authorial intention is a factor in determining what is true in the work, but it is not the whole story.[13]

II. MUTUAL BELIEF PRINCIPLE

The Authorial Intention Principle gives the author too much control over the contents of her fiction, but the Reality Principle may not give her enough, since she may well be unaware of features of reality that determine what is true in the story according to RP. Several critics argue that what Kendall Walton calls the "Mutual Belief Principle" (MBP) has the advantage of avoiding this difficulty. Here is Lewis's version of the principle:

> "In the fiction F, Φ" is true if and only if whenever w is one of the collective belief worlds of the community of origin of F, then some world where F is told as known fact and Φ is true differs less from the world w, on balance, than does any world where F is told as known fact and Φ is not true.[14]

"The collective belief worlds of the community of origin" are possible worlds where things are pretty much as the author and the majority of his contemporaries believed things to be and believed one another to believe things to be, and so on. So collective belief worlds for *The Divine Comedy* would be worlds where (among other things) the following are true: God exists, the earth is flat, the earth is the center of the universe, blasphemy and adultery are wrong, and the sky is blue. What is true in *The Divine Comedy*, according to this principle, is what is true in those worlds where the words of *The Divine Comedy*, expressed with the same meaning, are told as known fact and which are closest to the collective belief worlds of the community of origin of *The Divine Comedy*.

One question that arises immediately is, What if there are no collective belief worlds? What if, as surely happens often, the collective beliefs of the community of origin are subtly contradictory?[15] Or what if the author is radically mis-

---

[13] Another difficulty is that AIP is circular, in that it uses the notion of truth in fiction to analyze truth in fiction. Perhaps it will be argued that the circularity is not vicious. If the author thinks to herself, "I hereby intend that Φ is true in F", then by this principle, Φ is true in F. Whether or not she has this thought is a straightforward matter. (Discovering it may be less straightforward.) This raises further questions. Suppose she doesn't have any explicit intentions of this sort, that is, she doesn't formulate the thought of this intention in these words or others closely related to them. Does that mean that nothing is true in F? Presumably not. Presumably, we have to look for other signs of her intention. But if so, it seems that we need an account of *what it is* to intend that Φ is true in F. And that suggests that we need a better understanding of the content of the intention. In other words, we are back where we started.

[14] Lewis, "Truth in Fiction," 273, calls it "Analysis 2". Wolterstorff, *Works*, 126, calls a slight variant on this idea the *b*-principle.

[15] I'll leave aside this problem here and simply note that the Reality Principle faces a related problem of dealing with contradictions which I discuss later.

taken about the beliefs of his contemporaries? Why, moreover, should the author's *contemporaries'* opinions have so much weight? The answer, presumably, is that the author's contemporaries constitute his intended audience, and his beliefs about their beliefs enable him to carry out his intention of directing their imaginings. But what if he is writing for posterity rather than for his contemporaries? As an extreme example, suppose he writes a novel and then leaves it to be opened after his death—or even several hundred years after his death (like the character in *I Claudius*). In such a case, it would seem arbitrary to pay attention to what the author's contemporaries believed. A natural alternative is to consider simply what the author himself believed. A difficulty for this is that it makes the content of the story depend on sometimes inaccessible and seemingly irrelevant facts about the author's beliefs. (MBP at least sticks to beliefs in the public domain.)

Here's a more troubling objection. Walton describes a story about a friendship between members of different racial groups in which the friendship is viciously suppressed by the authorities. He supposes that it is mutually believed—by the author and his contemporaries—that the mixing of the races is evil.[16] MBP, therefore, implies that the friendship described in the story is evil. Walton argues that the friendship is not evil and hence that MBP gets the wrong result in this case. He is surely right about this. Friendship between the races is not evil, or at least not simply in virtue of being friendship between the races, and it is not evil *anywhere* it occurs—here or in China, in the actual world or another possible world, in reality or in the story.

Since it may be objected that "the story" is not a place like China or Mars, that what holds everywhere may not hold there, I shall not rely on this simple argument for the claim that the friendship in the story Walton describes is not wrong. Here's a better argument. Many authors try to convince us of moral claims by way of fiction. For example, the author of *Cider House Rules* tries to convince us that abortion is sometimes permissible; the author of *Breaking the Code*, that persecution of homosexuals is wrong; Wilfred Owen, that war is evil; Shakespeare with *Henry V*, that war is sometimes glorious; with *Macbeth*, that ruthless ambition is its own punishment; with *Hamlet*, that one oughtn't be like Polonius. Often they succeed. Teaching and learning about morality is not a by-product or a sneaky, secondary agenda of fiction but an important and central aspect of it. I believe, however, that this phenomenon is impossible or incomprehensible if MBP (or some principle like it) is true. Here's why. Moral learning through fiction proceeds by way of our forming beliefs about events and characters in the story and extrapolating those beliefs to events and people in reality. For example, I come to believe that the executions portrayed in *The Green Mile* were wrong, and I extrapolate from that to the belief that some or all actual executions are wrong. Mary comes to believe that Goneril and

---

[16] Walton, *Mimesis as Make-Believe*, 155.

Regan's treatment of their father is morally abhorrent, and she realizes that her own (similar but not as monstrously cruel) treatment of her mother is also morally wrong, and so on.

But if this is so, it seems that the moral qualities of people and events in the story must depend on the same sort of factors as the moral qualities of people and events in reality. The moral qualities of people and events in reality do not depend on the moral beliefs of some author and his audience. So the moral qualities of people and events in the story cannot depend on the moral beliefs of the author and his audience as MBP implies.

> More formally:
> 1. We learn about morality through fiction.
> 2. If we learn about morality through fiction, then the moral qualities of people and events in the story must depend on the same sorts of factors as the moral qualities of people and events in reality.
> 3. But the moral qualities of people and events in reality don't depend on the beliefs of an author and his audience.
> So the moral qualities of people and events in the story don't depend on the beliefs of an author and his audience.

The second premise of this argument is the one most in need of defense. As it stands, it is perhaps a little strong. There may be other ways in which we can learn about morality through fiction (a character might offer a little philosophical argument in the middle of the text, for example), but an important and distinctively literary way of learning about morality through fiction occurs when the author makes us see that a character is good or bad or a fictional action is right or wrong (in the story) and we then infer, or simply come to believe, that similar actual people are good or bad or similar actual actions are right or wrong. If we suppose that this phenomenon does occur, it is difficult to see how it could occur if it were not a general assumption—implicitly common to authors and readers—that the same sort of factors underpinned the moral qualities of fictional and actual states of affairs.

It may be objected that the argument just stated relies on the controversial assumption that there are moral truths. I believe, however, that the point of this argument should be convincing both to moral realists and to moral noncognitivists who rely on fiction to help form their moral attitudes. Moreover, note that the point of my argument applies not just to moral truths but to other general truths that authors try to teach us by way of fiction—prudential truths, psychological truths, aesthetic truths, philosophical truths. I believe that fiction's ability to teach us such truths is, along with its beauty, pleasingness, and other aesthetic qualities, what makes it most valuable. If so, then it is important that our theory be able to explain this ability.

III. CURRIE'S FICTIONAL AUTHOR PRINCIPLE

Gregory Currie rejects both RP and MBP, primarily because of how they treat texts that contain contradictions. It sometimes happens that each of two contradictory claims is true in the story, although their conjunction and much of what follows from it are not true in the story.[17] For this and other reasons, Currie argues that truth in fiction has the structure of a belief system rather than a possible world or set of worlds. For example, it sometimes happens that someone believes each of two contradictory claims although she does not believe their conjunction or much of what follows from it. To exploit this analogy, Currie offers the following principle of interpretation:

> "In the fiction F, Φ" is true if and only if it is reasonable for the informed reader to infer that the fictional author of F believes that Φ.[18] [I call this the Fictional Author Principle, or FAP.]

"The fictional author . . . is that fictional character constructed within our make-believe whom we take to be telling us the story as known fact."[19] He is not the actual author, who does not believe that the story is true. Nor is he (at least not always) the narrator, who is sometimes deceived about what is true in the stories and so whose beliefs cannot ground truth in fiction. The fictional author, then, must be fully informed about what is true in the story (although we must be careful not to define the concept of a fictional author in this way or else the account of fictional truth will be objectionably circular).

An *informed reader* is one who knows about the text, the genre, and the community of origin of the text. It is interesting to note that different informed readers might reasonably infer different things about what the fictional author believes. In that case, two incompatible claims would be true in the story. For example, I might reasonably conclude that the fictional author of "Shall I compare thee to a summer's day?" believes that the sonnet is addressed to a young man whereas someone else might reasonably believe that it is addressed to a young woman. FAP seems to imply that it is true in the fiction that it is addressed both to a young man and to a young woman, although of course, it is addressed to only one person. This does not automatically refute FAP, since any theory of truth in fiction must deal with contradictions in fiction, and as I have indicated, FAP is partly *designed* to deal with them. But it is somewhat worrying that FAP introduces a whole new source of contradictions.

This could be avoided if FAP excluded all reference to the reasonable beliefs of an informed reader and simply defined fictional truth in terms of the beliefs of the fictional author. Currie doesn't explain why he does not do this, but he hints

---

[17] Gregory Currie, *The Nature of Fiction* (Cambridge: Cambridge University Press, 1990). I shall discuss his objections in more detail later.

[18] Ibid., 80.

[19] Ibid., 76.

that he doesn't think the fictional author has enough objective reality over and above what we reasonably believe about him for this suggestion to make sense.

The fictional author is a rather mysterious figure.[20] Currie might point out that RP relies on the notion of a fictional author too, since it defines fictional truth as what is true in worlds where the fiction is *told as known fact.* In those worlds there must be someone who knows the story and tells it. This person sounds like a fictional author. So any reason to reject the fictional author will count equally against RP and FAP. Currie's use of the fictional author creates a difficulty for him that does not arise for RP, however. This is because although RP implies the *existence* of a fictional author, it does not *rely on crucial features,* such as beliefs, of the fictional author for interpreting the story. FAP, in contrast, makes features of the fictional author crucial to the interpretation of the story. As Currie himself says, "To make this proposal plausible we must . . . show how it is possible to build up a belief set for the fictional author in a nonarbitrary way."[21] As an example, consider the question of when the fictional author lives. If he's a first-century Roman, he believes one set of propositions; if he's a twentieth-century Englishman, he believes a very different set. But what he believes (or can reasonably be supposed to believe) determines what is true in the novel.[22] Fixing the fictional author's approximate date of birth might seem a relatively straightforward matter. The fictional author of *Little Dorritt* presumably lives in the middle of the nineteenth century; that of *Primary Colors,* in the late twentieth century. But what about historical novels, like *I Claudius* or the Brother Cadfael mysteries? Currie says that the fictional author is sometimes a contemporary of the actual author and sometimes a contemporary of the other characters in the story.[23] How is this settled? He thinks we determine what the fictional author believes by examining the text and using background beliefs to fill in the gaps.

> But the text alone isn't enough. . . . Speakers often simply assume that, in a given context, some of their beliefs can be inferred. When we infer a person's beliefs from what he says or writes, we do so against a background of assumptions that help us choose between alternative hypotheses—assumptions about what someone *like that* would probably believe. . . . When it comes to interpreting the beliefs of the fictional author, the text itself will be one of the things that gives us clues as to what kind of person he is. . . . But the text provides these clues only against a background of assumptions for which there might be no warrant in the text itself.[24]

---

[20] As Phillips argues in "Truth and Inference."

[21] Phillips, "Truth and Inference," 76.

[22] Similar questions arise for moral beliefs. Are we to suppose that the fictional author shares the moral beliefs of the actual author or of the narrator or something in between? What if the story portrays itself as written by someone with moral beliefs very different from those of the actual author (perhaps *Lolita* is like this)?

[23] Currie, *Nature of Fiction,* n. 32.

[24] Ibid., 77.

So to determine what is true in one of the Cadfael stories, say, *Monk's Hood*, we rely on the text against background assumptions of what the fictional author can be expected to take for granted. But which background assumptions— those of a twentieth-century person or those of an eleventh-century person? Currie says this is to be settled by considering attitudes expressed in the work. But the text itself may well not determine the matter. Perhaps the text doesn't settle the question whether the fictional author is an eleventh-century Welshman ahead of his time or an old-fashioned modern. We are supposed to use background assumptions to resolve these indeterminacies, not use the text to determine which background assumptions to appeal to. Currie could simply *stipulate* that the fictional author be a contemporary of the actual author or simply stipulate that the fictional author be a contemporary of the characters described—but these suggestions raise their own problems.

Note that RP doesn't have this problem. It doesn't matter what the fictional author believes. In some of the closest worlds where *Monk's Hood* is told as known fact, the fictional author lives in one century; in another, he lives in a different century. But his date of birth makes very little difference to what else is true in these worlds and hence to what is true in the story.

Far more important than any of this is that FAP faces a morality objection analogous to the one I raised for MBP. According to FAP, a fictional character has some moral quality if the informed reader believes that the fictional author believes that she does. But if, as I have argued, the moral qualities of characters and events in the story must depend on the same sorts of factors as the moral qualities of people and events in reality, then they do not depend on what the informed reader believes about the fictional author's opinions.

IV. PHILLIPS'S ACTUAL AUTHOR PRINCIPLE

Attracted to Currie's account but hoping to avoid the mysterious and unnecessary "fictional author",[25] Phillips offers a variant principle that appeals to psychological states of the actual author:

> "In the fiction F, Φ" is true if and only if it is reasonable for an informed
> reader to infer from the text that, under ideal conditions, the author of F

---

[25] "In the story *To Build a Fire*, there are, on the face of it, only two characters, a man and a dog. The story is not told from the point of view of the dog, and the man dies toward the end of the story. The fictional author, then, must be some mysterious third character in the story, a character who has full access to the thoughts of the man and the dog as well as complete knowledge of the events of the story. The fictional author thus appears to be in the same epistemic position with respect to the story as the real author. Indeed, the only discernible difference between the author and his fictional counterpart is that the author is a real person whereas the fictional author is a character in the story. . . . There is virtue in economy, and it would be better, it seems to me, if we had a theory which could mimic the successes of Currie's theory without positing the existence of the fictional author in the story." Phillips, "Truth and Inference," 275–76.

would agree that Φ is part of F.[26] [I call this the Actual Author Principle, or AAP.]

By "ideal conditions" he means "if the author is cooperative and clear-headed, and able to specify each proposition which is a part of the story he has imagined."[27] But what does he mean by the phrase "Φ is part of F"? Presumably, he means, "In the fiction F, Φ". In other words, this account amounts to:

> "*In the fiction F, Φ*" is true if and only if it is reasonable for an informed reader to infer from the text that, under ideal conditions, the author of F would agree that *in the fiction F, Φ*.

That looks objectionably circular. Well, perhaps he is not attempting to give the meaning of "In the fiction F, Φ" but rather attempting to give truth conditions for it, that is, in order for it to be true, someone must think (that someone would think) that it is true. But like accounts of goodness in terms of whether someone or some group thinks about goodness, this raises the question what is going on in the head of the thinker. Do the informed reader and the author under ideal conditions have a theory about truth in fiction? Is it Phillips's theory? Is it a different theory such as RP or MBP? If they have a different theory, then, first, why should Phillips take their opinion so seriously? And second, won't they end up accepting a lot of implications that Phillips rejects? For example, the author of F might think that all the minute details of general relativity are part of his story—even if he couldn't articulate them and even if they don't appear in the text (perhaps it is clear from the text that the author has this theory about fictional truth, or perhaps the reader reasonably takes RP for granted). Third, in applying this theory, in thinking about what an informed reader would conclude that an author under ideal conditions would think is part of F, aren't we simply thinking about what a reasonable person would include? We are reasonable people, so doesn't this just amount to what we are intuitively inclined to include? Is there any wonder, then, that the theory is more or less impervious to counterexample? But that's because the account is close to being empty.

It's not entirely impervious to counterexample, however, since it too faces the Morality Objection. On AAP, in order to make the adultery in the story permissible, all the author has to do is make his opinions apparent enough for an informed reader to discern. But if, as I have argued, the moral qualities of characters and events in the story must depend on the same sorts of factors as the moral qualities of people and events in reality, then they do not depend on what the informed reader believes about the author's opinions.

---

[26] Phillips, "Truth and Inference," 287.
[27] Ibid.

V. THE REALITY PRINCIPLE AGAIN

I have argued that the most serious problem faced by a variety of accounts of truth in fiction is the Morality Objection. The Reality Principle doesn't face this problem.[28] It has the added advantage of considerable initial plausibility. Think how natural it is to start or describe a story in terms of, "What would happen if . . ." For example, a television movie about Y2K (produced and shown before the year 2000) was advertised with the slogan, "What if they're right . . ." Similarly, the movie *Deep Blue Sea* was advertised with the question, "What if sharks evolved high intelligence?" Presumably, these questions are partly answered by the explicit content of the movies, but audience members are supposed to fill in some of the details imaginatively by thinking about what things *would* be like in the circumstances described. When we imagine what would happen if . . . , we don't want to think about what the author and his contemporaries thought. That puts too much distance between us and the fiction by making us hold front and center the thought that it is a piece of fiction.[29] We want to think directly about the characters and so on as the Reality Principle directs us to do.

Natural and plausible as the Reality Principle is, however, it faces some formidable objections. I shall discuss seven of these.

VI. THE EXCESSIVE PROLIFERATION OBJECTION

Walton writes:

> The real world is a very big place. If fictional worlds are as much like it as their primary fictional truths allow, most of them will include most of it. So the world of even—or rather especially!—the sketchiest story . . . will turn out to be vastly richer, vastly more detailed, than anyone would have dreamed. It will be fictional in "Goldilocks and the Three Bears" that Tenzing and Hillary achieved the first ascent of Mount Everest and Neil Armstrong the first landing on the moon.[30]

Depending on the correct account of counterfactuals, "Goldilocks" may not be quite as rich as Walton imagines, even if the Reality Principle is true.

---

[28] What if the author explicitly says that M for some M that is false? For example, suppose the author of a children's book concludes with the line, "The moral of this story is that little girls shouldn't play with boys' toys"? In that case, RP seems to imply it is true in the story that little girls shouldn't play with boys' toys. This seems an unattractive implication of the view, but perhaps it is acceptable to bite the bullet since this sort of example is fairly rare.

[29] It is sometimes important to focus on the work *as* a work of art. For example, in a study or critique it will often be important to point to how the author achieved various effects or how impressive it was that she used this or that technique, but when we are simply enjoying it, entering into the spirit of it, we want to think directly about the characters and events depicted. The Reality Principle doesn't forbid us to focus on the text as a text or as the production of an author, etc., but it doesn't require us to do so.

[30] Walton, *Mimesis as Make-Believe*, 148.

It probably won't include Hillary and Tenzing's ascent of Everest or Armstrong's landing on the moon, but it will include all the laws of science, astronomical facts, prehistoric facts, and much of human history.[31] This sounds a bit odd, but is it really a problem? As Walton himself points out, these extra truths will not be emphasized in our thought or discussion of the story since they are common to most works of fiction and aren't in any way to be attributed to the author's skill.[32] Discussion of the work will focus on what is distinctive about it.

All right, the objector might continue, perhaps this objection is not devastating to the Reality Principle, but it certainly constitutes a *cost* that must be paid for in other intuitive advantages of the principle.

Although on the face of it this appears to be a prima facie strike against the Reality Principle, on closer inspection it appears less repellent. Consider Elizabeth Bennet, the heroine of *Pride and Prejudice*, who reads a lot and has been reasonably well educated. Ask yourself: can she recite passages from Shakespeare like other characters in Austen novels? Can she speak French? Italian? Zulu? Does she know that Socrates taught Plato who taught Aristotle who taught Alexander? Does she know much about the lives of the Caesars? It seems natural to suppose that there are answers to some of these questions (although as we shall see, some answers may be indeterminate). Of course, she can recite passages from Shakespeare. Of course, she knows some French. Of course, she knows about Socrates and Caesar. Of course, she can't speak Zulu. But that means that it is true that Socrates taught Plato and true that Julius Caesar died in 44 B.C. and true that the French word for "bread" is *pain*, and so on. And when we say, unadornedly, that Elizabeth knows that Socrates taught Plato, what we really mean is that *in Pride and Prejudice* it is true that Elizabeth knows that Socrates taught Plato. So it is also true *in Pride and Prejudice* that Socrates taught Plato. And the same is true for facts of which Elizabeth is ignorant. We might think to ourselves, "Poor girl, she is ignorant of facts about sex or childbirth that may affect her future life", or, about a bumbling fictional detective, "What a fool! Surely he should have known that . . ." If someone is ignorant of something, there are facts of which she is ignorant. This means that, simply in recognizing that Elizabeth is well informed but not excessively so, we

---

[31] On Lewis's account, the counterfactual, if A then B, is true if and only if the closest A-worlds are also B-worlds. One factor that makes one A-world closer to the actual world than another is if a tiny miracle would be sufficient to transform the actual world to the A-world. This means that A-worlds are typically exactly like the actual world up to shortly before the time of A but then diverge in order to make the antecedent true and continue in accordance with laws of nature, perhaps diverging quite radically from the actual world as time goes on. The closest worlds in which "Goldilocks and the Three Bears" is told as known fact are ones that diverge from the actual world at some point shortly before its events are supposed to have taken place. There is no reason to suppose that all such worlds would contain Hillary and Tenzing's ascent. See Lewis, *Counterfactuals*.

[32] Walton, *Mimesis as Make-Believe*, 149–50.

import vast amounts of detail about history, literature, politics, and the like into the story. Where does this detail end? Does it include everything that would be true if *Pride and Prejudice* were told as known fact (most of which is in fact true); does it include everything that would be true if the world were more or less as Austen's contemporaries believed it to be and *Pride and Prejudice* were told as known fact; does it include everything the fictional author of *Pride and Prejudice* can reasonably be expected to have believed, or does it stop somewhere short of that? RP, MBP, and FAP all imply that *Pride and Prejudice* includes vast numbers of facts that are not in any way relevant to the story. The Excessive Proliferation Objection works against all of them if it works against any. The thought experiment about Elizabeth Bennet suggests, I hope, that it does not work against any of them. Can considerations of this sort be used to choose between them? Perhaps. I find myself inclined to believe that a vast array of facts about the past, relative to the early nineteenth century—facts about Elizabeth I, for example—are available for Elizabeth Bennet to be knowledgeable or ignorant of, but I feel much less confident about facts about times much later than the early nineteenth century—facts about Elizabeth II, for example. This might be thought of as a reason to prefer MBP or FAP to RP, but that is not so. Lewis's semantics of counterfactuals implies that this is what we should expect on RP.[33]

VII. CONTRADICTION OBJECTION

Here's a more serious problem. Stories often contradict themselves, sometimes because of a slip and sometimes because of the author's deliberate intention. A contradiction entails all propositions and counterfactually implies whatever it entails. This means that everything true in *The Time Machine* is also true in *Alice in Wonderland* and vice versa—in other words, that they have the same content. It also means that all positive claims of interpretation about these books are correct. Several strategies have been offered for dealing with these consequences. They can be divided into those that bite the bullet and simply deemphasize the unwanted implications, on the one hand, and those that block the inference from P and not P to all propositions, on the other hand.

The method of deemphasis accepts that everything is true in inconsistent fictions but notes that we can ignore most of what is true since it is not important to the story. This enables us to distinguish *The Time Machine* from *Alice in Wonderland*—they emphasize different things—but it has the disadvantage that if a critic claims that *Hamlet* is about Martin Luther or incest at the court of Elizabeth I, the strongest objection that can be raised is that, though true, these are not very interesting or central parts of the story. (Suppose that *Hamlet* is contradictory—for example, in claiming that Hamlet is a teenager in the first act and a thirty-year-old a few months later.)

Lewis attempts to block the inference by modifying RP, by asking us to con-

[33] Ibid.

sider consistent *fragments* of the inconsistent fiction.[34] In his original presentation of the matter, he claimed that a fragment would be a maximal consistent proper part of the story. If the only contradiction is P on page 1 and ~P on page 700, then one of the fragments will include everything in the story except P and another will include everything the story except ~P.[35] In a postscript to "Truth in Fiction", Lewis suggests a different way of dividing up the text—for example, into the first and second halves.[36] Once we have the fragments, what do we do with them? Lewis describes two functions from truth in fragments to truth in whole fictions. The first is *the method of intersection*: what is true in the fiction is what is true in all the fragments. The second is *the method of union*: what is true in the fiction is what is true in some of the fragments. Both these methods avoid the crazy implications. Even if P is true in one fragment and ~P is true in another, it does not follow that P&~P is true in the fiction as a whole.[37]

If the hero is said to have blue eyes on page 1, and his eyes are never mentioned again, we want it to be true in the fiction as a whole that he has blue eyes. If the fiction contains the second half as a fragment, then the method of intersection will imply that it is not true that he has blue eyes. Perhaps the method of intersection should be modified to read:

Φ is true in F iff Φ is true in *some* of the fragments and *not false* in any.

Moreover, if P is true in one fragment, and P→Q is true in another fragment, then Q should be true in the fiction as a whole. Suppose we learn in the first chapter that the murderer was left-handed and in the third chapter that none of the Jones boys was left-handed. Aren't we entitled to conclude—even if this conclusion is never explicitly drawn—that none of the Jones boys was the murderer? This suggests that we should allow that whatever is jointly entailed (or counterfactually implied) by other propositions true in the fiction is also true in the fiction. Let's modify the method of intersection to make this explicit:

Φ is true in F iff Φ is true in *some* of the fragments and *not false* in any, or Φ is counterfactually implied by some proposition or set of propositions true in F.

The method of union cannot be similarly modified, however, without immediately returning us to the problem we started with. If one fragment contains P and another ~P, then if we make the method of union closed under implication,

---

[34] Note that Wolterstorff does something similar in *Works*, 128 ff.

[35] Lewis, "Truth in Fiction," 275.

[36] Ibid., 277.

[37] If it is impossible to separate the strands—if, for example, the author has a character devise a mechanism for making contradictions true—then P&~P will be true in the story, and perhaps in this story everything that follows (i.e., everything) will be true too. Authors who devise such fictions may even welcome such paradoxical implications.

it will follow that P&~P and everything else is true in the fiction. This seems a good reason to prefer the modified method of intersection.

VIII. CURRIE'S DEGREES-OF-TRUTH OBJECTION

Currie presents the following set of claims about Sherlock Holmes:

> He was a detective.
> He had a full set of fingers and toes.
> Sometime in his early life he suffered a serious illness.
> He had a full set of teeth.
> Sometime in his early life he suffered from diphtheria.
> Sometime in his career he visited Minsk.
> He was moonlighting as a gentleman cracksman in the style of Raffles.[38]

The items on this list have decreasing plausibility. Currie claims that any attempt to divide them up into those that are true in the story and those that aren't would fail or be intolerably arbitrary. And this isn't an epistemic problem. It's not that we just don't know whether Holmes had diphtheria as a child. That "is to be seduced by the picture of a determinate fictional reality to which we have greater or lesser epistemic access. When it comes to truth in fiction there is no distinguishing an epistemic from an ontological difference. There is no sense to the suggestion that although total evidence may leave the question undecided, a proposition is either true in the story or not. . . . This strongly suggests that our intuitive notion of truth in fiction is the notion of something that admits of degrees."[39]

Currie then argues that his Fictional Author Principle can easily accommodate the idea that truth in fiction admits of degrees but that RP cannot (at least, not easily and, I assume, naturally) be adjusted to deal with it, since on RP, "the right-hand side specifies a condition that simply holds or fails to hold, not a condition that holds to a greater or a lesser degree. There is thus no quantitative variability on the right-hand side that could be exploited to explain the variability we detect within [in the fiction, F, Φ]."[40]

I think Currie is right that we need to allow for some sort of degrees of truth-in-fiction. Here's a list of claims that more obviously and simply exemplifies the degree notion he wants. Lady Macbeth had fewer than fifty children. She had fewer than forty-nine. She had fewer than forty-eight . . . she had fewer than twenty . . . ten . . . eight, seven, six, five, four, three, two, one. The first of these

---

[38] Currie, *Nature of Fiction*, 90.

[39] Ibid., 91. I shall grant that truth in fiction admits of degrees, but not the premise that there is no distinguishing epistemic gaps from ontological ones. It seems that the text may leave it open—to be decided by reality—whether God exists, whether ghosts exist, or whether Goldbach's conjecture is true.

[40] Ibid., 92. Note that Currie raises this objection for MBP rather than RP, but the point applies exactly as much to RP.

is clearly true. The last is clearly false. We find ourselves unable to say at what point the items on the list go from being clearly true to being merely very likely. And it seems, as Currie supposes, that our inability to say is a matter of metaphysical indeterminacy rather than mere ignorance. Can RP accommodate this? That will depend on the true theory of counterfactuals, but it seems that a similar phenomenon occurs with counterfactuals that have nothing to do with fiction. Consider the six-year-old child who was shot to death in Michigan recently. We might wonder—sadly—what this child might have done had she survived to adulthood. Consider the claims that if she had survived to adulthood, she might have had at least fifty children, she might have had at least forty-nine . . . she might have had at least twenty . . . ten . . . five, four, three, two, one. The first two of these are false. The last five are true. What point, between fifty and five, is the cutoff? Six seems a better candidate than sixteen, and sixteen a better candidate than twenty-six, but there seems to be no fact of the matter. How can a semantics of counterfactuals accommodate these two facts: some counterfactuals (or truths of fiction) seem more true than others, and there is often no nonfuzzy line between the least true and the false ones?

Like this: for any counterfactual, if A, then C, there will be many, probably infinitely many, closest A-worlds. If all these A-worlds are C-worlds, the counterfactual is true; otherwise, it is not true. But sometimes most of them will be C-worlds and sometimes most of them will be ~C-worlds. For example, all the closest *Macbeth* worlds are worlds in which Lady Macbeth has at least one child; most of the *Macbeth* worlds are worlds in which she has at least two; a smaller subset are worlds where she has at least three, and so on.[41] This means that it is true that if *Macbeth* were told as known fact, she would have at least one and not true that she would have at least two. But if we think of the proportion of C-worlds as a measure of probability, then it is more probable that she had at least two than that she had at least three, and so on. Similarly, it is highly probable that Holmes had some serious childhood illness and less probable that he had diphtheria. Varying probabilities are not quite varying degrees of truth, but they are close enough. What about the fact that there is no sharp line between true and nontrue claims or between very unlikely and definitely false claims? A counterfactual is true if and only if all the closest A-worlds are C-worlds and not true otherwise. But imagine a band of closest A-worlds that are all C-worlds. Add to this picture an A-~C-world that is neither determinately within this band nor determinately outside it. In that case, there will be no fact of the matter whether the counterfactual is true or not. Does this happen? Why not? Closeness of worlds is often considered to be a matter of similarity between them, and surely there is sometimes no fact of the matter whether A and B are as similar as A and C. For example, are William and his dad as similar as Peter and his dad? There may well be no answer. In this way,

---

[41] If you are bothered by the question how one subset of an infinite set can be bigger than another, consider all the points on a bulls'-eye compared with all the points on a dartboard.

RP can easily and naturally make sense of the degrees of truth data that Currie invokes, and thus avoids this objection.

IX. PHILLIPS'S *EMMA* OBJECTION

Phillips raises an intriguing objection.[42] He argues that RP cannot account for various fictional facts, such as that the character Isabella, in *Emma*, takes after her father, Mr. Woodhouse, more than Emma does. He believes that the counterfactual or possible-worlds analysis of such propositions implies that "Emma takes after Mr. Woodhouse more than Isabella does" is just as true as "Isabella takes after Mr. Woodhouse more than Emma does."

Phillips uses this example to make the point that "if there is a preponderance of textual evidence that points towards a proposition's being true in a given fiction, we take the proposition to be true in the fiction", whereas a strong inductive argument is not enough to secure with certainty that a claim is true simpliciter.[43] I'm not sure what to make of the general claim and so will tackle his particular claim about *Emma*. To facilitate discussion of his argument, I shall lay it out in numbered premises. Suppose that w^* is some world where *Emma* is told as known fact and Isabella is more like her father than Emma is; and w^{**} is a world where *Emma* is told as known fact and Emma is more like her father than Isabella is. w^* and w^{**} are as alike as possible except for the relevant facts about Emma, Isabella, and Mr. Woodhouse.

1. If RP is correct, then w^* is closer to the actual world than w^{**} is.
2. If w^* is closer to the actual world than w^{**} is, then there must be some proposition true in both the actual world and w^* which is false in w^{**}.
3. But by hypothesis, w^{**} is just like w^*, with the exception of certain propositions concerning Emma, Isabella, and Mr. Woodhouse, none of which is true in the actual world.
4. So there is no proposition true in both the actual world and w^* which is false in w^{**}.
5. So w^* is not closer to the actual world than w^{**} is.
6. So RP is not correct.

The third and fourth premises of this seemingly plausible argument are vulnerable to attack. To see this, first note that when we say that a woman "takes after" or resembles her father closely, presumably we mean that they share interesting, salient personality or character traits, not simply that they share a large number of properties. Now let's distinguish two different levels of propositions about Emma, Isabella, and Mr. Woodhouse. First, there are the propositions about what they do and say. At this level, 4 is correct. w^* has everything

---

[42] In "Truth and Inference," 280–81. Like Currie, Phillips takes MBP as his target, but the objection applies with equal force to RP. I shall alter his statement of the objection accordingly.

[43] Phillips, "Truth and Inference," 280–81.

that is explicit in *Emma* plus extra propositions about their (offstage) words and actions, b*. w** has everything explicit in *Emma* plus different extra propositions about their (offstage) words and actions, b**. Neither b* nor b** is true in the actual world. So at this level w* and w** *are* both equally distant from the actual world. But consider another level of propositions about Emma, Isabella, and Mr. Woodhouse that are partly implied by facts at the first level. At this level we note that in w*, Emma's behavior is consistent (as is the behavior of her family members) since b* depicts her as behaving in ways consistent with the ways she is explicitly portrayed as behaving in the novel. If she is tough on Monday, as represented in the novel, she is tough on Tuesday, offstage. If she is intelligent on Wednesday, she is intelligent on Thursday, and so on. In w**, however, her behavior, intelligence, and so on are radically inconsistent. She goes from being bright and tough one day to being feeble the next (whenever she is offstage). If the behavior of at least one character is not radically inconsistent in this way, then we must imagine Emma's interesting characteristics differing dramatically from her father's offstage as well as onstage while Isabella's resemble his offstage as well as onstage, in which case it seems that Isabella does take after her father more than Emma does. But if Emma's personality (or that of one or more of the other characters) is radically inconsistent in this way, then her behavior does not fit in with normal psychological laws. That means that those psychological laws are true in w* but not true in w**. This suggests that some propositions true in the actual world—those expressing the true psychological laws—are true in w* and false in w**. So RP implies that Isabella does resemble her father more than Emma does. Similar points apply to myriad other propositions not made explicit in the story but obviously true in it. The *Emma* Objection is not a reason to reject RP.

X. AUTHORIAL CONTROL OBJECTION

RP implies that authors are ignorant of much of the content of their stories. Jane Austen's ignorance of the superstring theory element in *Emma* may not matter much, but some philosophers worry about what happens when facts about geography, zoology, or psychology actually make a difference to the central events in a story, undermining what the author intends to convey. Walton illustrates this point by describing a story written by an author who believed, along with all his contemporaries, that the earth was flat. In the story a group of mariners set out across the ocean believing that in so doing they risk falling off the edge of the earth. Walton asks us to suppose that the success of this story depends on the earth's being flat. But

> according to the Reality Principle, it is fictional that the earth is spherical and that there is no danger of falling off. But to insist on this, to wrench the story from its original context and force on it an interpretation neither the author nor the most perceptive of his intended listeners could have divined, would seem contrived and gratuitously uncharitable. And to do so would ruin a

good adventure story; the tale (let us assume) depends on the danger for its dramatic effect. Better to go along with the misconception about the shape of the earth for purposes of understanding and appreciating the story, and allow that fictionally the earth does have a dangerous edge. In making implied fictional truths depend on facts of nature, the Reality Principle loosens the artist's control over them. If he happens to be mistaken about the relevant facts, his fictional worlds will not turn out as he intends. This would be unfortunate in many instances, since artists whose works are worth experiencing at all can be expected to have good judgment about what sorts of fictional worlds are likely to be interesting or valuable. Why not give the artist a free hand in constructing fictional worlds, rather than permitting chance in the form of unknown facts of nature to help shape them?[44]

Here's a simple statement of the argument:

    1. If RP is true, then authors lack a certain kind of control over their fictions.
    2. Authors do not lack this kind of control over their fictions.
    So RP is false.

How much and what kind of control do we reasonably want the author to have? The following principle will maximize authorial control:

Authorial Control Principle (ACP): If the author wants to make Φ true in the fiction F, and believes that if δ then Φ, and makes δ an explicit part of F, then Φ is true in F.

If ACP is correct, then the Reality Principle is obviously wrong. But is it correct? Recall an objection I raised for the Authorial Intention Principle. Suppose that Jane Austen—without altering the text of *Pride and Prejudice* one jot—had intended Mrs. Bennet to be a great wit and Mr. Collins to be a profoundly good

---

[44] Walton, *Mimesis as Make-Believe*, 151. Several other philosophers have made the same point with different examples. For example, Lewis writes: "In an article setting forth little-known facts about the movement of snakes, Carl Gans has argued as follows:
    In 'The Adventure of the Speckled Band' S.H. solves a murder mystery by showing
    that the victim has been killed by a Russell's viper that has climbed up a bell rope.
    What H. did not realize was that Russell's viper is not a constrictor. The snake is
    therefore incapable of concertina movement and could not have climbed the rope. Ei-
    ther the snake reached its victim some other way or the case remains open. (Carl Gans,
    "How Snakes Move," *Scientific American*, vol. 222 [1970]: 93.)
We may well look askance at this reasoning. But if [RP] is correct then so is Gans's argument. The story never quite says that Holmes was right that the snake climbed the rope. Hence there are worlds where the Holmes stories are told as known fact, where the snake reached the victim some other way, and where Holmes therefore bungled. Presumably some of these worlds differ less from ours than their rivals where Holmes was right and where Russell's viper is capable of concertina movement up a rope. Holmes's infallibility, of course, is not a countervailing resemblance to actuality; our world contains no infallible Holmes." Lewis, "Truth in Fiction," 271.

but much misunderstood man. Suppose Austen wrote *Pride and Prejudice* the way she did in part because she wanted Mrs. Bennet to be a great wit and believed that people who made the remarks Mrs. Bennet makes were great wits. If ACP were correct, it would be true in *Pride and Prejudice* that Mrs. Bennet is a great wit. I think it is obvious, however, that Jane Austen couldn't make this proposition true simply by intending (or wanting and believing) it to be true. ACP is clearly false. This doesn't mean that Walton is wrong about the mariner tale he describes, but it suggests that he needs a different and weaker principle of authorial control than ACP. One thing that distinguishes my imaginary Jane Austen's belief from Walton's author's belief is that the first is crazy and the second is reasonable. This suggests:

> Reasonable Authorial Control Principle (RACP): If the author wants to make Φ true in the fiction F, and reasonably believes that if δ then Φ, and makes δ an explicit part of F, then Φ is true in F (even if the author is mistaken in believing that if δ then Φ).

To evaluate this principle, we need to clarify the notion of reasonable belief. Does it depend on how the author arrived at her beliefs, or is it something about the nature of the beliefs themselves, or is it a combination? If it depends on how the author arrived at her beliefs, then what is true in the fiction may depend on esoteric epistemological facts about the author. For example, suppose that some of Conan Doyle's apparently respectable beliefs were arrived at by examining tea leaves. That seems an implausible ground on which to disqualify these beliefs. But if it's something about the nature of the beliefs themselves, shouldn't we disqualify them? If a modern author wrote a novel while believing that the earth was flat, for example, then I believe Walton would want to disqualify her crazy belief, but not if an ancient author did. Note that Walton and Lewis both raise this argument in the context of motivating MBP, which suggests that they would want to disqualify the belief if it was in conflict with what was widely believed by the author's contemporaries but that they would want to allow it if it were not. This suggests that if an author is guided by beliefs that *it is reasonable for someone in her situation to have*, then she can use those beliefs to determine the content of her story.

But this is still problematic. Consider a variant on the Jane Austen example above. Suppose an author creates a character, Little Tom, whom she believes to be worthy of our sympathy and affection because of his suffering and his poignant reflections on his suffering. And suppose, moreover, that this is *a reasonable guess* as to what a sympathetic and lovable person would be like. But suppose that she just misses: people like Little Tom are sickly sweet, wheedling wimps. In that case, in spite of her reasonable belief, the author doesn't succeed in making Little Tom sympathetic and lovable. So RACP is false.

If this is correct, it suggests that writing fiction is a risky business—even with the best will in the world, an author doesn't have complete control over events and characters in her stories. But why is this a problem? We know that writing fiction is a difficult business that takes considerable skill. RP still is not refuted.[45]

XI. SLITHERGADEE OBJECTION

Walton cites Sheldon Silverstein's poem "Slithergadee" and argues that it has an implication not licensed by RP.[46] In the poem, the speaker describes a sea monster, the Slithergadee, that has attacked other people or animals. The speaker insists that, while the monster may catch all the others, it will not catch him. He repeats this confident assertion a couple of times, but the poem ends abruptly, mid-sentence, even mid-word, leaving no doubt in the reader's mind about the results of that overconfidence.

Walton points out that the Slithergadee did catch the boastful speaker but that if RP were true, this would not be true. If a speaker uttering these words were to stop midsentence, it wouldn't be true that he had been eaten by a sea monster. More likely, he would have spilt his coffee or remembered an important meeting or some such thing. Both premises seem correct: the Slithergadee did catch the speaker, and RP does not imply this. So we must grant that RP, as stated, is false. But perhaps we can reconstrue it as having prima facie force:

> "In the fiction F, Φ" is prima facie true if and only if were the story told as known fact Φ would be true.

Or:

> "In the fiction F, Φ" is . . . prima facie true if and only if some world where F is told as known fact and Φ is true differs less from our actual world, on balance, than does any world where F is told as known fact and Φ is not true.

I mean the prima facie qualification like this: RP is the default principle of interpretation, but it can be overridden by explicit or implicit conventions that either block inferences that RP sanctions or add new inferences that RP does not sanction.

It might be objected that this is an ad hoc move, but I think not. Walton offers a plausible model of what authors are doing (at the most general level) when they write stories. They are inviting or instructing or encouraging us to imagine certain things. The issue of this chapter is a coordination problem: how do authors and readers arrive at the same things to imagine? How do authors direct readers' imaginings? How do readers figure out authors' instructions? Surely

---

[45] It may be objected that my counterexamples to ACP and RACP involve necessary falsehoods. A modified version of RACP may try to capitalize on this fact, but I believe the result will be ad hoc.

[46] Walton, *Mimesis as Make-Believe*, 162–63. Sheldon Silverstein, "Slithergadee," in *Uncle Shelby's Zoo: Don't Bump the Glump* (New York: Simon and Schuster, 1964).

some part of this could be achieved by explicit convention. For example, there might be a well-recognized convention—agreed to by all writers and made known to all readers—that whenever a page is left blank in the middle of a book, sex will be understood to be taking place between the main characters. Could we (critics or philosophers) prevent this convention from taking effect? Should we do so if we could? These are odd questions—a bit like asking, "Suppose a group of people wanted to adopt a convention to use the word 'bad' to mean 'exciting'. Could philosophers or language purists somehow prevent them from doing so?" By invoking this convention, an author would succeed in directing the reader's imagination—the very thing fiction is supposed to do. This suggests that it would be absurd to deny conventions a role in determining what is true in fiction.

A different objection: once you allow this role to convention, haven't you effectively made RP redundant? I don't think so. Convention—either explicit or implicit—cannot (or cannot easily) do more than a tiny fraction of the work of generating truth in fiction. RP constitutes a very natural default mechanism. As such, it plays a significant role in determining truth in fiction. As my discussion of the Excessive Proliferation, the Degrees-of-Truth, the *Emma*, and the Morality Objections suggests, RP, even with the prima facie qualification, has some very interesting implications.

XII. THE LEVELS OBJECTION

According to RP, truths of fiction are generated in two ways, or at two different levels. Primary truths (as Walton calls them) are generated directly by constituting the meaning of the sentences of the text. For example, if the text includes the sentence "An owl and a pussycat went to sea in a beautiful pea-green boat", then if someone had uttered that sentence as known fact in English, it would have been true that an owl and a pussycat went to sea in a beautiful pea-green boat. Indirect truths in fiction are generated indirectly by being counterfactually implied by primary truths. Walton objects that the 'told as known fact' account of primary truths does not work. He concedes that the essence of RP is its account of indirect generation of fictional truths and that an adjustment in its account of direct generation would not alter its spirit, but he argues that no systematic account of the generation of primary truths is possible.

The most obvious difficulty of this sort for the original statement of RP is the phenomenon of the unreliable narrator. Anticipating this objection, Lewis gives the example of Flash Stockman:

> I'm a stockman to my trade, and they call me Ugly Dave.
> I'm old and grey and only got one eye.
> In a yard I'm good, of course, but just put me on a horse,
> And I'll go where lots of young-'uns daren't try.

Lewis adds, "The boasting gets ever steeper: riding, whipping, branding, shearing . . .

In fact, I'm duke of every blasted thing.

Plainly this is fiction. What is true in it?"[47]

If the poem were told as known fact, then it would be true that the speaker was very skilled at every blasted thing. But presumably that is not true in the story. What is true is that the speaker is a braggart and a liar.

A related problem is that even reliable narrators often use metaphor and irony. When Jane Austen writes, "It is a truth universally acknowledged that a single man of large fortune is in want of a wife", we know that she is to be trusted but that she means something other than what those words literally say.

Walton suggests an alternative account of directly generated or primary truths: what is primarily true in the fiction is that someone is uttering the words of the story. This primary truth together with various other facts generates secondary or indirect truths that most of what is said in most cases is true, or that some of what is said is ironic, some of what is said is wishful thinking, and so on. But further difficulties arise for this suggestion. First, it sometimes seems that nobody is *uttering* the words. Sometimes they are written down, sometimes they are the content of someone's thoughts or dreams. Sometimes there is more than one speaker. Second, sometimes there seems to be no narrator at all. And finally, there is what we might call the *Macbeth* Objection, as expressed by James Thurber:

> "I don't think for a moment that Macbeth did it . . . I don't think for a mo-
> ment that he killed the King," she said . . . "Who do you suspect?" I
> asked . . . "Macduff," she said, promptly.
> "Oh, Macduff did it, all right . . . Do you know who discovered Duncan's
> body? . . . Macduff discovers it . . . Then he comes running downstairs and
> shouts, 'Confusion has broke open the Lord's anointed temple' and 'Sacrile-
> gious murder had made his masterpiece' and on and on like that . . . All that
> stuff was rehearsed . . . You wouldn't say a lot of stuff like that, offhand,
> would you—if you had found a body? . . . You wouldn't! Unless you had
> practiced it in advance. 'My God, there's a body in there!' is what an innocent
> man would say."[48]

The point, of course, is that it cannot be true at the primary or any other level that Macduff says, "Confusion has broke open the Lord's anointed temple." For one thing, he wouldn't be speaking Elizabethan English. For another, he wouldn't be speaking in blank verse and using metaphors worthy of the greatest poet of the language. He was an ordinary fellow in a state of severe shock and grief. Aware of the difficulty for the original statement of RP, Lewis writes:

---

[47] Lewis, "Truth in Fiction," 279.

[48] James Thurber, "The Macbeth Murder Mystery," 81–82, quoted in Walton, *Mimesis as Make-Believe*, 150.

The thing to do is to consider those worlds where the act of storytelling really is whatever it purports to be—ravings, reliable translation of a reliable source, or whatever—here at our world.[49]

Most authors purport to be presenting a reliable account of events, so in most cases the 'told as known fact' version works perfectly well. But sometimes they purport to be offering unreliable accounts, boasts, ironic statements, metaphors, and so on. In the case of Flash Stockman, we are invited to consider a world where someone is offering an unreliable report about his own behavior. In this world it is true that the stockman exists and perhaps that he is old and gray, but it is not true that he is a magnificent horseman.

This would take care of the problem of the unreliable narrator. What about irony and metaphor? The story here is a little more complicated. When an author of fiction uses a metaphor, she is purporting to use it to do something else—paint an accurate picture, tell a pack of boastful lies, express genuine or insincere feelings, and the like. So here the thing to do is to consider a world where someone uses metaphor to do what the author here purports to be doing with it.[50]

What about the problems Walton raises for his own variant account? Do they spell trouble for Lewis's? What about a story in which no one seems to utter the words of the story—because, for example, someone dreams them or writes them in a diary instead? This is not a problem for Lewis's account, since "whatever the author is purporting to do" can include dreaming or writing in a diary. What about stories that don't appear to have a narrator at all? Lewis's account talks about what *the author* purports to do—and there is always one or more author. But perhaps this objection could be recast as the claim that it's not so plausible that the author is always *purporting* to do something. What is a playwright purporting to do? It is tempting to think of a play as an abbreviated novel—with everything except the dialogue left out—so the playwright is purporting to give us an accurate (or maybe partially inaccurate) account of what a group of people said. How about the *Macbeth* problem? Well, sometimes the author is purporting to tell us what the characters said using direct quotation and sometimes using indirect quotation. With *Macbeth* it's clearly understood by playwright and audience that the characters don't use the exact words that come out of their mouths.

This all raises a further big question: What makes it the case that the author purports to be doing one thing rather than another? Walton points out that

[49] Lewis, "Truth in Fiction," 266 n. 7. Note that this footnote appears in the essay's original version.

[50] I don't mean to take sides in the debate over the *meaning* of metaphors. Whatever they mean—whether they mean what they say on their faces, and hence are usually false, or whether they mean what they are meant to suggest or convey—their authors use them to *convey* something different from what they literally mean.

readers are often uncertain as to which of various things is going on. To avoid confusing epistemology and metaphysics here, perhaps we can put the point like this: sometimes there just seems to be no grounding for one purport rather than another. A possible response here is to appeal to authorial intention. If the author intends to purport to be telling the story as known fact, then she is purporting to be telling the story as known fact. If she intends to be purporting to be telling a pack of boastful lies, then she is purporting to be telling a pack of boastful lies. Usually—especially in successful fiction—these intentions are accessible, but sometimes they are not. I'm not endorsing the Authorial Intention Principle I disputed above. Rather, I would endorse a more qualified principle:

> "In the fiction F, Φ" is true iff Φ would be true if the author were actually doing what she purports to be doing (and what she purports to be doing is what she intends to purport to be doing).

It might be objected that this appeal to authorial intention has to rely on some more general principle such as the Authorial Intention Principle if it is to avoid being ad hoc. Perhaps not. Remember the other cases where it seemed plausible that authorial intention should play a role—in determining which word was used, which meaning of a word was understood, whether a chapter should be included or not. It seems that the role I give to authorial intention here can explain those examples too. For example, if Burgess intended to purport to tell as known fact the version of *A Clockwork Orange* in which Alex reforms, then he does purport to tell that version as known fact and hence it is true in *A Clockwork Orange* that Alex reforms. The effect is that authorial intentions determine what is true at the primary level but not at higher levels since these, by definition, supervene on what is true at the primary level.[51]

XIII. CONCLUSION

At the start of this chapter I took on the challenge of defending realism about statements of the form "In the fiction F, Φ." To do this, it was necessary to provide a satisfactory account of the truth conditions of such statements. I discussed five principles that attempt this and showed that the first four face insuperable difficulties, most strikingly, the Morality Objection. The fifth, namely,

[51] Currie claims that what makes it the case that the author is being ironical or using understatement may well be what else is true in the story (at higher levels) (*Nature of Fiction*, 70). This, he thinks, creates a difficulty for the distinction between primary and secondary levels since what is true at the primary level depends on what is true at the secondary level. I think my suggestion avoids this difficulty since it claims that whether the author is being ironical, etc., depends on the author's intention. In *figuring out* what is true at the primary level, however, we may well rely on what we believe about the secondary levels. We may, for example, start out assuming that the author is speaking literally, purporting to tell known facts, draw inferences on the basis of that, and then have to go back and adjust our beliefs about the primary level if necessary.

the Reality Principle, faces seven objections but, I argued, has resources to respond to four of these and can easily be modified to respond to the other three. In brief, in response to the Contradiction Objection, I follow Lewis and Wolterstorff in distinguishing whole fictions from fragments of fictions. In response to the Slithergadee Objection, I argued that we should treat RP as determining what is prima facie true in fiction and that whatever is made true in this way can be overridden by explicit or implicit convention. In response to the Levels Objection, I follow Lewis in shifting from the "told as known fact" version of RP to the "told in whatever way the author purports to tell" version of RP. These modifications are not ad hoc, and they preserve the spirit of the Reality Principle in spite of depriving it of some of its elegant simplicity.

.15.

Fiction as a Kind of Philosophy

KELLY JAMES CLARK

In this chapter I defend the importance of narrative to moral philosophy, in particular to moral realism. Moral realism, for the purposes of this essay, is the claim that there are moral truths independent of human beliefs, attitudes, desires, and feelings.[1] Contemporary philosophers typically focus on discursive arguments and exclude narrative. But narrative is considerably more powerful than argument in effecting belief-change. I shall argue that through such belief-change one can attain moral truth.[2] This account is opposed to that of fellow narrativalist Richard Rorty, who denies moral realism. Since I believe the clash between realists and antirealists resolves into a clash of intuitions, I don't propose to offer a convincing argument in favor of moral realism. Instead, like Rorty I will draw a word-picture, one that stands in stark contrast to the word-picture he draws about stories.

PHILOSOPHY AS A KIND OF WRITING
In "Philosophy as a Kind of Writing: An Essay on Derrida" Rorty contrasts the traditional, realist way with his own antirealist way of looking at both philosophy and morality.[3] Traditional moral philosophy, which typically assumes moral realism, holds that moral truths are discovered, not made. Rorty summarizes this traditional view as follows: "Here is a way of thinking about right and wrong: the common moral consciousness contains certain intuitions concerning

---

[1] This entails that some moral beliefs are true and some are false. Geoffrey Sayre-McCord defines realism as follows: "Realism involves embracing just two theses: (1) the claims in question, when literally construed, are literally true or false (cognitivism), and (2) some are literally true." In Sayre-McCord, "The Many Moral Realisms," in *Essays on Moral Realism*, ed. Geoffrey Sayre-McCord (Ithaca: Cornell University Press, 1988), 3.

[2] A narrative understanding of reality is often opposed to the 'Greek', rational understanding of reality. See, for example, Mark Edmundson, *Literature Against Philosophy: Plato to Derrida* (Cambridge: Cambridge University Press, 1995). This is a misconception: some of the greatest philosophers in the West—Plato, Augustine, Boethius, Descartes, and Kierkegaard, for example—rely heavily on narrative.

[3] Richard Rorty, "Philosophy as a Kind of Writing: An Essay on Derrida," in *Consequences of Pragmatism* (Minneapolis: University of Minnesota Press, 1982), 90–109.

equality, fairness, human dignity and the like."[4] Denying the power of human intuition to grasp moral truths, Rorty rejects traditional moral philosophy. The traditionalist views philosophy as the "vertical" discovery of trans-cultural and trans-historical, perhaps eternal, moral truths. Rortian "horizontal" philosophy "is best seen as a kind of writing."[5] The kind of writing Rorty has in mind eschews the insidious desire to discover 'the truth'; rather, it contents itself with commenting on, developing, reinvigorating, and reinventing previous texts. Texts, beliefs even, relate to one another, not to something beyond sociohistorically conditioned human beliefs and desires—not to something "out there"—that gives them a truth value.[6] The difference between the vertical and horizontal approaches reveals Rorty's decided antirealism: "it is the difference between regarding truth, goodness, and beauty as eternal objects which we try to locate and reveal, and regarding them as artifacts whose fundamental design we often have to alter."[7] There is, for Rorty, only contingent and ironic human language, dialogue among texts, and increasingly useful metaphors; the best one can hope for is "metaphoric redescriptions," not insight into the nature of reality. Rorty denigrates orthodox notions of truth only to subsequently reinvent truth. Truth is, Rorty claims, "a mobile army of metaphors."[8] But for the Rortian ironist, there is nothing "beyond" the metaphors before which they must bow down.

Rorty's reconception of truth requires the rejection of the dichotomies enshrined in orthodox conceptions of truth. In "Science as Solidarity" Rorty considers and rejects the modern division of knowledge into hierarchical classes: science v. humanities, objective v. subjective, fact v. value.[9] The former member of each class is, according to our culture, the more valued. Although Rorty protests that he doesn't intend to downgrade science, he does seem to relegate it to useful fiction. And his claim that he is beyond such distinctions seems little more than the claim that humanities and science belong in the same subjective/value boat. Since there is no nonhuman world to which our beliefs are accountable, human agreement is the source of 'truth'. Science is "just one cultural manifestation among others."[10] There is no fact; everything is fiction. Rorty affirms Derrida's claim that all writing—scientific, philosophical, moral, and fictional—is not about the world but about texts.[11] Texts do not represent (metaphysical, moral, objective, factual) reality; they simply comment on previous texts. Texts (including scientific texts) are, to use a quaint phrase, fancy.

If all writing is about writing, we cannot play off our beliefs, moral or other-

---

[4] Rorty, *Consequences of Pragmatism*, 90.
[5] Ibid., 92.
[6] See Richard Rorty, *Contingency, Irony, and Solidarity* (New York: Cambridge University Press, 1989), esp. xiii–xv.
[7] Rorty, *Consequences of Pragmatism*, 92.
[8] Rorty, *Contingency*, 7–9.
[9] Richard Rorty, "Science as Solidarity," in *Objectivity, Relativism, and Truth* (New York: Cambridge University Press, 1991), 35–45.
[10] Rorty, *Consequences of Pragmatism*, 67.
[11] Ibid., 95.

wise, against reality. Rorty views philosophy as a dialectical process of text commenting on text. The method of philosophy, therefore, is literary criticism. Literary criticism, à la Rorty, should not be confused with the traditional view of literature as a channel of moral or religious truth. The kind of literary criticism that Rorty espouses involves nothing more than placing books within the context of other books: "In the course of doing so, we revise our opinions of both the old and the new. Simultaneously, we revise our own moral identity by revising our own final vocabulary. Literary criticism does for ironists what the search for universal moral principles is supposed to do for metaphysicians."[12]

Rorty's unflagging antirealism is clear. Although Rorty claims that the realism/antirealism distinction is rooted in an outmoded view of the world, it is clear that he is antirealist in the sense defined at the beginning of this essay; that is, Rorty clearly denies that there are moral truths independent of human beliefs, attitudes, preferences, or feelings. He is intent on rejecting moral realism, as defined, replacing moral intuition with fiction. He writes: "Not until Kant did philosophy destroy science and theology to make room for moral faith, and not until Schiller did it seem possible that the room cleared for morality could be occupied by art."[13] Art, according to Rorty, precludes traditional, robust moral fiction that aims to put the reader in touch with belief-independent moral reality. Rather, fiction provides the imagination with new images and reinvigorates old images of the possibilities of the human self and human society, none of which is (morally) better or worse than any other. If science is useful fiction, fiction is useful fancy.

The goal of Rorty's narrative philosophy is self-creation, the rejection of anyone else's description of oneself. Rorty proposes that we see our lives as poems that each person is in the process of writing.[14] One must write one's poem without the consolation of rules. There are no nonhuman constraints on this kind of writing. Previous texts may inspire, but plagiarism is forbidden. By carefully attending to (contingent and ironic) language, one gives linguistic birth to one's self. Thus Rorty's insistence on the importance of narrative becomes clear.

PHILOSOPHY OF NARRATIVE

Like Rorty, I believe that narrative is important to philosophy and that narrative can be an effective means of belief-change. And like Rorty, I believe that philosophy can profit from employing narrative. Unlike Rorty, however, I believe that narrative can help us grasp moral truth. Before we come to that, I briefly develop a philosophy of narrative, primarily of fiction. This philosophy

---

[12] Rorty, *Contingency*, 80. A final vocabulary are the words that one uses to justify one's beliefs, actions, and existence. The ironist (1) has deep doubts about the adequacy of her own final vocabulary because of her sympathetic awareness of the final vocabularies of others, (2) believes that arguments are not adequate to ground her own final vocabulary (and undermine the final vocabulary of others), and (3) does not believe that her final vocabulary is closer to the truth than others (Rorty, *Contingency*, 73).

[13] Rorty, *Consequences of Pragmatism*, 67.

[14] Rorty, *Contingency*, 35.

of fiction is not the only plausible philosophy of fiction. And although not all fiction is moral fiction, this philosophy of (moral) fiction helps explain fundamental belief-change in the sphere of the ethical. Next I argue that our willingness to accept or reject premises of an argument is in large part a function of our sentiments. The appreciation of some arguments may require the reorientation of our passions. This may require the sympathetic hearing of a story.

Fiction poses challenges both to the attentive reader's understanding of the world and to the reader's self-understanding. The challenge often comes through the depiction of new worlds, different perspectives, or novel interpretations of reality. In good fiction the challenge often comes as a surprise that startles the reader and initiates her reevaluation of self and world. Fictional narratives are transformative only when the reader integrates these insights into her self-understanding and worldview. How does (or can) literary narrative exert such power? I shall rely, in this section, on some suggestive comments by the philosopher–novelist–literary critic C. S. Lewis.[15]

The power of literature lies partly in its ability to enable us to enter into the world that it creates. Lewis writes: "It is irrelevant whether the mood expressed in a poem was truly and historically the poet's own or one that he also had imagined. What matters is his power to make us live it."[16] The narrative has power to make us live it—to get us out of the limitations of our self and our understanding of the world, and to enter into the world of the writer. But we cannot, even the most romantic among us, enter fully into the world of another. We can no longer believe that the reader's "temporary suspension of unbelief" is possible. Nor can the reader stand naked before the text. We are too invested in our beliefs to become transparent before the text. Nonetheless, a partial suspension of disbelief is possible, as is a partial disrobing of our historico-cultural clothing. We read about cultures distant in space or time, and we imagine ourselves in those cultures. It is still our self, informed by the narratives of our own time and place. But we can gain at least a partial perspective (from the inside, so to speak) of what it might be like to be a cowboy in nineteenth-century America, or a woman in eighteenth-century China, or a warrior in eighth-century B.C. Greece, or an alien in twenty-fourth-century Alpha Centauri.

In what does the power of the story to coax us into its world consist? There is, initially, the skillful craft of the writer to write an enticing story. But the reader, in order to enter into the fictional world, must sympathetically respond to the story. Lewis suggests the following are involved in the sympathetic hearing of a story:

> Good reading, though it is not essentially an affectional or moral or intellectual activity, has something in common with all three. In love we escape

---

[15] C.S. Lewis, *An Experiment in Criticism* (Cambridge: Cambridge University Press, 1961).

[16] Ibid., 139.

from our self into one other. In the moral sphere, every act of justice or charity involves putting ourselves in the other person's place and thus transcending our own competitive particularity. In coming to understand anything we are rejecting the facts as they are for us in favour of the facts as they are. The primary impulse of each is to maintain and aggrandise himself. The secondary impulse is to go out of the self, to correct its provincialism and heal its loneliness. In love, in virtue, in the pursuit of knowledge, and in the reception of the arts, we are doing this.[17]

There are, according to Lewis, affectional, moral, and intellectual elements involved in the sympathetic hearing of a story. Let us consider the moral dimension.

There is as Lewis claims a subtle and not so subtle tendency in humans to favor themselves. This selfish tendency finds expression in myriad ways: gossip, for example, and self-deception, racism, ethnocentrism, elitism, and jingoism. These and countless other lies are involved in creating the delusion that I am infinitely valuable. We are, Thomas Hobbes claims, glory seekers: life is a race with no other good but to be foremost.

Here is a way of putting the matter in the first person. I favor those particulars that uniquely define and exalt me (my "competitive particularity"). Since I alone am the unique intersection of these particulars (and the narrative that embeds and, therefore, values them), I alone am supremely valuable. I enlist the myths and traditions that have shaped me into the service of self-glorification. This self-glorification prevents me from fully valuing others—indeed, my natural instinct is to devalue others because, perhaps, of their skin color, foreign or primitive culture, lack of education or religious convictions. We are infinitely creative in the systematic devaluation of the other.

But we are also social beings eager to be in relationship with people who love and are loved by us. In love we rise above the glory-seeking self to seek human connection. In order to love another, therefore, I must be willing to set aside my self and put myself in the position of the other; I must view the world from the other's perspective given the other's particularities. Only thus can I know how to treat the other with love and justice. In love I sympathetically assume the other's particularities.

Good reading embraces the human tensions of self-interest and the need to love. Here is a way of putting Lewis's point about the moral nature of reading literature. Our incessantly demanding and particular self stands in the way of understanding both our self and reality (which includes other selves). The sympathetic reading of a story involves partially entering into the particularities of another time or place, or even of another person. We can do so only if we have silenced or quieted the clanging self that clings to its particularities. Good reading is like a dying to the self. On a small scale, the self is set aside as it sympa-

---

[17] Ibid., 138.

thetically entertains another self. In some cases one imaginatively becomes another self.

The power to imaginatively and sympathetically enter into a story is exemplified in Nathan's confrontation with King David. In the narrative David has seduced Bathsheba and arranged for the death of her husband. The prophet Nathan, seeing David's moral blindness, tells him a story that captures his heart:

> There were two men in a certain town, one rich and the other poor. The rich man had a very large number of sheep and cattle, but the poor man had nothing except one little ewe lamb he had bought. He raised it, and it grew up with him and his children. It shared his food, drank from his cup and even slept in his arms. It was like a daughter to him. Now a traveler came to the rich man, but the rich man refrained from taking one of his own sheep or cattle to prepare a meal for the traveler who had come to him. Instead, he took the ewe lamb that belonged to the poor man and prepared it for the one who had come to him. (2 Samuel 12:1–4 NIV)

David sympathetically enters into the story while remaining blissfully unaware of his own injustice. By temporarily setting aside his own particularities—rich, handsome, powerful, king—David is enabled to enter into the story on the side of the poor man. In so doing, he sympathetically grasps the injustice in the story and indignantly denounces it: "David burned with anger against the man and said to Nathan: 'As surely as the Lord lives, the man who did this deserves to die.'" Nathan counters, "Thou art the man." By entering into the story of the oppressed poor man, David is prepared for this new ending, which enables his own moral transformation. Only when David's lusty and powerful self is set aside could he hear the cry of injustice. Going beyond the particularities of injustice in Nathan's story, David is brought to see Injustice (capital "I"); he brings the moral insight back into his own life, aware now of his own reproach and shame.

Like David, when the self is stilled, one can hear the voice of the other (in all its particularities): the voice of the oppressed, the downtrodden, the lonely, and the needy. Sympathy is not the only appropriate moral response to stories; one may also find oneself revulsed by the unjust, miserly, angry, hate-filled, and racist. With revulsion (to wickedness) one may see, as perhaps David did, injustice as inhumanity; or one may see that the oppressor is more dehumanized by injustice than the oppressed. This may occasion the reorientation of one's moral likes and dislikes, which involves our passions or feelings as much as our intellect.[18]

When narrative gets one out of one's own particulars and into another's, one

---

[18] We must concede the ignoble potential of narrative. We might, for example, be sympathetic to the racist or rapist and be revulsed by the righteous or humble. Or we often find ourselves sympathetically entering into the life of the murderer in films.

may see the universal: for example, that rights extend to everyone regardless of color, race, creed, or religion; that humans are intrinsically valuable; that injustice may have short-term benefits but in the long term destroys our humanity; or that the category 'human' extends to people of different color, social status, nationality, or religion. Literature forces the good reader to experience the universally human through the particulars of the other.[19] Not every reading of literature is so transformative; if this were so, literature professors would all be saints! But on those occasions of significant belief-change, brought about by seeing things from new perspectives, we may be morally transformed.

FICTION AS A KIND OF PHILOSOPHY

Here's a way to look at the psychodynamics of significant belief and belief-change. Evidence in matters of fundamental human concern is often difficult to decipher or ambiguous. Some pieces of evidence are deemed weightier than others. But deeming is in the eye of the beholder. We must rely on our intuitions, but none of us is so metaphysically astute that we can reliably intuit the evidence in, say, an argument for the existence of God, for moral absolutism, or for idealism. It is difficult to see clearly the true propositions. Is it so clear, after all, that an infinite regress of finite causes is absurd, that there are universal moral truths, or that sensory appearances cannot be adequately accounted for without reference to a material world? Discussions in political theory, social policy, ethics, the meaning of life, the nature of human persons, and many other issues likewise rely on crucial premises that are not universally discoverable by rational intuition. The views of John Henry Newman and William James on these matters are instructive.[20]

Disagreement is interminable because there is, as Newman writes, no "common measure between mind and mind." Arguments rely on premises, the acceptance of which depends on the commitments of each person. Newman observes "how little depends upon the inferential proofs, and how much upon those pre-existing beliefs and views, in which men either already agree with each other or hopelessly differ, before they begin to dispute, and which are hidden deep in our nature, or, it may be, in our personal peculiarities."[21] Because of these conceptual uncertainties and lack of a common measure between mind and mind, we are forced to bring all that we value to bear on our assessment of the evidence. We are forced because, at least with respect to certain philosophical issues, not to decide is to decide. So we bring our whole person to bear on the assessment of the evidence. But different persons with different values will

[19] One might, through narrative, move from particulars to particulars.

[20] For an excellent discussion of these issues and thinkers, see William Wainwright, *Reason and the Heart: A Prolegomenon to a Critique of Passional Reason* (Ithaca: Cornell University Press, 1995).

[21] John Henry Newman, *An Essay in Aid of a Grammar of Assent* (Notre Dame: University of Notre Dame Press, 1979), 82 and 221–22.

make different judgments about the relative weightings of the various bits of evidence. Evaluating evidence is person-specific. As Newman writes, "We judge for ourselves, by our own lights, and on our own principles; and our criterion of truth is not so much the manipulation of propositions, as the intellectual and moral character of the person maintaining them, and the ultimate silent effect of his arguments or conclusions upon our minds."[22] Newman does not deny that there are arguments, indeed very good arguments, for certain philosophical positions. Rather, he believes that our intellectual and moral character affect our ability to see the truth of the premises and, therefore, our ability to judge rightly. Who we are determines what we are inclined to believe. Two obvious moral obstacles to perceiving the truth aright relate to the argument of the previous section; Newman claims that our perception of the fundamental premises of an argument "is enfeebled, obstructed, perverted, by allurements of sense and the supremacy of self."[23] Other obstacles to perceiving true beliefs are prejudice, passion, and self-interest. In certain cases of significant human beliefs, seeing the truth requires moral rectitude.

James, like Newman, holds that philosophical arguments are expressions of temperament and reason.[24] James claims that inquiry in the humanities and social sciences, in everyday life, and even in science unavoidably reflects our 'willing' or 'passional' nature—our temperament, needs, concerns, fears, hopes, and passions: "Pretend what we may, the whole man within us is at work when we form our philosophical opinions. Intellect, will, taste, and passion co-operate just as they do in practical affairs."[25] We rely, fundamentally, on the way things seem to us, not on theory-free rational intuition. Every philosopher, James claims, "has taken his stand on a sort of dumb conviction that the truth must lie in one direction rather than another."[26] We come to philosophy with our 'dumb convictions', prephilosophical presuppositions about the way things seem to us. And the way things seem to us is a function of both our sentiments (temperament or tastes) and reason. Our willingness to accept or reject premises of an argument is, therefore, affected by our sentiments.

We have been discussing the psychology of believings, but for James these descriptive claims are epistemic claims because of his affirmation of what has come to be called 'the underdetermination of theory by data'. Underdetermination holds that for any set of data, there are many hypotheses which adequately explain the data but which are mutually incompatible. James writes:

---

[22] Ibid., 240.

[23] Ibid., 247.

[24] James puts reason and the sentiments in a dichotomous relationship. I don't think it is a simple matter of "either-or." There is a sentimental (evaluative?) side of reason and a rational side of sentiments.

[25] William James, "The Sentiment of Rationality," in *The Will to Believe and Other Essays in Popular Philosophy* (New York: Dover, 1956), 92.

[26] James, *Will to Believe*, 93.

There is nothing improbable in the supposition that an analysis of the world may yield a number of formulae, all consistent with the facts. In physical science different formulae may explain the phenomena equally well. . . . Why may it not be so with the world? Why may there not be different points of view for surveying it, within each of which all data harmonize, and which the observer may therefore either choose between, or simply cumulate one upon another? A Beethoven string-quartet is truly, as some one has said, a scraping of horses' tails on cats' bowels, and may be exhaustively described in such terms; but the application of this description in no way precludes the simultaneous applicability of an entirely different description.[27]

Most of our theories of the world—philosophical, commonsensical, religious, or even scientific—are underdetermined by the evidence that supports them; they are consistent with the facts, but the facts are not so compelling that they logically exclude their competitors. Therefore, when two such theories are in competition, no appeal to the evidence could determine the winner. In order to assess our beliefs, we must bring all that we as human beings have to bear on these matters. In such cases, James suggests the following for deciding what to believe: "Well, of two conceptions equally fit to satisfy the logical demand, that one which awakens the active impulses, or satisfies the aesthetic demands better than the other, will be accounted the more rational conception, and will deservedly prevail."[28] Different persons, with differing dumb convictions, will find different active impulses awakened and different aesthetic demands satisfied. So radically different beliefs are or could be rational for sincere inquirers after the truth.

Newman's and James' claims about the perspectival nature of the human believing condition create a serious problem for the human prospect of grasping the truth. Either one is properly disposed to the truth or one is not. One's temperament orients one in one direction and prevents seeing truth that may lie in another direction. Newman pointedly raises the problem: "I am what I am, or I am nothing. I cannot think, reflect, or judge about my being, without starting from the very point which I aim at concluding. My ideas are all assumptions, and I am ever moving in a circle."[29] How can we get out of this self-imposed circle of belief to see the truth? How can we rise above the passions or temperaments that seem to ineluctably determine our conclusions? This cannot be done without involving the whole person in a way that engages both the intellect and the passions. And belief-change, at least on matters of fundamental human concern, will involve the reorientation of our passions. As Newman writes, "Deductions have no power of persuasion. The heart is commonly reached, not through the reason, but through the imagination, by means of direct impres-

---

[27] Ibid., 76.
[28] Ibid., 75–76.
[29] Newman, *Grammar of Assent*, 272.

sions, by the testimony of facts and events, by history, by description. Persons influence us, voices melt us, looks subdue us, deeds inflame us."[30]

How is our heart reached through the imagination? Narrative can assist in the process of getting our hearts properly disposed. The sympathetic hearing of a story is one of the most powerful ways of orienting and reorienting our passions and is, therefore, relevant to the practice of philosophy proper. How does narrative assist in the orienting and reorienting of our passions?

Let me suggest, briefly, the following. Our storied lives have already determined, to a large extent, the affections that we have. We start our quest for understanding already situated within a context that fixes our passions and, therefore, orients our reason in a certain direction. We come to any question already valuing this and discounting that; we have a decided preference for this kind of explanation and an aversion to that sort of explanation. Our passions have been shaped in such a manner that we are oriented toward this sort of truth but opposed to that sort of truth (fill in your favorite rational preferences and aversions: for the rational or the empirical, for the logical or the narratival, for the material or the ideal, for theism or naturalism, for moral absolutes or relativism, for free will or determinism . . .).

One might think, therefore, that we are simply stuck within the circle, or to use Newman's helpful metaphor, circumscribed by our desires and aversions. Are our worldviews ineluctably determined by our perspectives? Here I optimistically opine, no. How, then, do stories reorient our passions or desires (if and when they do)? I suggest the following. Suppose we are confronted with a fictional story. Our sentiments set the limits of our own believing circle. The story that confronts us attempts to move us into the story's circle. These circles may overlap, or they may be entirely distinct. Insofar as we are able to die to our self (the self that tends to keep us fixed in our own circle), we sympathetically enter into the story's circle. If we resist entering into the story's circle, then either it has not effectively engaged our passions or we have not permitted our passions to be engaged by the story. On certain occasions, the story, with our (perhaps unwitting) permission, reorients or incites our passions to enable us to see truth. In moving our passions and desires, it shifts the center of our own circle toward the story's circle. And in cases of moral fiction, it may shift our perception away from the self toward moral truth.

Rorty might agree with my philosophy of narrative and its importance for philosophy. We disagree, however, because I view narrative as a vehicle for moral and philosophical truths. That is, I hold the antiquated view that Rorty believes impossible to hold of thinking of "plays, poems, and novels as making vivid something already known, of literature as ancillary to cognition, beauty to truth."[31] In the narrative discovery of moral truth one may, contra Rorty, think

---

[30] Ibid., 89.
[31] Rorty, *Contingency*, 79.

that one's moral vocabulary is closer to reality than others.[32] One may, and should, have doubts that one has fully grasped this or all moral truths and should, therefore, be open to refutation and continual transformation. But the recognition of contingency does not entail that one does not have a better grasp of moral truth than one had previously.

Rorty would reduce all philosophy to fiction—useful fiction or fancy—with no connection to Reality. In so doing, he not only denigrates philosophy; he fails to take fiction seriously. Writers of moral fiction, such as Dickens, Dante, and Virgil, believed themselves to be communicating moral truth, not mere fancy. Their fanciful worlds manifested their moral vision. Their fictional and fanciful writings are not typically literally true. Dickens did not intend for sentences including 'the artful dodger' to refer to some actually existent artful dodger. And even if he did, that sort of truth is irrelevant to the truth of the story. For the primary truth of the story is moral: about, among other things, inhumane working conditions, unfair wages, the breakdown of the family, human flourishing, the moral blindness of unbridled capitalism and the like. Yet Rorty would reduce these so-called truths to ephemera: words speaking to words. What begins as an upgrade for fiction (by downgrading science to fiction) is really a downgrade. Rorty simply does not take fiction seriously.

REASONS FOR PREFERRING MY STORY TO RORTY'S STORY

In good Rortian fashion, two stories of moral philosophy have been placed beside each other. So far, no arguments, conclusive or otherwise, have been offered in favor of either story. Let me conclude by offering four reasons for preferring my story to Rorty's.

1. *Innocent until proven guilty.* Here's my view: Our moral intuitions are occasionally transformed by the power of narrative (fictional and otherwise) such that, in some cases, we grasp moral truth. Here's my claim: These moral intuitions have some presumption to truth unless one has adequate reason to believe otherwise.[33] This "innocent until proven guilty" principle has prominent defenders in the field of epistemology. Knowledge, if it is possible at all, begins with trust, not with doubt. If we cannot trust our hearing, sight, and the like, we have nothing upon which to reason, and to build up our view of the world. We are so constructed that we believe what others tell us or that the future will resemble the past. The presumption of guilt in epistemology invariably leads to skepticism. Parity suggests that we should extend the presumption of innocence to our moral beliefs as well. If we don't, moral skepticism seems inevitable. Since Rorty has not argued in favor of his view, he has not offered a case, let alone a compelling case, against taking our moral intuitions as true; he hasn't

[32] Ibid., 73.

[33] I don't have the space to defend this here, but it has been amply defended by Alvin Plantinga, philosophical heir to Thomas Reid and G. E. Moore; see Plantinga, *Warrant and Proper Function* (New York: Oxford University Press, 1993).

provided any compelling reason to believe otherwise.[34] Indeed, Rorty eschews argument (and the philosophical tradition that enshrines argument) in favor of showing *how things look if* you make or reject certain assumptions.[35] But absent argument one is under no compulsion to accept his assumptions and, therefore, under no compulsion to look at things the way he looks at things. Here I speak with understatement: one should expect compelling reasons before giving up one's fundamental beliefs about truth, reality, and morality.

2. *The antirealist Euthyphro problem.* If moral values are created and then imposed on the world by one's choice (individually or communally), then an antirealist Euthyphro problem arises. Socrates, in Plato's *Euthyphro*, discusses divine command theories of ethics. Divine command theories locate the source of goodness in the will of God. This view creates a dilemma:

(i) Something is good because God wills it.
or
(ii) God wills it because it is good.

If (i) is true—that is, if something is good simply because God wills it—the problem of arbitrariness arises. According to (i), God could have willed anything—say, torturing babies for fun or eating human flesh for dessert—and it would have been good. In order to bestow goodness on an action, state of affairs, character trait, or property, all that is required is that God wills it. "Goodness," if (i) is true, is arbitrary. And if (ii) is true, then it seems that God is superfluous. According to (ii), God discovers what is good and simply endorses it by his willing. But (ii) suggests that the moral standard is independent of God, and God must accede to it. If (ii) is true, then God is not necessary as the standard of goodness.

A version of the Euthyphro problem arises for the Rortian antirealist. This is not surprising since the individual as self- and world-creator assumes a godlike role in Rorty's moral theory.[36] The antirealist Euthyphro problem is analogous to the dilemma in the classical Euthyphro problem:

(iii) Something is good because a godlike person wills it.
or
(iv) A godlike person wills it because it is good.

If (iii) is true, the arbitrariness problem rears its ugly head. If a godlike person were to will any x, x would be good. This is not merely a counterfactual problem for persons. On various occasions humans have willed that torturing children, eating human flesh, enslaving blacks, killing Jews, and so on and on are

---

[34] Insofar as Rorty does make a case, it is based, I believe, on unfounded inferences and false dichotomies.

[35] Rorty, *Contingency*, 44.

[36] Ibid., 18–22.

good. Indeed, entire communities have reached a consensus on these matters. The arbitrariness problem is exacerbated by the relevant disanalogies between God and godlike persons. God, should God exist, is love, essentially other-regarding, just, holy, and so on. God's character would constrain the kinds of things that God would will. But there are no such characterological constraints on the willings of human persons. Humans are often self-centered, self-regarding, unjust, competitive, and so on. The lack of essential and essentially good character traits make the Euthyphro problem considerably more vicious in the case of godlike persons.

In order to avoid the arbitrariness problem, the antirealist might embrace (iv). The antirealist can accept (iv), however, only by ceasing to be an antirealist. (iv) entails that there is a standard of goodness independent of human willing. (iv) is simply a restatement of moral realism, the claim that there are moral truths independent of human beliefs. Clearly, for humans (and perhaps for God) the dilemma raised by the Euthyphro problem should warn off any antirealist attempt to locate goodness in the will.

3. *Theism and antirealism*. Theists, and perhaps other sorts of religious believers, have good reason to reject Rorty's decidedly antitheistic worldview. Although Rorty eschews metaphysics and denounces the pretensions of science to the truth, he seems clearly to base his philosophical views on a naturalistic metaphysics allied with an evolutionary understanding of development. His "de-divination of the world" grounds his moral theorizing. His *how things look if* approach when allied with his naturalism lead him to ask "*how things might look if we did not have religion built into the fabric of our moral life.*"[37] When Rorty says, with Nietzsche, that God is dead, he denies that we have a higher purpose or a created nature that need to be discovered as part of the moral project of acting in accord with that purpose or fulfilling our nature. Rorty's moral project begins with rejecting a Creator and becomes one of self-creation. His moral philosophy follows upon his metaphysical commitment that we are simply creatures of time and chance.[38] Viewing human beings as created not in their own image but in the image of God has implications for one's moral views. If one is a creature, not a creator, then one is likely subject to creaturely norms related somehow to the Creator.[39]

4. *Demoralization*. And finally, Rorty's moral theory, if accepted, would prove demoralizing. That is, if it were accepted, people would lose some of their motivation to be moral, thus reducing the *demand* of morality. Morality is often demanding, asking us to forgo selfishness for the interest of others. Given the clamor of desires, morality must speak sufficiently loudly for us to hear and

---

[37] Rorty, *Consequences of Pragmatism*, 98; his emphasis.

[38] Rorty's belief that we are creatures of time and chance is perhaps not metaphysical. His claim that we are *merely* creatures of time and chance is. For the latter entails that humans have no essence, that humans were not created, that there is no preexistent human telos, etc.

[39] I take no position here on how the theist might conceive of such creaturely norms.

heed its call. Morality must be able to move us, at least occasionally, from self-ish desire-satisfaction to altruism; it needs the motivational force to move us from self to other. But the denial of objective morality, with the requisite impli-cation of subjectivity or relativity, reduces morality's motivational force. William James, one of Rorty's inspirations, sounds the warning:

> The subjectivist in morals, when his moral feelings are at war with the facts about him, is always free to seek harmony by toning down the sensitiveness of the feelings. Being mere data, neither good nor evil in themselves, he may per-vert them or lull them to sleep by any means at his command. Truckling, com-promise, time-serving, capitulations of conscience, are conventionally oppro-brious names for what, if successfully carried out, would be on his principles by far the easiest and most praiseworthy mode of bringing out that harmony between inner and outer relations which is all that he means by the good.[40]

Rorty suggests that the way to eliminate suffering is to sympathetically expand the definition of humanity to include fellow sufferers, for example, blacks, Jews, or women. But why do that? According to Rorty, when we make judgments about humanity, there is no fact of the matter concerning human nature to rec-ognize; it is simply our choice: "personhood" is "a matter of decision rather than knowledge, an acceptance of another human being into fellowship rather than a recognition of a common essence."[41] Why not keep one's circle of hu-manity closed, thereby achieving an exaltation of self? Indeed, if one is tempted to view the other sympathetically as fellow sufferer, why not simply tone down one's sympathies? If one were to choose not to include blacks, Jews, or women in the category of human being, one would not have a false belief, according to Rorty, because there is nothing to be wrong about. One has not failed to grasp some moral truth or some metaphysical essence of humans. Rorty concedes the seriousness of the problem:

> This means that when the secret police come, when the torturers violate the innocent, there is nothing to be said to them of the form "There is something within you which you are betraying. Though you embody the practices of a totalitarian society which will endure forever, there is something beyond those practices which condemns you." This thought is hard to live with.[42]

From Rorty's ethnocentric perspective it seems to him that the fascist has done something wrong. But from a different ethnocentric perspective, the Nazi might be judged right. If the game is perspective versus perspective, everyone's a win-ner! The problem is that if Rorty's philosophy is correct, there is no moral or

---

[40]   James, *Will to Believe*, 104–5.
[41]   Richard Rorty, *Philosophy and the Mirror of Nature* (Princeton: Princeton University Press, 1979), 38.
[42]   Rorty, *Consequences of Pragmatism*, xlii.

metaphysical reality standing over human history according to which certain actions are (objectively) right and others wrong. Ideal observer theories in ethics attempt to preserve the neutrality and universality of the moral point of view. If there is no such moral point of view, humans will be tempted to make moral judgments that show a decided preference for their self. Indeed, Rorty's insistence on virtually limitless[43] self-creation would reduce the moral demand and thereby reduce morality to self-interest.

CONCLUSION

A philosophy of literary narrative makes clear why fiction and other narratives (autobiographical, anecdotal, sacred, filmic, musical, etc.) have the power to redirect our lives. They can put us in a position where, by setting aside the clamoring self, we can see the other and, through the other, understand the universal, which can reorient our passions. If our passions are reoriented, we may find ourselves in a position to understand and grasp moral truths to which we were formerly blind. Our new moral intuitions have a presumption to truth unless we have adequate reason to cease believing them. Rorty has simply not provided adequate reason, because he has not provided reasons at all, for people to cease believing their moral intuitions. The antirealist Euthyphro problem, especially when it concerns human willing, creates an untenable dilemma. In addition, a theist ought not accept Rorty's naturalistic assumptions and should refuse to accept what follows from such assumptions. And finally, if accepted, Rorty's moral theory would prove demoralizing.

The practice of philosophy proper involves the passions. Thus narrative is essential to philosophy properly so-called. We need to be rightly disposed to see and grasp the truth of certain propositions. Narrative is essential to philosophy because its power lies in the reorientation of passions even toward the Truth.

[43] One is limited only by harm to others. But 'others' is perspectivally determined and may or may not include blacks, slaves, Jews, women, animals, etc.

Select Bibliography

Alston, William P. 1996. *A Realist Conception of Truth*. Ithaca: Cornell University Press.
———. 2001. *A Sensible Metaphysical Realism*. Milwaukee: Marquette University Press.
Cortens, Andrew J. 2000. *Global Anti-Realism*. Boulder: Westview Press.
Devitt, Michael. 1984. *Realism and Truth*. Oxford: Basil Blackwell.
Dummett, Michael. 1991. *The Logical Basis of Metaphysics*. Cambridge: Harvard University Press.
Fine, Arthur. 1986. *The Shaky Game: Einstein, Realism, and the Quantum Theory*. Chicago: University of Chicago Press.
Goodman, Nelson. 1978. *Ways of Worldmaking*. Indianapolis: Hackett.
Horwich, Paul. 1990. *Truth*. Oxford: Basil Blackwell.
James, William. 1909. *The Meaning of Truth*. Cambridge: Harvard University Press.
Lynch, Michael. 1998. *Truth in Context*. Cambridge: MIT Press.
Plantinga, Alvin. 1982. "How to Be an Anti-Realist". *Proceedings and Addresses of the American Philosophical Association*, 46–70.
Price, Huw. 1988. *Facts and the Function of Truth*. Oxford: Basil Blackwell.
Putnam, Hilary. 1981. *Reason, Truth, and History*. Cambridge: Cambridge University Press.
———. 1987. *The Many Faces of Realism*. La Salle, Ill.: Open Court.
———. 1990. *Realism with a Human Face*. Cambridge: Harvard University Press.
———. 1978. "Realism and Reason". In *Meaning and the Moral Sciences*, 123–40. London: Routledge and Kegan Paul.
Rorty, Richard. 1979. *Philosophy and the Mirror of Nature*. Princeton: Princeton University Press.
———. 1991. *Objectivity, Relativism, and Truth*. Cambridge: Cambridge University Press.
Vision, Gerald. 1988. *Modern Anti-Realism and Manufactured Truth*. London: Routledge.
Wolterstorff, Nicholas. 1983. "Are Concept-Users World-Makers?" *Philosophical Perspectives* 1:233–67.
Wright, Crispin. 1992. *Truth and Objectivity*. Cambridge: Harvard University Press.

Notes on Contributors

WILLIAM P. ALSTON is Professor of Philosophy Emeritus at Syracuse University. The main fields in which he has published are philosophy of language, philosophy of religion, epistemology, and philosophy of mind. Recent books include *Divine Nature and Human Language, Epistemic Justification, Perceiving God, A Realist Conception of Truth*, and *Illocutionary Acts and Sentence Meaning*.

DAVID LEECH ANDERSON is Associate Professor of Philosophy at Illinois State University. He works in metaphysics, philosophy of language, philosophy of religion, and cognitive science. His publications have appeared in *The Journal of Philosophy, American Philosophical Quarterly*, and *Philosophical Topics*. He is founder and director of The Mind Project (www.mind.ilstu.edu), an international research and curriculum project in the cognitive sciences.

KELLY JAMES CLARK is Professor of Philosophy at Calvin College, Grand Rapids, Michigan. He earned his doctorate at the University of Notre Dame. He is the author and editor of numerous books and articles, including *Return to Reason, When Faith Is Not Enough, Our Knowledge of God*, and *The Story of Ethics*.

GAVIN T. COLVERT is Assistant Professor of Philosophy at Assumption College in Worcester, Massachusetts. His areas of research include ethics and medieval and political philosophy. He has a special interest in the dialogue between Aquinas and contemporary analytical philosophy. He has published articles on Aquinas's ethics and action theory as well as William Ockham's epistemology in such journals as *The American Catholic Philosophical Quarterly* and *The Modern Schoolman*.

ANDREW CORTENS has been fascinated by realist/antirealist debates since the time of his undergraduate work at the University of Manitoba. He earned his doctorate at Syracuse University in 1995. Now an Associate Professor of Philosophy at Boise State University, he is the author of *Global Anti-Realism: A Metaphilosophical Inquiry* (Westview Press, 2000). He lives in Boise, Idaho, with his wife, Caroline, and their four children.

ANNE L. HISKES is Associate Professor of Philosophy at the University of Connecticut, Storrs. Her research interests include the philosophy of science, theories of space and time, and interactions among science, values, and religion. She is coauthor of *Science, Technology, and Policy Decisions* with Richard P. Hiskes (Westview Press, 1986). Currently, she is writing *New Empiricist Perspectives on Science and Religion*.

FRANCES HOWARD-SNYDER received a B.A. and M.A. from the University of Cape Town and a Ph.D. from Syracuse University. She has published articles on ethics, metaphysics, and the philosophy of religion. She is Associate Professor of Philosophy at Western Washington University in Bellingham, where she lives with her husband, Daniel, and her twin sons, Peter Edward and William Payne.

MICHAEL P. LYNCH is Associate Professor of Philosophy at Connecticut College, New London. He is the author of *Truth in Context* and the editor of *The Nature of Truth: Classic and Contemporary Perspectives* (both from MIT Press).

MARK S. MCLEOD is a priest with the Communion of Evangelical Episcopal Churches, Abbot of the Community of Christ the Teacher, and Professor of Philosophy at George Fox University, Newberg, Oregon. He is author of *Rationality and Theistic Belief: An Essay on Reformed Epistemology* and the forthcoming *Repairing Eden: Mysticism, Humility, and the Existential Problem of Religious Diversity*.

CALEB MILLER is Professor of Philosophy and Chair of the Department of Philosophy at Messiah College in Grantham, Pennsylvania. He has published articles in ethics, epistemology, and philosophy of religion.

MICHAEL J. MURRAY is Associate Professor of Philosophy at Franklin and Marshall College, Lancaster, Pennsylvania. His published essays have appeared in a variety of collections and journals including *American Philosophical Quarterly*, *Faith and Philosophy*, and *Religious Studies*. He is the editor of *Reason for the Hope Within* (Eerdmans, 1999) and *Philosophy of Religion: The Big Questions* (Blackwell, 1999).

PHILIP A. ROLNICK is Professor of Religion at Greensboro College, where he teaches theology and is Director of the Ethics Across the Curriculum program. He has written *Analogical Possibilities: How Words Refer to God* (Oxford University Press), edited *Explorations in Ethics* (Greensboro College Press), and is currently working on a manuscript, *The Theology of the Person*.

LAURA A. SMIT is Assistant Professor of Theology at Calvin College in Grand Rapids, Michigan. She did her doctoral work at Boston University, and her dissertation explored the intersection of aesthetics and epistemology in Bonaventure. She is currently writing a book on the ethics of romance, focusing on experiences of unrequited love. Dr. Smit is also a minister in the Presbyterian Church (USA).

CHRISTOPHER TOLLEFSEN is Assistant Professor of Philosophy at the University of South Carolina. He works in normative, meta, and applied ethics. His recent publications have appeared in *Ethical Theory and Moral Practice*, *The Journal of Applied Philosophy*, and *The Journal of Value Inquiry*.

RENÉ VAN WOUDENBERG is Professor of Philosophy at the Free University of Amsterdam. He has published in metaphysics, epistemology, and philosophy of language. With Terence Cuneo he is the editor of *The Cambridge Companion to Thomas Reid* (2003).

Index